Michael and

Chris Duke

12/2014

VISIONS OF DYSTOPIA
IN CHINA'S NEW HISTORICAL NOVELS

VISIONS OF DYSTOPIA
IN CHINA'S NEW HISTORICAL NOVELS

JEFFREY C. KINKLEY

COLUMBIA UNIVERSITY PRESS   *New York*

COLUMBIA UNIVERSITY PRESS
Publishers Since 1893
NEW YORK   CHICHESTER, WEST SUSSEX
cup.columbia.edu

The author expresses appreciation to the Schoff Fund at the University Seminars at Columbia University for their help in publication. Material in this work was presented to the University Seminars: Modern China.

Library of Congress Cataloging-in-Publication Data

Kinkley, Jeffrey C., 1948– author.
 Visions of dystopia in China's new historical novels / Jeffrey C. Kinkley.
   pages cm
 Includes bibliographical references and index.
 ISBN 978-0-231-16768-0 (cloth : acid-free paper)—ISBN 978-0-231-53229-7 (e-book)
  1. Historical fiction, Chinese—History and criticism.   2. Chinese fiction—
20th century—History and criticism.   3. Dystopias in literature.   I. Title.
 PL2419.H57K56 2014
 895.13'509—dc23

                                                      2014011654

COVER DESIGN: CHANG JAE LEE
COVER PHOTO: © ED FREEMAN/GETTY IMAGES

References to websites (URLs) were accurate at the time of writing. Neither the author nor Columbia University Press is responsible for URLs that may have expired or changed since the manuscript was prepared.

In memory of my mother, Emily Jane Robinson Kinkley (1918–2014)

CONTENTS

PREFACE

I N THIS BOOK I hope to make at least two contributions to the study of modern history and literature. One is the identification and exploration of a recent phenomenon in Chinese intellectual history: a new kind of narrative in which China's most celebrated in-country writers have conveyed original and yet mutually reinforcing grand ideas about twentieth-century Chinese history. For convenience and comparative purposes, I refer to the writers' epics by a literary term in use outside the China field, though it is a term bound one day to expire: "new historical novels." These works make a statement not just about modern China, I believe, but also about the human condition. That finding leads to my other intended contribution: identification in these works of a new kind of dystopian vision.

The melding of historical fables with the dystopian novel may seem improbable to Western readers, who expect to see dystopia embodied in stories of future technology and society. Deducing a bad future from patterns of the past is a different pursuit. Latin American, Caribbean, and Chinese writers have excelled at it, creating narrative wonderment for readers even while leading them to contemplate terrible human outcomes in actual history.

A classic example is Cuban novelist Alejo Carpentier's *El reino de este mundo* (The kingdom of this world; 1949), a tale of Haiti's eighteenth-century revolution and its horrific aftermaths. The same novel finds beauty in time-honored Haitian spiritualism; Carpentier's prologue to the work is a manifesto not of history- or apocalypse-based lament, but rather of a much brighter "marvelous real" that he thought characteristic of the Americas. Critics later called it "magical realism." Revising the essay years later, Carpentier added that the

Old World was marvelous, too—endowed with a wondrous baroque sensibility, as he learned during a 1967 visit to Cultural Revolution China and Brezhnev's USSR, of all places. Their less exquisite, more conflict-ridden and prefabricated sides might have escaped his notice, but not that of Russian and Chinese novelists. Writers of all hemispheres have depicted societies that aspired to transcend the marvelous itself, by creating a secular utopia. The result, say the novelists, is always dystopia—history shows.

The historically themed Chinese epics I discuss should intrigue literary scholars if they see in them a literary subgenre or at least a collective practice in Chinese writing. Historians may be surprised to see how deeply China's most creative literary minds have grappled with historical thinking, beyond the a priori paradoxes of existence and epistemology that captivated the philosophical imagination of China's avant-garde in an earlier phase of the post-Mao era, when authors first confronted the propagandistic nature of Maoist views of history. That avant-garde included those who went on to become the "marvelous" rewriters of Chinese history featured in this book: Mo Yan, Su Tong, Yu Hua, Han Shaogong, Ge Fei, Wang Anyi, Zhang Wei, and Li Rui.

Critics in China and Lin Qingxin's and Howard Y. F. Choy's monographs in English write of a broad category overlapping mine (and yet not necessarily cognate with it) that they call "new historical fiction," starting with short stories of the 1980s. Xudong Zhang, Xiaobing Tang, and Xiaobin Yang, attracted to ideas of modernity, modernism, and postmodernism (as those terms are defined in China) likewise celebrate the 1980s as the great turning point in Chinese literary culture; they see the 1990s as an era of decline into commercialism. I shift the focus to *full-length* novels that directly examine change across generations, generally written after the 1989 Tiananmen massacre, though pioneering novels by Mo Yan, Zhang Wei, and Su Tong appeared earlier. To me, the 1990s historical epics are still experimental, and yet "post-avant-garde" in the Chinese context—aware of patently old and patently new narrative modes, but disposed, by the 1990s, to use them selectively. I do not hold their popularity against them. Meanwhile Shelley Chan (on Mo Yan) and Hua Li (on Su Tong and Yu Hua) have bridged the gap between the 1980s and 1990s by analyzing those writers' earlier lives as reflected in their works, perhaps preparing the way one day for a prosopography of literary rewriters of Chinese history. Dissertations by Christopher Payne and Alastair Morrison, respectively, point to metafictional historical writing in greater China and in the mainland still today.

This book reflects my position as a practicing historian in North America (where history has long quarreled with philosophy of history) who feels informed though not directed by Paul Ricoeur's and Hayden White's studies of history as narrative, and finds comparative literary methods indispensable to reading any kind of text. I do not, like Lin Qingxin and Howard Choy, detect a major shift in China's highbrow historical fiction from emphasis on time to emphasis on place, and from big events to individual bodies, with historical placement thereby demoted to a mere setting. China's "new" historical novels intrigue me because of their fresh perceptions of history. Newness, of course, is contestable. Ideas of historical cyclicalism, of utopia and utopia lost, of family and fate, are ancient—and recurring.

Analysis of recent Chinese fiction with themes of past tragedies is well established, and in North America it tends to draw on "history and memory" critiques. That approach, which many historians identify with sociology, is generally deployed in the China field by literature scholars such as David Der-wei Wang, Ban Wang, Yomi Braester, Xiaobin Yang, and Jie Lu. All but Jie Lu focus on violence and trauma in Chinese fiction, and they do not restrict themselves to historical fiction. Like Michael Berry and Sylvia Lin, I attribute the surfeit of violence in modern Chinese fiction to the writers' interest in exterior twentieth-century events rather than their search for metaphors of figurative violence and crises of representation, although depicting violence may now have become a literary or subliterary fad. Real violence punctuates and "organizes" history, I believe, instead of simply disordering individual sequential memories and reconstructions of the past as trauma may do (to paraphrase Ban Wang's view). Our Chinese authors see history as a "monster," in David Der-wei Wang's words, but not so much due to a priori causes as to their own observations. Cruelty in history appears to the novelists to be intermittent, even cyclical; flaws in human nature are the constant. That emphasis sets these writers apart from most of their Chinese predecessors.

Chinese science fiction, whose study has been revived by David Der-wei Wang and Mingwei Song, lies outside the scope of this book. So do dystopian narratives with premises very directly derived from Huxley and Orwell, like Chan Koonchung's best seller, *The Fat Years*. Douwe Fokkema's magisterial *Perfect Worlds* is a global literary history of the utopian impulse, delineating how dystopian visions from authors as different as Dostoevsky, Orwell, and Michel Houellebecq appear to respond dialectically to utopias, from Thomas More and Tao Yuanming down through H. G. Wells and Mao Zedong. Fokkema's analysis features two post-Mao novels, Wang Shuo's *Please Don't Call Me Human* and Su Tong's *My Life as Emperor*, works I mention mostly for comparison with those at the center of my study. While affirming the idea of a global dystopian literary practice, I shall argue that China's recent dystopian historical novels constitute a fresh and distinctive strain within it. Fokkema and I agree that China's recent dystopian visions (except for Ge Fei's) react against modern historical developments, notably Mao Zedong's utopianism, more than China's native, pre-twentieth-century utopian thinking. I do, however, suggest a strong exterior literary and thematic influence on China's new dystopian novels: Latin America's "new novel," with its powerful stories of rural utopias collapsing into dystopia and annihilation, and not always due just to exterior material forces or even "modernity."

Because the Chinese novels at issue are works of literature, one can enjoy and find enlightenment in them without reference to their apparent historical views or commentary. One school of North American criticism tends to see China's best writing, even China's leftist and revolutionary literature, as primarily "about writing." Yi-tsi Mei Feuerwerker has fruitfully deployed this approach to explicate works by Han Shaogong, Mo Yan, and Wang Anyi, as Roberto González Echevarría has for novels by García Márquez and Carpentier. The Chinese novelists' images of historical stasis might on the other hand be seen as not a probing of history but a renewal of "anthropological" or cultural (history-averse) analyses of Chinese life. These began a century ago, with Lu Xun's concerns about Chinese "national character," followed in the mid-1980s by Chinese writers' imaginings of a telluric romanticism or, conversely, a determinism of decline and dementia in China's "original" cultural "roots."

Above all, politics may explain many of the novelists' narrative choices, including their reticence about Mao Zedong and the Communist Party, perhaps even the setting of their plots "safely" in the past or in particular years that are less "inconvenient" than others. The novelists' celebrated use of magical realism, fantasy, allegory, and burlesque may help them evade censorship, and some writers may avoid historical criticism because of shame as much as fear. Censorship and self-censorship might thus *force* the novels' narratives to be abstract—panhuman rather than national—and, *therefore*, "grand." Given the commercial, faddish, and competitive trends in elite and popular literature alike, one might even wonder if Mo Yan's financial success or the obsessive goal of winning a Nobel Prize, the subject of a book by Julia Lovell (Mo Yan has since won the prize, in 2012), has encouraged certain trends in the novels discussed below.

These alternative explanations for the novels' peculiarities (and similarities) are not mutually exclusive, with my views or with one another. Han Shaogong's *A Dictionary of Maqiao,* a book narrated as a series of dictionary entries, is the most structurally unconventional of the works, but it is still a novel, even a historical novel broadly defined. It is "about China" and humanity, and its (our) history, not just about writing, linguistics, epistemology, or a transhistorical "Chinese culture" or predicament, any more than it is just about village life. To recover Han Shaogong's historical and metahistorical vision, while explicating his literary approach, is surely proper and necessary work for historians, social scientists, and literary critics. That all the novels here implicitly take history seriously does not compromise their status as what the Chinese call "pure literature." It is also true that works with historical themes are not these major writers' only important works. A preliminary study like this, with focus on the writers' ways of writing about history, cannot detail the entirety of their literary talents: their inventive imagery and language, the full range of their intellectual breadth, or even all facets of their pessimism about human nature. Gender inequalities may appear particularly understated in these novels. Latin America's Boom was criticized for having a male bias, and so sometimes was Chinese fiction "of the new era" (1979–1989); the Latin American Post-Boom has notable female practitioners, but the Chinese "post–new era" field of avant-garde *historical* novelists is mostly known for male writers. Wang Anyi is an exception.

I present my argument in six chapters. Chapter 1 clarifies what I mean by historical novels, new historical novels, and dystopian visions. This chapter also compares the Chinese novels with other critical and historical narratives of literary merit, and with Chinese textbook history, the better to differentiate the epics that are the main subject of this book and their unique historical vision. What first interested me about China's new historical novels was not their optimism or pessimism. These works not only deny expectations of progress and other historicist conceptions (overemphasis on "A-type phenomena" as occurring in Era A and "B-type phenomena" as belonging to Era B); they often relate standard historical events without recourse to the idea of historical periods. Chapter 2 thus explores the unusual ambiguity of some of the novels' temporal settings, particularly in light of conventions in more orthodox Chinese literary and historical writing. Although the novelists clearly comment on recent history, suggesting cause and effect in plots that span generations, the reader often enters the worlds they have created, and those of certain narrower, period novels and novellas, with considerable bewilderment about the setting. The reader feels lost in time, or in some works, suspended in time out of time, thanks to diverse narrative devices and inconsistencies or ambiguities of setting and detail. Evils of the past are not necessarily past.

The very anomie of being lost in time can be unsettling and evoke uneasiness about the past and future. Chapter 3 then analyzes several kinds of temporal circularity in particular novels. They are by no means comforting, unlike the kinds of historical circularity that earlier Chinese generations believed in. Dystopia is eternal rather than futuristic. This goes beyond pessimistic views of a future era that might itself be bounded or tragic in the Aristotelian sense, with a beginning, middle, and end.

The next two chapters relate China's new historical novels directly to international traditions of dystopian writing. Chapter 4 notes an absence of group ties in the Chinese novels, indeed a general alienation from or fear of the group. The reader observes anxieties about, even antipathy to, that most given, most sacred of groups, the family. The village, town, and neighborhood do not fare any better in these works, whose settings are usually constricted and isolated, as is generally true of utopias and dystopias. Following the examination in chapter 4 of this patently un-Confucian ethos, chapter 5 addresses the awful visions of chaos and social-moral disorder in the novels and finds that the works also lack any kind of "Legalist" (traditionally Chinese statist) grounds for optimism. There is no benevolent or even order-conferring leader, no justice under penal laws, nor any ideological rationale to buttress society. Divine interventions, whether from invasive "magic" or pervasive fantasy, do little to alleviate the situations. Chapters 4 and 5 thus examine Chinese variations on two classic dystopian syndromes: stifling of the individual under totalitarianism and terror under anarchy. The novelists appear to fear the latter more than the former. Chapter 6, the conclusion, discusses the place of China's high literary historical novels in the twenty-first century, in light of politics, postmodernism, national allegory, and the ascendancy of Mo Yan. Will these trends hasten or postpone the arrival of a post–Mo Yan Chinese literary era, comparable to Latin America's post-Marquezian ("McOndo") era and India's post-Rushdie era—a time possibly less hospitable to baggy, fabular, "hallucinatory" historical epics?

Yearning for "social harmony" seems natural in light of the appalling conflict in twentieth-century Chinese history. But "social harmony" is a shibboleth the Communist Party now uses to suppress competing ideas and forms of citizen self-expression. The Chinese novelists, even more than citizens in capitalist societies, have grown up with notions that struggle, competition, creative destruction, and other "Darwinian" contests are progressive. That is a doctrine now of China's new marketplace society, without the Maoist celebration of destruction through revolution, liquidation, and dialectical transcendence. Novelists educated during the heyday of Mao Zedong can trace such ideas to capitalism *and* Marxism-Leninism. That contributes to their special historical visions, and to their ambivalence about them.

Because many of these novels are available in excellent English translations, I shall refer to the translated ones and their characters by their names as previously translated. My parenthetical in-text page references are to the relevant Chinese editions named in the bibliography, followed by a slash and then the corresponding page number in the English translation. As to the "original" Chinese texts, critical practice typically privileges final editions, but sometimes a fuller previous edition published in Taiwan to avoid censorship is the best text. Translators, editors, and marketers of overseas editions occasionally introduce their own abridgments and alterations, including the renaming and reordering of chapters. The translated version may even contain passages not found in major published Chinese versions, due to changes in the Chinese text after a prior version went to the translator. This is notably the case with Su Tong's *The Boat to Redemption*, whose English translation, rendered by Howard Goldblatt, won Su Tong a Man Asian Literary Prize.

I am greatly indebted to Howard Goldblatt, Perry Link, Julia Lovell, Stanley Rosen, and Jonathan Spence. Special thanks go to Jennifer Crewe, Kathryn Schell, Anne McCoy, Kathryn Jorge, and my editor Jan McIlroy of Columbia University Press for their advice and corrections. The University Seminars of Columbia University provided much-needed scholarly and financial support. My dear wife, Susan Corliss Kinkley, supported me with love, inspiration, and valuable editorial assistance; she and my son, Matthew Kinkley, endured my lengthy engrossment in this project. For institutional support, I thank the John Simon Guggenheim Foundation for a scholarship and St. John's University for a yearlong research leave, release time from teaching in earlier and later stages, and enthusiastic support from its librarians, including William Keogan, Arthur Sherman, and Tian Zhang. Princeton University, Columbia University, and the Academia Sinica in Taiwan provided materials, and so did colleagues Zhang Zhiqing, Xue Chaofeng, Klaus Mühlhahn, Dale LaBelle, and my students Liu Chang and Zhang Ruicheng. Alina Camacho-Gingerich of St. John's helped me understand Latin American literature. Xudong Zhang, Pat Laurence, and other members of Columbia University's Modern China Seminar offered many helpful comments, as did anonymous Columbia University Press readers. Christopher Payne and Alastair Morrison generously lent me their insightful dissertations. In years past, Mo Yan, Yu Hua, Li Rui, Wang Anyi, and many of their friends and colleagues graciously met with me for discussion and interviews. It is my loss that I have not always kept up those contacts. Yet media and academic pursuit of China's famous authors for comment on the record is so intense now that I fear some writers are already "overexposed" as interpreters of their own writing.

VISIONS OF DYSTOPIA
IN CHINA'S NEW HISTORICAL NOVELS

1 INTRODUCTION

Chinese Visions of History and Dystopia

C HINA'S PREEMINENT CONTEMPORARY novelists—foremost among them Mo Yan, Su Tong, Yu Hua, Ge Fei, Zhang Wei, Wang Anyi, Li Rui, and Han Shaogong—tell astonishing tales of modern Chinese history. Family sagas, village histories, coming-of-age narratives, and stories of enduring feuds fill these synoptic works. Reviewing one of Mo Yan's most "wildly visionary and creative" novels, Jonathan Spence, reading as historian as well as critic, still found it to be "a kind of documentary."[1] Mo Yan's generation, after all, grew up with novels that depicted "social forces." Their own works are more avant-garde, and yet appear to embody "lessons" from history. These epics enrich history with myths and dreams, as in the politically and stylistically "dangerous" "total novel" of the Latin American Boom. Anthropology, old books, travelogues, and personal journeys into the wild inspired the Spanish Americans' new myths of history.[2] The Chinese authors experienced China's hinterlands before they became writers. Several were *banished* to the countryside, after having experienced freedom, chaos, terror, and boredom in the Cultural Revolution.

The Chinese novels discussed here and their film adaptations depict awful bullying, beatings, executions, murders, rapes, suicides, and torture. So it was in history. Ingenious plotting, imaginative language, and satire are more in evidence than character development or psychological depth in most of these works, but the settings are memorable. Typically limited in geographic scope and often rural, they give these tales a different perspective from most other avant-garde Chinese novels and films.[3] Yet it is movement through time, not space, which takes the novels' pent-up characters into different worlds. In this book I shall refer to a work set in one particular bygone era as a "period" novel or film, reserving the designation of "historical" novel or film for multi-era epics that unfold across generations or critically and self-consciously reinterpret the past from a vantage point in later times. These may be called historical novels if we note that they are first of all literary novels, with cinematic adaptations that are art films, and that the history retold is relatively recent. Story lines set in the Mao era often reenact scenes from the novelists' own memories. Narratives that continue into post-Mao times become, at that point, contemporary social satires, buttressed by hints that the past shapes the present and perhaps an ingenious use of one era to comment on another. These works are not heavily researched for history buffs who read for "facts," as American readers once sought from novels by Kenneth Roberts, Leon Uris, and James Michener, or as college students may still be asked to learn from *Middlemarch*. The Chinese works do not serve readers who want to lose themselves in a past age or pursue antiquarian interests, as one might in a novel by Mary Renault or Robert Graves. Nor do the Chinese writers reappraise founding patriarchs and dictators, a predilection of modern Latin American novelists. The persons and even the legends of Mao Zedong, Chiang Kaishek, and Sun Yatsen are practically invisible in the Chinese works.[4] Few would call these novels romantic or chivalric either, like the historical novels of Walter Scott, James Fenimore Cooper, or Jin Yong. On the contrary, the Chinese narratives discussed below conjure up broadly dystopian visions of a society that never literally existed in the past, even in China's cruel and bloody twentieth century, but can be taken as portents of a dark human future. If utopias are inspired by hopes for the perfectibility of human life, these works seem inspired by fears of its capacity for unlimited degradation.

Seventeen novels and novellas that portray twentieth-century Chinese history with broad brushstrokes and epic, highly imaginative story lines occupy center stage in this book. I take these works, among the most influential written by authors living in China, to be a new, Chinese variation on the historical novel *and* the dystopian novel. The major works are by Mo Yan: *Red Sorghum* (1986–1987), *Big Breasts and Wide Hips* (1996), and *Life and Death Are Wearing Me Out* (2006). By Su Tong: *Nineteen Thirty-Four Escapes* (1987), *Opium Family* (1990), *Rice* (1991), and *The Boat to Redemption* (2009). By Yu Hua: *Cries in the Drizzle* (1991), *To Live* (1992), *Chronicle of a Blood Merchant* (1995), and *Brothers* (2005). By Zhang Wei: *The Ancient Ship* (1986) and *September's Fable* (1992). By Li Rui: *Silver City* (1990). By Wang Anyi: *The Song of Everlasting Sorrow* (1995).[5] By Han Shaogong: *A Dictionary of Maqiao* (1996). And by

Ge Fei: his *Southlands Trilogy*, consisting of *Bygone Beauty* (2004), *Land in Dreamland* (2007), and *Southern Spring Played Out* (2011). Zhang Yimou, China's most famous film auteur of China's "Fifth Generation" of cinematographers (the first cohort to graduate from the Beijing Film Academy after Mao's death), promoted the historical trend through film adaptations of *Red Sorghum* (*Hong gaoliang*, 1987) and *To Live* (*Huozhe*, 1994, still banned in China).[6]

For comparison, this book will cite other works with historical and dystopian themes, most of them by the same authors and filmmakers or others of their generation, the "children of Mao" who participated in or witnessed the Cultural Revolution.[7] Early inspirations for historical reassessments were Fifth Generation director Chen Kaige's period film about the pre-1949 Communist movement, *Yellow Earth* (*Huang tudi*, 1984; cinematographer Zhang Yimou), and Zheng Yi's *Old Well* (1985; film, *Lao jing*, 1986, starring Zhang Yimou and directed by Wu Tianming), which is set in post-Mao times, with backstories. The critique of Chinese history in Su Xiaokang and Wang Luxiang's television documentary series *Deathsong of the River* (or, *River Elegy*, 1988; banned in 1989) was particularly influential.[8]

Novels set in relatively fantastic, futuristic, or alternative worlds and that pay homage to Western dystopian classics, if only in their titles, include Wang Xiaobo's *2015* (1997), Chan Koonchung's (Mandarin: Chen Guanzhong's) *The Fat Years*, whose Chinese subtitle is *China 2013* (2009), and Wang Lixiong's *Yellow Peril* (1991).[9] The last two works are post-apocalyptic popular fiction blockbusters, heavily indebted to devices from Huxley, Orwell, and science fiction. Wang's *2015* is a high-literary period novella concluding a trilogy called *The Age of Silver*, which itself is the conclusion of a triple trilogy that in its entirety (nine volumes) conveys a discontinuous historical progression from the Sui dynasty to future times. Wang's writing is more devoted to 1980s-style "ontological" (metaphysical) interests and absurdist critiques of the present than the twentieth-century historical interests at the heart of the seventeen aforementioned core novels.[10]

Other period masterpieces, which despite their limited historical purview are not simply costume dramas, include Ye Zhaoyan's *Nanjing 1937: A Love Story* (1996), whose backdrop is the Rape of Nanking,[11] and other novels by Mo Yan. His *Sandalwood Death* (2001) unfolds during the cataclysmic 1900 Boxer Rising. Mo Yan, Yan Lianke, and Wang Anyi have in recent years written exposés of health crises, famines, the one-child policy, and other unhappy phenomena that by now feel historical.[12] My book mostly restricts itself to Mo

Yan's relatively allegorical *The Republic of Wine* (1992), one of the most dystopian (and magical or fantastic) critiques of post-Mao China in China's new literary canon.[13] That work, like Wang Shuo's *Please Don't Call Me Human* (1989), is a contemporary satire whose historical themes are relatively minor. Both novels are closer to *national* allegories as conceived by Fredric Jameson than the less nationally obsessed core epics discussed in this book.[14]

More central to my analysis of the fictional treatment of historical change are four other period pieces by Su Tong. Three are novellas: *The Gardener's Art* (1992), *Tattoo* (1993), and *Wives and Concubines* (1989), whose film version, *Raise the Red Lantern* (*Da hong denglong gaogao gua*; 1991, dir. Zhang Yimou), has since its Oscar nomination lent its title back to the novella in many reprint and translated editions. Su Tong's longer novel *My Life as Emperor* (1992) is set in no identifiable dynasty, century, or millennium. Surely it is not the twentieth century, though it seems to reflect symbolically on modern times. That there can be a novel set in China's past and yet in no particular century is cause enough for controversy.

Liu Zhenyun, whose biography is comparable to that of the core authors (apart from his 1980s adherence to "neo-realism" instead of technical experimentalism), in the 1990s published a *Homeland Trilogy* of epics with pessimistic and cyclical historical views like those of the seventeen core novels. The later volumes of the trilogy have been so heavily criticized as outlandish or simply tedious that I skip down to Liu's widely praised 2009 epic, *One Word Is Worth a Thousand*, for discussion in my conclusion as an "anti-historical" foil to the earlier highbrow novels set in China's past, including Liu's own.

The appearance of dystopian and utopian themes, which tend to be speculative, in historical works like the seventeen core novels might seem unlikely. But precedents in Latin American and former Soviet bloc literature are well known to Chinese writers. In European culture, Andreas Huyssen feels, the supposed postmodern "death of utopias" has redirected utopian literary energies from the future to the past.[15] Literary dystopias, likewise, can be concretely grounded in visions of history, particularly if that history has been harnessed to enact utopian plans. David Cowart considers future fiction and science fiction in principle to be subtypes of historical fiction. Georg Lukács, he points out, attacked the very "distinction between the novel and the historical novel."[16] But Lukács was a Marxist critic who saw history as progressive, dialectical, and revolutionary; to him, any *novel* worthy of the name must "realistically" embody social forces having origins in History, a History whose future course is fixed and knowable. None of the seventeen core novels, or any of the other works just cited, is Marxist. Most are determinedly non-Marxist, skeptical of revolution, and dubious of progress.[17]

The Chinese writers would probably agree with Lukács that "severance of the present from history creates an historical novel which drops to the level of light entertainment."[18] Many critics feel that China's new historical novels are as much about the present and events of living memory as the past.[19] The allegorical and "presentist" nature of the works is evident, but these novelists try to understand—or rationalize—their own memories in historical terms. Depictions of vengeance and violence in the first half of the twentieth century can be an oblique way of addressing the same phenomena in the Maoist era, when such terror was justified as class struggle. This violence may also represent injustices that Chinese leaders excuse in the name of rational development still today.

One may ask if such complex novels are "simply" dystopian. That is fair, and yet, as chapter 5 will make clear, most of the works are obsessed with endemic evils of human nature and its seeming penchant for quasi-Darwinist struggle for dominance. The Chinese word for "utopian" has in the last decade become a cliché for a sense of the mere "impracticality" of Maoism, now that it is becoming a fading memory. To younger urban generations who know only an industrialized China with superhighways and bullet trains, Maoism seems unreal, incredible. Some use the word ironically, as if Maoism had been a put-on from its inception. Even those old enough to harbor vague memories of a time when all citizens wore blue pants and there were no street vendors may attribute such things to China's former third-world poverty instead of Mao's unique zeal to create a "new socialist man." One mission of the aging children of Mao, who once accepted Mao's utopianism as a living faith, is to make the fanatical beliefs of their youth believable, so that these beliefs' historical culmination in dystopian outcomes (some of which are already superseded by market forces and their problems) can be taken seriously. Whether the authors have sidetracked that mission by letting their own inhibitions and creative excesses, aided and abetted by censorship, make recent Chinese history seem simply absurd and improbable may still be asked.

CHINA'S "NEW HISTORICAL NOVEL"

The seventeen core novels above and others like them[20] will be called here, for convenience, China's "new historical novels." In English- and Spanish-language critical discourse, "new historical novel" (often capitalized) or "*nueva novela histórica*" typically refers to historically situated epics of the 1960s–1970s Latin American Boom that arose within the Latin American "new novel" of Carlos Fuentes, Julio Cortázar, Gabriel García Márquez, Mario Vargas Llosa, et al., and the Post-Boom associated with the aforementioned and later authors.[21] One alternative European lineage claims that Umberto Eco's *The Name of the Rose* (1980) laid "the foundations for the so-called New Historical Novel—a genre that has inspired emulation throughout Europe in recent decades."[22] Günter Grass's *The Tin Drum* (1959), 1970s works by Margaret Atwood, and Salman Rushdie's allegories of India and Pakistan (*Midnight's Children*, 1981; *Shame*, 1983) could also be called new historical novels. Novels in English by India-born writers, many of them depicting the past century as the Chinese works do, experienced a boom of their own, little noticed in China until the late 1990s.[23]

Even when applied just to Latin American and Caribbean works, without the later postcolonial epics, the idea of a "new historical novel" is contested, variously defined, and historicized, for the new cannot remain new forever. I use the term "new historical novel" because I see stylistic, thematic, and intellectual similarities between particular Chinese and Latin American/Caribbean novels, general and particular influences of the latter on the former, and even certain parallels between recent Chinese and Latin American literary history, though the similarities may be coincidental and were not simultaneous.

During the 1990s, critics like Lei Da called such works "allegorical," "symbolic," or "fabular" (*yuyan*) fiction, to distinguish them from costume-drama historical and period fiction.[24] Allegory can refer to concrete political and historical events represented through fanciful figurations in the manner of García Márquez and Rushdie, or criticism of the present through depictions of the past—a time-honored practice in Chinese literature. Alternatively, allegory can embody more universal and abstract morals about human nature in the manner of Jonathan Swift. Chapter 5 will argue that the latter sort of allegory applies generally to the Chinese novels discussed in this book; allegories of the first type, pointing to specific events and phenomena, will be noted as we examine individual novels. The term "metahistorical novel" might describe the Chinese works at issue, but that suggests a programmatic philosophy of history that these works lack. "Postmodern historical novel" seems inconsistent with these novels' dedication to grand narratives of history.

Many Chinese critics speak of *xin lishi xiaoshuo* (new historical fiction), which includes the core and subsidiary works listed above and many more besides. The Chinese term is exceedingly broad and variable, and not just because it includes short stories as well as novels.[25] The term is not necessarily cognate with Western ideas of "new historical" writing.

Chinese scholars tend to see in their "new historical fiction" an emphasis on the individual, hardship, everyday life, and perspectives from lower social strata. That fits the works discussed in this monograph, but some Chinese scholars proceed to link the objects of their study to "new historicism," meaning either post-Mao historiography or the Western school of *literary criticism* so named.[26] Any connection to the latter, whose roots are in a poststructuralist skepticism conjoined with a focus on anecdotes and Marxist and *Annales* school historicism, and whose subject is not primarily "historical fiction" or even narrated history, is problematic. Even more confusingly, an early statement from the eminent scholar Chen Sihe, still echoed in online Chinese encyclopedias, claims for "new historical fiction" practically any work that overturns official Chinese revolutionary historical discourse.[27] Such a broad definition excludes very little; revision of the Marxist-Leninist historical narrative by China's creative writers and university-level historians has gone on for three decades now, and longer than that in the Chinese Diaspora. Chen also wrote that this fiction depicts the Republican period (1912–1949), which is too narrow to capture the scope of highbrow historical fiction today. He feels that new historical fiction derives from "neo-realism," evidently because of its dispassionate narration and concern with the little people (what Spanish speakers might call the *pueblo*, referring also to the village, the indigenous, and the lower classes, but not the glorified "proletariat" of Maoist idealism).

China's most celebrated 1980s short stories with historical themes by authors of the Mo Yan, Ge Fei, Su Tong, and Yu Hua cohort are known not for realism but for experimental style, metaphysical questioning of the epistemology of historical knowing, and interest in the semiotics, philosophy, and paradoxes of historical writing.[28] Those arty, sometimes surrealistic approaches diminished in Chinese historically themed fiction when the longer novel began to flourish in the later 1980s and 1990s. Their allegorical impulses remained.

In this book, "new historical novel" refers to full-length historical novels (a few are novellas) that deny and defy previous national historical narratives, typically with a political edge that bears heavy implications for the present and future, and that also reflect familiarity with, even when rebounding from, magical realism, surrealism, fantasy, allegory, metahistorical questioning, parody, self-parody, pastiche, the absurd, and various experimental, dissociated, and nonlinear representations of time and plot that were avant-garde in 1980s China. China's new historical novels continue the meta-critique of Chinese culture characteristic of the 1980s, even as they construct new grand narratives of history in comprehensible, sometimes even mimetic forms. Several writers ultimately adopted folk narrative structures. This was part of the global magical realist tendency but not China's own 1980s avant-garde short stories, which were on guard against "proletarian" or "poor peasant" pseudo folkishness.[29] The new historical novel differs not just from modern costume-drama epics, but also from the tradition of romantic, nationalistic, and programmatic works with linear plots and linear assumptions about national development that dominated both Latin American historical novels prior to the Boom[30] and Chinese literature in an ideologically different, Marxist-Leninist national form during the Mao years (1949–1976). Mao-era "red classics" of socialist realism are epic historical novels of a different kind, still read with pleasure (though in a different frame of mind) by many Chinese, as are truly classic historical novels written centuries ago, such as *The Romance of the Three Kingdoms*.

The early post-Mao creativity in what mainland Chinese call the "new era," 1978–1989, is mainland China's Boom. It was then that Chinese fiction "broke out" and won international attention, due to the political criticism and startling experimental styles of its most famous authors. Some Latin American Boom authors were sympathetic to the Cuban Revolution, but writers of the 1980s Chinese Boom eschewed left-wing perspectives and some took pains to avoid overt political commentary. The Chinese Boom began to lose influence in China during the later 1980s, just as Chinese intellectuals grew impatient or disillusioned with Deng Xiaoping's reforms. Commercially attractive "popular" works were stealing the avant-garde's hold on the public imagination, although controversial political commentary burgeoned in late-1980s reportage, until the 1989 Beijing ("Tiananmen") massacre. Many public intellectuals then made peace with the state and embraced commercial fiction and globally distributed art films, calling them "mass literature" or "postmodernism."[31] China's major creative writers nevertheless felt compelled to keep writing, if only for the drawer or publication in Taiwan, even during the difficult 1989–1992 post-massacre period. The maturation of the Chinese new historical *novel* was one of the happier products of the transition. Other full-length subgenres flourished, too, including popular and conventional costume-drama historical novels.[32] Film adaptations of the "new" historical novels, however, were few. That may have been a nuanced aspect of the post-Mao regime's evolving tactics of controlling literary and mass media discourse.

The seventeen new historical novels at the center of this book are a major efflorescence of a Chinese Post-Boom, a rebirth of serious-and-popular fiction with a political edge following the late 1980s split between Chinese intellectuals and their political leaders that culminated in the massacre.[33] The 1990s can be seen as a post-avant-garde age mostly dominated by the same authors, with "post" meaning having known, not necessarily rejected, the prior experimentalism. Engagement with history as a grand narrative helped the new epics of the Chinese Post-Boom ("post-new era," in Chinese parlance) win favor with contemporary readers at a time when literature was newly in competition with popular fiction and could no longer enjoy éclat simply by entering "forbidden zones" of sex and violence, precincts already breached in the 1980s.[34] This epic narrative strategy accommodates dramatic story lines and subplots, presented in ways that are variously linear, fragmented, fantastic, allegorical, and of mythic proportions (sheer length attracts some contemporary readers), but on the whole more realistic than China's high literature of the 1980s—not so absurdist or mind-numbingly labyrinthine as to be detached from familiar twentieth-century historical concerns. A "return" to realism and a "move towards re-establishing the so-called 'mimetic contract' between writer and reader,"[35] using more "popular" narrative techniques, is also counted as a characteristic of Latin America's Post-Boom. Some critics of Latin American fiction see "the New Historical Novel" as "perhaps the most important form of writing in the Post-Boom."[36]

There is hardly a more "important" body of Chinese fiction in the 1990s than the new historical novels, and they remain in print and online. Their critical reputation and mass appeal, even in competition with history-themed potboilers and Internet and television productions, remain strong.[37] The Chinese works' position might be compared with historical and period novels about the USA by Don DeLillo, Gore Vidal, and E. L. Doctorow in their market, or in an earlier era, John Dos Passos's U.S.A. trilogy. China's new historical novels do not overtly embrace youth or mass culture, like the Latin American Post-Boom, but they feature the love interests, graphic depictions of sex and violence, comedy, and burlesque found in popular Chinese magazines of the 1990s. Like the Latin works, the Chinese novels are less explicitly "cosmopolitan" (less modernist in the European sense) than the highbrow fiction that preceded them, and more connected to local continental history.

The new historical novels are known and sometimes criticized for the pervasive violence in their plots. That might be attributed to Chinese history itself, though critics see depiction of violence as integral to global magical realist and postmodern critiques of modernity.[38]

Providing further inspiration for a new Chinese historical imagination, as Chinese avant-garde "pure literature" slipped into the doldrums, were international plaudits won by cinema from China's Fifth Generation filmmakers. That response confirmed global interest in the mythic proportions of China's twentieth-century history, its vast landscapes, and the cruelty and compounding tragedies of its modern social upheavals. This was the "new" wide-screen, Technicolor story that China's narrative artists were eager to tell about their people's past, of which they were prideful, and which also evoked sympathy and a horrible fascination. Yet the subject was China's twentieth-century past, when China remade itself as a nation, not its nineteenth-century semicolonial past.

China's new historical novels as I define them are widely translated and now enjoy global appeal as transnational works about the human condition. These novels are neither chiefly "national allegories" of an externally oppressed and belatedly modernized, unified, or liberated Chinese people, nor are they "obsessed" with China,[39] though all the plots take place in China and only China. This is not to deny that China- or even Han-obsessed novels exist (e.g., Jiang Rong's *Wolf Totem*), or that foreign and indeed many Chinese readers and critics may *read* what I call new historical novels as national allegories. But the focus of these works is not Chinese identity as the converse of the identity of an "Other," China's place in the world, or an organic Chinese nation, despite their quasi-biological images of humanity in the throes of struggle. For comparison, one thinks again of the Latin American and Caribbean epics that can be read as allegories not just of national histories but of regional (New World) and human history. Even with their limited geographical settings, odd folk customs and idioms, exotic flora and fauna, and occasional magical realism, the Chinese works are not (small-scale) regional novels (*novelas de la tierra* or *xiangtu xiaoshuo*, a term that Sinologists often translate as "rural" or "native-soil fiction"). These novels have some dialect and local color, but they are deployed idiosyncratically and may not always be authentic; they are not the works' major drawing cards. (Certain novels by Liu Zhenyun, Mo Yan's *Sandalwood Death*, and Zhang Wei's *September's Fable* make heavier use of northern dialects. But Mao-era novels written in those northern Mandarin variants have practically made them into native, even if passive, second dialects for avid Chinese readers.) The new historical novels eschew earthbound romanticism and telluric fatalism. Such feelings might be attributed to the films *Yellow Earth* and *Old Well*, or Zhang Yimou's film adaptation of Mo Yan's *Red Sorghum*, a novel originally set in Shandong to which the filmmaker imparted an atmosphere of semiarid Northwestern grandeur appropriate to the presumed "cradle of Chinese civilization." Mo Yan avows close emotional ties to his native Northeast Gaomi Township in Shandong, his Yoknapatawpha;[40] he even feels nostalgic about propagandistic Mao-era "red" films because he saw them there during childhood. However, "in reality, [my] Gaomi is only a literary construct," he has said. "I can put events from Hong Kong, Taiwan, France, or America, even from my dreams, into my writing about Gaomi, or have them occur in Beijing, no matter. I've become used to situating them in Gaomi from inertia."[41]

Some of China's new historical novels have allegorical subplots that reflect their having been written after the 1989 Beijing massacre, but that episode proved easy to assimilate within the works' larger historical pageants of violence; it was even prefigured in a subplot of the Chinese writers' favorite foreign novel, *Cien años de soledad* (One hundred years of solitude; 1967), about the slaughter of three thousand striking banana workers in Macondo's central plaza, subsequently forgotten by the people and denied by the government. And yet, unlike García Márquez's masterpiece, or China's mid-1980s roots-seeking literature, the newer Chinese novels do not go in quest of Chinese cultural origins. They are "post-roots-seeking"[42] and not focused on "exotic," "indigenous" culture. Alai, Tashi Dawa, and Zhang Chengzhi have written historically themed fiction, but Tibetans and China's Islamic peoples consider their cultures either that of a proto-nation or an ethnic segment of Chinese culture, not an indigenous mestizo or creole (*criollo*, in Alejo Carpentier's usage) palimpsest that gives the dominant Han culture its national or regional peculiarities, as Gu Jiegang, Shen Congwen, and some of the roots writers once imagined. Nor is there in China's new historical novels a quest for cultural or existential new beginnings in *modern* times, despite the modernism of the authors' prose and Maoism's former zeal to remake China and its people. In the works that concern us here, China has always been and always will be; Mao did not transform human nature. The new market forces are not historically unprecedented, and the current "Beijing consensus" or "China model" is just mishmash. The new historical novels reflect on culture, but it is human culture, and their tales of history begin in medias res. They see no need to go back before the twentieth century to the great age of imperialism, or before that, to ponder Chinese regional hegemony. The novels' rural settings may reflect the social science and ideological "discovery" of rural China as a world unto itself that in history awaited the Republican and Communist eras. But the works do not clearly argue for a new policy, revolution, or reformism—not even an explicit reversal of Maoism. The art of domestic survival is of primary concern. In this, the novels reflect a common anxiety of ordinary people *and* leaders of many nations—that the center may be at home, and it cannot hold. In this, the Chinese novels join a global discourse of dystopia.

Five Traditions of the Global Dystopian Novel

Chinese critics define the dystopian literary tradition with the West's canon of *We, Brave New World,* and *Nineteen Eighty-Four.* Some online Chinese encyclopedias call them "the dystopian trilogy," though one website for popular readers gives pride of place to *Lord of the Flies* and contains works heavy with science fiction—all foreign.[43] Chinese common readers have not been so thoroughly exposed to *Nineteen Eighty-Four* as the Anglophone world, but Orwell is no longer banned in China, and authors including Mo Yan claim that Orwell (author also of *Animal Farm*) influenced them.[44] (H. G. Wells's *The Time Machine* [1895] and Charlotte Perkins Gilman's *Herland* [1915], which are critiqued as both utopian and dystopian, are little discussed in China.) Bootleg DVDs long ago introduced Chinese audiences to the *Mad Max* and *Terminator* films, as well as book and film versions of Suzanne Collins's *The Hunger Games* and its Japanese predecessor, Takami Koushun's *Battle Royale. Lord of the Flies* captured nationwide attention in Chinese intellectuals' 1980–1981 debates about "human nature." William Golding won the 1980 Booker Prize and the 1983 Nobel Prize in Literature; numerous Chinese translations of his masterwork ensued, which may have stimulated images of struggle in Chinese allegorical fiction writing in the next twenty years. Following the 1989 crackdowns, *Lord of the Flies* reentered debates about the baseness of human nature.[45]

In the early twenty-first-century climate of Chinese triumphalism, Chinese critics seldom speak of a Chinese dystopian novel, and post-apocalyptic visions are rare outside of popular fiction. Pre-1949 Chinese futuristic and fantasy fiction about alternative societies that reflect badly on the author's current times are thought-provoking and well known, but were never a dominant tradition.[46] Crises of the late Qing, 1895–1911, and Edward Bellamy's utopian *Looking Backward* (1888), "one of the first English-language novels translated into Chinese" (in condensed form; published serially beginning in 1891, and as a booklet in 1894), led to an outpouring of futuristic fiction writing at that time. Those works are little read today.[47]

I refer to the "classic" tradition of dystopian writing (and filming) as the Slavic and Anglophone stream, founded by Zamyatin, Čapek, Huxley, and Orwell, further developed by Golding, Vonnegut, Bradbury, Atwood, and a host of science fiction authors, including Bulgakov. There were earlier dystopias; many modern readers see Plato's *Republic*, with its controlling guardians and their auxiliaries, as a plan for dystopia rather than utopia. The canonical stream of modern dystopian speculation dwells on the dangers of totalitarianism and mindless social conformism furthered by technological progress, or on chaos and civilization regression as the aftermath of apocalypse, likewise furthered by technology run amok. Classic utopias tend to be situated on a self-contained and inaccessible island, sometimes literally.[48] The totalitarian one-world government of the classic modern dystopia is existentially equivalent, for escape is nearly impossible.[49] The Anglophone stream also considers the threat of authoritarianism in works of "soft" science fiction or social-science fiction set in worlds not so technologically different from when they were written, from authors as diverse as Jack London, Sinclair Lewis, Gore Vidal, and Anthony Burgess.[50] Lesser authors a century ago prognosticated about a future American evil oligarchy,[51] even adding presumed perils of Chinese immigrant coolie labor, Eric Hayot points out.[52] The more canonical dystopian works have been called tragic, but classic tragedy ends with the hero (here, society) recognizing the error of his (its) ways.[53] The dystopian novel lacks such a resolution. The hero may hope to flee to an outside world. More often, the plot ends with the trial and condemnation of the hero, notes Erika Gottlieb.[54]

Technological development is not the emphasis of the dystopian Chinese novels under discussion here; they are social-science fiction set mostly in the past. More surprisingly, their emphasis is not totalitarianism or authoritarianism, either. Literary control in China is surely a major cause of that.[55] A more accepting attitude toward authority may be another factor, leading writers to censor themselves. Moreover, China lacks the Christian and thus the anti-clerical traditions whose ghosts inform many Anglophone, Slavic, and Latin American dystopias.[56] The Euro-American world can see images of total control in the medieval "One Church," before Lenin, Stalin, and Hitler—even before the Inquisition and church collaboration in colonizing New World indigenes. The Chinese see Maoist totalism as an aberration in Chinese culture. China's ancient religions, teachings, and state were seldom so ambitious. Chinese obsession with modernity as a non-relative, historicist concept carries with it materialist worries about global capitalism as a recent incursion from the West, absent the Western idea of modernity as liberation from pandemics of religious and ideological totalism and fanaticism. The Chinese novels also lack trials, despite the fascination with them in ancient Chinese drama and fiction. (Interest in criminal trials seems to many modern Chinese a low-class taste.) The relative occlusion of our common fears of dictators and out-of-control technologies differentiates the Chinese dystopian vision all the more from Western, Eastern European, and indeed Latin American versions, even as the Chinese novelists continue the mission of dystopian writers everywhere: social criticism and satire.

Erika Gottlieb's monograph *Dystopian Fiction East and West* splits off the post–October Revolution Russian and East European dystopian novels of Koestler, Zinoviev, Aksyonov, Voinovich, Klíma, and others into a second stream of dystopian writing, separate from the "Western" canon. (She deemphasizes Pasternak and Solzhenitsyn, who are known to contemporary Chinese, because she feels that those Russian writers put individual psychology above social concerns.) This "Eastern" dystopian stream imagines the worst of all possible worlds in a Stalinist society that the authors had already experienced when they wrote. Their tradition contradicts the notion that the dystopian novel must be hypothetical or futuristic. My chief displeasure with Gottlieb's category comes from its preemption of the term "Eastern." And one wonders where to place great progenitors like Kafka and diverse anomalies caused by censorship. Zamyatin's *We* was first published in English, in 1924. Reflecting the author's experience not just of the USSR (where it was published only in 1988), but also England, it influenced Huxley and Orwell. Čapek's play *R.U.R.* premiered in Prague in 1921 and became influential through English-language productions in New York, London, Chicago, and Los Angeles in 1922–1923.[57] Hence the idea of a "Slavic and Anglophone" tradition, which has a counterpart in science fiction writing.

A third dystopian stream comes from much farther "east" and is relatively unstudied: that of Japan, pioneered by Akutagawa Ryūnosuke and continued by Abe Kōbō, Murakami Haruki, and Ōe Kenzaburō.[58] The not-so-famous dystopian works[59] of these world-famous authors partake of fantasy and sometimes science fiction, but without the focus on totalitarianism and surveillance in the "classic" Western tradition.

The greatest influence on contemporary Chinese novelists, however, is a less pervasively fantastic and technology-obsessed, yet often "magical," fourth tradition—that of Latin American and Caribbean writers, most famously Gabriel García Márquez. This stream of dystopian writing draws on epic historical fable making and is a bridge between the literary historical novel and dystopian novel.[60] One could define the fourth stream more broadly as Hispano-Lusitanophone, adding certain magical, surrealistic, and "baroque" novels of the Portuguese Nobel laureate José Saramago to the Latin American and Caribbean epics.[61] One might even speak of a fabular, magical realist and dystopian critique of recent history and politics written outside the Iberian languages, including Salman Rushdie's *Midnight's Children*, whose elaborate prose narrative culminates in Indira Gandhi's "Emergency," much as Isabel Allende's popular *The House of the Spirits* (1982) climaxes with the Chilean military coup that overthrew her relative, Salvador Allende. In China, however, it was particularly "Latin American literature" of high literary register that writers and critics of the late 1980s and 1990s looked to for inspiration. The Spanish American epics seemed like a blueprint for a new kind of novel, one big enough to encompass allegory and social criticism with a partly realist, partly magical or fantastic historical plot—and a dystopian outlook. The result, almost immediately, was a *fifth* stream of dystopian and highbrow historical novels: a Chinese one, buttressed by foreign techniques for making Chinese institutions seem strange.

The big event for China was the award of the 1982 Nobel Prize in Literature to García Márquez. This generated García Márquez, Latin America, and magical realism literary "fevers";[62] a Chinese translation of *One Hundred Years of Solitude* in 1984; a 1985–1988 "roots-seeking" tendency in Chinese literature;[63] and intensive study and translation of other Latin American authors and poets, including Jorge Luis Borges, Alejo Carpentier, Miguel Ángel Asturias, Pablo Neruda, Julio Cortázar, and Mario Vargas Llosa. It reinvigorated yearnings by Chinese authors to win a Nobel for their nation and themselves.[64] Mao-era conceits of China as the miles-ahead world *leader* of oppressed (and "backward") peoples of "Asia, Africa, and Latin America" were melting away, as official propaganda now acknowledged that China was only in the preliminary stage of socialism.

García Márquez's outsized influence is evident in China's (like the world's) lack of comparable attention to Asturias and Carpentier, who preceded the Boom writers in deploying magical realism to create dystopian fictions of

history. Both authors had after all visited China during its era of high socialism, Carpentier as a diplomat for Castro.[65] But China during *its* Boom was
becoming "post-socialist." García Márquez, regardless of his friendship with
Castro, appeared as a modern Cervantes and successor to the Golden Age of
Spanish literature—a return to past glory that China desired, after tidal waves
of successive Western and socialist influences.

One Hundred Years of Solitude represents the history of the author's native
Colombia (and perhaps Latin America and the Caribbean) through an allegorical tale, variously critiqued as nostalgic and anti-nostalgic, about the fortunes of seven generations of a family named Buendía. The work can be read
as a parody of the conventional historical novel that fragments the historical
story line with a "schizophrenic journey backwards and forwards in time."[66]
The novel's setting is the fictional town of Macondo, founded in the wilderness as a classic utopia. The Buendías and their burgeoning town (*pueblo*)
become prosperous enough to last through thirty-two civil wars started by a son
of their founding patriarch, but ultimately and inexorably Macondo and the
Buendías decline into a decadent and dystopian condition that ends in the
annihilation of both. Modern Colombian history has some elements in common with modern Chinese history: civil wars over ideological differences,
revolution and counterrevolution, suffering under militarism and imperialism, and nostalgia for past glories. There were government lies about its misdeeds, disruptions caused by the introduction of modern technology, and, like
China in the first half of the twentieth century, misfortunes of anarchy as well
as authoritarianism.

Yu Hua recalls, "We were obsessed with the Márquez-led Latin American
literature movement. . . . Every one of us, the so-called 'literary youth,' can recite the first paragraph [of *One Hundred Years of Solitude*] by heart."[67] Li Rui's
Silver City opens, like García Márquez's masterpiece, with a portentous looming execution by firing squad and events that will be clarified much later in the
novel.[68] In Mo Yan's *Red Sorghum*, the narrator frequently "recollects" an earlier character's future turning points that the character will never know (92/104).
The novel's first paragraph, like *One Hundred Years of Solitude*'s, retrospectively
ponders a father-son event yet to be fully related. In fact, paying homage to *One
Hundred Years of Solitude*'s premonitory opening is a global phenomenon.[69] Mo
Yan both admits influence from García Márquez and confesses that he finished
One Hundred Years only on the third try, years after he started it![70]

Marquezian elements (sometimes simply homage) in China's new historical novels go beyond opening paragraphs and "magical realism," even though

that term is used so broadly in China (and elsewhere, as discussed in chapter 5) that it has come to signify any surprising flight of imagination in a Latin American, third world, or other contemporary novel. Mo Yan delights in startlingly rich (some would say, trivial), seemingly Marquezian or Asturian, though not always "magical" detail. He invents characters with special gifts, including visionary or telepathic powers. The narrator of Su Tong's *Nineteen Thirty-Four Escapes* is another example.[71] Zhang Wei writes of a stranded, inland "ancient ship" in his novel by that name, like the antique, earthbound Spanish galleon in *One Hundred Years of Solitude* (which may be an evocation of the Ark, if the novel is a rewriting of Genesis).[72] Zhang Wei's *September's Fable* tells of the rise and fall of a mythic town, caught like Macondo between utopia and dystopia. Mo Yan's signature oxymoronic description of his native Northeast Gaomi Township near the start of *Red Sorghum* recalls the contradictory truths and dueling nostalgias facing one another in Macondo, the *pueblo* of facing mirrors. He named the mother of *Red Sorghum's* narrator "Beauty," seemingly the same tribute to Macondo's Remedios the Beauty paid by Isabel Allende when she created Rosa the Beauty in *The House of the Spirits*. One of Tashi Dawa's novels about Tibetans has recurring personal names in successive generations, another peculiarity of *One Hundred Years* (and *The House of Spirits*).[73] The opening image of a dead man, possibly executed, among a child's oldest memories in Yu Hua's *Cries in the Drizzle* recalls a subplot of *One Hundred Years of Solitude*. Ubiquitous in the Latin American and Chinese novels are intimations of historical circularity within a larger syndrome of political-moral dysfunction and social entropy that feels allegorical and predestined.[74]

China's new historical novels continue *One Hundred Years of Solitude's* episodic interest in epochal family, clan, and community evolution and devolution through tragedy, as well as the voracious sexual appetites and deviances of the characters. Incest figures prominently in *One Hundred Years of Solitude* and also in Su Tong's and Mo Yan's fiction; sadism is on display in Yu Hua's and Su Tong's works; bestiality and necrophilia in Mo Yan's.[75] Whether the scene is Colombia, Haiti, or China, with all their respective national and supra-national peculiarities and lyrical warmth as well as humorous absurdity in customs, some real, some invented (in works by Han Shaogong, Mo Yan, and perhaps Su Tong)—unlike the cold anonymities of *We, Nineteen Eighty-Four, Brave New World*—the new historical novels' tales situate all humankind, not just a nation, within an abstract utopian/dystopian literary figuration in world literature and historical thinking.

Hombres de maíz (Men of maize; 1949; full Chinese translation, 1986) by Asturias, not coincidentally another Nobel laureate (1967), had a lower profile influence on China's young authors.[76] *Men of Maize* relates a half-century (ca. 1899–1949) of historical conflict between highlands Mayan indigenes of Asturias's native Guatemala and encroaching Hispanic ladinos (mestizos) who seize and privatize their tribal lands for commercial plantation agriculture. The novel's Indian rebel heroes, their gods and totems, and their profane landlord, sharecropper, and military nemeses come from history and pre- and post-Columbian Mayan books, myths, and legends. So does much of Asturias's language, directly or through analogous imaginary tropes. The Indians and their way of life (without private property, an ideal of Thomas More's and numerous subsequent European utopias) are wholly and unjustly ruined, particularly in spirit. The disjointed historical story line is thus dystopian, and the plot, in the work as a whole and in each of six discontinuous chapters, suggests recurrent destruction, even apocalypse. Like Carpentier, Asturias was an interwar partisan of surrealism in Paris. He studied ethnology there and intended to write an anthropological novel. That is the project of an outsider, but Asturias was no dilettante. He spent decades, beginning in Paris, translating the sacred Mayan *Popol Vuh* into Spanish. It maintains that humans were made from maize; so does Asturias's novel.

As with *One Hundred Years of Solitude*, the opening prose and themes of *Men of Maize*, or the mere idea of them, may have been sufficient to stimulate Chinese fiction, including works by Su Tong, Zhang Wei, and possibly Han Shaogong. Asturias's first chapter conjures up an utterly alien worldview that can be read simultaneously as surrealistic—modernist—and also "tribal" and "non-rational." Years can pass within moments. Later chapters revert to "rational" European-style notions of cause and effect, still adorned with baroque detail, in alternation with the Indian worldview. *Men of Maize*, like Carpentier's *The Kingdom of This World*, is a precursor of "ontological magical realism," or the empathetic representation of an alien worldview or subjectivity (here including indigenous notions of time and the cosmos) holistically, from the inside[77]—"roots" culture, to China's writers. When Mo Yan's first epic appeared in book form in 1987, it was titled, literally, *Red Sorghum Clan* (or *Clans*). Zhang Wei's *September's Fable* is virtually a *Men of Yams*. Males in Su Tong's *Nineteen Thirty-Four Escapes* can shape-shift into bamboo.[78]

Latin American novelists were not the only experimental authors heralded by China's young writers as they began to see dystopia in history. Franz Kafka (who, like Borges, influenced later magical realists) was greatly esteemed in

1980s China;[79] so were William Faulkner, James Joyce, Umberto Eco, and Milan Kundera, a sometime magical realist, though not (apart from anthropomorphic pig and dog characters) in his novel most loved in China, *The Unbearable Lightness of Being* (1984).[80] Mo Yan's character Speechless Sun in *Big Breasts and Wide Hips* is capable of a single utterance: "strip!" That word, meaning "disrobe," is a famous command voiced by Kundera's hero, Tomas. Some Chinese critics faulted Han Shaogong's *A Dictionary of Maqiao* for being a novel written in dictionary form without credit to the 1985 Serbian novel by Milorad Pavić, *Dictionary of the Khazars* (Chinese translation, 1994).[81] But Han Shaogong had co-translated *The Unbearable Lightness of Being* into Chinese for publication in 1987. Its third part, titled "Misunderstood Words," is a lexicon in which words have opposite meanings when used by people of different cultural backgrounds, just as the "Maqiao" folk reverse the meanings of many words in Modern Standard Chinese. The Chinese novel suggests to me homage to, not plagiarism of—Kundera.

The Unbearable Lightness of Being, set in Communist Czechoslovakia during and after the 1968 Soviet invasion, examines the hypocrisy of a Communist state that puts its intellectuals under constant surveillance,[82] the "totalitarian kitsch" of the state's arts and its ideals, and the anguish of intellectuals as they try to stay true to themselves, their ideals, and their friends and lovers—all challenges with Chinese counterparts. The work is also a philosophical novel; its first sentence invokes Nietzsche's contemplation of the idea of the "eternal return" (recurrence) of lived experience. Hence the novel broaches the idea of repetition, though its idea of cyclicalism is more philosophical and speculative than historical. The work also considers the nature of love, sex, fidelity, and betrayal; it was read in China just as the country was experiencing a sexual revolution. Kundera's novel explicitly refers to utopias, paradises, and idylls, from Eden to the early years of Communism, and lets the characters muse about how intended utopia becomes dystopia or perhaps *is* dystopia. "Communism" ruins the character Tereza's idyll even of country life.

China's new historical novels, however dystopian, fabular, magical realist, surrealist, or concerned with recurrence, seldom convey a "transgressive" or alternate history, as do certain novels by Carlos Fuentes, Salman Rushdie, and Toni Morrison, which alter major past events.[83] The Chinese writers play with parody and anachronism, but only Wang Xiaobo and Liu Zhenyun add characters from ancient times who speak modern slang or words from Mao Zedong, as an eighteenth-century character in Carpentier's *Explosion in a Cathedral* speaks of a specter haunting Europe (as in the opening of *The*

Communist Manifesto).[84] China's new historical novelists are noticeably loath to create fictitious Maoist political campaigns; they keep to the real ones. Nor do they depict the Nationalists defeating the Communists as the outcome of the Chinese Civil War. Modern characters' lives unfold amid familiar political history, giving the Chinese novels that "documentary" sense remarked on by Jonathan Spence. The novels startle the reader not through "mythomania," but by telling outlandish "truths"—truths taboo in official histories. The works' larger subject is the dark side of human nature, and not just in the past.

THE DYSTOPIAN NOVEL IN POST-MAO CHINA

China's new historical novels do not create a dystopian world extrapolated from technological development or apocalypses. In colloquial speech, on the other hand, any unpleasant and unjust society may be called dystopian. That is too broad; it is the vocation of all Chinese intellectuals to "worry about China"[85] and the world. I seek a middle definition. A dystopian novel of the Chinese stream is one that conveys inexorable and unbounded social-moral decline, particularly if that decline was engendered by would-be utopian social schemes. M. Keith Booker indeed feels that "dystopian literature is specifically that literature which situates itself in direct opposition to utopian thought, warning against the potential negative consequences of arrant utopianism."[86] China's contemporary writers have added a fifth stream to the global dystopian literary tradition. It is prophetic, based on reinterpretation of the past.

Chinese intellectuals sometimes see the present, or "modernity" itself, in the Chinese past. Our novelists, who like most Chinese today are allergic to the idea of revolution (though Mo Yan, for one, is given to portraying mass uprisings that are righteous and sometimes fantastic),[87] deny modernity instead of "subverting" it. (Modernity in China means increasing prosperity, not the postulated future mass poverty of *Nineteen Eighty-Four*, *Brave New World*, and the 1973 film *Soylent Green*.) The Chinese authors were brought up in a system that was relatively stagnant economically and technologically, but which insisted on, and among their generation actually inspired, belief in a prosperous socialist utopia and the creation of a new socialist human being. The collapse of that worldview did not lead to its just apocalyptic end, or any kind of revelation, but instead, to yet another utopian faith, that economic growth and a "harmonious society" dictated from above would lead China to the best of all possible worlds. And this new utopian faith seemed, perversely, to be succeeding.[88] Capitalist utopia, like the Maoist, was said by others to follow from simple extrapolation of current trends, accelerated by *skipping stages* of historical progress. Might not the ex–Red Guard generation then have its own alternative dystopian visions transcending Communism and capitalism, of pervasive Darwinian struggle for dominance, as in William Golding's *Lord of the Flies*?[89] Many Chinese intellectuals now see the 1980s of their youth as a lost "utopian decade of their own making," writes Jing Wang.[90] It was a time of unprecedented ideological freedom, decisively terminated by the 1989 massacre and the coming supremacy of market economy values. To intellectuals, the 1980s springtime was the biggest failed Chinese utopia since the Cultural Revolution.[91]

The idea of fate's operating with circularity, driven by human and cosmological forces rather than by machines, mines a deep vein in the Chinese tradition. Circularity, stasis, and return to the past need not in principle evoke pessimism, certainly not in most traditional and ancient Chinese worldviews, but in the novelists' modern Chinese visions, there is no Golden Age in the past, hence no optimism accompanying images of stasis, suspended time, or the recurrence of events. The writers tend to conjure up instead a deep fear that humankind's "original nature" is not in fact good, pace Mencius and all his orthodox Confucian successors in the two millennia since. Nor is human nature potentially ameliorable by reasoned regulation from above by wise absolute rulers, pace the Confucians' ancient Legalist ideological opponents and modern-day cheerleaders for the "China model." This distrust of human nature brings the Chinese novelists' world into closer alignment with the aftermaths of Original Sin and expulsion from the Garden of Eden developed in *One Hundred Years of Solitude*, *The Unbearable Lightness of Being*, and the "Western," Judeo-Christian tradition. China's new historical novelists purvey an unexpectedly dark side of national consciousness in the midst of China's age of triumph. Some of them might have us think that they (and we) are on the road to a dog-eat-dog, *Mad Max*, *Lord of the Flies* world, even without a third world war, One World State, or artificial intelligence gone rogue.

OTHER NARRATIVES OF MODERN CHINESE HISTORY OFFICIAL

Modern Chinese history as dictated to the general public in China's textbooks, mass media, and museums (unlike the better monographs produced in universities and research institutes) is shockingly retrograde, even in, and particularly in, the early twenty-first century. Revision of widely held official views of history has been a primary mission of China's new historical writers. In this section I scrutinize a standard required 2011 high school textbook on "modern and contemporary Chinese history," which is nearly unchanged from its 2002 edition.[92] The textbook deemphasizes internal class struggle and tones down the moralizing rhetoric of Mao-era history books that the Red Guard generation might have read in the 1960s and 1970s. The Cultural Revolution–era view of Chinese history as governed by peasant rebellions[93] is now replaced by focus on developments in the cities and on the battlefields. The official line remains the old nationalist narrative of China progressing and overcoming victimization by imperialist powers, superimposed on an economically determinist Marxist-Leninist framework. As Mao proclaimed, "modern Chinese history" began precisely in 1840, with the Opium War; from then until the Communist revolution, China was a "semicolonial and semifeudal society."[94]

Like Japan's textbooks, China's textbooks have provoked diplomatic complaints about their nationalistic bias.[95] The aforementioned high school textbook depicts the Taiping Rebellion and the Boxer Rising as revolutionary movements with few fanatical or even religious underpinnings. The northern warlords of the 1920s appear to have flourished because of foreign imperialist backers; hence the internal dynamics of civil war that intrigue China's new historical novelists are invisible. The Japanese empire appears to have been defeated in the 1940s primarily by Chinese Communist army victories on Chinese soil (Ch. ed., 2:42/Eng. ed., 2:74). China also "won the war" in Korea (2:84/2:143). There is no reference to China's onetime "leaning" toward the USSR's socialist bloc, hence no need to refer to the Sino-Soviet rift. The new historical novels likewise seldom acknowledge China's past Russian affinities (most writers were toddlers or unborn in the 1950s).[96] Some of the novels, notably Zhang Wei's *The Ancient Ship*, unlike textbooks and national battle monuments, do make veiled references to China's 1979 incursion into Vietnam.

Quotations from Marx, Engels, and Mao are fewer in the current version of history than in 1970s history books (though still present), but economic determinist themes have become overwhelming. Chinese modern history appears as the story of proletarian (Chinese Communist Party) maturation, minus class struggle, except as it occurred in wars and civil wars. It is as though social classes arose through gradual enlightenment and economic development. Taiping leader Hong Ren'gan wanted in the 1860s to establish a government with "capitalist hues" (1:29/1:42–43). The narrative about *nineteenth*-century China features sections titled "The Birth of the Chinese Proletariat" and "The Characteristics of the Chinese Proletariat." Kang Youwei's 1898 reforms featured "capitalist ideas of reform" (1:56/1:90).

Description of the Rape of Nanjing is surprisingly brief (2:29/2:51)—only half as long as coverage of the 1937 skirmish that began the Sino-Japanese War and accounts of other *battlefield* campaigns—but Japanese atrocities have been deemphasized in earlier, Mao-era, discourse.[97] Today the emphasis is on economics, nation-building, war-making, and triumphs of the Communist Party. The main damage of the Great Leap Forward was not deaths from famine, but economic imbalances. Successful construction projects and the exploits of Mao-era heroes Wang Jinxi, Lei Feng, and Jiao Yulu appear to have offset economic difficulties (2:101–103/2:168–170). The role of young people as Red Guards in the Cultural Revolution is erased, despite a later section about their rustication, titled "Educated Urban Youth Going and Working in the Countryside and Mountain Areas." Again, one could conclude that the main damage of the Cultural Revolution was to economic production (2:109–119/2:180–181).

Political struggle is subsequently replaced by policy options, culminating in Deng Xiaoping's reforms. Final chapters list Chinese achievements in science, technology, education, historical research, and culture.[98] The only literary achievements acknowledged are Maoist "red classics," Ai Qing's poetry, and the "eight model plays" of the Cultural Revolution. No post-Mao work is mentioned, except for certain movies and TV series of the historical potboiler and "main melody" type. It is as if Mao Zedong's arts policy were still in command.[99] It appears that even China's lifestyle improvements are due not so much to changes in the last three decades as to the revolution that created New China in 1949.

China's new historical novels do have points of similarity with the old-fashioned official narrative of history. Focus on the material content of history as a series of wars, civil wars, invasions, and general mayhem makes the "content" of the new historical novels not unlike that of China's textbooks, and also the "red classic" novels of the Mao period, which depict, and justify, vengeful violence against oppressor classes. Yet the conflict-based "isms" that motivated the turmoil are largely invisible in the new novels and the textbooks alike. The material emphases of the textbook do not deny the general lack of human kindness depicted in the novels.[100] And the novels hardly contradict the main story line of increasing prosperity when they come to post-Mao times—less so than China's equally epic "anticorruption novels" of 1995–2002.[101]

The crux of the revolution, in the textbooks, in novels by the northern Chinese writers Mo Yan, Zhang Wei, and Li Rui, and in the works of many Western social scientists, is not just the 1947–1949 civil war, but the great land reform of those and surrounding years, during which the Communist Party gained control of the countryside.[102] The difference is that the novelists emphasize the violence of the land reform. The novels, in a way truer to Maoism and even Deng Xiaoping's original 1980s policies than the more classically orthodox Marxist textbook writers' stance, have not written off the Chinese countryside as a place whose historical role is to be superseded in the march of progress. And yet the novels, more than the textbooks, tend to conflate Maoist policies with Communism; there are no hints of Communist crosscurrents from other leaders, such as Liu Shaoqi, Peng Dehuai, and the Cultural Revolution Group. Peasants' and workers' memories of the past (subjective, nostalgic, and contradictory though they seem when read collectively) often differ from standard textbook periodization more than the new historical novels do;[103] the distinction of the latter is their tendency to transcend periodization, even as they write of familiar political movements and wars.

Lin Qingxin notes that the "new historical fiction" of the 1980s and 1990s originally shocked Chinese readers by reversing the ideologically appropriate class backgrounds of the heroes and villains.[104] This is not to say that the novels embrace the values of capitalism, as some critics have charged.[105] Novels like Mo Yan's *Red Sorghum* created images of "third forces," Lin adds. They are not really people in the ideological middle, but autonomous armed forces struggling for power on their own terms: "bandits," who in Mao-era histories and novels were lumped together with feudal or imperialist enemies. Emphasis on heroics is not a deep-structure reversal of the old Maoist "revolutionary history." I will note that ideological struggle as such is deleted in the novels' historical depictions.

More fundamentally, Lin Qingxin notes, China's new historical novels eschew any post-Enlightenment confidence in progress—the global discourse of modernity. By my readings, the novels deny the very concept of "liberation." To that extent these works may share some ground with the worldview of Michel Foucault. Yet the novelists refuse to portray China as a victim. This may have led them to narrow the scope of their historical inquiry to the twentieth century or the latter half of it, without the necessity of starting in the nineteenth century, the seedtime of Western imperialism in East Asia. Revolution in the novels appears sui generis or like a traditional uprising. Chinese society looks like a special case, but then, imperialistic exploitation in the textbooks also appears unique to China rather than global.[106] China stands only for itself, or all humanity. It is a people without a cause. China remains a microcosm of the pain inflicted by and on abstract humanity. *a symect* ~~

OTHER NARRATIVES OF MODERN CHINESE HISTORY: NONOFFICIAL

Memoirs and other nonofficial narratives with varying degrees of fictionalization have surely influenced China's new historical novel. I think of these other accounts as narratives of lamentation, accusation, or nostalgia. The personal lamentations cover the same historical ground as the new historical novels, recalling individual and collective suffering during decades of war, revolution, and political persecution. They delve deeply into historical particulars and often describe changing mores in courtship, education, and women's rights, even as they construct their own moral fables. The earliest blockbuster was Nien Cheng's melodramatic damning of Communism in her memoir, *Life and Death in Shanghai* (1987). Reminiscences by ex-Rightists, former Red Guards, and victims of the Cultural Revolution, when published abroad, often in English, benefited not only from freedom of speech but also from professional editing.[107] Jung Chang (Zhang Rong) brought the genre into the realm of multigenerational family saga with her *Wild Swans* (1991). Heavily or wholly fictional works, such as Dai Sijie's *Balzac and the Little Chinese Seamstress* (2000), Anchee Min's *Red Azalea* (1994), and her *Becoming Madame Mao* (2001), bring one full circle to the sensational anecdotal biographies of Mao Zedong, such as the memoirs of Li Zhisui, his personal physician. Some of China's top leaders, sensing a possible sea change in store for China and a need to justify themselves in the eyes of history, are writing their own memoirs for publication abroad.[108]

China's autobiographical authors are often suspected of covering up their complicity in their tales of victimization. That is a burden that authors of fiction are not expected to bear, and they seldom do; their characters, likewise, seldom exhibit survivor guilt.[109] On the other hand, without historical perspective, even those who confess to persecuting others in the Cultural Revolution may be blind to its historical similarities to earlier campaigns against class enemies. There, the new historical novelists shine.

Typifying the second, less self-centered and more accusatory category of narrative is *A Small Town Called Hibiscus* (1981) by Gu Hua, who is a little older than the new historical novelists (b. 1942), and Xie Jin's (1923–2008) major film (*Furongzhen*, 1986) based on that novel. These works feel more conventionally realistic and melodramatic than the "new" historical novels, and yet less dystopian, because their implicit call for political change seems not only old-fashioned but also optimistic in its implication that politics can bring a solution to what ails China. Such novels and films are the direct inheritors of the critical anger of the highly political scar and introspective literature of 1978–1980. Gu Hua's later novels, composed in Canada, go further in their social criticism while broadening the panoptic historical scope.[110] Later accusatory narratives might include Mo Yan's own *The Garlic Ballads* (1988), about rural protest and corruption, and the explosive 1998–2002 trend of "anticorruption novels." Accusatory novels capture public attention by exposing policy horrors and the disintegration of basic moral codes. Hong Ying's *Summer of Betrayal* (1992) and Ma Jian's *Beijing Coma* (2008), composed in exile, remember the 1989 Beijing massacre. In China, Yan Lianke has written about China's AIDS epidemic in *Dream of Ding Village* (2005). His *Four Books* (published in Hong Kong in 2010) tells of the famine caused by the Great Leap Forward.

The third category of critical narrative, the nostalgic, condemns recent events by preferring an idealized past. That past can include even the Cultural Revolution, preferred by some who scarcely knew it and by others who did; fond memories of 1966–1967 began for the ex–Red Guards almost immediately after they were banished to the countryside.[111] As they matured and rethought the role of the Cultural Revolution proper (1966–1967) in causing their predicament, the whole revolutionary gestalt began to seem dystopian. A different nostalgia is for the "old society" before the Communist revolution, a time of ostensibly purer and more stable rural values, compared not just to Maoism, which had its own "pastoral" values, but to industrializing China today. Some of the first expressions of rural nostalgia might be sought in the 1980s roots-seeking fiction, though more in the works of Li Hangyu and Wang Zengqi than of Han Shaogong, whose *Pa Pa Pa* (1985) is dystopian.

Since the 1990s, one of the most popular forms of nostalgia has been for old Shanghai and its grandeur as the Paris of the East, a fictional subgenre plied in the 1980s by Cheng Naishan.[112] Wang Anyi's *The Song of Everlasting Sorrow*, with its early chapters re-creating the ethos of an "Old Shanghai" (whose lost virtue is, paradoxically, a modernity or up-to-dateness in that relatively new metropolis that became "old" only due to its subsequent destruction by socialism), is called nostalgic by some. One can also find period nostalgia in art films of the 1990s such as *Shanghai Triad* (*Yao a yao, yao dao waipo qiao*; Zhang Yimou, 1995), and perhaps even the pessimistic *Temptress Moon* (Chen Kaige, *Feng yue*, 1996; banned in China). Zhang's later period films, set in more ancient times, such as *Hero* (*Yingxiong*, 2002) and *Curse of the Golden Flower* (*Mancheng jindai huangjinjia*, 2006), and Chen Kaige's *The Emperor and the Assassin* (*Jing Ke ci Qin Wang*, 1998), evoke a sense of the gorgeousness of the past. Some critics argue that they further a conservative, nationalistic, and statist cause.

Differences in tone and level of abstraction help to define the new historical novels against these other works; the historical novels are not just pessimistic, maudlin, or tragic, but also dystopian. They convey a view of human nature that manifests itself socially in history, and that can be extrapolated into the future. There is no Golden Age in the past, no need to name names and settle past scores, and nothing to be gained from self-pity. History is not just a set of events or the fulfillment of an ideology, but an ever-recurring pattern—moral or amoral, as the observer may judge.

The Writers

China's dystopian new historical writers have a unique perspective on China and the world. Born after the 1949 Communist revolution, they were socialized to see the Maoist worldview as normal, in schools and society rather than in the reindoctrination "study classes" and labor camps endured by comparably intellectual members of their parents' and grandparents' generations. They were already in or soon to enter young adulthood when Mao died in 1976, and they have their own mixed memories of the mid-twentieth century. Before leaving young adulthood, they saw the Maoist worldview utterly overthrown. Not only were the old ideology and values repudiated in state propaganda and open citizen discourse, but they were also undermined by China's burgeoning new prosperity—even though, from any standard Marxist-Leninist viewpoint, China was moving backward in the eyes of "history." Yet the political structure remained the same, and in 1989 proved that it could stop reform and "bite back."

These authors surely are ambivalent about the older generations that commanded them and also aware that younger generations are molded by pervasive public erasure, denial, and selective remembering of much of China's revolutionary past (and now, of the failed democracy and protest movements of 1989)—and moreover, they are content to be so molded. The writers hope to compensate for these selective views of history by taking critical and oppositional approaches.

The authors at issue in this book, of both the core seventeen works and the aforementioned subsidiary ones, were born between 1950 and 1964, except for Zheng Yi (b. 1947). Chan Koonchung is another outlier; he was born in Shanghai in 1952, but grew up in Hong Kong. The new historical authors were too young to have studied Russian, like Gu Hua (b. 1942). Most of them personally experienced country life and the hunger that went with it. Mo Yan (b. 1955), Yan Lianke (b. 1958), Liu Zhenyun (b. 1958), and Ge Fei (b. 1964) were born and raised in rural villages. The first three escaped the countryside by entering the People's Liberation Army, and it was as army propagandists that they learned "creative" writing; Ge Fei, who once considered becoming a carpenter or a peasant, was born late enough for a natural transition to college through the newly established entrance exams of 1978.[113] Li Rui (b. 1950), Han Shaogong (b. 1953), Wang Anyi (b. 1954), Zhang Wei (b. 1956), and Wang Xiaobo (1952–1997) were sent down to "learn from the poor peasants" under the youth rustication program of 1969—famously so[114] (likewise, filmmakers Zhang Yimou, b. 1951, and Chen Kaige, b. 1952). Han Shaogong went to West Hunan of his own volition in 1984 to search for "roots" and indigenes; it was quite unlike northeastern Hunan, the location of his rustication and his fictional town of Maqiao. Mo Yan was still in the countryside during the Cultural Revolution, which was a factor in the interruption of his rudimentary schooling, though he found work in a local factory before entering the army in 1976. Ge Fei, Yu Hua (b. 1960), Su Tong (b. 1963), and Ye Zhaoyan (b. 1957) were able to graduate from high school at the proper time (Yu Hua practiced as a dentist for five years before turning to writing), but even so they claim personal knowledge of Cultural Revolution turmoil, having witnessed it or heard tales from friends and family.[115] That era's legacy of hyper-politicization and focus on organizing for purposes of conflict affected Chinese life for decades. For Wang Shuo (b. 1958), it was his parents who were sent to the countryside in the Cultural Revolution, leaving him alone in Beijing with his siblings during his adolescence.

Most of the writers went to college after regular higher education was restored in the late 1970s. That includes not just the younger writers Ye Zhaoyan, Su Tong, and Ge Fei (college graduates of 1983, 1984, and 1985, respectively), but also some of the older cohort whose secondary education was disrupted or denied them: Li Rui graduated in 1984, after six years as a peasant and two years as a worker; Liu Zhenyun, in 1982, after his stint in the army; Han Shaogong, likewise in 1982; and Wang Xiaobo, about the same time. Like Liu Zhenyun, Yan Lianke followed his initial years in the army with college, graduating from a civilian university in 1985, and in 1991, like Mo Yan in 1986, from the People's Liberation Army Art Institute. Zhang Wei also had some college education.

Most of our novelists had educated parents and escaped their rustication ahead of time, into the arts, if only through the army. Wang Anyi, the daughter of famous novelist Ru Zhijuan (who, like her daughter, wrote works of lasting importance only in the post-Mao period), won a transfer to work in a cultural troupe already in 1972. Wang Xiaobo, the son of a famous academician, also got an early release to return to Beijing in 1972. Sent-down youths Li Rui and Han Shaogong were able to secure transfers to cultural workplaces in 1977, two years before most rusticated youth were freed to return to their old homes in the cities. Mo Yan's father was a production brigade accountant, and his elder brother, a particular inspiration for his literary pursuits, attended college.[116] Wang Shuo was raised in Beijing, in an army compound. Liu Zhenyun grew up in poverty, but an uncle was the village Communist Party secretary "for several decades."[117] Ye Zhaoyan, younger than the sent-down cohort, is the son of a writer and the grandson of one of the great novelists of the May Fourth era, Ye Shengtao.

The other notable aspect of these writers is a two-stage writing career, transitioning from a career in the Chinese Boom to one in the Post-Boom—or, for the older writers, a double rebirth, as they passed from Pre-Boom (late Mao era) to Boom and then to Post-Boom. (Only Wang Xiaobo was little known before the 1990s.) The older writers' 1970s works naturally followed tried-and-true "socialist" formulas. Their first creative turnaround occurred during the passage from Mao to Deng. They gained fame as experimentalists, some in the roots-seeking movement, in the mid-1980s (when Wang Shuo, Liu Zhenyun, and Yan Lianke also emerged, though not as avant-gardes but as realists and satirists). Major experimentalists of the earlier 1980s, like Zhang Xinxin, Liu Suola, Can Xue, Chen Cun, and the older Wang Meng, were known for satire, but not historical themes.

The second transition of the core writers, from avant-garde Boom to post-avant-garde Post-Boom, is better known and seminal in the formation of the new historical novel. Yu Hua and Ge Fei epitomize the trend. Yu Hua's youthful works of the mid-1980s are seemingly absurdist short stories shorn of modifiers but full of senseless and unmotivated violence. Enigmatic, faceless, unnamed characters in his stories sometimes refer repeatedly to very precise calendar dates of no apparent historical significance. The language is basic—stripped down—and one sentence does not always logically or thematically follow another. But even these stories are full of "events"—which is to say, plotted. One line of interpretation reads Yu Hua's early stories allegorically, comparing them to *Lord of the Flies*.[118]

In the 1990s, after the massacre, Yu Hua gained fame all over again, from his best-selling masterworks *To Live* and *Chronicle of a Blood Merchant*. These "new historical novels" were powerful in their own right and also notorious because they marked the author's turn away from difficult, enigmatic, some would say nonsensical highbrow prose toward strong realistic narratives with intriguing story lines and characters, tragic or pathetic suffering, and "a point."[119] It was also a transition from short stories to full-length fiction. Yu Hua's later works, too, are open to allegorical readings.

Labyrinthine plots with missing information gained Ge Fei a reputation in the 1980s as "China's Borges."[120] His later works retain his nonlinear plotting, puzzles and mysteries, and the interest in dreams and madness he shares with Naguib Mahfouz (Nobel laureate of 1988), whose *Cairo Trilogy*, a realistic, if nostalgic, multigenerational epic about changing social mores influenced the *Southlands Trilogy* (2004–2011). However, an overall more "realistic" and straightforward trend in Ge Fei's post-1980s writing disappointed his old aficionados. Not all the imaginary flourishes in his *Southlands Trilogy* are modernist; they include use of classical Chinese (in the first volume), allusions to ancient Chinese poems and parables, and references to works of Western classical music (in the final volume).[121]

The passage from Boom to Post-Boom was similarly transitional for other budding new historical writers, notably Su Tong (as in his later and less avant-garde *Rice* and *The Boat to Redemption*) and Han Shaogong. Some adopted more realistic styles, some went from short stories "seeking roots" to full-length novels, and some, like Mo Yan (and ultimately Yu Hua), developed skills in comedy and farce. They did not take up the thesis fiction of China's May Fourth and socialist realist classics. Most tended toward epic novels that viewed the past synoptically or allegorically, portraying it with intriguing plotting that won them a broader readership.

Wang Anyi, the most prominent of the writers in the early 1980s and perhaps later in the decade, too, joined the experimentalists only in the late 1980s, when she took up feminist themes, and in the 1990s, when she penned experimental works like *Uncle's Story* (*Shushu de gushi*; 1990, first published in Taiwan).[122] Her aficionados felt that she had always created her own sensibility. In *The Song of Everlasting Sorrow*, she turned to the full-length fictional form, now with historical themes, still accompanied by complexities of narrative viewpoint.

Not all the writers forsook experimentalism. That would include Zhang Wei in his *September's Fable* (1992), though he began writing that work in 1987, during the high tide of the avant-garde, and Li Rui's *Trees without Wind* (1996), a period tragedy set in the Cultural Revolution. Its multiple narrators and themes often replicate those of *As I Lay Dying*, right down to the carpentry of coffin-making. These Chinese works and Mo Yan's *Sandalwood Death* (2001) are notable for another tendency that gained momentum in the later high-literary novels set in the past: use of dialect, likewise a Faulknerian attribute.

Something happened in the late 1980s, and more comprehensively in the 1990s, that nurtured the birth of China's new historical novels and their special breadth of vision. The 1989 massacre, the clampdown on freedom of expression that followed, and the subsequent restructuring of the Chinese intellectual scene played a role. So did the commercialization of literature, which gave high literature new competition while also suggesting how to reach new audiences. The 1989 calamity could not have influenced *Red Sorghum*, *The Ancient Ship*, *Nineteen Thirty-Four Escapes*, or *Old Well*, but the malaise of China's intellectuals and students was apparent before the massacre. Equally important were the early signs of China's global rise, amid change and no change. Another clue comes from the novels: the reappearance, after the death of Mao, of so many characteristics of the "old society" from before 1949 that had been denounced throughout the novelists' formative years, conjoined with a newborn, unconditional optimism among the general public that was quite in line with official propaganda. At times, novelists of the Red Guard generation must have seen China as moving backward.

R EADERS OPEN A historical novel expecting a quick orientation to the era of the plot. Chinese readers are no different, and they are no less predisposed than the rest of us to see history unfold in discrete periods. Marxist ideas of stages of historical progress die hard. Even anciently, Chinese historians (far more than the Indians, for instance) scrupulously recorded dates. Standard dynastic histories of the past two millennia and local histories ("gazetteers") still written by Communist Party–appointed committees begin with chronologies of major events. Chinese historians of practically any political persuasion agree and insist that "modern Chinese history" is a non-relative term that starts with the Opium War in 1840. In the Mao era, political movements were clearly demarcated and unfolded in a now well-remembered sequence.[1] Each had its own "saddle-shaped" history, like a sine curve, intensifying and dying off. Literary scholars, too, create literary histories and taxonomies of the nation's finest writers (to their great annoyance) according to their allegiance to period and faction (*pai*).[2] Historicist concepts of "post-" this or that are everywhere in scholarly and popular writings.

Luke S. K. Kwong argues that late nineteenth-century Chinese reformers from Xue Fucheng to Liang Qichao initiated China's transition from cyclical to linear concepts of time, frequently resorting to "'block-time' phrases." Their chief concern was the relatively recent, post-Taiping "block" of time, with its cascading national crises, but they accommodated concepts from the Chinese classics by having their current era follow a long series of other eras. Going backward, they were the recent-ancient, middle-ancient, and high-ancient eras, sometimes with a paleo-ancient era at the start.[3] Since recent-ancient times began before or after the Han dynasty (206 BCE–220 CE), the first two or three ancient eras necessarily told of mythological events, increasingly conceived as "prehistoric" after modern theories of evolution took hold.

Historians across the globe take the 1949 revolution and the 1976 death of Mao to be great divides in Chinese history, though they do not speak of China's pre-1949 history as that of "the old society," as is still common in China. To young people, Maoist Communism is just another superseded period in China's march toward "modernity," conceived as a historicist concept, not a relative term. It is primarily academic historians who write of historical tendencies not wholly reversed in 1949, or even 1976. Such revisionism is not found in Chinese textbooks. Yet these watersheds and other standard dates, like 1911, 1919, and 1937, are not so clearly demarcated in China's new historical novels.

This chapter asks what happens when the reader opens a new historical novel from China and seeks bearings in time. Most readers will wonder if the action occurs before or after the Communist revolution. And if it postdates 1949, is it "contemporary"—"post-socialist"—or a reflection of the "old" Maoist era?

Most of China's notable *memoir* literature locates biographical events within larger historical events and trends, including famines, revolutions, warfare, and political movements. Politically charged art films such as Tian Zhuangzhuang's *The Blue Kite* likewise depict the lives of characters being fashioned and destroyed by successive political upheavals. A more melodramatic example, initially banned in China (*The Blue Kite* is still banned), is the film version of *Farewell My Concubine* (1993), directed by Chen Kaige. The complicated and highly allegorical relationship among the three starring roles develops in tandem with the political winds of the Mao era.[4]

China's new historical works often deny the reader or viewer such clear chronological bearings, without, however, engaging in the kind of labyrinthine shifts and paradoxes about chronology that are characteristic of militantly avant-garde fiction. The works at issue below display at least four potentially unsettling treatments of historical time. (1) Protracted ambiguity about the temporal setting of the era being recollected or the era from which it is being recalled, achieved through misdirection and mixed or missing clues. (2) Defamiliarization of a temporal setting that *is* specified, due to missing or discordant supporting details, so that the context and meaning of history appear altered, unknowable, or allegorical. (3) Conscious elevation of the historical narrative to the level of myth or legend: to a world whose most important reality exists in a time out of time, despite references to the past, even a recent past. (4) Defamiliarization of past *and* present, or of a farther past and a recent past, through visions of life as a repetition of past events.

Particular novels, of course, transcend and straddle any such categories, while still being similarly ambiguous in chronology. Liu Zhenyun's *One Word Is Worth a Thousand* so calculatingly avoids historical markers that I leave it for the conclusion, for consideration as an "anti-historical novel" about a culture seemingly beyond influence by historical vicissitudes. The opening pages of Zhang Wei's *September's Fable* speak of an adult character named Little Red Guard, but subsequent, not always chronologically arranged, chapters offer extreme puzzles in temporal ambiguity. However, I discuss that work under the third tendency, for it seems to me a modern myth (or fable, as its title says), narrating events outside of historical time. Ge Fei's *Bygone Beauty* goes on for pages with another narrative set in a timeless "rural China," like the two aforementioned works, and Wang Anyi's *The Song of Everlasting Sorrow* immerses the reader in an "eternal Shanghai." I discuss those novels in chapter 3, the better to emphasize their themes of historical cyclicalism. Yu Hua's *Chronicle of a Blood Merchant*, for its part, leaves the reader long suspended in temporal limbo before finally revealing the time of the action. I will discuss it in this chapter under the second category, since its temporal defamiliarization continues even after the setting is clarified. This chapter opens with works by Su Tong, a pioneer in the art of historical ambiguity, even in his early, shorter works.

Modern Chinese history has, to be sure, been divided up in different ways by imaginative authors, critics, and historians, suggesting continuities between times as disparate as the Cultural Revolution and post-Mao marketized socialism. Bonnie S. McDougall and Kam Louie, followed by Yibing Huang, see continuities between the fictions of those very eras. The one followed the other, after all; I, too, have argued that China's epic "realistic" "anticorruption" novels written not much more than ten years ago show continuities with the epic fiction of the Mao era.[5] Huang and many other younger writers and critics, however, tend to identify the Cultural Revolution and only the Cultural Revolution with "Maoism," either overlooking or exaggerating differences between the 1950s and 1960s. This is not the viewpoint of China's new historical novelists; whatever their view of history as an epic process, their "memory" (whether they were old enough personally to understand the early Communist years) does not conflate the Cultural Revolution and the Maoist society that preceded it, nor does it see the Cultural Revolution as an aberration

not prefigured by the "seventeen years" preceding it. To see continuities, similarities, and repetitions is of course their choice, as novelists with a historical
vision.

Ambiguities about the historical era of the action that unfolds in these
novels may reflect several factors: the authors' avant-garde narrative prefer-
ences; pessimism about history, social change, and human nature; the reappearance of pre-1949 institutions and social practices in "post-socialist" China;
or constraints of self-censorship in writing about what is really the present.
The idea that Deng Xiaoping's vision of progress was, in Marxist historical
terms, reactionary was argued by leftists in the 1980s and may remain persua-
sive to generations educated by Maoism. Visions of history running backward
can suggest dystopia itself as a recurring phenomenon.

How then might the new novels' treatment of historical time influence the
common reader to reconsider modern Chinese history as dystopian? It is not
the same for all works. Dissonances with standard conceptions of historical
time or of historical progress may in some cases create a sense of anomie and
discomfort, a protracted uneasiness. Awful conflicts of the past persist or recur. If the events related reflect a brutish vision of society, culture, or human
nature, then even when the author or filmmaker provides clarity about the
era, the narrative's detachment from history as the reader "knows it" allows
projection of these unsettling visions indefinitely into the future. In works that
self-consciously transplant canonical historical events to a mythologized time
out of time, temporally universalist (even if at times nationally "tribal") visions can turn dystopian if the moral of the myth is one of decadence and
decline. Modern-day myths can demolish or parody Maoist accounts, or result in self-parody if the heroism is sufficiently exaggerated. Maoist myths
pointed toward utopia; counter-myths of dystopia become all the clearer, by
transposition, as one descends from the mythic heights. Still other works, of
the fourth tendency, create a sense of dystopia by conjuring up explicit visions
of historical circularity conjoined with pessimism. They are examined in the
next chapter.

LINGERING TEMPORAL AMBIGUITY IN CHINA'S NEW HISTORICAL NOVELS AND NOVELLAS

China's avant-garde short fiction of the 1980s was already known for its historical fabrications, blurring of boundaries among eras, chronological paradoxes
and non sequiturs, diverse factual contradictions, and vacillations in view-

point. From the later, new historical *novels*, however, one can usually construct a linear storyline or *fabula* behind the most puzzling plot (*suzhet*) even as the novels continue to question the validity of historical judgments, the personal memories, and the competence of the narrative viewpoint, as would any serious historian and most common readers. Several of the later and longer works are fascinated with the conventional subject of genealogy, for instance; others detail the effects of time on particular people or places. The temporal settings of the storylines seldom remain ambiguous for chapters on end, as in Gabriel García Márquez's *One Hundred Years of Solitude*, and different technologies and social formations are not "out of sync," like the railroads in Ayn Rand's dystopian and futuristic *Atlas Shrugged*. Even so, chronological reference points in the Chinese novels may remain indeterminate long enough into the tale to be disquieting to the reader who seeks historical bearings. The cognitive disorientation of temporal anomie, particularly when the events at hand are violent or inexplicable, can lead to a sense of disquiet, vertigo, even horror. In life, the reappearance of prerevolutionary social phenomena such as servants, pedicabs, child labor, and prostitutes, not to mention private property, advertisements, and other commercial phenomena once castigated as morally odious and condemned to "the ashcan of history," can create disorientation and discomfort. Such multi-era phenomena make it easier to write a novel without specifying the era. Characters in the novels, even rugged individualists, seldom change psychologically in relation to the political environment—developing separate private and public selves, for instance.

Su Tong's *The Gardener's Art* (1992) and *Tattoo* (1993) may serve as bookends illustrating converse types of temporal defamiliarization: the past as present and the present as past. One is sure only that the setting is modern and urban. Both tales are told in Su Tong's characteristically modern colloquial voice: direct and often mordant in its description of unattractive realities. In the former work, a major theme is a young woman's revolting underarm body odor, which comes from an abnormal medical condition. The work is punctuated by poignant visual images and symbols in which beauty emanates from the damaged or ugly. It finally becomes clear that the setting is prewar Shanghai, but the unpleasant subject, family discord and disintegration, continues to develop in a way that has a more contemporary feel and relevance. The atmosphere seems perforce almost anachronistic. *Tattoo*, by contrast, is peopled by young hooligans, as if it were a common tale about prewar Shanghai gangsters. Yet this story's setting turns out to be a southern Chinese city in the waning days of the Cultural Revolution, if not after the death of Mao. Only the political slogans are lacking.

The Gardener's Art is a tale of petty but escalating domestic and generational disputes among four parties: a middle-aged, middle-class urban married couple and their daughter and son, both of whom are in their twenties and unmarried. Each of the first three, perceiving their individual autonomy to be at risk within the household, cultivates a plant that the rest of the family finds repugnant. A picture of "eternal" Shanghai begins to emerge in the early pages, though in fact the setting is never identified as Shanghai. It could be unfolding in old neighborhoods of Shanghai that preserved their shabby but distinctive prewar character through the socialist era into post-Mao times. The houses are "dilapidated" and in "bad repair" (95),[6] appropriate to the Mao or post-Mao era. The tale is told in a simple, contemporary voice; old bourgeois terms for "Mr." and "Mrs." could be simply construed as slightly satiric if the setting is the 1990s instead of the 1930s. Only gradually does it become apparent that the story really does take place in prerevolutionary times. The daughter reads the popular novel *Fate in Tears and Laughter (Ti xiao yinyuan)* by Zhang Henshui, but that 1930 classic was revived and popular again in the 1980s. Mentions of rickshaws, a bowler hat, a private eye, a Charlie Chaplin film, and a play by Guo Moruo finally offer overwhelming evidence that the setting must be in the past. Even so, the "postmodern" ethos of a cosmopolitan Shanghai as we know it today, absorbed in entertainment, sexuality, snobbishness, and voyeurism, never dissipates.

The atmosphere of *The Gardener's Art* (1992) indeed prefigures the lengthier description of "eternal bourgeois Shanghai" in Wang Anyi's masterwork, *The Song of Everlasting Sorrow* (1995). That more famous full-length historical novel, discussed in chapter 3, begins with equally colloquial, very chatty disquisitions that go on for pages describing in individual subchapters Shanghai's enclosed alleyway compounds of row houses (*longtang*), the nature of gossip, pigeons and their bird's-eye view of society, even the heroine-to-be of the novel, who is introduced not as an individual but as a generic type: "Wang Qiyao is the typical daughter of the Shanghai *longtang*" (20/22). Later the translators, not unreasonably, have Wang Anyi writing of "Wang Qiyaos," in the plural. Still, one cannot be sure if these young Wang maidens are historical or contemporary. The row house neighborhoods, or *longtang*, were built in old (prewar) Shanghai and were an appropriate setting for contemplative 1990s fiction about Shanghai's still unique ethos; they were the subject of celebratory academic research, much of it from Shanghai academics. It is not until chapter 2 that Wang Anyi divulges concrete information about the temporal setting: "Four decades the story spans" (24/27), and even then it is merely the reader's presumption that the story most likely begins "at the start," with references to cheongsams representing contemporary 1940s fashion instead of a 1980s retro trend (which the novel also treats, in later chapters). Finally one reads that "Shanghai in late 1945 was a city of wealth, colors, and stunning women" (39/45)—which is also to say that it was then very much as it is when Wang Anyi wrote about it, in the late twentieth century. Just as disconcertingly, part 2, after the heroine's neighbors' flight from Shanghai as the Communist armies reach the gates of the great city at the end of part 1, opens in another temporal limbo, with the heroine in a rural village. It takes a chapter before the reader can be sure that novelistic time has indeed progressed chronologically into the socialist era. One never does learn exactly how many years it takes the heroine to return to Shanghai and resume her urban life in the new era of socialism.

Returning to *The Gardener's Art*, the reader notes that this work is a highly symbolic piece about family life set in the past; it is not a long novel or directly a meditation on history. However, the tale gradually turns dark and in the end does not differentiate past from present so clearly after all. The husband goes missing for several days, which in principle introduces the intrigue of mystery fiction, but Su Tong deflates (perhaps satirizes) this interest with comic portraits of the two separate detective agencies the family son attempts to engage. Both agencies appear inept or worse and the subjects of their investigations inconsequential—moreover, the son's visits to them are in both cases interrupted by social diversions irrelevant to the case. Both the son and the daughter quickly lose interest in their father's disappearance, assuming that he has simply run off with a mistress after they saw their mother humiliate him. The story concentrates on the disintegration of the family, a garden that has been very badly cultivated. The gracelessness of married life is accentuated by the fact that everyone suspects infidelity rather than foul play. In the end, since the husband was indeed murdered and buried in his own flower bed, this turns out to be one more indication of the whole family's inattention and insensitivity. The tale is not ultimately a historical period piece, but an examination of the meaner side of humanity (in a family surnamed Kong, like Confucius) that surely is about the past, present, and future. A 1990s un-Confucian urban family is not much more distant from the era of the Sage who provided family rules than the 1930s—or should one say that the 1930s, before the revolution, was just as un-Confucian as the 1990s? One may look for progress in technology and "history," but in the "history" of families and morals, a modern tendency in many other cultures besides China's is to see decline and decay.

Su Tong's *Tattoo* is like *The Gardener's Art* in its opening mystery about the historical epoch of the action, but the discord between atmosphere and the era of the plot is the opposite of the other work in regard to the 1949 divide. *Tattoo's* opening pages tell of the tragic birth of a boy destined later in childhood to be given the cruel nickname of a cripple, Limpy. His mother froze to death when she fell into an ice-covered river while carrying him across it shortly after he was born. Miraculously, the baby orphan survived. Frightened neighbors had heard the anonymous mother's screams out on the ice, but "no one even dared open their rear window" (133/153) to learn the cause of her panic. This opening conjures up images of hardhearted bourgeois Shanghai of the old society; later, the reader is thrust into scenes of a dirty industrial city that could have been inhabited by characters from Dickens or the Little Match Girl. (The street name where the story unfolds, by association with similar places in other stories by Su Tong, suggests that the location is an industrial area of Suzhou.[7]) The reader is told that the mother awakened on the last day of her life to the sound of an alarm clock, ostensibly a sign of modernity, but as an indication of the era that would be misleading. Prewar urban China had its clocks. It was later on, in the impoverished Mao era, that timepieces became scarce, so much so that in the early 1980s wristwatches became standard wedding or dowry gifts.

A few pages into the story, the narrator offhandedly gives away the era by speaking of a game played with copper coils in the early 1970s, and of how Limpy lost his leg and got his nickname at the age of nine. It is unclear, however, exactly when Limpy was born; the reader can only guess that the setting of the rest of the story is the 1970s or perhaps the early eighties—either before or after China's opening up. From there the plot turns on gang violence, family discord, the death of Limpy's elder brother—a gang member killed in a rumble—and Limpy's grand dream of resurrecting the gang after the police break it up. None of this social disorder suggests either China's "socialist" violence during the Cultural Revolution (the "real" Cultural Revolution of 1966–1967) or the rosier and nearer memories of the period after 1976, when China came out from under the officially defined period of "madness." The gangs in *Tattoo* are named the Boars and White Wolves, not the East Is Red or Protect the Helmsman factions. The young thugs take names like Commander Tang and Bornkiller; initiation is with the traditional chicken blood of the old secret societies and triads. Is it the late "Cultural Revolution" (the eve of

China's reforms), the chaotic Red Guard years after all, or the start of the Deng Xiaoping era? A satiric masterstroke is that Limpy, having been brought up in a society with nothing but street rules, in order to create gang rules for the resurrected gang turns to the People's Liberation Army's Three Main Rules of Discipline and Eight Points for Attention as the only model he knows (146/179). In Su Tong's practiced "gothic" manner, the story proceeds onward, drearily and horrifically. There are more rumbles and hints of incest between Limpy's father and his sister. Tortured by his rivals, Limpy declines in health until he becomes an eccentric recluse, a near invalid living in his father's attic.

Tattoo invites a reading as an allegory of the turmoil of Chinese politics. The story is told in retrospect by Limpy's one friend (and that single known aspect of the narrator's identity is revealed only midway through the novella), indicating that the action is all in the past, associated with the disorders of the Mao years and/or their immediate aftermath. And yet, in this retrospective vision of an era shorn throughout of clear identifications of time and place, one can easily imagine that this horrible story of a ruined human being has its eye on the present and future. It bears the horrors of a dystopian vision. Concludes the narrator, in a mordant voice: "For people like us, who grew up on Mahogany Road, the warm, happy memories of childhood always end in disagreement. It's perfectly normal" (157/203).

Of Su Tong's longer novels with historical themes, *Rice* (1990) is perhaps the most famous.[8] Like the novellas just mentioned, it is written in a very contemporary vernacular and begins with ambiguous or conflicting signals about the era, even as it develops Su Tong's forte, precisely described by David Der-wei Wang as "family melodrama with a gothic touch; looming behind the façade of his domestic tales are decadent motives and unspeakable desires."[9] Hunger is the unifying trope of this novel, as in so many other works by Su Tong—hunger for food (as again in his novella *Opium Family*), sex, and the power of life and death over others (particularly of men over women)—all of which are satisfied by rice in this novel. Rice can and in the novel does adorn a corpse or suffocate a person thrown into a stockpile of it.

Childhood hunger makes rice into a fetish for the hero, Five Dragons, as he flees famine in his village and worms his way into a city rice merchant's family. Five Dragons is driven to eat rice uncooked, sleep on it, and put it into a woman's cervix before and after her death. Learning to enjoy the power of humiliating others instead of being humiliated, he marries the rice merchant's daughter when she becomes a fallen woman. He abuses her, forces himself on her sister as her replacement, becomes an underworld don after committing mass murder by arson, and fathers a son named "Rice Boy" who suffocates his little sister in rice. Finally Five Dragons betrays all his former gangster associates to the authorities so that he can return to his village on a boxcar of rice, proving that he has permanently conquered the "rice problem."

Hunger, desire, gangsters, and prostitutes are universals of Chinese history and are literary themes in stories representing pre-1949 and 1980s society. Certainly the trend of history in *Rice* is downward and horrific; Howard Y. F. Choy (150) links the dystopian theme to Su Tong's focus on the unhealthiness of city life in contrast to rural life, though he also sees the city as utopian because of its plenty. But what exactly is the era in the novel?[10] Is this, shorn of any allegory, a tale of prerevolutionary decline ready to be reversed by revolution, as in the official Communist Party discourse? The opening scene, in which a hungry young orphan boy who has migrated from Maple Village to the big city with his bedroll is dazzled by its streetlights, gaudy advertisements, and the hum of textile mill machinery, could be entirely contemporary. Details such as rickshaws and reports of a general famine in the countryside, as well as some traditional names for the characters and family appellations such as "Sixth Master" begin to suggest a setting in the "old society," but China today is no stranger to private enterprise, wealth, greed, poverty, and obsessive desire. Finally, halfway through the novel one meets a Sixth Concubine (115/132). Still later, in chapter 8, a concrete date finally appears—1930 (119/137)—and, near the novel's end, the coming of Japanese planes "one day in July" indicates that the story has progressed to 1937, the beginning of the Sino-Japanese War (163/191). The raw intervention of the grand narrative of "history," in the form of war itself, brings horrors that nevertheless seem paltry compared to the horrible awakening of Five Dragon's sadism and uncontrolled urges in the pages preceding. The war simply provides Five Dragon an opportunity to settle scores with his old enemies and for other enemies to have him tortured one night by the Japanese. But then the war recedes from view. It is Five Dragon's own rotting away from venereal disease that brings an end to his story. His greedy son yanks gold teeth from his gums before the corpse completes its last trip home to Maple Village. This is a tale of cosmic, metaphorical destruction born of eternal, self-perpetuating human greed and weakness, above and outside of the "history" in textbooks. There can be no optimism about the human race, with or without the revolution that is still to come in the novel's belatedly clarified historical setting.

Su Tong's *My Life as Emperor* (1992) is the emblematic work of ambiguous temporality in his oeuvre, for it is about the fall of a purely imaginary state called Xie in a century, indeed a millennium, that is unidentifiable. Standard Chinese accounts of imperial life revel in dates and places. Su Tong's novel is written as the memoir of a boy prince named Duanbai who at the age of fourteen succeeds to the throne, due to schemes that may remind the popular reader of tales about the historical Yongzheng Emperor's ascent in 1722. Duanbai is deposed after eight years, yet manages to remain alive to see his former kingdom vanquished after he has enjoyed marvelous adventures while on the run as a commoner with his servant companion Swallow, eventually to seek solace as a monk. The language is Su Tong's usual modern Mandarin, with few concessions to formal court language or archaic grammar of any century (unlike the archaisms favored by China's many television historical drama series). Su Tong writes in the author's preface: "I hope my readers do not approach *My Life as Emperor* with the idea that it is historical fiction; that is why I have set the novel in no particular time. Identifying allusions and determining the accuracy of events places too great a burden on you and on me. The world of women and palace intrigues that you will encounter in this novel is but a scary dream on a rainy night; the suffering and slaughter reflect my worries and fears for all the people in all worlds, and nothing more" (vi).[11] Su Tong's truths about history are not to be found in the details. He has written, "What is past? What is history? To me, it is a stack of torn pieces of paper; since it is so torn, I can use my own style to pick it up, patch it up, and fold it up to reconstruct a world of my own."[12] Yet, in 1993, only one year after he penned *My Life as Emperor*, Su Tong did write a historical novel about a real person, China's female emperor of the Tang dynasty; the work takes her name, *Wu Zetian*. *My Life as Emperor* was reprinted in a volume together with *Wu Zetian*. Su Tong has intimated that neither work told more truth about history than the other.[13]

My Life as Emperor is yet another tale filled with inhuman, senseless, casual violence, much of it perpetrated by the almost nonchalantly brutal boy emperor, Duanbai. Upset by the nocturnal wailing of concubines shut up in a nearby palace, he ends their irritating sounds by ordering that all of their tongues be cut out. Due to his own queasiness more than sangfroid, he also orders a loyal injured general put to the sword. During a picaresque second life, as a pauper now that he is no longer a prince, Duanbai seeks to fulfill a childhood dream of becoming a tightrope walker—childish and absurd, and obviously symbolic—and so the hero finally does, in this work, attain a degree of internal peace in a monastery, where he incongruously seeks instruction not from teachings of the Buddha but from the *Analects* of Confucius.

The novel can be read as one more variation on Su Tong's common theme of moral degradation and decline due to obsessive desires for sex, food, and domination. In this work, women's machinations are the root of much evil and political instability, as in traditional Chinese readings and writings of dynastic and indeed later Maoist history. *My Life as Emperor*, narrated from the start with stark portents about the coming destruction of the Xie dynasty (or *state*, or empire?), can be seen either as a fulfillment of traditionally cyclical dynastic history or as a portent of the end of it. The message is not religious, however. The reformed ex-emperor-monk ends his tale ambivalently: "Sometimes I think [the *Analects*] holds all the wisdom of the world; sometimes I don't get anything at all out of it" (189/290).

A more likely reading of the temporally ambiguous *My Life as Emperor*, given the oddly comforting resolution, is as allegory, and yet it is more clearly dystopian if one takes the ending as purposely absurd. The novel's scenes of imperial abuse of power evoke both eternal and recurring problems of imperial power-lust leading to political decline, and also the recent excesses of Chairman Mao. It is interesting that Su Tong's novel preceded the scandalous exposure of the chairman by his personal physician,[14] but Mao's abuses were already the subject of gossip. Critic Sabina Knight finds in the work's "descriptions of the cutting out of tongues to silence dissent, the severing of a musician's ten fingers, or the details of eleven gory tortures inflicted on a peasant leader" echoes of atrocities perpetrated by the Red Guards in the Cultural Revolution.[15]

SPECIFYING THE DATES, BUT DEFAMILIARIZING THE ERA

Anachronism makes its appearance in various ways in China's new historical novels. Mo Yan's *Life and Death Are Wearing Me Out* features a peasant protagonist who farms independently, outside the collective, throughout the Maoist period. He is the lone holdout from collectivization in the locality—perhaps in all of China proper, one imagines. But this figuration is absurd, almost farcical. The later volumes of Liu Zhenyun's *Homeland Trilogy* are notorious for inserting real and parodied Maoist slogans into the mouths of figures from ancient history.[16] Wang Xiaobo's period novels have Tang dynasty characters speak modern slang.[17] Wang Anyi's *The Song of Everlasting Sorrow* has several characters who appear, in the days of socialism and then post-socialism, as relics of the past, but these anachronisms are to be taken on faith as at least somewhat plausible. They suit Wang's purpose in delineating Shanghai's resistance to socialist change and its love of fashion, including retro fashion, as a way of resisting politics. Han Shaogong's A *Dictionary of Maqiao*, with its quasi-scholarly analysis of a putative local dialect, contains examples of anachronistic speech, too, but again the trope of a rural backwardness so profound that it ultimately defeats totalitarianism is common in post-Mao literature; it simply reverses the old Maoist discourse of resistant backwaters finally being overwhelmed by the righteous winds—and putative rewards—of social change, typically coming from still poorer, thus more righteous, rural areas of China.[18] The film *Yellow Earth* originally broke ground in portraying the immovability of peasant tradition (superstition, in this case); that the setting is the relatively recent 1930s, indicated by the appearance of a Red Army uniform, seems anomalous. The Mao-era and post-Mao villagers in Mo Yan's *Life and Death Are Wearing Me Out* still think in terms of imperial visits, imperial edicts, and imperial wardrobes, and cite the names of ancient gods. Han Shaogong's village of Maqiao exists in its own mythical time out of time, but its peculiarities are not the stuff of legend, as in a Mo Yan novel. What concern us in the pages below are novels that specify the era clearly enough, creating expectations in almost any reader old enough to have common historical knowledge, but that fail to reinforce and even seem to contradict these expectations, despite a certain realism in the telling. The new sense of history, in the presence of so many horrors, may suggest dystopia—the possibility, even probability, that these events will come again.

Su Tong's *Nineteen Thirty-Four Escapes* (1987), which played a major role in introducing the author to the public, is a bridge between China's avant-garde Boom and its already dawning Post-Boom. It is also a bridge between those works whose temporal subject is vague from the outset and those with a temporal setting as explicit as "1934," which nevertheless manage to defamiliarize it. This work is a novella with an epic sensibility; it ranges broadly and self-consciously over the fate of three generations of the narrator's family. Like Su Tong's other fiction, *Nineteen Thirty-Four Escapes* accentuates the harshness of China's "old society," and yet it can also be read as damning human nature and its inveterate perversions in every era.[19]

The novella ostensibly explores a very linear phenomenon—genealogy. From start to finish, however, the first-person narrative is solipsistic, nonlinear, and at times irrational. Only offhandedly and well into the story do we learn that the narrator has gotten his story not just through some sort of psychic communion with spirits, including those of inanimate objects, as he intimates early on, but also from the usual method of returning home and interviewing old-timers. Still, he admits that much of the family history he writes is imagined (147–148/134). It contains contradictions and invokes oddly recurring visual images (evidently from free association) and putrid olfactory images, as of the narrator's favorite uncle, Dingo, who devoted his life to picking up dog droppings.

The year recollected may be precise, but the time at which it is recollected is disconcertingly vague. The opening sentence is mysterious, even stupefying: "Perhaps my father was a mute fetus." (When? How long? How was this silence any different from other fetuses', if "fetus" has a literal rather than figurative meaning—and why would one mean it literally, since the next sentence says, as if blaming him, "His profound reticence left my family shrouded in a murky gray fog for fully half a century"?) It is only pages later that one learns he was born in 1934; he might, then, have literally been a fetus, necessarily mute, in earlier months of 1934. The time of the narration seemingly would be the mid-1980s, when the story was published, but the narrator has said at the outset that he is *not* Su Tong. Moreover, the narrator fictionalizes *the readers*, reminding them (us), "You are my good friends." We are said to have watched the narrator try to write a poem about his ancestral background "last winter" (130/102–103).

A subjective, seemingly schizophrenic confession comes in the second paragraph, when the narrator admits to having a "congenital fear" of seeing his own elongated shadow, which during one urban night took on "the image of a fugitive"; this accentuates the narrator's self-identification with the inadequacies of his "mute" and runaway father, who one night chased him in what the narrator himself calls a "surrealistic pursuit" (129–130/102). The father and all his male relatives now and hereafter will be explicitly associated with phallic images of straw, bamboo, and their own elongated shadows. The straw embodies ancestral memory and the smell of deceased ancestors born on top of it, says the narrator. Straw, moreover, allows his father to "transform himself into a wizard." The narrator realizes that in fleeing his shadow and his father he was making an escape, and it comes to pass that his entire home community, Maple Village, has made its own escapes. The nonlinear narrative, surrealistic body consciousness, and sense of local apocalypse remind one of Asturias's *Men of Maize*. Su Tong's obsessive images can be read either as surreal and solipsistic[20] or as esoterically coded in an alien belief system that the story never decodes. Humans become "shadows" (important also in Su Tong's *The Boat to Redemption*), as in the Mayan world, in which shadows represent souls. "Magic" dancing "house mice" in the narrator's old rural homestead prophesy human affairs, recalling the Mayan yellow rabbits and firefly wizards. Men are made not of maize but bamboo. And numbers, notably "139" and "1934," appear to have a cabalistic significance. The year 1934 is personified and, as the novella title might suggest, can "escape," like a human. Stalks of straw and bamboo are like vegetable *nahuales*, or living protector spirits (animals, in Central America) that local males can change into through shape-shifting.

The story proceeds throughout with these disquieting, sometimes magical touches, including nightmare images and hallucinations. Family and friends include scarred and grotesque characters, notably an omnipresent blind man who is alternately benevolent and malicious. The mostly tragic and horrific main events, which quite improbably all occurred in 1934, include the birth of the narrator's father, Uncle Dingo's flight from home, the overturning "everywhere in Maple Village" of "the rules of morality" (159/118), and other instances of seeming mass hysteria. Then came a bout of excessive prosperity when Maple Village (like the Guatemalan highlands upon the advent of maize-growing capitalism) became rich from growing bamboo, leading 139 males to migrate to a distant city to sell bamboo handicrafts. Then, still in 1934, there came a horrendous cholera epidemic, a conflagration at the bamboo craft shop of the narrator's grandfather, his death and that of Dingo, the miscarriage of a family pregnancy, and the theft of the narrator's father from his home. The grandmother, always at home, is a positive character, like the grandmother of Mo Yan's equally anonymous narrator in *Red Sorghum*, but she leads a subhuman life even before her only surviving child ("Father") is kidnapped.

Even when rationally weighing different accounts, the narrator feels compelled to interrupt his speculations with his own fantasies and hallucinations (my italics):

This is the first time the little woman Huanzi appears in my family history. *Inevitably she appears in front of Dingo, the two of them being separated by the wet, humid city street and a huge pig-iron kettle.* I think this has concrete historical implications; the little woman Huanzi was fated to become a singularly important guest in our clan, one who established an eternal connection with us.   (161/156)

I never saw that big-handled bamboo knife handed down to my ancestors. I don't know. I'm only thinking of the element of bamboo in the blood of the Maple Village men. *If my grandfather Chen Baonian and my uncle Dingo were both stalks of bamboo, if all their emotions were stalks of bamboo, everything would surpass our thoughts about it.* (162–163/159)

Thus does *Nineteen Thirty-Four Escapes* combine Su Tong's avant-garde mystical, extrasensory, and macabre explorations with a realistic interest in history—in events, characters, causation, and coincidence. This is a profoundly disquieting work about human events that finds history to be decadent and ruled by human failings destructive of all "rules of morality" and of life itself. The era is allegedly "1934," fetishistically so, but is "historical causation" a force actually in operation in such a phantasmagoric world?

The only partially satisfied desire (of both the narrator and the reader) to learn the "true" stories of the family and 1934 leads to an anomie of indeterminate meaning, as in many an avant-garde work, yet the narrator learns a historical lesson: that all of his relatives "together made up one particular link in the great teeming chain of human life" (131/104). Memory can be inherited—not from the ancestors, but from the straw on which they were born (131/104). Family and community history stand on their own, outside of and as if unrelated to any larger national history. This suggests that life does after all have a direction and a cause and effect—but its meaning cannot be happy for the human race. It is indistinguishable from a nightmare.

Su Tong's more conventionally narrated novel written a decade later, *The Boat to Redemption* (2009; winner of the 2009 Man Asian Literary Prize), retains a less unsettling sense of temporal ambiguity. A reference to a revolutionary martyr in the first pages indicates early on that the action unfolds after 1949; from there, occasional use of language about counterrevolutionaries and so forth, often so gratuitous as to appear humorous to a reader in post-Mao times, suggests that the story's action, when the unfortunate narrator is fifteen and twenty-six (in two succeeding parts of the novel), must take place after the late 1950s radicalism and during the Cultural Revolution, respectively. There are hints that things are changing later in the novel, but no clear indications that the post-Mao era has arrived. As we shall see in chapter 4, the plot delivers a dark, generalized picture of society and human nature, more than any particular political era. It applies to all of post-1949 China and has much broader applicability to the human condition than that.

Another novel (or novella) that names a particular year in its very title is Wang Xiaobo's *2015*. Yet this bizarre and dystopian work contains no other markers of the time, and no explicit or implicit indications that the plot actually unfolds in the future (the work was published in 1997), other than certain surrealistic extrapolations of current social ills that might suggest future developments. Technological innovations are not evident. This is appropriate to what might be near-future fiction, but the ambiguity of it all, particularly since the narrator tells his story as reminiscence, raises all the more the question of how the year 2015 relates to any of the narration. The sense of defamiliarization and temporal anomie lifts the tale out of history altogether, into metahistorical or fantastic speculation.

Yu Hua's *Cries in the Drizzle*, that writer's first full-length work of fiction, is another personal stylistic bridge, like Su Tong's *Nineteen Thirty-Four Escapes*, between the author's 1980s avant-garde short stories and his more conventional and epic 1990s historical novels. *Cries in the Drizzle*'s narrator tells a logical and relatively linear, though episodic, tale of pervasive suffering, bullying, and sudden, inexplicable death in his family and village as he grew up. In his earlier works, Yu Hua would baffle the reader by repeatedly inserting into his plots exact calendar dates that had no clear historical or even plot significance (though some dates occurred during the Cultural Revolution). The novels Yu Hua wrote in the 1990s, by contrast, have been heralded by critics as relatively "realistic."

Cries in the Drizzle names the year 1965 in its first sentence. Yet the narrative connects the date not to larger events (1965 was the eve of the Cultural Revolution), but instead to a very personal, subjective feeling attached to a general fear of the dark: "It was in 1965 that nighttime began to stir in me a nameless dread" (3). The early events unfold in just such a nervous and mysterious existential fog, for the basis of the story is childhood memory and incomprehension of the social, indeed familial, surroundings. Like Su Tong's boy emperor, Duanbai, whose sleep is disturbed by wailing concubines until he cuts out their tongues, Yu Hua's anonymous narrator, who is identified by name only several chapters later when a friend addresses him as Sun Guanglin (82/86), finds his sleep disturbed during a night of drizzle by "the sound of a woman's anguished wails. . . . Surely there is nothing more chilling than the sound of inconsolable cries on such a desolate night" (3/3). The narrator, adult at the time of the recitation but no more inclined to fill in the social context, next muses over his second childhood recollection, of being scared by the rustling clothes of an approaching stranger dressed in black that he somehow comes to associate with the woman's wailing. On another occasion, he and his playmates come upon his corpse. He is six years old at the time and "that must have been the extent of my reaction then: that dying was like falling asleep" (4/5). Is this unattributed death of an unidentified man related to known "history"? It is a mystery never solved.

An often-cited passage in this novel takes historical time more seriously than Su Tong's dismissive pronouncements. Says Yu Hua's narrator, "Our lives, after all, are not rooted in the soil as much as they are rooted in time. Fields, streets, rivers, houses—these are our companions, placed like ourselves in time. Time pushes us forward or back, and alters our aspect" (31/34). But the reader must put his full life story together like pieces of a puzzle, partly due to the episodic plot. Each chapter, and even subchapter, can stand alone as a separate reminiscence with its own theme and plot; some consider *Cries in the Drizzle* a book of linked stories by a single narrator. This, together with his musings about the nature of time and questioning of the reliability of memory and testimony (as in Su Tong's *Nineteen Thirty-Four Escapes*), indicates continuities with Yu Hua's avant-garde short stories of the 1980s. However, the memories add up to a coherent storyline. The episodes are not always in chronological order and there is some doubling-back; individual chapters may be flashbacks, but they are often clearly marked at the outset by the year, the narrator's age, or concurrent events. This allows the novel as a whole to be taken as a coming-of-age novel. (The fourth chapter, "Birth," begins in the autumn of 1958, before the narrator's birth, so the work cannot be wholly based on reminiscence.) The novel relates Guanglin's remembered childhood fears, strained family relations, the first awakenings of his and his brother's sexual desire, disappointments of adolescence, odd village events including a wedding followed by a suicide, the way he and his brothers made friends and enemies, and finally his schooling in the city. Guanglin's history is mysteriously complicated because his natal family for some reason (never explained) lent him out to a couple several miles away in the village of Littlemarsh, in 1966, when he was six; he returned to Southgate at twelve, reappearing the very day his family lost its home to fire. That initiated his life as family scapegoat and village outcast. The story takes him up to college in 1978, when he is eighteen. Constructing this chronology requires some calculation by the reader; the flashbacks between the two villages of Guanglin's early childhood are confusing to sort out in the plot.

Cries in the Drizzle is filled with unsuspecting victims and unsavory, often frustrated passions. Yet the suffering is almost completely detached from any Cultural Revolution context. An urban family's moves into and then out of Southgate may be interpreted ominously, but as far as the youthful Guanglin can see, the family is under no particular supervision "by the masses."[21] He has, after all, spent the violent years of the Cultural Revolution, 1966–1969, tucked away in Littlemarsh village, a place of memories much happier than those from Southgate. Politics is abnormally absent from this reminiscence, except in a tragicomic episode in which Guanglin's younger brother drowns trying to save a playmate. Guanglin's irresponsible and sexually unfaithful father buys new clothes for the family in the expectation that the sacrifice of his youngest "might well elevate them [the survivors] to some kind of official status in the county" (38/42). On closer inspection, however, this chapter, titled "Passings" and containing the aforementioned pronouncement about the importance of one's times, reads like an allegory of the Mao years, and of the Great Leap Forward and its aftermath in particular. With that, the novel as a whole, set during the larger "Cultural Revolution era," takes on the cast of a larger allegory.

Guanglin's younger brother, Guangming, "walked complacently toward his demise, while the boy behind. who would have many more years to live, carried a basket in each arm and trailed wearily in the footsteps of his ill-fated mentor" (32/35). When the "subordinate" was drowning, Guangming jumped in, failing to understand the danger, and not even acting selflessly. "It was his authority over the other boy that prompted his action. When death threatened his sidekick, he jumped to the conclusion that saving him would be easy" (32/36). In time the passive follower developed amnesia about his near-death experience: "Several years later, when people raised the topic with him, he seemed unconvinced that the accident had ever occurred, as though the story was all cock-and-bull. If one of the villagers hadn't witnessed the incident, people might well have thought that Sun Guangming drowned all by himself" (36/33). Here Yu Hua contests the truthfulness of public memory, not on psychological or epistemological grounds, in the manner of the avant-garde, but symbolically, to speak obliquely of the erasure of memory in *history*. (China's "masses" likewise took no responsibility for having enabled the suicidal actions of their foolish leaders.) Then came the days when the narrator's family waited fruitlessly for glory, which caused it to be "rent with divisions" (43/47). The outcome: "Now that he had lost hope of becoming a hero's father Sun Kwangtsai [the father] drew inspiration from the prospect of monetary gain." (44/47) He takes up a doctrine of sybaritic cynicism of the sort attributed to current times: "While you're still young you should make the most of it and sleep around as much as you can" (47/51). This leads to still more family dissension. The father and brother carry on with the same widow and they come to blows; the brother goes to jail, the mother dies, and the father dies a hopeless drunk, pushed into a cesspool, the same fate as befalls Mo Yan's hero detective in *The Republic of Wine*.

Yu Hua's acclaimed second novel, *To Live*, is not only written in a much simpler, realistic vein, with simple—indeed, limited—vocabulary, but its major events are framed by major named historical events, including the civil war between Nationalist and Communist armies (1945–1949), the Great Leap Forward and the famine it created, and the Cultural Revolution, with a cameo appearance of Red Guards who drag away the village's production team leader. The main protagonist from start to finish is Fugui, the once dissolute son of a rich landlord who, during his young manhood before the revolution, gambled away the entire family fortune, including all its land and dwellings, leaving his old father, pregnant wife, and child homeless.[22] Fugui in the narrative's present time, as an elder in the post-Mao era accompanied by an old ox who serves as his symbolic double, tells his life story episodically but mostly in chronological order to a youngster who has come down to the countryside to collect folklore. The younger man, in framing passages, expresses his awe of Fugui's self-understanding.

The time of Fugui's early years is not dated by means of numbers or events, but it is clearly the stereotyped "old society" of rich, irresponsible landlords and rice merchants, with servants willing to obey their "master" unto death; this affirms the Communist narrative of misery ended by the revolutionary Liberation of 1949. What is remarkable about this novel, besides the simple, honest values of old Fugui, chastened by his life of misfortune (though, if one looks for it, also good fortune),[23] is the simplicity of the themes of life, death, and ordinary rites of passage such as marriage, illness, and neighborly help extended to the unfortunate—a very different world from that of *Cries in the Drizzle*. The major historical disconnect of this moving work of ordinary humanistic heroism is the fact that so many awful deaths and tragedies unfold in Fugui's life as a result of "fate." Unlike in the movie version, it is not really the Chinese Civil War, the post-Leap famine, or persecution that kill Fugui's family members (and the team leader, who survives being beaten in the Cultural Revolution), but the poverty, hardships, and diseases of everyday life.

Yu Hua's third, particularly influential novel, *Chronicle of a Blood Merchant*, fits our first category—of prolonged and utter temporal ambiguity—for the time setting is indicated only retrospectively, halfway through the novel's fairly long chronological narrative, with references to the Great Leap Forward and the Cultural Revolution. Family misfortunes such as near starvation and rustication of the young, to the detriment of their health, follow from those big events, and this time the main characters are a city family: Xu Sangui, his wife, and their three sons. The broad narrative of a family trying to cope with repeated misfortunes, as political movements of the larger society keep time for the reader and directly cause much of the suffering, has led Yu Hua's second and third novels to become emblems of his turn to "realism." *Chronicle of a Blood Merchant* is narrated relatively conventionally in the third person and divided into chapters, unlike *To Live*. The episodes of suffering can be enumerated in tandem with Xu Sangui's repeated efforts to save himself and his family by selling his blood—his "energy," as his rural friends call it—twelve times, though without success in the last attempt. Xu Sangui's penultimate blood donation nearly kills him as he tries to save his eldest son.[24] Yu Hua's third novel ends more happily than his second, for in this case not only the hero but his whole family manage "to live."

The deeply flawed heroes of *To Live* and *Chronicle of a Blood Merchant* manage to redeem themselves morally by the end of the story. Fugui, the onetime prodigal landlord's son who ruined his family, in various later episodes inadvertently or purposely saves or at least lengthens the lives of others. In the end he emerges as a morally chastened figure, a man who works his fingers to the bone even in old age and out of the goodness of his heart has rescued an old ox from being slaughtered. As his double, also named Fugui, the ox represents Fugui the man saving himself. In a final twist reminiscent of a famous plot device from Shen Congwen, Fugui turns his ox into a double for each of his deceased family members, by referring to him by each of their names.[25] Xu Sangui is a simpler, less corrupted character at the end of his life story, too, after having shamefully disowned and humiliated his eldest son upon learning that he was fathered by another man. He even uses the "unfaithfulness" of his wife (though she was not yet married when impregnated) as an excuse for a tryst of his own, with a helpless woman on her sickbed. The subsequent redemption of Xu Sangui is uplifting and even gut-wrenching.

Yet, there are three major departures from such a "logical" interpretation, including two discrepancies about the novel's setting in time. To begin with, the dating is internally inconsistent. In the early chapters, a young man named Xu Sanguan learns from more experienced friends in the countryside that he can sell his blood for money in the city; he accompanies them, "just that once," and learns the rituals associated with it. There is no reason to doubt, from either the plot or Yu Hua's extremely simple language, that the setting is after the 1949 revolution. In fact, the sale of blood by peasants really took off in the post-Mao years. (It was only after 2000 that reporting on an AIDS epidemic brought China's unhygienic mass blood-selling practices to national and international attention; Yu Hua was "ahead of the news.") Allegorically, a citizen's selling of his or her blood might represent the limitless sacrifices of a toiling, and poor, peasant or worker in any decade of the twentieth century, but the Mao years were among the harshest, and the recent post-Mao years the mostly openly accepting of trafficking in whatever might sell. In Yu Hua's rural world, going to sell blood is a prized indication of good health—as fine an emblem of one's marriageability and social status as wealth (unlike the urban view, expressed later, that selling blood is a shameful indication of poverty). And yet, the narrative's mentions of grain- and sugar-rationing coupons, many chapters into the story (75/36, 118/78), indicate that the time has even then progressed to no later than the early 1980s. Chapter 18 begins (149/110), oddly, in a manner out of character with the realistic tone of most of the dialogues: "Xu Sanguan said to Xu Yulan: 'This year is 1958. We've had People's Communes, the Great Leap Forward, Backyard Steel Furnaces, and what else?'" The previous action has therefore occurred within the first nine years of the revolution. Xu Sanguan's introduction to selling blood, then, must have occurred *before* 1949. Yu Hua elsewhere allows the reader to calculate that Sanguan and Yulan got married before the revolution, evidently around 1948. That was after Sanguan's first sale of his blood and certain other subplots.[26]

The novel at this point has started to take note of the passage of time through multiple reference points (136/96), so it seems unlikely that Yu Hua muddied up his time line through a failure of concentration. The result is that the role of major Maoist political movements is duly noted in the last half of the novel, yet the biggest political change of them all, the 1949 revolution, has occurred within the time of the story without any notice taken of it. Even the 1948 manager of the blood bank is unchanged, despite the overthrow of the old regime—still less so, the texture of country, indeed city, life. Xu Sanguan's very employment, as a worker at a silk factory in town, is the same before and after the great revolution.

The second anomaly, then, is that social change does not appear to reflect "the times," which are after all oddly marked when characters, not the narrator, make superfluous statements like "This year is 1958." The pattern of history being referred to here, whether Yu Hua means it to be taken realistically or didactically, is a paradox or a mystery.[27] It does, surely, cause the reader to ponder the importance of the "times." And the seeming political meaning of Xu Sanguan selling his life blood in serial trips to the hospital, following one misfortune after another, is also at odds with a closer analysis of just why Xu

Sanguan sells his blood. His first three trips to the blood bank have nothing to do with politics. He sells blood the first time to have the means to marry. The second trip is occasioned by his financial need to redeem household furniture. The third trip is to have the means to buy restorative foods for an injured woman named Lin with whom Xu has just had illicit sex. *Then* come the trips occasioned by a need to save his family from Maoist political excesses and so forth. The second and third trips are the result not of "fate," but really of human folly, indeed Xu Sanguan's. Xu Sanguan has created much of his own bad luck. He has cheated on his wife and for a time left his son without a caring father. The greater, of course, is Xu Sanguan's moral redemption in the end, when he is willing to risk sacrificing his own life by giving away his lifeblood for the son he once disowned.

The novel also fails to note the reverse historical watershed that is almost as important as the invisible 1949 revolution, not to mention 1958: China's post-Mao reforms. There is no mention of political change or its consequences, or any fluctuations in social customs and institutions. Even the institution of selling blood has not changed; Blood Chief Li has only passed away and been replaced. Xu Sanguan's final attempt to sell blood comes at a time when his family is prosperous and he considered too old to donate. But the family prosperity is attributed to the sons' having grown up, not to any post-Mao social change, even in this urban setting. Xu Sanguan's final attempt to sell blood is the first time he has ever done so to fulfill his own needs; he looks forward to the blood-restorative feast after the blood-drawing. On previous occasions it has been coded as a social ritual as well as a fulfillment of a personal desire. Yet this final, self-gratifying selling of blood is not allowed. This lends an ironic touch to the rosy ending. Having fulfilled his social duty, Xu Sanguan is not allowed to please himself through his own efforts. This puts the new "market socialism" in almost as bad a light as the old collectivized society that forced Xu to sell his blood to keep his family alive.

A third oddity is that *Chronicle of a Blood Merchant* exhibits stylistic and even thematic resonances with Yu Hua's earlier, absurdist, avant-garde stories, such as "One Kind of Reality."[28] The characters' speech is so bare (scholars have done numeric studies showing that Yu Hua's prose, even in or particularly in his novels, uses very few Chinese characters)[29] that it often seems unmotivated—inane, almost moronic. One cannot really imagine a worker saying, particularly to his spouse, "This year is 1958. We have now experienced this social institution and that social institution." The use of dialogue here to convey information reminds one of some forms of Asian opera. Nor would an ordinary person evaluate Great Leap Forward mess halls with unintended humor like this: "I didn't burp once after I ate at Heavenrest Temple canteen, and I didn't burp after eating at the canteen at the theater either. But when I ate at the silk factory, I was burping all night long" (150/111). At times, Xu Sanguan is almost outlandishly honest and direct in confessing his misdeeds and betrayals. *Chronicle of a Blood Merchant* also reminds one of Yu Hua's earlier work "One Kind of Reality" in its stupefying and mindless vengeance. Xu Sanguan, before his moral enlightenment, tells his young sons that their duty is to exact vengeance on the man who cuckolded him; they must grow up, so they can rape the man's daughters. "When Xu Sanguan's two sons listened again to his instruction that they should rape He Xiaoyong's daughters, they began to giggle. Xu Sanguan quizzed them: 'So what are you going to do after you grow up?' The two sons replied, 'Rape He Xiaoyong's daughters.' Xu Sanguan broke into roars of laughter" (116/76).

Yu Hua's third novel is a puzzling commentary on China's modern history. Surely it is critical of the course of events and damaging to Communism's self-image. Remarkably, Xu Sanguan observes of collectivization, "The state is just like the landlords before" (149/110). Indeed, the fields belong to the state, not the peasants. The happy ending is not what it seems, either. There are grounds for hope of human learning and redemption, but the overall view of human events is not rosy. Yu Hua's devastatingly uncomplicated prose lives on, mesmerizing readers with its simple repeated rhythms much as it did in the 1980s—and still tending to make a mockery of the humane, indeed the human side of the characters.

CREATING PRESENT-DAY MYTHS IN A TIME OUT OF TIME

Mo Yan's *Red Sorghum*, prized by Chinese readers since 1986 as an exemplary product of "roots-seeking literature" even before the release of Zhang Yimou's world-famous film adaptation the next year, is widely viewed as a foundational work of China's new historical fiction. The original, 1986 version of the saga had two episodes, called "Red Sorghum" and "Sorghum Wine,"[30] which together form the basis of the film (Mo Yan collaborated in writing the screenplay). It was so successful that Mo Yan fleshed out the tale with three more, largely backfilling episodes, "Dog Ways," "Sorghum Funeral," and "Strange Death." The five pieces were printed in succession as the book *Hong gaoliang jiazu* (lit., "Red sorghum family" or "families" or perhaps "clan" or "clans"), which Howard Goldblatt translated as one epic novel under the title *Red Sor-*

ghum (the title I use here in reference to the longer work), as did a 1987 mainland edition and a 1988 Taiwan edition that presumably best represents Mo Yan's intentions. The Taiwan edition does not identify armies in the story as Nationalist or Communist, unlike the mainland editions and the still more "politically correct" film.[31] The complete work set a precedent for the "new historical novel" by creating a full-length narrative from shorter works having a common narrator, characters, and setting (Shandong's Northeast Gaomi Township).[32] The plot, even of the initial chapter, is already so complex that the later chapters clarify the general story line. Such complexity suited the avant-garde taste of Chinese readers seeking "roots" in the 1980s, and perhaps the work was composed for filming from the start, though it is hard to imagine the inner complexity of the original plot surviving in any audience-pleasing film narrative. Zhang Yimou's film adaptation is chronological and declines even to use flashbacks, except insofar as the whole tale is told in retrospect. Because of multiple flashbacks, flash-forwards,[33] and changes of viewpoint in the original novel, one may say that Mo Yan's plot, at both the macro level and the micro level, continuously intercuts events and memories from different years in several decades. In the uniquely complex opening chapter, an unnamed narrator, who is consistent throughout the novel, reimagines through free association a stream of consciousness from his father, Yu Douguan, when Douguan was just a boy, lying in wait to do battle with the Japanese. The boy soldier's mind flits back and forth between people and places who contributed to his growing up, even as his own yet-to-be-born son freely enters the minds of two generations before him and provides the larger narration.

The plot may be circuitous, but the era is clear enough. At the core of the initial long chapter is a drawn-out account of an actual 1939 battle in Northeast Gaomi Township that claimed the life of a Japanese general.[34] It is intercut with the backstories of several local heroes on the Chinese side and with scenes, likewise delivered piecemeal, of a Japanese massacre of hundreds of villagers in retaliation. A year before the attack, the Japanese had conscripted, then publicly skinned alive, one Uncle Arhat, a servant of the narrator's forebears. (The final chapter fills the reader in on another Japanese outrage that preceded Arhat's troubles, a massacre at the village of Saltwater Gap. Lack of reference to it in earlier chapters suggests the subsequent improvisation of the later chapters.[35]) The Chinese are mostly fated to die during their 1939 attack, including the narrator's grandmother, whom we know at first only as Grandma. Chinese critics and readers considered it avant-garde and titillating to have a narrator, both self-dramatized and omniscient, enter the mind of a grand-mother whom he had never met.[36] Certainly it is arresting to hear the grandson state, with a triumphalism common to the texture of the work, that he knows "Grandma" better than his father ever did: "Father . . . never knew how many sexual comedies my grandma had performed on this dirt path, but I knew. And he never knew that her naked body, pure as glossy white jade, had lain on the black soil beneath the shadows of sorghum stalks, but I knew" (5/6).

This epic makes the time explicit in the first line: "[It all began in] 1939, on the ninth day of the eighth lunar month; my father, a bandit's offspring, had just passed his fifteenth birthday."[37] Two pages more, and it is clear that the Sino-Japanese War is in full progress in Northeast Gaomi Township and that the heroes—"Father" and Father's father, or at least Father's foster father (grandiloquently referred to as "Commander Yu Zhan'ao," though he is really a legendary bandit chieftain)—are on the patriotic, "Chinese" side. The story of Yu and his common-law wife, Grandma (actually the first of two concurrent common-law wives, who after their deaths are replaced by a third) is itself told in pieces, intercut by scenes of the ragtag militia waiting for battle. In the retrospective subplot, Granddad murdered a rich sorghum winemaker and his leprous son, to whom Grandma was married at age sixteen, after first saving her from rape by bandits in the sorghum fields, only to ravish (most readers would say rape) her three days later among the same stands of sorghum, so as to take charge of her as his wife, and the distillery she had just inherited.

Amid these many complications and ambiguities, the characters' ages and the number of years passed are occasionally mentioned. One has the means to calculate, as early as the first chapter, that Grandma was born about 1907 or 1908; she was about thirty-two at the time of the legendary battle.[38] It is a little odd that when she was betrothed at sixteen, about 1923, her father-in-law-to-be still wore the queue that became unfashionable after the Qing monarchy was overthrown in 1911. The peculiarities of time in this novel do not come from the numbers, though part of the novel's strangeness lies in the narrator's penchant for exact enumerations of people and things, as in *Nineteen Thirty-Four Escapes* and *One Hundred Years of Solitude*. Most observers would tell of these things in round numbers.

There is no major thematic mismatch of *Red Sorghum*'s storyline with other histories of the time. Historian Diana Lary finds that "Mo Yan's account closely parallels the war in Gaomi and other counties" (129). Later chapters of the novel continue occasionally to cite the year or the age of a particular character. The fourth chapter allows a reader to assemble from its pieces a capsule (partly fictitious) history of warfare and warlordism throughout that entire neck of Shandong province, though the beginnings of some subchapters tease the reader at first about which thread of the narrative is being picked up. Shandong was divided among many petty armed groups in the 1920s and 1930s, and it was the province where the Boxers ("spirit soldiers," in the novel) originated. In the Taiwan edition preferred by Mo Yan, Nationalist and Communist ideologies do not explicitly come to blows; ambiguity about political affiliations is managed to heighten suspense.[39] The fourth chapter and many of its numerous subchapters end just before a pitched battle, like a premodern Chinese chapter-driven novel or a contemporary mystery story—one does not learn which enemy army is set to appear on the horizon until a few subchapters later. And yet, like a modern mystery, by the end of the fifth chapter Mo Yan has tied up most of his loose ends, and without introducing many new characters.[40]

Red Sorghum is an exercise not in writing a conventional historical novel but in Marquezian mythmaking for the modern scions of Gaomi, and the world—and more self-consciously so than *One Hundred Years of Solitude*. The unnamed narrator, grandson of Commander Yu Zhan'ao and Grandma Dai Fenglian, frames the narrative at the outset as the fruit of materials he gleaned during a homecoming in post-Mao times. Of special prominence is a clapper tale about the battle with the Japanese chanted by a ninety-two-year-old woman who knew the characters. It recalls the modern folk songs that begin chapters of *The Garlic Ballads* and the "opera lyrics" that would begin early and late chapters of *Sandalwood Death*, distilling the action to come. The old woman's words are legend, not history. "Her narration was choppy and confused, like a shower of leaves at the mercy of the wind." She adds her own commentary: "Your dad was a capable boy, killed his first man at fifteen, eight or nine out of every ten bastard kids turn out bad" (14/13). Here she has altered her rehearsed clapper talk (which still contains interjections of "Aiyaya") to directly address the novel's narrator. His father, literally a bastard, fits the old lady's description.

Certainly Mo Yan satirizes the standard Communist Party narrative of the Sino-Japanese War that he as a former army propagandist knew by heart. Even more than the general histories, China's "revolutionary recollections" industry, which led to the publication of anthologies such as *A Single Spark Can Start a Prairie Fire*,[41] appears to be under Mo Yan's satiric scalpel. His chief male anti-Japanese heroes, however brave or foolhardy, are ragtag highwaymen of no certain political affiliation. Granddad has in years prior to the battle personally kidnapped for ransom both Nationalist- and Communist-affiliated leaders, and unintentionally led eight hundred of his own troops into a massacre by provincial soldiers. Granddad has taken three women to wife and murdered the first's husband in order to seize a winery and make it prosper as a *capitalist* enterprise. As a boy he murdered the monk who was his mother's lover. Even the narrator admits that the grandfather he lionizes was a "black-hearted, ruthless bandit" who lived "an existence of moral degeneracy and fickle passions" (371/273). Mo Yan dares the reader to evaluate him as heroically as the narrator does. Northeast Gaomi Township is a den of iniquity. Only the stalks of red sorghum are without sin—and they are bloodstained, providing refuge from, but also cover for, killings and rapes.

The wine's genesis in the red sorghum peculiar to the locality—with the addition of Granddad's piss as a secret ingredient—symbolizes the rough, unstoppable vigor of the local peasantry, as do their bawdy folk songs and outrageous folk superstitions.[42] It is here that Mo Yan's epic tale departs from the novel that is "about history," opening itself up to metahistorical and ultimately dystopian readings, even as it connects local family history to national history and moreover mimics, facetiously, the Communist Party's grand narrative of technologically primitive Chinese heroism being so strong in collective spirit that it can triumph over Japanese spirit and technological superiority. The time is the early twentieth century, but Mo Yan is really creating a modern myth for China to take the place of the standard Communist Party one. Myths are eternal, existing in time out of time.

Life in these gallant times pulses with energy and unimaginable violence, rendered by Mo Yan in horrible detail in chapter after chapter, to inspire posterity. The ancestors' ignominious defeats as well as their victories, retreats, and mere misunderstandings appear superhuman in retrospect. Even the errant character Big Tooth Yu, a rapist, goes to his execution bravely, in the old operatic manner, winning plaudits from the community, or so the narrator imagines. Northeast Gaomi Township is itself heroic; if *feng shui* that produces legendary heroes had not existed already, Mo Yan would have invented it, as in his famous combination of contradictory superlatives (the superlatives are sometimes taken by Chinese critics as satire of Maoist superlatives—but they also retain a connection to the old heroic mode of expression). Says the narrator of *Red Sorghum*,

> I didn't realize until I'd grown up that Northeast Gaomi Township is easily the most beautiful and most repulsive, most unusual and most common,

most sacred and most corrupt, most heroic and most bastardly, hardest-drinking and hardest-loving place in the world. . . . Tall and dense, [the red sorghum] reeked of glory, cold and graceful, it promised enchantment, passionate and loving, it was tumultuous. (2/4)

The very landscape comes alive through Mo Yan's extravagant synesthesia and his pantheistic and romantic natural metaphors, which render even the repulsive and gangrenous beautiful. The red of the sorghum and the incessantly spilled blood of the people may be appreciated as a satiric perversion or a patriotic inheritance of the color red in the Communist vision, but it is also the traditional Chinese color of joy, marriage, and triumph. The ribald songs and absurd beliefs of the folk further attest to their hyperbolic vitality in this township's state of nature, independent of the political state and rising above both tyranny and anarchy. These images, too, undermine the orthodox Communist view of the folk as embodiments of a social class motivated by progressive class consciousness, while on the other hand preserving the myth of vigor rising up spontaneously, self-sufficiently, and also unfathomably, from the uneducated masses, through struggle and opposition to powerful adversarial forces. *Red Sorghum* shows the ancestors to be deeply flawed or worse, yet it also creates a credible basis for worshiping them. Great deeds of the folk have been passed on by word of mouth, the narrator avers, becoming "beautiful legends" (lit., "beautiful sanctified legends") within the legend (46/37). The deceased live on as specters, as martyrs to the locality. Perhaps the bedrock belief from the "old society" most thoroughly upended by Mo Yan's great novel is the idea that heroes cannot emerge in "bad times"—except that the larger, dystopian context blurs the line between heroism and antiheroism. The narrator, by his ebullient, fever-pitched *attitude*, creates a sense of excitement and heroism whether the events told are heroic or not, and whether they are true or not. (Yi-tsi Mei Feuerwerker suggests that some instances of the narrator's ebullience may be self-parody; 222.) The particular attention to the progress of real historical time that is left conveys a sense of the difference between past and present: a vision of a time of yore when the gods still ruled.

When the myth of the past descends to the real present, however, the vision is dystopian. The present is characterized by decline in the human stock. Confides the narrator, "The young men of [Granddad's] generation were as sturdy as Northeast Gaomi sorghum, which is more than can be said about us weaklings who succeeded them" (53/43). More generally, "over decades that seem but a moment in time, lines of scarlet figures shuttled among the sorghum stalks to weave a vast human tapestry. They killed, they looted, and they defended their country in a valiant, stirring ballet that makes us unfilial descendants who now occupy the land pale by comparison. Surrounded by progress, I feel a nagging sense of our species' regression" (2/4). A vision of human regression into bestiality concludes the third section, "Dog Ways," or the ostensibly philosophical "Way (*Dao*) of Dogs." That section describes a dog-eat-dog battle and a battle of dogs against humans.

The eternal symbol of Northeast Gaomi's vitality, its red sorghum, has in contemporary times been replaced by a hybrid variety from outside "with a bitter, astringent taste" that "is the source of rampant constipation. With the exception of cadres above the rank of branch secretary, all the villagers' faces are the color of rusty iron. How I loathe the hybrid sorghum," concludes the still unnamed narrator after his return home in the 1980s (495/358). In one stroke, Mo Yan damns the evidently counterrevolutionary tendencies of a society previously created in an image of revolution. China has changed color—away from red. Nor is any hope for the future dangled before the reader. Yet the heroic age of bygone days is steeped in terror and horror.

Ten years later Mo Yan carried his legends of rural Northeast Gaomi Township historically forward and backward in *Big Breasts and Wide Hips*, a novel that covers the entire twentieth century. Shangguan Lu, or "Mother," is the main protagonist, and quite as heroic as Grandma and Second Grandma in *Red Sorghum*. Unlike Grandma Dai, this Mother outlasts the Japanese, the Chinese Civil War, land reform, the Great Leap Forward, the Cultural Revolution, and China's post-Mao decollectivization, giving birth along the way to seven daughters and one son (Jintong, the major narrator), none of them sired by her legal husband, and some of them conceived rather haphazardly, and in Jintong's case, through intercourse with a foreigner. The management of time and viewpoint is as complex as in *Red Sorghum*, and this time the bloody and high sexualized plot, much of which is focalized through the consciousness of Jintong as a child, may have occasionally slipped beyond the control of the author. When translating the sprawling epic into English, Howard Goldblatt, a friend willing to serve as a Maxwell Perkins–style editor to rein in Mo Yan's Thomas Wolfe–style expansiveness, urged Mo Yan and was allowed by him to make cuts and reorder the baggy narrative.

Farcical moments intermingle with the solemn heroism that has built up the novel's status as a modern myth or anti-myth for a China that survived imperialism, the danger of national extinction, Communism, and more recently, unbridled greed, corruption, and consumerism. Certainly Mother is heroic; many critics have contrasted her competence and presence of mind to the fecklessness, incompetence, cowardice, and parasitism of the males in the novel. As allegory, "Mother" could be the motherland, though modern Mandarin prefers the term *zuguo*, the ancestral land. It is the Communist Party that is called the party members' mother (Mo Yan is a party member, but surely that has not influenced his female symbolism). In contrast with her lone biracial son, Mother embodies native, Chinese culture and its dogged perseverance. Since ancient times, the family has also stood as a symbol of the state. In this case, satiric ridicule of the symbolized object seems at least as strong as celebration of it.

Big Breasts and Wide Hips' many images of decadence and deterioration continue the theme of generational decline in *Red Sorghum*. The novel is comic, but also dystopian. In the analysis of Kenny Ng and many Chinese critics, "species degeneration" (*zhong de tuihua*) is a major theme in much of Mo Yan's work. In this novel, the odd and repellent narrating protagonist Shangguan Jintong, with his outlandish breast fetish, remains childish to the end of his days, ever more ill-adapted to adult life as China enters the globalized contemporary world.[43]

Zhang Wei's *September's Fable* (1992) is another allegorical tale ranging over the entire history of China under Communism, self-consciously creating modern myths and legends for contemporary readers starved for them after the Communist Party stripped them of their traditional myths, fed them new but shorter-lived proletarian myths, then consigned the people to unheroic post-Mao lives of struggle for petty monetary gain. *September's Fable*, like *Red Sorghum*, and Miguel Asturias's *Men of Maize*, can be read as a series of linked chapters. Repeat appearances of the same dirt-poor peasant characters with their own peculiarities and stories in an unnamed village, presumably in Shandong, like Gaomi but closer to the northern seacoast, allow accumulating knowledge of the community, and later chapters refer to events previously told, but the chapters' tales are individual fables, told out of order. A Marquezian omniscience about ultimate outcomes emphasizes the status of the stories as legends and parables. Says the narrator in the voice of a seer rather than an omniscient narrator, of the character Ox Pole, "He was almost dead, but the time of his decease was still far in the future." (59/97)

Zhang Wei's relatively avant-garde writing in *September's Fable* seemingly reverses the trend of diminishing experimentalism seen in Yu Hua's and Su Tong's 1990s literary careers, but Zhang began writing his 1992 novel in 1987. The critic Yan Min sees in the work a romantic, we might say, noble savage syndrome. I believe the novel is influenced by Miguel Asturias's *Men of Maize*. The structure of both novels is episodic; the passage of time from one chapter to the next is indeterminate, and each chapter is filled with tales and legends that are themselves fables. Recurring themes of both novels include a unique village identification with the local staple (maize or yams) and local tales of males undertaking dangerous treks to find runaway wives (reflecting tensions of ancient patriarchy and of newly modernized male-female relations in the Chinese and Guatemalan novels, respectively). A collective village ethos of "tribal" solidarity is almost a character unto itself. Zhang's folk, the local dispossessed, fortify themselves against depredations of antagonistic surrounding villages and an outer, more modern world through community practices, including an odd freedom of the young—at night—that seems rather un-Chinese.[44] The villagers are relatively recent immigrants to their living space—northern equivalents of Hakkas in the south—such that the better-established "original" villagers in the environs despise them with an intensity characteristic of racism.[45] Both villages are defined by peculiar lore, beliefs, and rituals beyond Han Chinese and Latin tradition, such as shape-shifting, so that even familiar Mao-era political rituals are assimilated into "native," "superstitious," at times frightening "native rites," as indigenous Central American gods and festivals were assimilated into Latin American Catholicism. Both communities are progressively destroyed by a new way of life. As foreshadowed at the start, engineers and coal miners steadily dig tunnels under the *September's Fable* village, destroying its habitability and forcing the community into another forced migration.

A few pages into the story, one hears of a peasant called "Little Red Guard," but how he got the name is never told. Direct references to the sociopolitical history of China and dramatized changes in the fabric of peasant life are so sparse that *September's Fable* feels as distanced from historical time as Su Tong's works analyzed at the start of this chapter. When peasants speak of landlords, they describe a world hardly different from the present. At the end of the novel, it is still unclear whether post-Mao times have arrived, for the "pure socialist" era had its engineers and miners, too. Until the last days of the village, a gypsy-like wandering community of "vagrants" (recalling the gypsies in *One Hundred Years of Solitude*) plays a major role in the plot (272–273/458–460), as if the era were still the "old society." Their ethic and that of the ordinary villagers are untouched by socialism.

Chapter 5 (of seven), "Wisdom of the Heart," appears to make a veiled reference to the Cultural Revolution when it tells how a war veteran and his friend the butcher plot a "war" against the village leader by disgracing him in a village meeting. When their plan misfires, they are locked up and tortured; the butcher commits suicide. But there is no named connection to the outer society or to class politics. One can surmise that peasants who died of famine might well have been victims of the Great Leap Forward, but that, too, is speculation. Politics is practically nonexistent here. The village head is known as a man who lives a little better than other villagers, not as a leader or even a taskmaster; his wife is a heartless bully, but her mission, revealed near the end of the narrative, is to root the girls in place, so they do not run wild. She prevails due to her size, strength, and personality, not her social or political status.

Indicating the syncretism of traditional and Maoist worldviews is the nature of "speak bitterness" (*suku*) sessions, here called *yiku*, or "remember bitterness," in which old-timers recount stories of how badly they were oppressed by landlords under the "old society" before Liberation. In this peasant world, these sessions are entertainment, a time of fabulous storytelling. (In life, peasants and workers found the ritual boring and sometimes fell asleep.) Even when Jinxiang, a storytelling specialist hardly old enough to remember the old society, tells fairy tales about a landlord whose monkey-spirit wife made him rich through theft by supernaturally moving objects from one place to another (a common folk belief), that does not diminish his credibility or status in his community. To be sure, the reader may attribute this to the anti-landlord discourse established by the Communist Party. Zhang Wei's simulations of "speak bitterness" sessions not only parody the Communist rituals, exploding the credibility of both historical and local memory, but also incorporate Jinxiang's "memory" sessions into the larger discourse of the novel, which is one of rustic, unsophisticated storytelling: a realm of myth and legend. The *truth* of "history" appears irrelevant to its social function.

All "events" in the novel are of legendary proportions—to the characters. Although much of the story is told by a traditional omniscient narrator, the viewpoint frequently shifts, after unmarked transitions, to allow the characters to tell and in effect dramatize their own stories in their own voices. The narrator often speaks in a breathlessly expectant, even exultant voice. At other times, the narrator speaks to and for the peasant community as a collective, like a Greek chorus.

What a long, storyless winter night, a winter night shrouded in smudge smoke, a winter night to listen to Jinxiang recalling hardships! But Jinxiang the bachelor has left the village forever, carrying with him a big pile of black pancakes. The whole village misses you! Having Flash alone is not enough. We can't bear listening to the rattling of the carts from outside the village coming to get our storyteller. Jinxiang won't ever wake from this long sleep. Oh Father Heaven, how could this have happened? We just want to cry, we just want to cry.   (127/211)

As in Homeric epics (or modern Balkan storytelling, made famous by Albert Lord), the rustic peasant characters' nicknames are joined by epithets—Jinxiang "the bachelor"; "short, stout Idiot," "long-braided Parrot Chaser" (the free-running wild "colt"), "the prissy girl Jinmin," and "beautiful Incense Bowl of the scarred eyelid."

As dirty and dusty as any peasant created by the May Fourth writer Zhang Tianyi (1906–1985), those in *September's Fable* cultivate and eat little other than dried yams, which put a fire in their belly, making them active and argumentative. An unpredictably randy and violent lot they are, sometimes submitting meekly to fate and other times running off to have affairs. Disabilities, genetic and man-made (two peasants have lost an eye in fights), illnesses, and fights that draw blood are prominent. Wife beating is described as a local custom, accepted by the wives and justified by the narrative voice (284–285/479). When the villagers venture outside their confined territory, the surrounding villagers, who are of a different, more dominant "tribe," assault them. Other major events in the village's "secret history" (155/259) are escapes from the community (interpreted as treachery), encounters with barefoot doctors, pregnancies and abortions, and opportunities simply to take a bath or wear a pair of boots. It is a superstitious, magical world in which dead relatives come back to provide warnings and guidance, or are cursed for not doing so.[46] Yet the peasants harbor a passion for freedom, counterbalanced by loyalty to their village. The young people run around wild at night. They have affairs, dream their own dreams, and ache for independence, often expressed in the figure of a free-running horse or colt, even as they remain tied to the village as their mother. Zhang Wei's style is ostensibly that of a peasant: rustic, simple, and repetitious. Nature appears charged with energy, in images a peasant might appreciate. The village exemplifies a perverse and perhaps anti-heroic persistence in its crude and materially deprived style of life. It is in the last analysis heroic because of its refusal to die, despite persecution by outsiders and the village's predestined collapse into the coal tunnels below—for this has always been a community of socially despised migrants that migrates together.

Life is Hobbesian: "poor, nasty, brutish, and short," and old age means living into one's fifties;[47] its "heroes," however, exist in time out of time.

Yet, as in *Red Sorghum* and *The Ancient Ship*, images of stasis in *September's Fable* are joined by figures of decline. Zhang Wei's later novel frequently repeats, in this case as peasant wisdom (132/221, 143/239, 202/340, 276/465), the epigram from his previous one[48] that transforms a positive Maoist slogan about humanity's boundless prowess into a censure of human nature: "There are things that people cannot imagine but nothing that people can [will] not do." The village disappears, as foretold at the start, and the mining society that replaces it is hardly uplifting socially or spiritually. As the narrative nears its end, the young, the village's one hope antithetical to the miners as told at the start, has eroded: "The young people in the village had all become so passive, no longer spending days and nights charging wildly through the fields. They had grown up, become older, and spent days on their own *kangs*" (255/429). Nor have they produced a strong third generation to carry on the struggle. The young beauty Parrot Chaser, the only villager admired by outsiders and the leader of the young people's independent strivings, by now "had not seriously recited her clapper tales even once, and people were gradually forgetting that she ever had. . . . Just like that pair of corduroy trousers that she had worn for so long, the good old days were truly gone forever" (262/440–441). In the end, says the narrator, after questioning and berating the village instead of speaking on its behalf: "Things get worse all the time. Young people aren't as good as their parents; parents aren't as good as their ancestors, and the bunch of bare-assed babies being born aren't as good as even the young people. . . . Look at the young people today: they're listless and lazy, and their hair isn't even as glossy as in the past" (285/480). The narrator's vision has the limitations of a peasant, but it also has the mythic authority of a Chinese epic balladeer. It lacks, however, *cosmic* resonances with a book like the Mayans' *Popol Vuh*, a book unassimilated by the Chinese literati tradition.

FILM ADAPTATIONS AND ALLEGORY

Certain original films and adaptations by China's Fifth Generation of filmmakers create their own modern historical myths, in settings sufficiently ambiguous as to suggest universality or allegorical reference to a further past. Ordinarily, costumes, hairstyles, backdrops, and props require choices that indicate a particular time and place, but when the setting is rural China or, from a modern Chinese perspective, simply the "old society," the era and location can be universalized. Zhang Yimou's film version of Red Sorghum (1987), whose impact on Chinese cinema was explosive, is a good example. Xudong Zhang feels it creates "both a sublimated world of peasant utopia and an unapologetic Social Darwinism unfolding according to the logic of desire and conquest."[49] (Few other great "new historical novels" from China won approval for domestic filming and distribution in the 1980s or even the 1990s.) The mythic and timeless ethos of the Red Sorghum film does not, however, stand alone among China's Fifth Generation films. Departing from the stagey cinematic practices of previous Chinese cinema, the new films' unprecedented emphasis on cinematography bends their visual images toward themes of stasis and universality, toward confusion about the very idea of historical epochs and a "direction" of history.

Zhang Yimou's cinematic revisions and simplifications of Mo Yan's novel heighten the saga's dramatic impact. In just ninety-one minutes, Zhang dramatizes, in a chronological order quite unlike the book's plot, Granddad's capture of Grandma and her winery, his triumph over local toughs, the skinning alive of Uncle Arhat, and the glorious but costly attack on the Japanese convoy. Voice-overs are spoken by an undramatized and faceless narrator in adulthood, as in the novel. The drama is so intense that the film is sometimes classified as melodrama, and it is also remembered for introducing frank sex and violence into Chinese cinema. Vying with the plot for the audience's attention are magnificent landscape shots. The sorghum, its many stalks eerily waving in unison under the wind in vast fields, becomes a living, pantheistic entity that wraps itself around the action, true to Mo Yan's vision. The mood is as ebullient and heroic as in the novel—perhaps even simplistically nationalistic, Xudong Zhang and others have charged. The Japanese have no redeeming qualities, Granddad is a peasant, not a bandit, and Grandma's inner strength is heightened. When Granddad forces himself on her at the winery, she at first fends him off, then consummates their sexual relationship on her terms, allowing a more feminist interpretation of Mo Yan's narrative. Missing from this and perhaps all of Zhang Yimou's films is Mo Yan's sense of humor and his farcical exaggerations that border on self-parody.[50]

The clothing, cloth shoes, old-style tavern, bare-chested men bearing Grandma's bridal palanquin (it is not filthy, as in the novel), winery heavily reliant on manual labor, and dirt paths through the sorghum bespeak a timeless, rural Chinese "old" society, until finally the Japanese invaders appear, forcing the locals to trample the sturdy sorghum to build a road.[51] As the narrator reverently recalls the deeds of his ancestors, making even the seduction of his grandmother seem daring and manly (and her submission, heroic), the film takes up Mo Yan's mission of creating a modern, non-Communist myth of Chinese vitality—in bygone times. The Japanese are hardly more than extras.

Breathtaking long shots of majestic yet desolate landscapes, with dusty wide-open spaces devoid of dwellings and other signs of human habitation, accompanied by scenes of long silences and rustic primitivism, evoke the great Northwest celebrated in China's most famous Fifth Generation films: besides *Red Sorghum, Yellow Earth* (Zhang Yimou, cinematographer) and *Old Well* (with Zhang starring in the leading role), and then Zhang Yimou's own films *Ju dou* (1990) and *The Story of Qiu Ju* (*Qiu Ju da guansi*, 1992). This region is the putative "cradle" of Chinese civilization and also of the Chinese Communist movement at Yan'an—a place belonging to history, but immune to change dictated by outside forces.

The antique, inward-looking, landlocked Yellow River region represents a "yellow" culture in the television series *Deathsong of the River*. Its opposite is the innovative and expansive "blue" culture of seafaring peoples. Chen Kaige's *Yellow Earth*, set in 1939, was controversial for depicting peasants as "feudal," passive, fatalistic, and culturally unmovable. That film is of mythic proportions, but far from heroic like *Red Sorghum. Yellow Earth* dramatizes a tragic gulf between the peasants, personified by a girl who yearns to escape to a new life, and the Communist Party, personified by a party folk song collector whose interventions in local life, though well-intentioned, lead ultimately to the girl's death because he cannot fulfill her hopes. *Old Well*, likewise, conjures up visions of an eternal Chinese peasant culture, so well adapted to its majestic but harsh environment as to exist beyond the heroic efforts of others to change it, until its happy ending.

Zhang Yimou's signature luscious cinematography re-creates these images and they nearly steal the show in *Red Sorghum*. The sorghum fields were planted (after much finagling) for filming,[52] but Zhang's many shots of the winery do not portray the black-soil Shandong marshlands of Mo Yan's novel; they are closer to the semiarid Northwest. *Red Sorghum*'s cinematographer was Zhang's Shaanxi fellow-provincial Gu Changwei, and the folk songs, original to the film, are from Shaanxi and celebrated as such. Small wonder the scenery and peasant culture, replete with Northwestern folk songs, are in sight and sound reminiscent of *Yellow Earth* and *Old Well*.

Zhang Yimou's film version of Su Tong's *Raise the Red Lantern* (*Da hong denglong gaogao gua*) seems thematically worlds apart. Set in an urban locale (though again, in a semiarid region bordering on Northwest China—the work was filmed in Pingyao, Shanxi), it tells the story of a college-educated girl forced by her mother and poverty to become the fourth concubine of a wealthy official. His house has many courtyards and the rooms are full of paintings and fine calligraphic presentations—the epitome of China's ancient high civilization. Even more than *Red Sorghum*, however, the film represents the "old society," though at a time when enough modern culture existed (in the person of the ex-student, who carries a modern suitcase to her new home) to be ground under by the weight of tradition. Old rituals and taboos wear the heroine down, until she inadvertently leads a fellow concubine on the path of death and herself goes mad. Acting according to "the rules" is fetishized, since not only Confucian representations of family obedience and reciprocity but also the proper activities and protocol for every hour of the day are closely examined and ostentatiously proclaimed to the newcomer whose education comes from a different world entirely.

Despite all this, the cinematography of *Raise the Red Lantern* bears remarkable similarities to Zhang Yimou's other early films. The giant compound where the four concubines, the master, and their servants live is bleak, brown, and dusty on the outside—unadorned in its exteriors except for the red lanterns that the master orders hung in the wing of the concubine he intends to favor that night. The lanterns are not permanent; they mark the exercise of power and are not primarily decorative. The compound is otherwise bleak and has an unlived-in look. As in Zhang Yimou's rural films, the pace is slow. Long silences and averted gazes at times take the place of speech. Shots alternate between wide-screen "landscapes" (in this case, aerial views of the whole compound, as one great walled-in prison) and close-up shots of faces. The plot initially revolves around the timeless rituals, which, like the compound walls (and the unforgiving landscape of *Yellow Earth*, more than the joyous fields of *Red Sorghum*), are absolutely confining. At the end of the film, there is even a hint of circularity: the fourth concubine, Songlian, having suffered so many vicissitudes and ultimately madness, returns to wearing the braids she wore at the start of the film, when she was a student. Once more, Zhang Yimou blurs the era and lifts the action out of historical time altogether.

Are these films, including *Yellow Earth* and *Old Well*, in their depiction of stasis in Chinese culture, more "anthropological"—about an eternal Chinese culture—than historical? Some critics allege that the films make China seem primitive. This does not fit *Raise the Red Lantern*, which depicts a cruel and static society, ruled by yang rather than yin, but with fewer overtones of actual decadence and decline than the novel *Red Sorghum*. (That novel's theme of decline, voiced explicitly by the narrator, is omitted from *Red Sorghum* the movie.) The alternative to viewing the films as depicting a timeless China is to see them not as period pieces but as allegories of another time.

Jerome Silbergeld notes that some critics and literary historians have questioned the prominence or the very existence of allegory in Chinese literature, even attributing this absence to monistic tendencies in the Chinese language and Chinese thought (108). But the importance of allegory in this Chinese  historical fiction and film can hardly be denied. The Fifth Generation films' images and relatively simple plots are concrete and visual, not intellectually abstract, hence easily interpreted as "about" something else. Censorship of film, harsher than that of fiction, stimulates both the writing of allegory and critical discoveries of it, but allegory exists in fiction, too. Li Rui's historical novel *Silver City* opens with the execution of 108 counterrevolutionaries at the beginning of the Communist revolution, recalling the 108 heroes of the Ming-Qing novel *Water Margin* or *Outlaws of the Marsh*; the number 108 has origins in ancient Buddhist iconography.[53]

A past dynasty stands for the present one in classic Chinese novels such as *The Scholars* and *Flowers in the Mirror,* so the practice is hardly exotic to Chinese readers, particularly now that prerevolutionary social customs and institutions have returned to China within living memory. In these times, allegory may seem almost superfluous. But for writers of the generation under discussion, if any particular era is up for criticism, it is the Mao era, which they may well see as "historically unprecedented," though they would not use that Maoist phrase. Jerome Silbergeld suggests that *Red Sorghum* may be viewed as "melodramatic masquerade"; this film (and also *Raise the Red Lantern* and *The Story of Qiu Ju*) mark a restoration of "popular melodrama," in which it is clear which characters are good and which are bad, and yet we "are left uncertain about who or what in modern Chinese society is being referenced by their moral struggle" (238). The film *Red Sorghum* has been interpreted by some as an allegory of the cruelty of China's Communist leaders, with the   Japanese standing in for the Communists.[54] *Raise the Red Lantern*, with its critique of the harsh discipline of Confucianism, is more convincingly viewed as an allegory of constraints on original human nature by the strictures of Communism. More abstract allegorical interpretations of the films have been voiced too; when the family is everything, it can be an allegory of the state. When the individual sacrifices everything for art, for family, or the state, then art, the family, and even the state can stand for something else.[55]

3 PROJECTIONS OF HISTORICAL REPETITION

I N CHINA AS ELSEWHERE, cyclical conceptions of history long predate views
of history as a record of human progress. A common phrase in the Chinese
language, often voiced by characters in the new historical novels, is that fortune flows this way for "twenty years" (or thirty years, or sixty), and then the
other way for the next twenty (thirty, or sixty) years.[1] At a more philosophical
level, Chinese scholars and folk have for millennia looked for cycles in nature,
the ascendancy of yin and yang, successions of reigning dynasties, families,
Buddhist kalpas, Daoist eons, and the rise and fall of morality and prosperity.
In the words of Nathan Sivin, the Chinese saw the cosmos, nature, and "the
liturgical order of both government and religion" as mutually enmeshed in "a
remarkably articulated nest of cycles, with the life trajectory of the mayfly or
the diurnal rhythm of the human body representing the smallest wheel, and,
as the largest, the practically infinite great cycle—from the beginning to the
end of time—integrating all the astronomical periods, all the smaller cycles
turning within it like a superbly complicated train of gears" (152).

The idea of an absolute beginning or end of time is rare in traditional orthodox Chinese philosophy, though faith-based Chinese concepts of time
have included strains of millenarianism outside mainstream thought. The latter might envision irreversible decline, culminating in a great salvation or utopia long awaited by previous generations, yet coming due in the lifetime of
contemporary believers.[2] More typically, Chinese scholars of the classics in the
orthodox mainstream believed in a Golden Age when the ancient sage kings
created an ideal society, a historical utopia. This was accompanied by visions
of social and moral decline in the centuries and millennia since, a historical

process with its own cycles of peace and disorder. The historical inability of the civilized to re-create the good society of the past might seem pessimistic, but the hope and rhetoric of restoration, coupled with a basic Mencian belief in the original (and in practice, recoverable) goodness of human nature, lent an optimistic and even utopian aspect to such strains of historical thinking. Visionary utopian programs were conceived by reformers from Wang Mang (ca. 45 BCE–23 CE) and Wang Anshi (1021–1086) to Hong Xiuquan (1814–1864) and Kang Youwei (1858–1927).[3] They were men of power and optimism, not dystopian thinkers.

Chinese historical thinking has led to further views of relatively "golden" ages in past eras such as the Tang and Song dynasties. Some old believers in China today, like Kundera's Czech character Tereza in *The Unbearable Lightness of Being*, imagine a golden age of early Communism in the 1950s. That view of a youthfully innocent, "good socialism" is not endorsed by China's new historical novelists. Li Rui, Zhang Wei, and Mo Yan, whose novels provide the initial basis for discussion in this chapter, trace their visions of dystopian society to the land reform that established Communist power in North China in the late 1940s, if not to revolutionary activities before that. This contrasts with much of the more recent epic memoir literature, which is based on personal experience and focuses on later political traumas. The novels of this chapter conjoin images of history's repeating itself with social-moral visions of inescapable evil and misery, unmitigated by Confucian faith in the goodness of human nature or Daoist belief in cosmic regularity. Buddhist figurations in the novels combine images of hell and reiteration. Li Rui addresses the seeming conundrum of secular decline within circularity in his preface to *Silver City*: "It is said: If winter comes, can spring be far behind? But my story begins in winter and likewise ends in winter."[4] Springs, including Beijing springs (the original one of 1977–1978, whose nickname was inspired by the Prague Spring of 1968, is now almost forgotten) are preludes to winters. One might wonder, in a reprise of Giambattista Vico's view of recurrent historical cycles, which influenced Hegelian and Marxian dialectics, whether history goes in circles along a single plane, or in spirals—a reverse-Vicoan, *downward* spiral, in the Chinese novels.

Recurrence is a common plot device in world literature. A poignant example among the recent Chinese works is Su Tong's novella about a modern girl student dragged back into "feudal" social customs to become a rich man's fourth concubine, a tale best known from Zhang Yimou's film adaptation, *Raise the Red Lantern*. Cultural recurrence is individualized when the young, ex-student Lotus (whose name recalls that of a famous concubine in *The Golden Lotus*) in the end goes mad, unable to escape the fate of her uneducated concubine "sisters" in their social misery. Her favorite companion, the third wife, is hanged for adultery, repeating past horrors in the mansion filled with women.

This chapter examines six monumental and influential novels (the last is a trilogy) that depict life as cyclical and dystopian at the "micro," plot level, which is in turn embedded in "big events" of history: disastrous wars, revolutions, and failed attempts to build utopia. In the explicit historical timelines of Li Rui's *Silver City* and Zhang Wei's *The Ancient Ship*, which share many of the temporal ambiguities of works discussed in the last chapter, vengeance motivates cyclical patterns of political violence within larger cycles of horrific dynastic or regime change. Violent, murderous "revolutionary" vengeance already abounds in the "red classic" novels that surely influenced Mo Yan's generation, Shelley W. Chan points out.[5] In the new historical novels, vengeance is inherent in human nature, and it is evil—a recurring evil.

Mo Yan's *Life and Death Are Wearing Me Out* is more discursive, often farcical. Its hero and main narrator is a landlord executed after the land reform who, by post-Mao times, has witnessed subsequent history thanks to repeated reincarnations in animal bodies. This novel, like Li Rui's, Zhang Wei's, and Mo Yan's own *Big Breasts and Wide Hips*, takes the Communist land reform and executions of class enemies to be the great watershed in modern Chinese history. *Silver City* moves backward in history to contextualize the violence from 1949 to the 1970s, whereas Mo Yan confines himself largely to the aftermaths. A quite different narrative is Wang Anyi's *The Song of Everlasting Sorrow*. It is set in prerevolutionary and postrevolutionary Shanghai, which was a modern city "from the start," though culturally marginal and hybridized—viewed patronizingly by both the Western core of global capitalism and imperialism, and the continental core of imperial and Maoist China. Cyclicalism in this novel is both symbolic and embodied in concrete historical events and characters. Han Shaogong's *A Dictionary of Maqiao* illustrates another kind of authorial ingenuity. It creates images of cyclical repetition within a larger pattern of Chinese culture, though the work is ostensibly unplotted. Like the other novels, it can be read in different ways, but its dystopian themes are noteworthy. Ge Fei's *Southlands Trilogy* is a saga spanning more than a century, from the end of the Qing to the present. True to his inveterate avant-garde inclinations, Ge Fei leaves "blanks" in his novel's logic of historical continuity and character development that likewise foster a sense of historical cyclicalism. He is also intrigued by repeated historical attempts to create utopia. In every era, they create dystopia.

DYSTOPIAN CYCLICALISM IN A LYRIC HISTORICAL MODE: LI RUI'S *SILVER CITY*

Li Rui's *Silver City* (1990) is an exciting, suspenseful, and lyrical novel, yet one of the most conventionally realistic in plot and technique of all the works analyzed in this book.[6] It continually names the year as it relates past events, which include major struggles with national counterparts recorded in the history books: rebellions, pacifications, workers' strikes, and armed clashes. These frame the fictional characters' marriages, courtships, betrayals, births, and deaths, including the suicides of five major characters. Li Rui's attention to the time of the unfolding action is repetitive and mesmerizing. The effect is to clarify the sense of historical repetition through successive generations, and the plot is notable for remarkable coincidences and turns of fate. On the very day that the novel's great gentry patriarch, Li Naijing, is set to mortgage his clan's greatest potential asset, a salt mine that has so far been unproductive, handing it over to their commercial rival, the Bai clan, the well comes a gusher. That day Li Naijing also acquires an heir, his long-awaited first male child. Decades later, on the day in 1951 when Li Naijing is executed (in the dramatization of events to come that makes up the novel's first chapter), Li Naijing's younger cousin, Li Naizhi, likewise acquires a son and heir, Li Jingsheng. He is Silver City's ranking Communist, rewarded after the revolution with an official job in Beijing.

In keeping with European and Chinese realist traditions, short poems, diary excerpts, and documents—from death certificates to newspaper clippings—carry the narrative at particular moments. Li Rui's outstanding virtue is the economy of his narration. The "primary materials" let his vividly drawn revolutionaries, lovers, and propagandists speak in the voices of their time: succinctly, dramatically, and in character. Brief citations of ancient poetry, folk songs, and local customs recall the lyricism of the May Fourth giant Shen Congwen, evoking other authentic period voices with hopes and fears that represent changes and continuities in values from decade to decade. Even the main, omniscient narrative voice that at the start of the novel tells of the 1951 mass executions at times mimics the rhetorical bombast of the 1949 revolution—though with a brevity uncharacteristic of the original propagandists.

The events thus told, often shocking enough on their own terms, become portentous when Li Rui, with his characteristic sense of the dramatic, reveals that they are but prelude to future reversals not visible at present. The novel begins: "Not until later did it occur to anyone that October 24, 1951 . . . happened to fall on Frost's Descent" (3/5).[7] On that day the local elite were liquidated through a mass execution. The self-conscious historical ironies of Li Rui's opening and later, similarly explicit foreshadowings, in a nonlinear plot, are what make *Silver City* a "new" historical novel to Chinese readers, in addition to his starkly alternative visions of what is good and bad in the history of Chinese Communism. García Márquez used the technique in his more magically plotted *One Hundred Years of Solitude*.

Silver City is a family saga stretching across several decades. Major historical events provide context and determine the fate of the characters, many of whom seek to change the course of events by joining or fighting the revolution while fending off warlords, as in Ba Jin's classic novel *Family* (1931). References to the larger historical context drop out of Ba Jin's work after his initial chapters, but Li Rui maintains the dramatic interplay of family and society, and familial and social conflict, to the end, with much richer lyricism in the telling—more in the style, again, of Shen Congwen than Ba Jin. The Silver City of which the novel writes is a fictitious town far up the Yangzi River with an ancient past as a center of salt mining. Chinese readers might identify it straight off as Zigong, Sichuan. Li Rui claims Zigong as his ancestral home, though he was born in Beijing and is now strongly identified with Shanxi, indeed, as a regionalist writer who once sought Chinese cultural "roots" in Shanxi. The local warlord of the novel, Yang Chuxiong, is fictitious, though the higher leaders and ideologists that the novel mentions (without dramatizing them), from Li Naijing's hero Zeng Guofan to Li Naizhi's hero Li Dazhao, are real, possibly as far down as the Commander Liu from whom the local militarist Yang Chuxiong gains his independence.[8]

Early chapters of the plot develop dialectically, alternating between stories of the ancient, landed Li clan headed by Li Naijing, who keeps to the ancient Confucian code of ethics—until the war with Japan, when he corners the provincial salt market (to the admiration of the local community even so, which sees it as shrewd)—and the clan's future adversaries in Communist times, the rising Bai clan. Their American-educated head, Bai Ruide, brings foreign business products and methods to Silver City prior to the revolution and is not content with his own riches; he schemes repeatedly to take over the declining Li estate. His son-in-law Li Naizhi of the rival clan joins the Communist movement. The near extermination of Li Naizhi's own clan in the 1949 revolution is the price of his being on the right side of history; yet he and his wife, Bai Qiuyun, will also perish before their time, in the retributive madness of the Great Proletarian Cultural Revolution.

The dialectics of opposites is multifold: Lis vs. Bais; declining "feudal" landlords vs. a rising modern, foreign-connected bourgeoisie; capitalist and feudal classes (Lis and Bais together) vs. revolutionaries; Buddhist asceticism vs. modern education; and young vs. old, the venerable Ba Jin concern. The opening chapter follows the dramatized 1951 executions with a flashback to a 1927 Communist insurrection in which fifty-seven underground party members perished while trying to ride the revolutionary wave that had risen in Wuhan. Li Rui explains the plot significance of the abortive 1927 insurrection in advance. "In point of fact, the demise of the Li clan can be traced further back, to December 1927, when peasants in the five counties surrounding Silver City rose in rebellion" (10/10).

The self-destructive society throws off all human restraints. The great Li clan is destroyed, along with its salt-production enterprises and architectural monuments; wretched and impoverished citizens replace them in their mansion. Further violence leads to a decline of the Communist victors of the 1927–1951 revolutionary movement in their turn. Even before the revolution, members of the Li clan had made horrible and ultimately futile sacrifices to stave off the inevitable fall of their fortunes. Naijing's cousin Li Zihen early on disfigured her face (in 1928, we know, precisely) to make herself unmarriageable and thus preserve family resources for the education of her younger siblings. Zihen's sister subsequently renounces her true love to marry the local warlord, again in hopes of staving off family decline. Zihen's brother Li Naizhi ends up a Communist Party official in Beijing, but even so dies in isolation in 1970 while incarcerated in a May Seventh Cadre School, falsely suspected of having betrayed the revolution. He is disowned by one of his daughters even in death.

The endless slouch toward universal suffering and destruction gains momentum as a great historical cycle that has lesser cycles nested within it. At the subcosmic, middle level of local history, the pattern is of ambition leading to failure and violence. This begets counterviolence, in an inevitable pattern. The 1927 uprising thus provokes a 1928 retaliatory extermination of all fifty-seven underground Communists involved. The blood debt on both sides is remembered in 1939, during a salt workers' strike, which in turn provokes a subsequent round of white terror. In the words of the novel, "in the winter of 1939, the 1927 Silver City massacre was reenacted" (168/175). The "final" retaliatory solution, meant to restructure society by destroying landlord power forever, is the 1951 mass execution that opens the novel. But thenceforth another kind of retribution comes into play, as if by Buddhist logic. The revolutionary hunters become the hunted as their revolutionary purity comes increasingly into question. Even when a Communist Party member, Li Naizhi, is on his deathbed, the party inquires not after his health but whether he is headed for revolutionary heaven or damnation: does the comrade have anything else to confess? Confession is not to absolve the sinner, but the Communist Party, which thereby damns itself.

In an equally long, if less cosmic context, all the insurrections and purifications of the twentieth century—traced back, in this locale, to a 1907 labor uprising (75/76), the 1911 revolution that overthrew the monarchy, down to the more recent Communist uprisings (160/166)—reenact centuries and millennia of "rebellions" past. Mongrel Chen, leader of the 1927 uprising, shouts the customary warning of a brave man about to be executed: "In twenty years, I'll be back, stronger than ever [after reincarnation]." The novel adds a violent twist and voices Chen's simple view that all political insurrections are part of a tradition of rebellion, and its essence is killing: "I'll be back, stronger than ever, and ready to fuck and kill again . . . I am the Bolshevik, I am the Soviet! I am the rebel . . . Zhang Xianzhong [a mass murderer of Sichuanese in 1601–1647] will return and the slaughter will start anew" (14/15). Even world war loses its distinctiveness, for it falls into a historical pattern; the estate of the Lis survived the Taiping rebels in the 1850s, and it survives the invading Japanese (175–176/182). It does not survive the Communist revolution, whose cyclicalism exists on a more epochal plane.

At the family level, after the grandam of the Bais, Lady Yang, poisons the son of a concubine, the concubine tries to poison her. Lady Yang had encouraged the same concubine to seduce her husband in the first place—with phraseology that she repeats, almost verbatim, in an abortive attempt to find a match for her daughter ("the rest is up to you"; 49/50, 111/117). She does not learn from her mistakes. Neither does the patriarch of the Bais; when at first he fails to finish off the financial empire of the Lis, he tries and fails, again. The Lis trump his machinations, at the cost of abandoning their old morality, through intermarriage with the warlord. When Li Naijing finally nears his end in a Communist prison, he has déjà vu: "The whole scene seemed familiar somehow, as if he had witnessed one exactly like it somewhere at some other time" (185/191). The reader likewise feels déjà vu when only two pages later Li's sister, Zihen, "could not shake the feeling that she had witnessed a similar scene [of soldiers escorting prisoners] before" (186/193).

Within these eternal cycles of violence begetting violence is a vision not only of stark reversals of fortune, of rises and falls, of riches and ruin, but also of a unity of opposites: of murder and love, the simultaneous death of yin and yang (as when Li Naijing loses both his wife and his adviser, 138/145), and most explicitly, a so-called "dialectic of grief and strength," which can "turn one into the other" (18, 19/19; Li Rui uses the Hegelian/Marxist term for "dialectic"). Grief for fallen comrades was originally the revolutionaries' way of stoking anger to motivate revolutionary action, but in this post-Mao period the "dialectic" is redefined by the Communist Party. It means "forgetting past mistakes" (i.e., persecutions of loyal comrades) so as to achieve the strength of unity—a United Front, in which differences and past sorrows are papered over.[9] This is, of course, ironic. Li Rui, in the novel's preface (and on 149/156), evokes the falsity of truth and the truth of falsity, originally stated in *The Dream of the Red Chamber*, a classic novel that lies behind his tale of two clans.[10] *Silver City* is also known for its Buddhist references, but the alternation of rise and fall is most powerfully symbolized in the figure of a well sweep (an ancient fulcrum device for lowering and raising a bucket in a well), seen by Bai Qiuyun at her commune near the end of the Cultural Revolution. The author reminds the reader that the well sweep is an ancient Daoist symbol of alternating motion, fully detached from human volition and emotion (236–237/241). Qiuyun completes another, more conventionally literary cycle of suffering by recalling her favorite line from the great woman poet and essayist Li Qingzhao (ca. 1081–ca. 1141): "Desolation, misery, and woe" (241/245).

Life will go on in the post-socialist era, but the great historical relics have been demolished, history is forgotten, and in post-Mao times those who might still preserve its memory have become feebleminded. The surviving Li Jingsheng makes a pilgrimage to see his old aunt, the widow of the warlord, who has survived to the present day in Taiwan exile. Her mind is now gone. History repeats itself, but one cannot learn from it if one cannot even remember one's own past.

SOCIAL DECLINE IN A LARGER SYMBOLIC MIASMA: ZHANG WEI'S *THE ANCIENT SHIP*

Zhang Wei's *The Ancient Ship*, epic in historical scope and narrative length, weaves strong images of historical circularity into a tale of a century of decline. The work's periodical publication was in 1986, a time of great political ferment in China; Zhang may have hoped it would be the great Chinese novel, replete with his philosophy of life. It is a long, baggy narrative, with digressions on Chinese cuisine (featuring dishes so esoteric and peculiarly named that the effect is satiric, as in Mo Yan's later novel *The Republic of Wine*), occasional citations of Chinese cosmology and great books of the past, and multiple though not fully developed subplots about the frustrated romances (highly sexualized by 1986 standards) of the novel's main characters, the most important of whom are male. The epochal deterioration in the quality of life and love that Zhang depicts is ameliorated in final plot developments, perhaps due to politics or his own sense of duty, but the repeated alternation of opposites in society, politics, families, and morality embedded in a larger, dystopian cyclicalism in history itself, is overwhelming.

The setting is a fictitious Shandong provincial town, with some rural characteristics, called Wali. More than two thousand years ago, Wali was the site of a notable city-state of the Warring States epoch. Later, it was an inland port trading with the South Seas. Early in the twentieth century, its famous factories used the water power of the (likewise fictitious) Luqing River to make glass noodles (bean-starch vermicelli). Now, "the old, stepped riverbed told the history of the decline of a once great river" (2/2). The river, factories, and town began their decline in the 1930s. The plot then ranges back and forth across four decades of Communist rule. The core dramatized action is post-Mao, but the exact year is ambiguous. The death of Mao goes unnoticed, as in most new historical novels. Flashbacks, on the other hand, recall political movements precisely located in time: the great land reform (1947 at this location), 1950s socialization of industry, Great Leap Forward, Cultural Revolution, and post-Mao reshuffling of property rights.[11] In this and other novels that detail the recurrence of Communist political movements—the removal of Mao's role in them serves only to heighten the sense of their inevitability—the cyclical character of the movements recapitulates the cyclicalism of the author's larger historical vision. Like *Silver City*, *The Ancient Ship* finds the land reform and counterterror of a Landlord Restitution Corps to be the root of all vengeful evil. The revolution was thus poisoned from the start, before cyclical recurrences of madness in the Great Leap and Cultural Revolution came to undo any lingering successes of the early socialism. In this novel, violence requires no precedents of war, civil war, or peasant rebellion. The focus on the land reform and subsequent liquidation movements puts the emphasis on elemental eliminations of populations instead of transformations of production and social organization.

Statistics are surprisingly prominent. The numbers of casualties in the land reform liquidations, post-Leap famine, and Cultural Revolution are told with exactitude, as in the angry memoirs and nonfiction works by expatriate authors. The reader is bound to assume that such figures must come from the history of a real time and place, so as to bear witness to tragedies that never "entered into the town's chronicle," as *The Ancient Ship* puts it more than once (e.g., 314/387). Yet, Zhang Wei also relates precise seven-digit numbers from the account books of the glass noodle manufacturing enterprise in town (96–98/121–122), and not just figures for "entertainment" and bribes, but also for raw materials and wages, as if he really intended to record, for posterity, how an enterprise functioned economically at the time of the initial post-Mao transition from socialism.

The Ancient Ship develops, at length, a symbolic dialectic between two brothers. The younger, Sui Jiansu, is weakened by alleged greed and a destructive desire for vengeance against those who ruined his clan, even as he tries and mostly fails to adapt to China's new post-Mao marketizing economy. His elder brother, Sui Baopu, born before Liberation, is a feckless socialist factory overseer, subordinate to the Zhao clan, who tries to claim the moral high ground over Jiansu by proclaiming the need for the common good. His authority is *The Communist Manifesto* (not Mao Zedong Thought). *The Ancient Ship* describes a left-right balance of evil. It savages post-Mao consumerism even as it details the noxious effects of Communist bureaucratic tyranny; some of the characters who use and abuse political power have their good sides, and the Communist Party secretary is described at first mention as "an honest, decent man" (21/28). The narrative explains, in more than one place, how the Landlord Restitution Corps temporarily wrested power from the Communists in 1947 to undo their land redistribution. The landlords tortured and mutilated local Communists and buried forty-two peasants alive in a yam cellar.

The unusual ordering of the plot at the macro level (not at the paragraph level, as in *Red Sorghum*), won Zhang Wei a reputation as not only a daring political commentator but also an avant-garde writer. The plotline keeps circling back to the stories of a limited number of characters and events, going into greater depth and revealing new information in each retelling. This offers the reader several delights of old-fashioned storytelling. One is character development. The main actors' motivations and backstories are gradually filled in, as in a traditional novel. Another is the pursuit of the mysteries of a small town. What exactly did the Zhao clan do to punish the Sui clan after the revolution of 1947–1949 came to Wali? How did the Sui clan of ex-capitalists survive the land reform, the Great Leap Forward, and the Cultural Revolution without being executed? Why does Sui Jiansu's younger sister Hanzhang visit Fourth Master Zhao, and why did she never marry?

Wali's once much larger noodle factory complex was originally constructed by the Sui clan. The first subchapter ends with a Marquezian foreshadowing: "This period, spanning the 1930s and 1940s, witnessed the beginning of the Sui family's decline. Sui Yingzhi's life would end in a sad fashion, and in the days before his death he would find himself envying his [seafaring] brother [the eccentric drunkard Sui Buzhao], but too late . . . [implied ellipsis in the original]" (4/5). The rest of the first chapter introduces the main characters of the local Sui, Zhao, and Li clans in what was in 1986 present or near-present time, but the year is ambiguous. Two major recent but undated events were almost simultaneous: a great earthquake and the takeover of the historic town noodle factory, the only one still operating, by Zhao Duoduo under a "responsibility" contract of the sort that emerged after Mao died in 1976. It is realistic that the man designated to profit from the factory, with all the privileges of running a patronage system and little risk of losing capital during that first stage of departure from socialism, is a member of the politically ruling Zhao clan. He is its long-standing local "enforcer," the reader later learns. The plot will advert to full chapters of flashbacks as the story goes on, but the core action of the novel keeps returning to this initial factory privatization and how it tempts Sui Jiansu to take the factory back for the Suis when Zhao's contract will come up for renewal. So what is the year? The "responsibility" contract system came to agriculture only in 1981 and to industry some years later. And if control of the factory went, acrimoniously, to a Zhao in the late 1970s, after the reforms, who was running it for the government during all those decades of full Maoist socialism? Not a Sui, at least for most of that period. A great deal of what went on in the factory during those long years remains a mystery, apart from an admission that the factory was shuttered after the Great Leap Forward, when agricultural materials grew scarce.

One need not, perhaps, insist on tight logic here; there were always regional exceptions in the vast terrain of Chinese socialist practice. But what about the earthquake? That would be the terrible one that destroyed Tangshan in July 1976, shortly before the death of Chairman Mao. Zhang Wei, departing here from the relatively careful chronological accounting in the rest of his novel, has symbolically associated the post-Mao *economic* transition (not the death of Mao) with the great Tangshan quake as equally epochal, earthshaking events.

The indirectness of partial and repetitive revelation is one key to Zhang Wei's narrative art. Instead of softening the tragedy of ongoing atrocities, it accentuates them. The leaders' acquired power to destroy is related almost nonchalantly. As Zhao Duoduo in a fit of anger imagines shooting his post-Mao subordinate Sui Baopu for refusing to help out at the factory with a spoiled vat of noodles, the narrator adds a thunderbolt in passing: "As commander of the Gaoding Street militia during land reform, Duoduo had already shot several people, and he couldn't think of a better candidate for a bullet than this member of the Sui clan" (30/37–38). This is the first real hint of the past terror of the 1940s land reform movement and the origin of clan enmity between the Suis and the Zhaos. Several hundred pages later, the full story of the land reform terrorism, the Great Leap, and the Cultural Revolution have been filled in, telling how the Zhaos, under the leadership of Fourth Master (Zhao Bing), clan elder and behind-the-scenes town boss, lorded over the town. Fourth Master alternately persecuted and protected the formerly capitalist Suis, while wisely refraining from taking a high official post himself.

Moral defects in the characters are thus revealed piecemeal. Onetime militia head Zhao Duoduo is only gradually shown to be a serial killer; he murdered his wife (revealed only in chapter 8) and executed many fellow townsmen in the name of class warfare during the land reform (detailed only in chapter 18). Sui Jiansu appears to be the novel's one true entrepreneur, but he cuts corners in his privately owned shop in the city by selling counterfeit goods. These and other easy accoutrements of "modernity," such as ear-piercing, spread back to rustic Wali.

Direct narrative comment makes the decline explicit: "Sui Hengde and his immediate family had been the leaders [of their Sui clan], but this branch had begun to go downhill in the 1940s, taking the rest of the clan with them" (198/247). Ultimately, Sui Baopu and Fourth Master themselves reflect that "Heavenly justice" and a bad "end" are inevitable in the wake of the community's extreme violence and lack of propriety (85/107, 167/208).

Most portentously, Zhang Wei peppers his narrative with heavy allegorical figurations. One is "the ancient ship," a local archaeological relic that proves Wali's past glories, but is quickly spirited away to the provincial museum. Besides the danger of missing the boat (not an ancient Chinese idiom, but see 200/249), the ancient ship recalls a once glorious "ship of state" now badly in need of repair.[12] That would mean, for one thing, bringing the ship from the museum back to where it flourished and served a useful purpose (170/212).

The ancient ship points to a lost seagoing spirit of seeking adventure, new knowledge, and self-betterment abroad, soon to be celebrated in the 1988 documentary *Deathsong of the River,* in which Zhang Wei has a speaking role.[13] The Luqing River that held the key to Wali's fame, prosperity, and vitality has nearly dried up, but late in the novel, geological surveyors discover a second Luqing River in the bedrock underneath the visible one, symbolizing the suppressed talents of the Chinese people.

China's maritime past is recounted by the unreliable and eccentric ex-sailor Sui Buzhao, who fortifies himself, and the town, with tales of the great Ming dynasty explorer Zheng He. Other allegorical tropes include the town's chop or seal, which to the townsfolk embodies power, authority and legitimacy. All those things are lost during the chaotic Cultural Revolution, along with the seal (348/428). A canister of radioactive materials brought to the town for geological exploration, representing a threat to the health of future generations, is also lost; it has not been found by the end of the novel. As the rediscovered river represents an underground hope for the people of Wali, the canister represents a still hidden danger. By the end of the novel the glass noodle factory has been mechanized, which adds a triumphal note, but the enterprise founders. Meanwhile, the adventurers and inventors of the older generation have all died off. The middle generation falls prey to unexplained illnesses and is frustrated in its ambitions, as in a May Fourth romantic novel. A younger generation is largely absent from Zhang Wei's narrative. Given his allegorical bent, when Zhang Wei writes, "Too many people had suffered as a result of insufficient lighting in town" (38/47), one is tempted to look for deeper meanings in that.[14]

The vision of dystopia is most clearly expressed by the novel's one idealist, Sui Baopu, who is mesmerized by *The Communist Manifesto*: "You can't make life easy for yourself, because those around you will take it away from you [referring to capitalism, though at this point in the novel one can find that fault in communism]. . . . I thought that suffering and bloodshed in our town would come to an end, but now I know I was just fooling myself" (216/269–270). The fault lies in human nature itself, observes his brother, ironically imparting a negative interpretation to a Maoist phrase that summed up the hopes of the Great Leap Forward: "There are things that people cannot imagine but nothing that people will not do" (223/278).

Cyclicalism in the telling of the story, returning to the same events over and over again to fill in the chains of causation, frustrates any sense that Wali or its main characters are progressing. The larger pattern is that whole social systems come and go in a cycle. China's capitalist "old society" was replaced by a socialist one that was equally flawed, only to be replaced by a new society with the "old" values of greed and selfishness. Even the common people of Wali can see history repeating itself. With the post-Mao reforms and their supposed miracles come "one shocking story after another," "revealed in the paper and on the radio," about 1,842 peasants flying in airplanes and a peasant entrepreneur earning 489,000 yuan. "The old folks in Wali could not avoid being reminded of their youth, an era of gigantic numbers [the Great Leap Forward], one that had been recorded in the town's chronicles. But the chronicles neglected to mention what had happened after the arrival of those gigantic numbers, except to brush it off as a 'natural disaster'" (139/172).

The clans, too, have replaced each other in a circular fashion, without any new members appearing to inject new blood. Likewise, the locality's enterprises. The Zhaos took over the Suis' noodle manufactory, only to lose control of it at the very end, to a Sui after all—a much weaker Sui scion, Baopu—whose life philosophy comes not from Adam Smith but from daily reading of the old *Communist Manifesto*. His brother, Jiansu, devoted to opening up private shops, is the neo-capitalist of his generation of Suis, but soon his businesses fail and he falls deathly ill. Even he, the one who wants to adapt to change, observes that "people in the past were so much better at pondering problems and issues" (230/286).

An emblem of recurrence that gives the lie to visions of progress is the fashion and makeup industry. The Communists abolished the old society's makeup and Jiansu restored it after the post-Mao reforms, but his sort of capitalistic sales are burdened by fraud and fake products. And what if communism should once more take the place of "capitalism"? Sui Baopu (347/426–427) finds a historical answer to this in *The Communist Manifesto* that inspires him to keep reading, but not to act: the French and English aristocracy, superseded by their new masters, the bourgeoisie, "took their revenge by singing lampoons of their new masters and whispering in their ears sinister prophecies of coming catastrophe." His current reference could be Chinese landlords of the 1940s or Chinese cadres of the 1980s. Baopu continues reading from chapter 3 of the *Manifesto*: "In this way arose feudal socialism: half lamentation, half lampoon; half an echo of the past, half menace of the future." That could describe Maoism, post-Maoism, or both.

The moral undercurrents of *The Ancient Ship* bespeak a vision of historical cyclicalism at the highest level, one expressed in both mechanistic and religious terms. Evil comes from extremism and revenge, which provokes more revenge in a never-ending cycle of terror and extremism on both sides that bears overtones of karmic retribution. The moral imperative to avoid extremes acquires a Confucian rationale as voiced by the Zhao elder early on when his clan's dominion, like socialism itself, is about to end: "When you take things to an extreme, you abandon all claims of propriety. Confucius once said that you can do whatever you please so long as you don't transgress" (167/208). During the Cultural Revolution, Fourth Master gave this injunction to his clansmen and townsmen as they ran riot: "Confiscating their property and driving them out of the house is enough. Don't overdo it" (246/308). Yet he also speaks his pious observations of propriety to a woman whom he has long sexually abused and whose aim in life is therefore to exact revenge by killing him. (She will make her move in the final chapter and be shot in the attempt, providing further evidence of the futility of such motivation.) In the background, as Fourth Master muses about the coming of "the end," the local intellectual, who has ridden out the storms by serving all masters and writing out their denunciations, intones Daoist pieties from China's most ancient supramoral treatise on the inevitability of opposites superseding each other: "It [the Dao] spreads and unfolds with the rough and the gentle, falling and rising with the yin and the yang" (168/208).

Folk Buddhist belief in retribution and the wheel of life provides an even more pervasive undercurrent of moral warnings about evil leading to a just recompense. Here the novel's many references to account books and meticulously documented "debts" come into play. When the old Sui clan patriarch, Sui Yingzhi, hands over all but one of his factories to the state early on after the revolution, he explains that it is because "we owe people" (42/52). That is not enough, of course. "We still haven't paid off all our debts," Yingzhi tells his son Baopu (46/57). This fits revolutionary rhetoric, which held that the exploiting capitalist class owed *the people*. Sui Jiansu is obsessed with the account books of the noodle factory in his quest to take it back from Zhao Duoduo, and then Baopu pores over the books ad nauseam, for no apparent reason—except that he finds a hidden connection between those, his father's from before Liberation, and his lodestone, *The Communist Manifesto*. "He could see that hidden in [one of its passages] was an even more important and complicated account. Stirred by this thought, he pushed his abacus to the side and thought about the subjugation of nature's forces and its application to Wali" (282/350). The scores of political killings are a blood debt, and as if that metaphor were not clear enough, during the land reform an old man hacks a palm-sized piece of flesh from the body of a landlord, proclaiming, "That evens the account" (241/301). Explains the narrator: "Each generation of the Sui clan had produced someone like him [Jiansu], as if God, in his balancing scheme, had given the honest, slow-acting clan someone who knew how to exact revenge" (262/326). This, inevitably, brings about Jiansu's downfall. It is his slow, idealistic brother who in the end takes over the noodle factory—when it is finally facing extinction. From a long historical perspective, Jiansu's abortive attempt to settle scores with socialism is not unlike the Communists' ultimately futile settling of scores with landlords and capitalists.

THE WHEEL OF LIFE: MO YAN'S *LIFE AND DEATH ARE WEARING ME OUT*

Mo Yan's *Life and Death Are Wearing Me Out* is a rollicking, often farcical, sometimes scatological comic novel like Wang Shuo's *Please Don't Call Me Human* (1989), which to Douwe Fokkema (338–344) exemplifies the contemporary Chinese dystopian novel. That work reflects on the past by implication; Mo Yan's novel ranges broadly across China's Communist history to satirize the present. His hero Lan Lian is allowed to farm independently in Northeast Gaomi Township (the usual setting of Mo Yan's novels) for more than a decade after the rural collectivization movement, never being forced to join a cooperative or people's commune. Local officials accept Lan Lian's citation of Chairman Mao, who said that joining the collective was voluntary. That local cadres would take the Chairman at his word on that is as improbable as a Modest Proposal for eating babies (the subject of Mo Yan's prior satiric novel, *The Republic of Wine*).[15]

The novel's marvelous narrative shtick is the passage of its main protagonist through different animal bodies after his death, in accordance with the Buddhist wheel of life—the transmigration of souls. This hero is named Ximen Nao, recalling the lustful Ximen Qing of the classic, anonymously written erotic novel *The Plum in the Golden Vase* (*Jin ping mei*, also translated as *The Golden Lotus*); Mo Yan's character's given name, *nao*, means "raising a ruckus," rather like the Monkey King in another classic novel, by Wu Cheng'en, *The Journey to the West* (*Xi you ji*). Ximen Nao, a landlord who grew wealthy through his own industry, is executed as a matter of political vengeance in the class struggles during land reform in early 1948, for this is Shandong again, as in the works by Zhang Wei, where Communists consolidated rural power prior to their "Liberation" of all China in 1949. After two years in hell, Ximen returns to earth in successive reincarnations, initially as a donkey born on January 1, 1950. The text calls him Ximen Donkey. Subsequently his soul is reborn into the bodies of an ox, a pig, a dog, and a monkey. Ximen ends up, at the time of the present narration (about 2005), occupying the body of an extremely precocious, story-telling millennial child, Lan Qiansui (Thousand-Year-Old Lan), who as a five-year-old human can speak again and tell the incredible story of everything he has seen and done in his previous reincarnations and the stints in hell between them. Ximen Nao in each reincarnation retains memories of his previous life as a human landlord, father, and head of household, and also his prior experiences as other animals, even as he lives and breathes the passions, desires, and frustrations of the real donkey, ox, or pig that he feels in his current animal body. The main narrator is thus the former Ximen Nao reborn into a human called Lan Qiansui, an identity clarified only late in the novel; the reader hears him mainly as the reminiscing voice of an ex-donkey, ox, pig, or dog, who can look at life from the perspective of several species. Mo Yan's metempsychosis device can be appreciated as another absurdist or fantasy touch, or simply as a narrative device to give the story access to multiple viewpoints of history. It taps into a belief system and source of ethics widely embraced in China the wheel of life in its cosmic grandeur makes years, decades, and centuries of political change, of all human endeavors, seem insignificant.

Mo Yan after many chapters provides a second narrator, and finally a third—an author called "Mo Yan," though his life and works are frequently inconsistent with those of Mo Yan in life, sometimes farcically so.[16] Among the other characters are Bai, Ximen Nao's surviving legal wife, who suffers throughout the Communist era because of her husband's class status; the foundling Lan Lian, future hero, whom Ximen Nao discovered in the snow, years before the revolution, then adopted and supported as a farmhand; Ximen Nao's good concubine, Yingchun, who bore him the twins Baofeng (girl) and Jinlong (boy), before taking Lan Lian as her lawfully wedded husband after Ximen's execution; and a bad concubine, Qiuxiang, whose false accusations of rape helped bring about the execution. She marries the executioner, Huang Tong, an ex-beggar and Ximen's nemesis. He emerges as a long-standing underground Communist Party member and becomes head of the local militia. There are so many other characters that Mo Yan begins his novel with a list of dramatis personae. Lan Jiefang, born the son of Lan Lian in 1949, the year of China's Liberation (*jiefang*, in Mandarin), at first sides with his father by staying outside of the collective, with Lan Lian's donkey, and then his ox, the reincarnations of Ximen Nao (All human Ximens change their surname to hide their landlord class background; Baofeng and Jinlong become Lan Baofeng and Lan Jinlong). The heroic independent farmer Lan Lian is of good class background, since he was a propertyless farmhand under the old society, but his closeness to Ximen Nao endangers that protected status even before he marries the deceased landlord's honest concubine. Lan Lian's new class status problem is passed on to Lan Jiefang, particularly after father and son resist the tide of collectivism. Lan Jinlong, né Ximen Jinlong, has a bigger, more natal, background problem; he compensates by becoming an extreme revolutionary. He heads a Red Guard faction in the Cultural Revolution and hopes to rise into officialdom—until he becomes an "active counterrevolutionary" for having accidentally dropped his Mao badge into a latrine. Long before that, Lan Lian's wife and "adopted" children have all joined the commune for self-preservation, drawing a line between themselves and Lan Lian; only Lan Jiefang sides with his father, until finally he, too, must cave in and cast his lot with socialism in the Cultural Revolution.

The combination of satirically exaggerated visions of dystopia (e.g., Cultural Revolution rhetoric that makes birds fall from the skies) with cyclical metempsychosis might at first seem a mere comic device.[17] Mo Yan satirizes numerous objects of reverence, from Communist officials to novelists and film directors. Treading on dangerous territory, the narrator as pig observes, "The death of Chairman Mao was a loss not only for humans but for us pigs as well" (310/331). At times, his narrators address the reader with the phraseology of a traditional Chinese novel or storyteller. But the overall direction of history, epitomized in the Ximens and their kith and kin, is one of decadence, decline, and injustice. At the outset, Ximen Nao, a benevolent and public-spirited landlord, has his head blown open by a shotgun and begins his odyssey with Lord Yama in Buddhist hell. Ximen Donkey is slaughtered for food by a peasant mob reduced to starvation after the Great Leap Forward. Almost a decade later, Ximen Ox, predictably, is the victim of Cultural Revolution cruelty. The pig, in the discursive mid-novel chapters, lasts into post-Mao times and dies saving children from drowning under winter ice. The dog commits suicide with his master, Lan Lian, in 1998, and the monkey is shot dead by Jiefang's son in a fit of rage; the mother who bears Ximen in his latest form, as the human baby Lan Qiansui, is an ex-prostitute.

The animal consciousnesses are "fully human," even superhuman; Ximen Dog is more loyal than a human, including some humans descended from Ximen Nao, and a pig may at times be smarter than humans. This is ironic, for according to a figure of speech Mo Yan likes to cite in his novels, in the "old society" one might avow one's gratitude toward a benefactor by hoping to be reborn as his ox or horse, to serve him in his next life.[18] The animals in their stubbornness and fury tend to disrupt human political ceremonies at historically inopportune times. As half-human witnesses to history, they encounter Ximen's surviving family members and old friends and nemeses. The animals are finally able to relate the injustices done to one and all when these shadows of Ximen in the end regain a human voice. In other chapters, the animals are true to their species. The donkey speaks of the lust he feels for a female donkey in heat; the pig struggles to become "king of the pigs," takes up residence in an independent pig colony beyond human control, and fends off a human counterattack in passages reminiscent of *Red Sorghum*'s fight between humans and wild dogs. The chapters in which the animals act fully "in character" may strike readers as a distraction from the main narrative, if not filler, but some of their outbreaks of stubbornness and outright rebellion, though apolitical in motivation, disrupt political activities or thwart social injustices. At other times, their acts can be read as allegories of human behavior; individual animals appear as a higher species than humans when the latter are collectivized. The animalian reincarnations not only bear witness to history, they fight for the Ximen descendants and end up dying for them, sometimes heroically. The cyclicalism of reincarnation is thus conjoined with pessimism about the human condition, the "higher" form of life reacquired at the end of the novel. The dystopian image of socialist bureaucratism in the early chapters turns to social climbing when Lan Jinlong and even the hapless Lan Jiefang become local officials under "post-socialism." In the end, Ximen Jinlong (who reclaims his old surname, which has become illustrious again) plans to turn little Ximen Village—likewise renamed—into a theme park of the Cultural Revolution. The villagers will mimic their shocking misdeeds of yesteryear for the amusement of tourists.

As in *Silver City* and *The Ancient Ship*, vengeance begets vengeance. The powerful go to jail in the end, and Jinlong is assassinated (privately, not by the state) for his turn from Maoism to commercialism. The local bullies of early socialism belonged to the dregs and bad elements of the old society to begin with, in a familiar reversal of values; when socialism dims, they return to power. Post-Mao society is the ultimate recycling of the "old," pre-socialist society. "After thirty hard, demanding years, we're right back to the days before Liberation," protests Hong Tayue, the old Communist Party secretary of the village (337/350). Mo Yan's narrators likewise observe that the destruction and vengeance of the Mao years remind them of "tales of wartime" (134/159).

The animals, too, suffer the indignities of generational change. Observes Xi-men Dog, in the 1990s, after retiring as chair of the County Dog Association—with possible allegorical implications for the 1989 Tiananmen massacre and perhaps even the demonstrators—"After stepping down, I seldom attended the gatherings in Tianhua Square. . . . My generation has celebrated the gatherings with singing, dancing, drinking, eating, and mating. But the new breed of youngsters were engaged in unusual and, to me, inexplicable behaviors" (481/478). Each generation, each reincarnation, falls into its own traps, repeating *human* folly. Says Jiefang, "That torrential rainfall of the early 1990s exposed much of the corruption masked by the false prosperity of the age" (468/467).

There is a moral to this long, complicated novel, and it is the same as that of *Silver City* and *The Ancient Ship*. Ximen's Sisyphean reincarnations are punishments meant to teach him to purge himself of his hatreds: " 'There are too many, far too many, people in the world in whose hearts hatred resides,' Lord Yama said sorrowfully. 'We are unwilling to allow spirits who harbor hatred to be reborn as humans. Unavoidably, some do slip through the net' " (512/510).

The irony, however, is that cyclical repetition of a cosmic sort is the cure for the human cycles of hatred, vengeance, and more hatred. After doing good deeds and gradually shedding his hatred, Ximen is reborn as successively higher animals and finally as a human again, but is there any *escape* from the wheel of life, into nirvana, or even utopia? Moreover, as Ximen is transitioning between ox and pig, Lord Yama suggests that Ximen must seek happiness through amnesia, by forgetting the past (191–192/219–220). But how can that bring about justice, which is essential for happiness? Surely amnesia negates the purpose of history books and historical novels. And is rebirth as a human being, subject to all too much amnesia already—as in creating happy images of the Cultural Revolution for tourists and others too young to remember the real thing—really an end in itself? Here we see the inherent contradiction between the utopian quest for a just and good final end and the imperfections and ignorant repetitions of real humans in the realm of worldly dust. Dystopia, on the other hand, can be achieved through repeating past mistakes over and over. Yet, can one really know that dystopia, any more than utopia, is necessarily the "final outcome" for humankind, when death itself is not fully understood? These are contradictions within linear and cyclical notions of time as such. Indeed, the concept of predetermination, of history unfolding according to fate, makes its way into Mo Yan's narrative.

Ximen Ox was not born into Lan Lian's household; Lan Lian and his son, Jiefang, were drawn to buy the ox at market. "In the end we bought the ox," Jiefang recalls while taking a turn telling the Ximen saga as an old man. "It was inevitable, all previously arranged in the underworld" (94/113; see also 510/507). The self-dramatized narrator "Mo Yan," before describing the ultimate demise of Ximen's descendants in degradation, madness, and death, pronounces an equivalent moral: "Don't think I'm happy [about the final resolution of the younger generation], dear reader. The characters' fates have made it inevitable" (529/52).

RECURRENCE AND DECLINE CONTENDING WITH NOSTALGIA: WANG ANYI'S *THE SONG OF EVERLASTING SORROW*

Wang Anyi's *The Song of Everlasting Sorrow*, like the monumental novels above, ranges across three distinct periods of twentieth-century Chinese history as conventionally conceived: the pre-Communist era, the Mao era (1949– 1976), and the post-Mao era. Indeed, the plot is divided into parts 1, 2, and 3, the boundaries of whose action are just so defined. After a long discourse on the ethos of "old" Shanghai (pre-evolutionary, but already "modern," as well as "eternal") and daily life in Shanghai's *longtang* row house neighborhoods, themselves a modern invention, Wang Anyi follows the fate of her young heroine Wang Qiyao from 1945 until the time of the 1949 revolution. Qiyao, a budding beauty, is discovered by a photographer, Mr. Cheng, and is fated to become the "second runner-up to Miss Shanghai 1946," a distinction that is historical and immutable, but of dimming, yet revivable significance—though never capable of recovering its full 1946 import. Just so, as second runner-up (like Shanghai in early post-Mao China, a runner-up to Beijing and Guangzhou), Wang Qiyao is a woman of distinction but also a perpetual also-ran, a woman of potential who can never achieve her highest aspirations—although she was always diffident about running for the honor. And aging is her future. Sadly, Wang Qiyao, despite her favorable 1940s public image, ends up merely as the kept woman of a Nationalist general. He gives her gold bars to keep. Part 2, which unfolds after the revolution, describes the heroine's necessarily low-profile life, initially lived in a nearby village, and later played out in Shanghai again, among a mostly new set of nonproletarian friends like herself.[19] Wang Qiyao, like Shanghai itself, is now generally forgotten, neglected, and isolated, left to find her own path while earthshaking events have moved elsewhere. She is not empowered, certainly not by socialism; she goes through three months' training so she can provide for herself as a nurse. Such empowerment as she enjoys (its extent is debatable) comes from the eternal "women's world," in the novel's own discourse, of gossip and networking in daily life outside and underlying the "men's world" of politics and great deeds. This empowerment is an inheritance from the old Shanghai—eternal Shanghai, as it turns out, though its survival was in doubt during the Mao years. Wang Anyi's evocation of this world of gossip, fashion, and quotidian bourgeois life is frequently compared to that of the novelist Eileen Chang (Zhang Ailing).

Part 3 then follows the lives of Wang Qiyao and her illegitimate daughter, Weiwei, during the market socialism era inaugurated by Deng Xiaoping, when Shanghai, like the former not-quite Miss Shanghai 1946 and her once-stylish dresses, comes out of the wardrobe again. Tragically, Wang Qiyao is strangled to death when she is robbed by a young acquaintance, a hustler and black marketer. This completes the historical symbolism of the title, "The Song of Everlasting Sorrow," which was the title of a narrative poem by Bo Juyi. The heroine of the original poem (807 CE) is the Tang dynasty emperor's favorite consort, Yang Guifei. The distraction of her allure almost led the empire and its leader to disaster until Lady Yang was strangled, the barbarians conquered, and the dynasty restored. She was "a victim of political intrigue," notes Michel Hockx. In his evocative reading, "[Yang Guifei's] death signals the end of rebellion and the return to order—and this analogy (that Wang Qiyao dies to end the rebellious rampage of the Communist revolution and herald a better era) is perhaps the strongest political message that the author has allowed herself."[20] One can also note a correlative, equally ironic analogy. Wang Qiyao and her friends are caught up in an eternal quest for *restoration*, of the old Shanghai. Restoration of the Tang dynasty was furthered by the strangling of Lady Yang, but the restoration of the eternal Shanghai is not advanced by the demise of Wang Qiyao.

Wang Anyi's plot follows clear and conventional historical periodization. However, in chapter 2 we considered how the novel leaves the reader adrift in a sea of temporal ambiguity in its initial pages. It is only on page 39/45 that the time of the action is announced as 1945. The rest of the novel is similarly cut adrift from connections to "great historical events," except by implication from the novel's tripartite division. Part 3 begins precisely in 1976, without any mention of the deaths of Mao Zedong and Zhou Enlai that year. Later the text comments, abstractly, that "1976 was a year of epochal change," but goes on to state its significance for the two-person Wang household thus: "The impact it had on Weiwei lay all within the realm of the aesthetics of living.

The return of classic movies was one area, of high-heeled shoes another, and of perms yet another. It was only natural that Wang Qiyao too should get a perm" (262/294). The War to Resist Japan that had just ended in 1945 is scarcely mentioned in part 1; the Great Leap Forward and the famine it created are alluded to at the appropriate time in part 2, but only through the scarcity of goods that the characters must deal with. The Cultural Revolution is acknowledged chiefly through the suicide of Mr. Cheng, who appears driven to it partly by a nostalgic sense that the old ways have been lost. The text briefly mentions the larger political turmoil, characterizing it as an abnormal explosion of gossip that "lays bare" all the secrets of the city. (In life, the Shanghai Commune of that era epitomized China's most radical fanaticism.) The foremost secret exposed is said to be a case not of political persecution, but of a headstrong girl who was discovered, during a raid on her residence, to have been imprisoned for twenty years by her family for disobedience.

Wang Anyi mentions the passing years in her chapters set in the Mao years, but seldom big events. She may have felt that her Chinese readers had no need for "history" to be spelled out (a presumption that might not be borne out among younger readers), but in this novel the flight from political history surely indicates not just a desire to maintain narrative subtlety and individual style, but also a "political" comment that politics is not the guiding factor in life. Quotidian realities that underlie the grand narrative are the eternal realities. Thus, in the passage that for the first time in the novel indicates the era (39/45), the omniscient narrator writes:

> Shanghai in late 1945 was a city of wealth, colors, and stunning women. After the Japanese surrender, the revelry that took place every evening in its nightclubs seemed justified and appropriate. In actuality, of course, merry-making had nothing to do with the affairs of the world; it stemmed from people's natural affinity for pleasure and delight. The fashions displayed in shop windows, the novellas serialized in newspapers, the neon lights, the film posters, the department store banners, and the flower baskets celebrating new company openings all brightly sang out that the city was beside itself with happiness.

Wang Anyi might be referring to the joy of liberation from war and foreign occupation. She might even be describing an inappropriate Shanghai hedonism that decades later would lead to decadence and decline. But in a short disquisition that opposes "gossip" to official biographies, the novel claims: "It is not that gossip takes a different political view, but that it does not take *any* political view" (10/11). With its characteristic ambivalence toward this substratum of public life, the narrative admits that gossip may be "baseless and unreliable." "The *longtang* of Shanghai are incapable of harboring the kind of suffering that inspires legends [which rather negates the significance of Wang Qiyao's coming tragedy] . . . [the people] don't want to create a place for themselves in history; they want to create themselves" (11/12–13). Just so, the coming Communist revolution makes itself known to Wang Qiyao only because she sees that her neighbors are beginning to move away, for at that point she lives in a "society girl" apartment (114/98), next door to but socially isolated from other kept women of the rich and powerful of the Nationalist years. The establishment is called the Alice Apartments, a name that evokes a sense of Lewis Carroll–style wonderland more clearly than the English, since "Alice" in Chinese is necessarily a transliterated English name. The Chinese text (only; 97) indeed calls it a *shiwai taoyuan*, or Peach Garden Outside the World of Cares, the name of an ancient Chinese utopia. The texture of the prose suggests the same illusory, artificial, and impermanent splendor, with its "long extended paragraphs and run-on sentences,"[21] lacking quotation marks to differentiate between dramatized speech and narration. Whether considered as an affectation or an avant-garde challenge to the reader, this sort of prose fits the work's mood of inner self-sufficiency, free of ties to conventional, discrete "events" in the larger world.

There is, on the other hand, a good deal of disconnectedness in the plot when one considers the action vertically *or* horizontally. Wang Qiyao lives an enclosed domestic life, in part 2 practicing even her new profession as a nurse inside her post-Liberation home. She has a very small circle of friends. In the phraseology of the age, she is truly "cut off" from the masses, the great Shanghai proletariat, whose teeming numbers filled the *longtang* under socialism. Even in her enclosed world, Wang Qiyao tends to drop her old friends and replace them. This habit starts during her young maidenhood, when she abandons her close friend Wu Peizhen, whose homeliness sets off her own beauty, for one Wang Lili. Within just a few months, Qiyao sees Wu Peizhen as being "like someone from a different lifetime" (42/49). Two years more, and she drops Wang Lili, hurting her in the process. Wang Qiyao encounters her dropped friends in the second and third stages of her life, but by then they are strangers. *The Song of Everlasting Sorrow* to that extent preserves the traditional sense that history unfolds in periods—except that the socialist period depicted in part 2 is not always recognizable. Michel Hockx is surely right that Wang Qiyao's preservation of her gold ingots through the entire Mao era is improbable. That she could also escape socialist criticism as a former bourgeois idol (and friend of Mr. Cheng), and nourish her own extra-societal coterie of ex-bourgeois and nonconformist characters (notably a half-Russian wastrel who lives off the legacy of his revolutionary martyr father) in playing the decadent game of mah-jongg also seems, to say the least unusual. There is little sense of historical causation, certainly of sins (or positive developments) in one era having repercussions in later times. *The Song of Everlasting Sorrow* negates the thematics of vengeance and retribution that lead to notions of historical circularity in the novels previously discussed. Yet Wang Anyi's plot is still dominated by images of historical cycles, and the work is dystopian, too.

Inevitable decline, slouching toward dystopia, is visualized most concretely in the person of the heroine Wang Qiyao, as well as the progressive deterioration of all her personal relationships, even those from later in her life, for her daughter leaves for America. Qiyao achieves her greatest triumph at about the age of seventeen. Even that moment of glory is measured, for she only comes in third. It is not only Miss Wang who fails, but also her patrons, such as Mr. Cheng. From there, the trend is further downward, despite Qiyao's periodic comebacks, until her ignominious and lonely end, strangled by a hoodlum in her home. As Hockx notes, this ending, tragic or pathetic, must seem inevitable to the Chinese reader, for as one of Qiyao's dropped friends, a country intellectual who dreams of being her boyfriend, reminds the reader, "All the famous beauties named in classical poetry came to a tragic end" (137/155).

Worried about her own aging, Wang Qiyao envies even the youthful vigor of her relatively unattractive daughter, Weiwei (260/292), and looks for aging in the face of Weiwei's girlfriend (302/341). The younger generation is already beginning to "look conservative" in comparison to still younger and more-fashionable girls (314/356). Aging symbolizes the fate of Wang Qiyao's double, the feminine city of Shanghai, including her morals and her style. They mirror each other, even in the early years of the revolution, when Qiyao is self-exiled to the village: "In the morning, as she combed her hair, she saw Shanghai in the mirror, but Shanghai had aged, with tiny wrinkles around its eyes. When she walked by the river, she saw a reflection of Shanghai, but it was a faded Shanghai. Every time she tore a page from the calendar, she felt how Shanghai had grown older, and the thought pained her" (140/158). Aging is the novel's theme from the first page, as the narrative ostensibly discourses about pre-revolutionary times: "Today, everything looks worn out" (3/3). References to

Shanghai's aging, and thus intimations of Wang Qiyao's own, recur as the socialist years wear on (242/270). Qiyao and many of her other bourgeois friends from the old society regard themselves as "people left over from a previous era" (218/241). Post-Mao times do not bring physical or spiritual renewal; the old marble steps are worn down and the elevators are in disrepair. As in the old Li mansion of Silver City, every living space is subdivided and chaotic. The stairwells are used for storage; the wood panels are eaten away by termites. Moreover, "the innermost heart of the *longtang* is actually more aged and worn than its appearance" (268/300–301; see also 346–348/393–395).

The downward trend is in fact a spiral—cyclical. Recurrence applies to politics, fashion, characters, and situations. Wang Qiyao herself, even before the 1946 beauty contest, "had always believed that fortune comes and goes, in cycles—nothing good lasts forever." And when history repeats itself, the copy is always inferior to that which went before. It is as if Wang Anyi, like more highly ideologized people of her generation, had taken to heart Marx's *The Eighteenth Brumaire of Louis Bonaparte*: "All great world-historic facts and personages appear, so to speak, twice [Hegel remarked]. He forgot to add: the first time as tragedy, the second time as farce."[22]

The eclipse and rebirth of Shanghai suggests a possible new eclipse in the future; but more immediately, post-Mao Shanghai repeats and even imitates prerevolutionary Shanghai in weaker form. The coffee shops, love of style, and variety of cuisines are reborn—but not quite up to the standards of the old days. In those days, "you could get food from any country! Shanghai back then was a little universe of its own," exclaims Wang Qiyao, as if to shock her guests at a party (another revived institution), who are too young to have known the old Shanghai. "Did you know that, forty years ago, when you ordered noodles, they would make them one bowl at a time?" (328/372). Qiyao, too, has revived, but she is shopworn the second time around. Never married, she has had three lovers since the death of her first, and in post-Mao times she will take a fourth—as a cougar. Her affairs have turned out badly for her and also disillusioned her partners, not to mention her female rivals. These loves, like her honor at the beauty pageant, are mere consolation prizes. The new age is, in Wang Qiyao's eyes, one of vulgarity and *gluttony* (270/303). And Wang Qiyao is an agent of the new cynicism; she hands it down to the next generation. She warns her daughter, just before giving her a wedding ring, "No good will ever come to you if you treat men too well" (313/355). Most ironically, the inferior quality of life in "the new era" creates in Wang Qiyao nostalgia for the darkest days of socialism: "Looking back, Wang Qiyao felt that people were much better off during the Cultural Revolution, when they had to wear the same blue cloth jackets rather than these outlandish outfits that did not fit them. At least back then they had the elegance of simplicity" (269/302). Judgment of the Cultural Revolution from the standpoint of fashion undercuts the reliability of Wang Qiyao as witness to history by the light of her own values.

Fashion, like other aspects of everyday life that the narrative prizes above the "men's" world of politics, epitomizes cyclicalism. Retro fashions are well known in capitalist society, though they may have been fresh to Wang Anyi's first readers. Wang Qiyao in post-Mao times puts away her old clothes, "but she knew that before long they would be back in fashion again. That is the law of fashion, which is based on the principle of cycles." She waits out the current cycle until the next one arrives—but then comes the discordant note of secular decline within which fashion cycles are but micro-phenomena: "Wang Qiyao was more than willing to wait [the current cycle] out, until the arrival of the next cycle, but she was getting older and knew all too well that time waits for no one" (265–266/298).

Characters are recycled, too. Old love triangles involving Wang Qiyao and her friends from part 1 resurface in part 2, along with the old jealousies and hatreds. Echoes or imitations of the old part 1 triangles also emerge in later sections, translator and critic Michael Berry points out: "Relationships, scenarios, and even characters serve as counterpoints to earlier incarnations of themselves" ("Afterword" to The Song of Everlasting Sorrow, 434). Thus, the triangle of "Miss Third Place 1946," Mr. Cheng, and the Nationalist official is recapitulated in a triangle of mah-jongg players in part 2. The fourth at the table is a female who is jealous of Wang Qiyao, and she, too, has a counterpart in part 1, Jiang Lili. In part 3, two young men admire the aging Wang: Old Colour and the hustler who will kill her, Long Legs; the female confidante is young Zhang Yonghong, a paler, inferior version of Wang Qiyao despite their similar tastes in fashion. Qiyao's daughter, Weiwei, is not as pretty as her friend; she plays the Wu Peizhen role to Yonghong, as Peizhen once did to Qiyao. Wang Qiyao herself, in her prime, was at times viewed by others as a visual recreation of the famous (and doomed) 1930s movie star Ruan Lingyu. She recognizes the recurrent patterns of friendship—or quasi-friendship, including the configuration of the four cardplayers—in moments of déjà vu (352/400).

"Old Colour" is another "type": the name is actually a generic term for those who seek nostalgia as a lifestyle—antiquarians, dandies, would-be aristocrats—in a word, simulacra (in Baudrillard's sense) of the prewar Shanghai fashionistas. This set prefers to hear its dated music from old Victrolas instead of the new stereos and boom boxes. Old Colour's very life is an exercise in re-cycling. Much of Shanghai is caught up in nostalgia for the old, prerevolutionary days, but this is almost inevitable, so much has the style of life declined. During the dreary years of socialism, even Jiang Lili, who has become a super-Communist purist to avoid the shadow of her bourgeois background, feels nostalgic for her old social networks. But Wang Qiyao herself realizes, as she snaps out of her dreams, that the ideal of re-creating past excellences is at heart a flight from reality (350/398). The problem is that nostalgia, retro fashions, and all attempts to *embrace* the circular repetitions of life ignore "the cruel reality—the corrosive power of time" (325/369).

Like the other novelists discussed in this chapter, Wang Anyi in the end adapts her plot to the ends of situational doubling. As Wang Qiyao lies dying on her bed, she has a flashback to a movie scene she witnessed as a young belle during her first screen test. In the studio she saw a film star "murdered" in bed: "Only now did she finally realize that *she* was the woman on that bed—she was the one who had been murdered" (376/429). Is this artifice, inspired again by themes of the interpenetration of illusion and reality as in *The Dream of the Red Chamber*, or are we to wonder if Shanghai, too, has been murdered? This is also a *mise en abyme*, a story within the story that suggests infinite repetition—and the nausea that goes with it. And yet, when the younger Wang Qiyao first fell victim to illusion and thought the film star might really be dead, it was not "terrifying or foreboding," "only annoyingly familiar" (28/31). Cyclical repetition, a banal form of evil, is its own dystopia.

Circularity and Cultural Pessimism in Han Shaogong's *A Dictionary of Maqiao*

Han Shaogong's *A Dictionary of Maqiao* is ostensibly a lexicon of the dialect of a northeastern Hunanese village called Maqiao. The entries take the form of anecdotes, narrator's observations, and tales, many long enough to have their own narrative structure. They bear comparison to the "strange stories" (*zhiguai*), jottings (*biji*), and familiar essays (*xiaopin*) that have developed in China over a thousand years and flourished in the Qing. Han Shaogong's penultimate entry, for "Vernacular/Empty Talk (*Baihua*)," argues, contrary to received opinion, that "the source from which Chinese vernacular springs" (343/311) is a corpus of work "from the *Tales of the Supernatural* [*Sou shen ji*] of the Wei-Jin period to the early Qing *Strange Tales from a Chinese Studio*

[*Liaozhai zhiyi*]" by Pu Songling (1640–1715). The "vernacular" aspect that Han sees in these tales must inhere in their form and content, for even Pu Songling's are in classical Chinese.

Sometimes the keywords that the dictionary entries ostensibly explicate pop up only halfway into the entry, and even then appear to be of marginal relevance to the "tale." Chinese intellectuals were quite familiar with keywords, and not only from Raymond Williams's book by that title; in the 1990s keywords already appeared at the start of Chinese academic journal articles to facilitate subject matter searches. Subsequently censors used them to search out subversive ideas. Each chapter of Zamyatin's dystopian novel *We* begins with keywords.

The Maqiao entries' dramatis personae address the self-dramatizing narrator as "Shaogong," and the real Han Shaogong is known for having been "sent down" to this region after the Cultural Revolution. But one quickly gathers that the village, the dialect, and "Shaogong" are not exactly like any presumed equivalent in life, and may be mostly reflective of the author's fertile satiric imagination.

Despite its odd structure and content, *A Dictionary of Maqiao* may be considered a novel constructed from linked stories—stories that are simply shorter, more numerous, and more varied than those making up *Red Sorghum*, *September's Fable*, *Cries in the Drizzle*, or the not-so-linked stories of Wei-Jin and Qing dynasty collections. The entries often have a moral, delivered in the voice of the self-dramatizing dictionary compiler/narrator, who at times digresses about his philosophy of life, language, and ethnographic "difference." The *Dictionary* is plotted—best read from front to back. Entries in succession sometimes constitute a tale, an episodic character sketch, or an adventure in speculative or free-associative thinking. Characters recur in the dictionary when it is read as a novel, and they include not just local informants but also the narrator's sent-down intellectual youth comrades. A module of several entries at the end dramatizes narrator Shaogong's re-encounters with Maqiao people some twenty years after his mandated reeducation in their village.

A Dictionary of Maqiao is thus not a conventional historical novel, but its plot has an overall chronological and synoptic pattern; its narrator, more than those of other novelists mentioned in this book, self-consciously plays the role of amateur historian, anthropologist, historical linguist, and philosopher. Three interspersed, mutually interrupting storylines relate Chinese history in three different durations: Maqiao under late Maoism, as personally experienced by the ex–Red Guards; the natives' historical memory, which "oddly" begins

only in the twentieth century and knows nothing of the fanatical and trau-
matic Lotus Flower Rebellion of the 1890s that the narrator/researcher considers the formative local historical event of recent centuries; and the narrator's own researches into local history, from before the Common Era down
through the ages of warlordism, Japanese invasion, and Communism, with a
post-Mao epilogue. The big events that matter to the Maqiao folk are disputes,
work disasters, extramarital affairs, and other antics, not the events that matter
to leaders and historians, much as in *September's Fable* and *Life and Death
Are Wearing Me Out*.

That these storylines sometimes do explain historical "events" is not to say
the events are authentic. The arbitrariness of the peasants' reasoning by association (e.g., snakes are thought to be lecherous, therefore they can be fended
off by the portrait of a woman [140/129]) applies equally to the narrator's own
etymological speculations[23] and association of peculiar local customs with
ancient texts. One cannot even be sure whether the "strange" local beliefs,
customs, and linguistic usages have genuine correlatives, are satiric variations
on actual usages, or, like some customs in Han's signature "roots" novella, *Pa
Pa Pa*, are borrowed from other cultures and transplanted to Hunan for shock
value.[24] For instance, mentions of a poison woman and of a taboo on marrying one's first love recall legends from West Hunan, the home of some of
Han's forebears, an entirely different world from northeastern Hunan.[25]

The passages that the narrator quotes from ancient classics appear to be
authentic, as are his references to contemporary historians' ideas about the
ancient Ba culture of Sichuan, but the Lotus Flower Rebellion is a fabrication,
as is the local gazetteer that he cites as his source.[26] Still, the characters, however insouciant of events like the Cultural Revolution that sent the ex–Red
Guards down to their locale, live their lives in a world reshaped by a revolution, the great land reform, and post-Leap famine as we know them,[27] unlike
the West Hunanese tribal folk who inhabit *Pa Pa Pa*. The former acreage of an
unpopular ex-landlord character in Maqiao, for instance, takes the name
"Taiwan," since the poor peasants wish to "liberate" it and make its fields their
own! Some peculiarities of Maqiao can be imputed to a broad satirical impulse to analyze the Chinese "national character," and many aspects of the
work may be allegorical. The Lotus Flower Rebellion, like local Maqiao dialect
words whose meanings have opposite meanings in Modern Standard Chinese, summons up thoughts of the Cultural Revolution, when some red stop-
lights meant "go." Observations about the unity of opposites may spoof Marxist dialectics. Themes of the perversions and power of language, its taboos, and

the reversibility of its meanings are at times obviously political. An entry near the end of the book, "Democracy Cells," calls it a usage unique to prisoners, having nothing to do with being jailed for advocating democracy. But the next entry, whose referent likewise is miles distant from its namesake in Beijing, is "Tiananmen."

Not wholly unlike *Pa Pa Pa*, the *Dictionary* depicts history as a story of cultural-historical stasis and recurrence. Entries or modules of entries that begin the narrative all over again from a new perspective, such as one about a beggar king called "Nine Pockets," leave the reader uncertain as to the era, like the beginnings of the novels described in chapter 2. Begging was a facet of the old society, but it has made a comeback in recent times; it takes time for the reader to understand that the entry is about the past—a flashback from the novel's general retrospective account of the Cultural Revolution years. The narrator, in one of his garrulous and philosophical moods, throws into doubt linear understandings of time and causation:

> All you have to do is think a little, and you realize that most of the time real life . . . doesn't fit into one guiding, controlling line of cause and effect. A person exists in two, three, four, or even more interlocking strands, outside each of which a great many other elements exist, each constituting an indispensable part of our lives. In this multifarious, scattered network of cause and effect, how valid is the domination of one main thread of protagonists, plot and mood? (64/58)

It is above all the *meaning* of history that is circular. This is exemplified in the entry "Bandit Ma [Wenjie] and 1948." In 1982, narrator Shaogong had learned that Ma Wenjie's reputation had already been reversed, from bandit to patriotic hero. Muses the narrator, "As far as all I knew about Ma Wenjie was concerned, 1948 wasn't actually 1948 at all. It had been postponed and postponed, had fermented and soured. In other words, it had been postponed until it reemerged on this rainy evening of 1982" (98/88–89). Plots of land, even after collectivization, revert to names recalling their prerevolutionary owners (120–124/110–113). Another example is a "reactionary" crime once imputed to the narrator. He was reading a book by Marx instead of Chairman Mao. Shouts the commune cadre, "What on earth is he thinking?" (158/145). The book in question is *The Eighteenth Brumaire of Louis Bonaparte*. As in *The Song of Everlasting Sorrow*, tragic history repeats itself, the second time as comedy.

The narrator observes that people fabricated quotations from Chairman Mao, just as the ancients fabricated sage words from Confucius and Laozi (164/152). In post-Mao times, the return to old ways is particularly shocking: "Betting was back, prostitutes were back, highwaymen were back, and now, to top it all, there were ghosts, too" (220/203). The sent-down intellectual youths, who during their six years' rural residence had the potential to impart to local society a new window on life, left no trace on post-Mao Maqiao: "Even the old, familiar scratches on the mud walls had gone" (264/242). Yet, conversely, in the 1990s, "a mass of old words which hadn't been used much between the fifties and the seventies all turned up again. Anyone who didn't know this might have mistaken them for new words" (299/271). But cyclicalism begins earlier than that. What impresses the narrator most are words referring to killing, bribing, and good-for-nothings; two expressions are said to have originated with the historical underworld Red Gang of pre-Communist times.

All this casts a shadow on human nature. But perhaps the main interest here in the *Dictionary*'s words about circular patterns in history, in a book that after all delights in many other patterns too, is that the narrator directly links historical repetition to visions of dystopia.

> As I see it, history's optimists insist on the division between beginning and end, viewing history as an ever-advancing straight line, in which all honor and disgrace, success and failure, praise and blame, gains and losses are always precisely recorded, ready to receive true and just final judgment. Perseverance will receive its final reward. History's pessimists, however, insist on the unity between beginning and end, viewing history as an ever-repeating loop in which their retreats endlessly advance, their losses are endlessly gained, everything is futile. (341–342/310)

There is little doubt about which side *A Dictionary of Maqiao* agrees with. Its next-to-penultimate entry, which contains the words just quoted, is titled, literally, "Return to the Beginning (Return to the End)." The final chapter of the novel dramatizes the narrator at the beginning of his adventure in Maqiao, when he first saw the village and inquired, fruitlessly, how it got its name. He began his encounter with the Maqiao people with the misapprehension that he could understand them by knowing their origin, as if they had an origin.

That the narrator sees history pessimistically because of its circularity is not to say that the Maqiao people do. To a *modern* Chinese intellectual, like the narrator, being in a never-ending loop evokes modern angst. For all his defenses of cultural difference in philosophical asides and discourses, the narrator, it seems, is compelled to see the Maqiao people as unfortunate and unenlightened.

RECURRENT DECLINE IN GE FEI'S *SOUTHLANDS TRILOGY*

Ge Fei's *Southlands Trilogy* may be enjoyed as a single work or as three separate novels, unfolding respectively during the last years of the Qing, the early Communist era, and a meretricious, super-prosperous "hyper-present" just short of futurism, when love is communicated through text messages. Each volume has its own literary technique, texture, and atmosphere, reflecting the ethos of the era and perhaps also the different times of composition: 1994–2004, 2004–2007, and 2007–2011.[28] In life, South China was by 2011 already physically almost unrecognizable from a 1994 viewpoint. Ge Fei's plots unfold in fictitious villages called Fuji and Xiazhuang and later in nearby fictitious towns of Meicheng and Hepu, just south of the Yangzi River, near the real town of Changzhou, Jiangsu, midway between Nanjing and Shanghai. This area was famous for producing innovative and reformist literati scholarship during the late Ming and Qing dynasties.

Bygone Beauty (2004) begins in a dreamy and timeless rural village called Puji. Gradually the era narrows to ca. 1898–1912, as an antimonarchist secret society conspiracy comes into focus. The narrative tone is poetic, allusive, mysterious, and often wistful. Characters in the novel write letters, notes, poems, and diaries in classical Chinese. Occasional parenthetical textual asides act as historical footnotes, explaining the objective "facts" about and often the ironic final outcome of a (fictitious) character, group, or "historical event" at their point of exit from the action, via citations of fictitious official pronouncements and local histories written much later, presumably by committee, in the Communist era.

Land in Dreamland shifts the era to the mid-1950s through mid-1960s and the locale to "Meicheng," which has become the county seat governing Puji and Xiazhuang. The plot and language are trendier and more prosaic, evidencing what critics call Ge Fei's most recent "exterior turn," toward concrete phenomena and realism.[29] Yet the narrative and dialogic languages that relate the quotidian romances, squabbles, and sexual aggressions in the plot are quite apolitical, even though the main characters are county magistrates, vice magistrates, and their wives and subordinates. The second novel is thus "realistic" according to a *post*-Mao sensibility. As in many other contemporary novels, actions of the state are evident, but the Communist Party that controls the state is almost invisible, and so is Beijing.

Southern Spring Played Out, less surprisingly given its twenty-first-century setting (in Hepu, which was the nearby prefectural seat in the preceding volume), is further shorn of political subjects—descriptive of a hedonistic and thuggish society ruled by the rich and powerful, who use and abuse the law. The novel is still focused on events in this little corner of Jiangnan ("South of the River"), apart from cameo references to Tibet, Yunnan, Shanghai, and Beijing, the latter the site of a conference—of twenty-first-century lawyers, not cadres. The novel's ethos is to this extent postmodern, spotlighting ingenious social manipulations, consumerism, and hyper-development of the land. The language is so utilitarian, contemporary, and to some of Ge Fei's fans pedestrian (despite occasional quotations of poetry) that this most extreme "exterior turn" disappointed them. Moreover, the focus on postmodern annoyances of daily life and *interior* reactions to them suggested to others a turn away from "big history."[30]

A common bloodline connects the three plots in their respective eras, but the linkages are thin and the heroes remain fundamentally loners. The *Southlands Trilogy* lacks the feel of a family saga, for the family is a fragile vessel in all eras. The three plots are snapshots of their eras: long period novels individually, an epic historical novel collectively.

In the first volume, centered on rural landlord families, it gradually becomes clear that the main character is a daughter, an educated woman named Lu Xiumi. Even more slowly and obliquely, one learns that mysterious local goings-on, including violent deaths and possibly the unsolved disappearance of Xiumi's "mad" father, are connected to an incipient anti-Manchu revolution and its suppression. Like "Grandma" in *Red Sorghum*, Xiumi is then beset by bandits while she is en route to her wedding. They hide her in an outwardly idyllic village called Huajiashe, or "Flower Family Haven." Xiumi escapes murderous intrigues among those who would control the hamlet. Later, she becomes the headmistress of a new school back in Puji. Its odd visitors, students, and stockpiles suggest conspiracy. Xiumi is betrayed and stays in jail even after the revolution finally topples the Qing in 1911. She bears a son in prison, who is spirited away and raised as an orphan.

That son, Tan Gongda, is the hero of *Land in Dreamland*. As this second novel opens, in the 1950s, he is the Meicheng county magistrate, an odd character with ambitious plans for socialist development, including a dam in his mother's old village of Puji to provide hydroelectric power. The dam bursts during a flood. He is demoted and given an inconsequential post under the surveillance of the masses, though not requiring hard labor, in Huajiashe, where his mother had been held captive. That isolated hamlet is now a self-sufficient rural socialist utopia. Unfortunately, his former secretary, twenty-something Yao Peipei, a nonconformist and pretty woman of bad class background, is driven to kill a provincial official to keep from being raped and forcibly married to him. She goes on the lam and writes love letters to ex-Magistrate Tan, but is caught and executed. Born in jail, Tan dies in jail, for the crime of not having turned her in. He is survived by a son from an inopportune midlife marriage to a widow. She naturally divorces him.

The marital and social lives of that son, poet Tan Duanwu, and his wife, Pang Jiayu (née Li Xiurong), are the subject of the third novel. Post-Mao life is bereft of any kind of idealism, altruism, or personal fulfillment, as in Yu Hua's *Brothers* and the satires of contemporary Chinese society by Wang Shuo and Mo Yan. When a brazen upper-middle-class squatter moves into Ms. Pang's new, vacant apartment before she can, abetted by a fraudulent, short-lived real estate agency, Pang hires underworld thugs to threaten the intruder's life and limb. The scenario recalls worldwide landlord tactics for scaring tenants out of their apartments, but Ms. Pang is a lawyer, her husband is an idealistic poet, and the plan is organized by Pang's old boyfriend—a policeman. These upstanding citizens agree that "going around" the law is their only choice in this new era. Another, unremitting theme of Ge Fei's third epic is ruin of the environment and erasure of all beauty from the landscape. Meicheng, the locale of the previous volume, is particularly despoiled, an industrial armpit ("anus," in Chinese) of the Southlands (3:221). As one of Duanwu's associates drives through the countryside, past piles of garbage and AIDS prevention posters, he realizes that "rural villages are disappearing." And the farmers are only too happy to see them bulldozed. "Like a typhoon, capital had flattened Jiangnan in mid-spring, dressing up decadence in a bustling and fashionable overcoat, even if it didn't fit too well and seemed like a false outer layer" (3:296).

Even considered separately, each novel ends in decline, failure, death, and disillusionment. Lu Xiumi and Tan Gongda work for their ideals and land in jail for their pains. They die single and alone. Xiumi stays mute in her last years; Gongda dies in jail of cirrhosis. Pang Jiayu's marriage dissolves and she leaves her profession; she, too, dies alone, of suicide, before cancer and her enemies can do her in. Even more starkly, the trilogy as a whole tells a story, if not of Mo Yan's "species decline," then of the dissolution of all laws, hopes, and ideals, and the ubiquitous poisoning of the land itself. Individual moral agency and capacity to alter the course of events dissolve. In the second volume, lovely fields of the hardy purple flowers of the *ziyunying* (milk vetch) adorn Puji and Huajiashe. They impart beauty and rescue the folk from death by famine that afflicts nearby communities. In the third volume, what looks at night, from a distance, to be a marvelous sight turns out, close up, to be a garbage dump. Progressive socialist Tang Gongda in 1956 comes to the still arcadian landscape of Puji and finds it almost perfect—except that it would be still better, he opines (having visited the USSR), if a smokestack topped it off (2:4). The generation of *Southern Spring Played Out* later gets what he wished for—smokestacks everywhere. Gongda wonders, when exiled to the rebuilt rural utopia in Huajiashe near the end of his own life, why a smokestack surmounts that village's highest summit. It is a crematorium, an ominous hint of socialism's unique addition to arcadia.

Frequent premonitions and common figurations such as these lend an air of recurrence rather than continuity because the novels' three eras seem so distant from each other. The gaps in history also further a sense of historical defamiliarization of the sort discussed in chapter 2. Besides the different styles, languages, and new casts of characters in each era, the changes that bring about the discontinuities are largely offstage. The connecting figure, Tan Gongda, has a backstory—he won his political position through service to the Communist revolution in the New Fourth Army in the 1940s—but that took place during the narrative gap. How his mother became committed to the earlier, Republican revolutionary cause is similarly sketchy. (She had been to Japan as a student.) Tan Duanwu's and Li Xiurong's separate stories prior to the 1980s are shrouded in mystery, and so is, for some time, Li's change of name to Pang Jiayu (in the end, she reverts to Li Xiurong again). Great events of history, including the Communist revolution, remain offstage. The Great Leap Forward, post-Leap famine,[31] Cultural Revolution, death of Mao, and opening up of China are wholly ignored. One might almost include the 1911 revolution for which Lu Xiumi sacrificed so much, since its success is invisible and immaterial in this little corner of the Southlands.

Even the heroes appear as onlookers to "real history." Tan Gongda, for all his visionary plans, epitomized in maps for future development projects, not only fails to bring about communism, he is always the last to know what is going on in the county he governs, including the failure of his precious dam. He is strangely powerless, too, to order his romantic life; there are suggestions that he is bewitched by women, a modern Jia Baoyu. His son, Tan Duanwu, is just as feckless.[32] Duanwu's grandmother, Lu Xiumi, is an unusually strong character in the trilogy, but her actions are hidden and unmotivated. Duan-wu's wife is a woman of action, but she abandons her profession and erstwhile ideals, and ultimately commits suicide. The anti-Qing revolutionaries, the flighty twenty-first-century professionals with their two residences, and above all the Mao-era county bureaucrats who talk mostly to each other in their compound and their chauffeur-driven jeeps, are in all circumstances utterly "divorced from the masses" of their respective eras. In all three novels, details of the characters' quite "bourgeois" marital and extramarital romances nearly steal the show, indicating, to me, not just an "external" but also a "popular" turn in Ge Fei's writing.

At the most abstract level, the trilogy depicts a grand cycle of history. The end of the Qing betokens societal disintegration. The bandits of Huajiashe, who are among the revolutionaries and engage in internecine warfare until all but one is dead, in a long chapter that seems inexplicable except as alle-gory, suggest what is to come in life (warlordism). Social and political unity is restored under Communism in the second volume, at least from the limited viewpoint of the county government compound. But by the start of the next century, social disintegration has returned, and the market economy is back, this time in hyperkinetic form. Chaos reigns in social, personal, and family values, and the state is nearly invisible again. Its rule of law—concretized in horrible cases that come before Lawyer Pang—catalog the ways in which in-terpersonal relations have degenerated in China's great age of prosperity and "harmony." This reiterates the rapes perpetrated by powerful cadres in the second volume and the rape of Lu Xiumi by one of the bandits in the first. She fends off the other bandits with wiles worthy of Scheherazade, and *The Thousand and One Nights* is favorite reading of the inscrutable master of Hua-jiashe in the next volume. Tan Duanwu's favorite reading, in the third novel, is Ouyang Xiu's *New History of the Five Dynasties*, which draws moral lessons from an age of Chinese disunity and chaos. He evidently believes that history repeats itself.[33]

Thwarted male-female romances are a major element of recurrence in the trilogy, suggesting a worldview like that of *The Dream of the Red Chamber*. Hid-den affections are realized too late, except in the lovers' dreams. While in ban-dit captivity, Lu Xiumi reads the diary of an intellectual revolutionary called Zhang Jiyuan; the revelations of his character bring out what she realizes was her developing subconscious love of him. But it is too late; he is executed. The bulk of *Land in Dreamland* is about Magistrate Tan's middle-aged efforts to marry. One Bai Xiaoxian plays Xue Baochai to his Jia Baoyu, but the flawed Yao Peipei is his Lin Daiyu, and she will ruin him. Tan's son Duanwu has similarly suppressed, extramarital, passions for lonely women of the twenty-first century, all depressed and suicidal, as befits the new age. These tragedies and mismatches play out again and again.

Each novel, moreover, is overwritten on a palimpsest of a previous time experienced by earlier generations. The failed anti-Qing schemer Zhang Ji-yuan, through his diary, awakens a love in Lu Xiumi not just of him but also of his revolutionary cause. In the second volume, Magistrate Tan's relations with his old war buddies of the 1940s at first further his career, then come back to help destroy him. In the third volume, Pang Jiayu awakens to the ex-citement of intellectual and social exploration through famous poets of the 1989 democracy movement. She first encounters the celebrity poet Tan Duanwu when he hides out from Shanghai in this low-profile corner South of the River. This follows the post-Tiananmen crackdown, which cannot of course be mentioned in the work. Each novel has a story of a romantic and/or intellectual awakening and enlightenment that represents a twenty-year re-currence. This is repeated, generation after generation.

Other circular figurations include Yao Peipei's flight from the police at the conclusion of *Land in Dreamland*, in which she travels in a circle, ending up in Puji, where she committed the murder. Madness (which Ge Fei, like Na-guib Mahfouz, associates with genius) and dreams also recur. Contemplating the original Chinese utopia, Taohuayuan, the Peach Blossom Spring or *shi-wai taoyuan*, the Peach Garden Outside the World of Cares, Lu Xiumi's fa-ther goes mad and wanders off. Members of Magistrate Tan Gongda's staff in *Land in Dreamland* opine that he goes mad (dumbstruck) in the presence of women. And it is Tan Duanwu's clinically mad elder half brother, Wang Yuan-qing, who is the genuine idealist and visionary of his era, like Xiumi and Gongda before him. Many dreams in the three novels are difficult to unravel, but Pang Jiayu has one in the third volume (3:323–324) that recapitulates Xiu-mi's experiences in the first.

UTOPIA INTO DYSTOPIA: A RECURRING PATTERN

Recurrence in Ge Fei's world is embodied above all in utopian projects that, as in the other new historical epics, are predestined to mutate into dystopias, repeatedly. Ge Fei's utopias have two guises, and he for one does not eschew the term "utopia." One type of utopia takes shape as grandiose material plans to reconstruct All Under Heaven. Despite its material emphasis and breadth of ambition, this plan is, paradoxically, utopia as "no-place," unrealizable. The other type is a small-scale "model" of the sort so common in the twentieth century, whether envisioned by Zhou Zuoren, Xu Zhimo, James Y. C. Yen, Liang Shuming, or Mao Zedong with his successive model communes and production brigades. The model community is an enclave going against the current in the larger society, and yet it exists, in books and in life. It is however unique, hence false—dependent on an artificial or hermetic environment. Ge Fei's novels embody it in Huajiashe: an idyll that is actually inhabited, but unsustainable and irreproducible. Like his colleagues, Ge Fei depicts Western-inspired materialism as the primary motivator of both kinds of failed utopia, but unlike the other novelists, he also mentions China's own literary utopia, the Peach Blossom Spring. Ge Fei links dystopia to the utopian impulse, but finds it dangerous only in modern times.[34]

China's modern revolutionaries in the initial novel—and they precede the founding of the Communist Party—have their visionary, nation-building projects, but these fail and are destined to fail, as if embodying the etymology of "u-topia" from the Latin, as "no-place"—a place that does not exist. The revolutionary vision of *Bygone Beauty*, laid out on a larger scale by Zhang Jiyuan than by the bandits who are content to rule Huajiashe, is the first failure. So was the actual 1911 revolution, as most Chinese saw it. Tang Gongda's plans to quickly realize communism and a modern, developed society also fail, as symbolized by his dam. That failure was embodied in Maoism. The twenty-first century, depicted in the third volume, is simply disillusioned—postrevolutionary, post-visionary—not just post- but trans-utopian in its dynamism and dystopian in its quality of life. Tan Duanwu, an idealistic celebrity poet before Tiananmen, is reduced in the era of prosperity to doing trivial compilation tasks with old fogies in a local history project. His half brother, the brilliant one (once full of the 1980s-style intellectual reformist plans that now seem juvenile to Chinese caught up in their economic miracle), has consigned *himself* (a symbolic figuration, that) to an insane asylum.

These materialist projects, however "practical," bear the seeds of their destruction. Zhang Jiyuan discloses a ten-article directive from Guangxu 27 (1901) that is macabre and yet prescient about excesses to come decades later:

> 1. Those with land holdings exceeding 40 *mou*, kill. 2. Lenders of money at high interest, kill. 3. Court officials with bad records, kill. 4. Prostitutes,

kill. 5. Thieves and robbers, kill. 6. Those with leprosy, typhoid fever, and like infectious diseases, kill. 7. Abusers of women, children, and the elderly, kill. 8. Those with bound feet, kill. 9. Human traffickers, kill. 10. Matchmakers, shamans, monks, Daoist priests, kill them all.   (1:120)

A half century later, Magistrate Tan's grandiose and premature plans to hasten collectivization, divert a channel of the Yangzi, and promote methane gas throughout the county, incur huge costs in labor, capital, and political capital. This aggravates local poverty, famine, and insurrection, even before the dam break and flood—social effects to which he is dangerously oblivious.

Tan Duanwu and other poet idols of 1988–1989 had played the "enlightening" Zhang Jiyuan role for Pang Jiayu (when she was still Li Xiurong), the reader learns by flashback. But the movement for democracy and enlightenment led to a massacre in Beijing and massive failure on its own terms, we readers know, from life. That failure ushered in China's great age of wealth and power, but it has no need for idealism or poetry, or therefore for wonder and hope.

In contrast to these grandiose plans for a total solution are the trilogy's three incarnations of a "utopia" called Huajiashe, each of them unique and beyond the bounds of ordinary society as known to revolutionaries and poets, and yet actually existent instead of being a "no-place" (existent in fiction, that is—a dreamlike fiction like *The Dream of the Red Chamber*, in which "the real's unreal when the unreal's real"). The existence of a Huajiashe in all three eras makes it all the more disillusioning, due to the decay it betokens that most concerns Ge Fei: that of the human heart and spirit. Huajiashe is his Grand View Garden gone wrong, and like the idyll in *The Dream of the Red Chamber*, it is destined for destruction, in this case serially. In a dream, Lu Xiumi comes to understand in the late Qing that Huajiashe is destined to be destroyed and rebuilt again and again, in a sixty-year cycle (1:115).

The original Peach Blossom Spring described by Tao Qian (365–427), though understood to be a legendary and literary construct, did exist, in the tale; it was simply lost—to the troubled outside world—never to be found again. Huajiashe, called a *shiwai taoyuan* by its fictional 1885 founder (and subsequent destroyer—possibly an oblique reference to Mao) in *Bygone Beauty* (1:115), is the idyll where Lu Xiumi is held captive for ransom. It is a lakeside village built on a gentle slope. The houses are identical, with whitewashed walls, black tile roofs, ornately latticed wooden windows, and fenced-in gardens. A lovely arbor-covered walkway (*changlang*) *connects* all the village

houses (fulfilling a "mad" dream that Xiumi's Taohuayuan-besotted father
had for Puji), so that villagers may commune with each other without fear of
sun or rain. Pavilions for resting and playing chess occur at intervals, and
alongside the sheltered corridor is a stream that provides water for each
kitchen (1:102, 1:139–140). The drawback? The capital to build these comforts
was stolen from the outside world, by bandits, who made it their lair—and a
prison for young women, on an island in the lake. (Its meaning is revealed to
Xiumi by an erstwhile prisoner and ex-nun: "In reality, the heart of each of us
is a little island, under siege" 1:115, 322; see the identical epiphany of Yao Peipei, 2:204). Huajiashe lies in ruins when Xiumi revisits it before her death. A
life of bliss based on theft seems an allegory of the "old society," which was
built on landlordism and capitalism; the partial destruction of the idyll by fire
that occurs before Xiumi's eyes just before she escapes captivity has resulted
from a power struggle among the bandits for leadership, which suggests revolutionary politics.

Huajiashe has been duly reconstructed as a socialist utopia by the time
magistrate Tan Gongda is exiled there at the end of the second volume, and
this of course is an allegory of the Maoist experiment, before it took a still
more extraordinary turn in the Cultural Revolution. (Mao appreciated the
"utopianism" of bandit brotherhood purveyed in China's old chapter-driven
novels—another literary link between the two incarnations of Huajiashe, and
a native one.) The new Mao-era hamlet has the same old whitewashed, black-
tile-roofed houses—oddly identical—a sameness that bears new implications
under socialism. Lu Xiumi already hoped to build a late-Qing "practical" utopia of identical houses for all, of the same size and design. The people would
have identical amounts of property, eat together, go down to the fields at the
same hour, and go to bed at the same hour, too. She allegedly wanted "to make
all the inhabitants of Puji into the same person" (1:234). That dream will not
be fulfilled, or its dystopian qualities made clear, until the final volume depicting the twenty-first century, when all places and people are in fact becoming similar, as *xinren* (the new human; 3:206)—a new and opposite incarnation of Mao's "new socialist man" (3:354).

In the middle volume, Huajiashe has accomplished the very dreams Magistrate Tan Gongda aspired to but could never realize in the "real world." A
covered walkway (now a brick-wood structure, instead of an arbor) connects
all the houses, mirroring his premature dream of building a road to connect all
the villages of his county. There is even a smokestack at the summit of socialist-
era Huajiashe to make it "complete." Huajiashe in this period is more generally

a Marxist rather than a Maoist utopia: work is an honor, there is a natural collective consciousness, and compensation is by "democratic" consensus, suggesting Mao-era work points, but with self-reporting as the basis (not very Maoist). There is a leadership, but it remains invisible, like the ideal Legalist sage who lets a perfected system of harsh laws and punishments run the kingdom for him. There is plenty for all to eat, and all of Tan's precocious plans for development—canals, electrification, and methane gas partout—are fulfilled (3:294–300).

And yet, after several months' residence, in which he has to *seek* work for himself, since there are no "orders," Tan Gongda discovers Huajiashe's dark side. The people have entertainments, but they seldom smile or laugh. His guide and handler, the latest bright young woman to catch his eye, turns out to have attempted suicide repeatedly, and her brother went mad over the guilt he felt after once committing a transgression. There are no punishments because the entire populace has internalized "boundaries"; they punish themselves, and moreover their every action is reported anonymously under a system of pervasive citizen surveillance. The villagers do not smile because the fear of wrongdoing has terrorized them and made them clinically depressed. Huajiashe is an unrecognized socialist dystopia, even while serving as a model and a tourist destination of, for example, Cubans (3:356–362).

In the twenty-first century, Huajiashe is a tourist destination all over again: site of a luxurious conference center and full-service adult entertainment complex with a bordello. Imperfectly trained young guides show visitors the ruins of the old, abandoned feudal-capitalist and subsequently socialist Huajiashe with its crumbling black-tiled roofs on the hillside. (*Hua*, or "flower," was a euphemism in the old society for prostitution. In the late Qing, one of Huajiashe's bandit masters already called it a bordello, because of the young girls raped there; 1:144.) The newest Huajiashe indulges all the senses as never before, and even antiquarian curiosity, but it also symbolizes the utter collapse of idealism, with its sacrifices, blueprints, and maps, and the general degradation of the land and the soul. This Huajiashe betrays the principles that led to Duanwu's "liberal" hopes of reengineering the human soul during the late 1980s democracy movement.

One of Duanwu's psychologically troubled and impressionable girlfriends is sucked up into a plan to create yet another utopia, a green ecotopian Shangri-La in the wilderness of Yunnan (3:351–354). The project appears to be a scam (preceded, in fact, by an episode about a wholly fraudulent scheme to raise funds for an environmental protection organization that does not exist;

3:232). The first step in Yunnan will be to drive the original hunter-residents off their wilderness hillsides with money. In life, an official Shangri-La Eco-tourism Region was actually founded in this area in 2002–2003; it failed, but was revived in 2010.

It is above all Huajiashe that has a counterpart in life, which is real and yet cannot be widely reproduced. It is Huaxi, "China's richest village," a global model of rural development in Jiangsu, south of the Yangzi and located within just a few miles of the fictional towns and villages where Ge Fei's trilogy unfolds.[35] Huaxi, not Ge Fei's fictional entertainment complex, is the real third embodiment of Huajiashe in China's time of contemporary prosperity.

Huaxi began in 1961 as a one-kilometer-square rural village. By the twenty-first century the "village" proper still had a population of only 1,800 or so, but had been engulfed by industrial and suburban development. It is now the Jiangsu Huaxi Group Corporation, the first commune listed on a Chinese stock exchange, with dozens of subsidiaries and holding companies manufacturing everything from steel and textiles to Chinese medicine. Reported annual revenue in 2008–2009 was more than $7 billion.[36] Labor was and is performed by 30,000 low-wage citizens from communities abutting the "village" proper and 25,000 migrant workers. (They staged a protest for better treatment in 2011, but it was put down.[37]) Huaxi is thus parasitic on society at large, like the bandit Huajiashe of *Bygone Beauty*, its prosperity enhanced by government loans and tax breaks. In 2011, the village added a seventy-four-story skyscraper, taller than the Chrysler Building, which in its unique non-urban location enjoys more aerial solitude than the new Tower of Babel in Fritz Lang's film *Metropolis* (1927). As if Huaxi were not already a theme park, visited by two million tourists annually, it has its own theme park nearby, with reproductions of the Great Wall, the Arc de Triomphe, the Tiananmen Rostrum, the Sydney Opera House, and the U.S. Capitol dome, "stacked on top of the White House and topped off with the Statue of Liberty."[38] This is for tourists and also the villagers, so that the latter can appreciate the world *without leaving*.

For the lucky 1,800, Huaxi is a material utopia beyond Magistrate Tan's imagination. The corporation's capitalist-style profits allow each family to be allotted, socialist-style, a luxurious new two-story, red-roofed "European villa" with a two-car garage, a car or two, a generous annual income (half or more of which must be reinvested in the corporation), plus free basic medical care, education, pensions, utilities, and retro Mao-era amenities like cooking oil. Family assets are said to average about $150,000.[39] The "village" resembles the gated communities in Chinese anticorruption films where venal cadres stash their mistresses. "White BMWs are ubiquitous and the murals, instead of depicting socialist realist muscled workers in overalls, have pictures of happy families living in wealthy villas."[40]

The culture, however, is retro-socialist. Mao-era "red song" Muzak is omnipresent, through loudspeakers. Until his death, when his fourth son took the reins, the village patriarch and permanent Communist Party secretary Wu Renbao (1928–2003) personally supervised the main village entertainment, an old-fashioned Mao-style song-and-dance troupe.

This is socialist kitsch, Kundera would say, though it evokes nostalgia among Chinese of a certain age and seems exotic to younger folk. The uniformity of the housing conjures up the specter of an upscale Levittown, and the center of town has neo-traditionalist ten-story high-rises that top off their modernist box-like uniformity with "pagoda" roofs. Chinese intellectuals see in Huaxi dangers for the human spirit like those in the second incarnation of Huajiashe in *Land in Dreamland*. Not to mention the permanent dictatorship of the corporation, monopolized by one family, there are harsh laws, including a 10,000-yuan fine for picking the flowers.[41] A decade ago, China's official press reported that "villagers are off-limits to the media, and no one from Huaxi is allowed to strike up a casual conversation with an outsider. Huaxi Village is managed as if it were an army compound."[42] In the daytime, "the streets tend to be deserted of residents because they are all off working,"[43] seven days a week. Under Wu Renbao, there was "no night life whatsoever. No Internet cafes or karaoke lounges. No bars or coffee shops. . . . Social interaction takes place in a wealth of meetings. Every morning before the work day begins, everyone studies the news and Wu Renbao's latest instructions; every weekend, a village assembly is held; and, every month, migrant workers who have jobs in the village have to sit through such a meeting."[44] Above all, one may not move out of Huaxi without forfeiting *all* the family property: house, car, and all savings and cash.

This conjures up the specter of serfdom, or a company town like Pullman instead of a New Harmony or Oneida Community. Chinese commentators criticize Huaxi as a place of brain-dead perfection among a lobotomized populace. But what if Huaxi—the China model, the Beijing consensus, the modern embodiment of Lord Shang and Han Feizi's Legalist universe—could actually be duplicated, minus its unsustainability and socioeconomic parasitism? What if the "final" Huajiashe were not a bordello but a no-nonsense fulfillment of a materialist utopia like Huaxi—perhaps with some "democratic" improvements? Would that, too, necessarily become a dystopia for the human spirit? This is the Huajiashe that Ge Fei has not analyzed. Such a Huajiashe, more closely reflecting the "real," *post*-Mao Huaxi of Jiangsu, would privilege linear development and decay over circularity. Ge Fei prefers to depict *cyclical* decay—until the final volume, which ends the trilogy with a vision of secular decay. By making the second, Mao-era Huajiashe the last "real" utopia-cum-dystopia, Ge Fei has remained faithful not to fantasy, speculation, or even local "reality" in Jiangsu, but rather to his own broad vision of historical cyclicalism.

THIS CHAPTER AND THE NEXT examine China's new historical novels in light of world dystopian thinking and writing. Set aside the wars, civil wars, class persecutions, domestic conflicts, murders, rapes, beatings, suicides, and mob violence that fill the Chinese novels; the frequent resort to trauma theory and Holocaust-influenced "history and memory" discourse in the West's academic studies of recent Chinese fiction and autobiography; and the sense of futility, angst, or unease engendered by the new historical novels as described in chapters 2 and 3. To what extent do these works share classic global dystopian templates?

The major Slavic and Anglophone tradition of dystopian imagination reverses utopian formulations traceable to Thomas More, Edward Bellamy, and fellow spirits. Even earlier precedents include Plato's *Republic*, whose system of governing guardians and auxiliaries seems both utopian and dystopian. The post-Enlightenment utopian and dystopian imagination creates fictions that resemble scientific experiments. Even early utopias were imagined as planned, rational, uniform societies isolated from the rest of the world, often on an island (or in an enclave, Fredric Jameson notes),[1] as immune to outside cultural and social contamination as a laboratory. Western utopias seek happiness in collective life. In dystopia, collective rationality and "protection" from individual, random, unregulated, even "magical" phenomena are so excessive as to be hellish. The classic dystopia is "rooted in 'a basic distrust of all social groups.'"[2]

In modern fiction generally, including China's, the narrative subject is the individual. In a conventional modern dystopia, the hero is besieged and under surveillance by "the group": top down, from a unitary, totalitarian state, and laterally, from surveillance and pressure to conform from peers. The hero loses not only freedom but individuality, all "humanity": moral feelings, sympathy, love, creativity, and in *Brave New World*, the right to procreate. Despite technological progress, there may be poverty for the proles and even for the guardians' auxiliaries, such as Winston Smith in *Nineteen Eighty-Four*. The governing ethos is enslavement: mindlessness, conformism, moral numbness; perhaps also fear, terror, paranoia, and exhaustion.

The classic Euro-American dystopian plot typically begins with explication and exemplification of the bad society. Rationalizing it is a historical backstory of how the new society came into being—a history that is an "alternative" to hoped-for future progress, and yet an equally logical extrapolation from human nature, social trends, and scientific advances. The main drama is typically about the hero's alienation from society, its rulers, and their controlling structures, followed by his or her attempts to rebel against or escape the system. The unitary, one-culture society of utopia, protected by its insularity and exceptionalism, is in dystopia extended or converted into a universal whole-world monolith, a Leviathan. There may yet be an outer zone of "savages," unprotected from environmental toxins and still uncolonized by the Leviathan. The hero may try to escape to it, with a companion, typically one of the opposite sex—most often a woman, in these novels mostly written by men (apart from Atwood's classic, *The Handmaid's Tale*).[3] The Chinese novels, except for Wang Anyi's, are no exception in that respect. The hero's companion will have awakened him to truths, desires, and other touchstones of humanity (and the spirit world, in some Caribbean novels) that are suppressed by the one-world, All-Under-Heaven order. The heroes need not be from the bottom of the bad society; as intelligent beings able to seek alternatives, they may well be among the guardians' auxiliaries, like Winston Smith (in the Ministry of Truth), Guy Montag (Bradbury's doubting "fireman"), Zamyatin's scientist and engineer D-503, and Offred, one of Atwood's slightly privileged "handmaids," though she is subordinate to gender-traitor auxiliaries called Aunts. The goal is no longer simple survival, but self-determination. The escape may be successful (*Fahrenheit 451*), possibly successful (*The Handmaid's Tale*), or a failure. Often it leads, Erika Gottlieb points out (10), to the trial and demise of the hero. A Chinese variation is an escape that occurs through the passing of time—survival and passage from the old, Maoist countryside to the "new era" in the city. But that is not so liberating after all.

An alternative construction of dystopia is regression to an uncivilized "state of nature," the subject of chapter 5. Like the dystopian vision of tyranny and totalitarianism, that of dystopian anarchy and social chaos tends to be a "post-progress" formulation that resembles an experiment in closed-system laboratory conditions. The bad new society may be the result of a nuclear holocaust that has collapsed the global technological superstructure and thus the underpinnings of the modern social and moral order. Small tribal colonies or scattered groups of individuals struggle against each other to survive; the hero or heroes seek refuge or escape. A classic of this type, William Golding's *Lord of the Flies*, available in China in translation by 1985,[4] revives the figure of the insular, one-world utopian society, for it begins with an idyllic portrait of young boys enjoying freedom from adult strictures on a Pacific atoll. One assumes that they were literally enisled to protect them from nuclear war in the larger, grown-up world. They end up creating their own inescapable world of terror. In these novels, and the *Mad Max* and *Terminator* films, terror comes from anarchy as well from tyranny and enslavement. Dystopian anarchy leads to a consolidation in tyranny, as the ancient Greeks theorized, and as in Wang Lixiong's mass-market trilogy, *Yellow Peril*. In that work, global ecological disaster leads to global chaos, a neo-Maoist totalitarian state in China, rebellion, separatism, and anarchy again, abetted by Taiwan, and ultimately a (mainland) Chinese salvation of the globe. In *Yellow Peril* and Chan Koonchung's *The Fat Years*, a highly modernized Chinese culture far from its traditional roots triumphantly colonizes the world by nonmilitary means. Chinese readers may see these popular works as ultimately utopian.

Another kind of dystopian novel, from Latin America, the Caribbean, and China, may accommodate magical realism and fantasy, but its storyline is grounded in a publicly recognizable narrative of the past. In most new historical novels it is a dissenting vision of the past, and not so rationally and precisely the projection of a controlled experiment, as in classic dystopias. The latter, given their setting in a hypothetical future, depict and sometimes insist on scientific and social-scientific innovation. Dystopias that instead revolve around a broadly recognizable history invert and controvert utopian plans formerly or currently implemented in life. The Chinese new historical novel that covers the Mao era names and exposes the folly of historical, not fictitious campaigns to reengineer society: the land reform, the Great Leap Forward, the Cultural Revolution, or socialism as such. This often leads to an equal and opposite exposure of the follies of post-Mao decollectivization and marketization.

In reciting the past that is within their own memory, the Chinese new historical novelists thus recite the history of one and often two social experiments,
socialist and post-socialist. Yet, those respective experiments' widely trum-
peted utopian *ideologies* are hardly visible.

García Márquez's story of Macondo begins symbolically and mythically.
The fictional town is a classic utopia—visionary, newly created, and virtually
inaccessible in the wilderness. At length, a police force and a banana company encroach from the outside, but Macondo declines into a dystopia mostly
due to internal flaws. Like the classic Euro-American dystopias, Macondo can
represent a nation or a continent, even All Under Heaven. Just so, the Chinese dystopias take shape as isolated part-societies. As recognizable national
history unfolds, the village or neighborhood under the microscope becomes
China. And China, however dystopian, is All Under Heaven. Neither its de-
composition nor its social differences come from the outside world.

The overlap of the Chinese and Latin visions of dystopia with those of the
classics is substantial. The subject is an individual struggling for survival, freedom, and self-determination, as in a relentlessly pessimistic coming-of-age
novel. The foe, if not totalitarianism, is injustice, embodied in abuse of power.
A common variation has a family or generations of families as the subject,
often with symbolic significance:[5] Mo Yan's Yus and Dais (*Red Sorghum*),
Shangguans (*Big Breasts and Wide Hips*), and Ximens (*Life and Death Are
Wearing Me Out*); Su Tong's Chens (*Nineteen Thirty-Four Escapes*), Lius
(*Opium Family*), family of Five Dragons (*Rice*), and Kus (*The Boat to Redemption*); Zhang Wei's Sui and Zhao clans (*The Ancient Ship*); Li Rui's Li and Bai
clans (*Silver City*); Yu Hua's Suns (*Cries in the Drizzle*), family of Fugui (*To
Live*), and Xus (*Chronicle of a Blood Merchant*); Ge Fei's Lus and Tans. They
are Chinese counterparts of García Márquez's Buendías (*One Hundred Years
of Solitude*), Allende's Truebas (*The House of the Spirits*), Vargas Llosa's Cabrals (*The Feast of the Goat*), and Junot Díaz's de Leóns and Cabrals (*The
Brief Wondrous Life of Oscar Wao*). Still, even in the family sagas, the subject
within the subject is the struggling hero, who often narrates the family saga as
he or she tries to understand his or her forebears and their times in order to
escape from a terrible predicament. It is chiefly in Mo Yan's and Ge Fei's historical novels, as in those of the Spanish American authors, that the hero may
be awakened by a companion or coconspirator of the opposite sex, as in the
Slavic and Anglophone classics. However, in the Chinese novels, the hero's
exemplars may be from a previous generation: the narrator's grandmother in
Red Sorghum, his mother in *Big Breasts and Wide Hips* (as also in Su Tong's

Nineteen Thirty-Four Escapes), and Lu Xiumi's mother's onetime lover, Zhang Jiyuan, in *Bygone Beauty*. Ximen Nao in *Life and Death Are Wearing Me Out* takes inspiration and courage from species-appropriate sexual partners, be they donkeys or pigs.

Tyranny and anarchy are not as antithetical as they may seem. In either case, the hero seeks escape from "All Under Heaven." Tyranny prevails in Latin American and Caribbean novels about Trujillo, Pinochet, eighteenth-century Caribbean Jacobins (in Carpentier's *Explosion in a Cathedral*; 1962), and assorted juntas and caudillos (as in Asturias's *El Señor Presidente*; 1946). Anarchy or "barbarism" is the subject of Sarmiento's seminal *Facundo: Or, Civilization and Barbarism* (1845), a mixed-genre portrait of regional *caudillismo* in Argentina's provinces that is also commonly viewed as the progenitor of Latin America's "dictator novel" (*novela del dictador*) tradition, an indication that tyranny and anarchy can coexist. *One Hundred Years of Solitude*, following Colombian history, depicts evils of both tyranny and anarchy. China's novels set in early twentieth-century history, such as *Red Sorghum*, *Big Breasts and Wide Hips*, *Silver City*, *Nineteen Thirty-Four Escapes*, *Rice*, and *Opium Family*, emphasize the chaos of the revolution and warlordism of those days (Ge Fei's *Bygone Beauty* allegorizes it in bandits' last-man-standing atrocities at Huajiashe), not the tendencies of one-man dictatorship and fascism that made a weak showing in Nationalist China (1927–1949). China has no dictator novel tradition.[6]

In both the Latin and the Chinese novels, the family may be struggling for its own survival. Under Maoism, the state displaced the father's authority and urban married couples were often assigned work in different cities. Yet the family is itself a major locus of oppression. The traditional patriarchal family had polygamy and other "perversions," in the novelists' modern view, even before Maoism remolded it, evidently without curing its ills. All the more important are romantic and companionable voluntary relationships that allow escape from the dystopian family.

The puzzle: Why is Big Brother still invisible in the Chinese novels when the storyline reaches the Mao era? China's new historical novelists, liberal and progressive as they all are, regard China under Mao as dictatorial and totalitarian; they require no insights from Orwell or Latin American dictator novels about that. Given China's continuing sensitivity to its national weakness in the recent past, it is unsurprising that no Chinese author has psychoanalyzed Sun Yatsen or Chiang Kaishek, as García Márquez has Simón Bolívar (in *The General in His Labyrinth*). But the Great Helmsman Mao

Zedong, and most of his unitary system and institutions, are simply missing from the Chinese novels.[7] Mao's presence is occluded above all as inspiration for a particular Chinese generation—the new historical novelists' generation—to "rebel" and ferret out enemies of the revolution among various Others and among themselves. Big Brother's words embody an *ideology*, however absurd; where is that—Mao Zedong Thought—in the novels? Why is oppression so political, and yet so abstract—at times, Kafkaesque?

The occluded institutions of Mao-era control—the Communist Party, state, and army—*are* major subjects of China's epic Maoist "red classics"; turn-of-the-twenty-first-century novels exposing official corruption; most of the memoir literature; and textbook history, including that written by friends and enemies of the Chinese Communist revolution. "Anticorruption novels" at the turn of the millennium often depicted the Communist Party from the inside, as a members-only group, though official prepublication instructions for self-censorship prohibited depiction of malfeasance above the level of deputy provincial Communist Party secretary or vice governor. However, Mao Zedong's *utopia* and the ideas of revolution and making revolution are missing—and therefore so is the ex–Red Guard generation's onetime hope of building it, and their participation in creating chaos. Here the new historical novels diverge from the memoir literature, even though the latter portrays its composers as victims more often than as perpetrators. Still, the Chinese novels at the center of this study resemble the Latin American new historical novels in their foregrounding of the evils of *fanaticism*.[8]

And yet mass violence in the new historical novels about the Mao era appears to come spontaneously from street mobs, in Yu Hua's *Brothers*, or from the elemental bullying of childhood and adolescence, in his *Cries in the Drizzle*—novels that we now read as reflections of Yu Hua's childhood.[9] Local Communist Party secretaries make an appearance in the new historical novels, and they have power and privilege, but even when they perpetrate injustice, their misdeeds appear to come from personal faults and motives. Zhao Duoduo in *The Ancient Ship*, for instance, who commits his worst evil as a militia head in the land reform, is empowered by his clan, not by the Communist Party as such. Magistrate Tan Gongda of *Land in Dreamland* is dreamily ineffectual; the corruption of his bureaucratic subordinates is also personal. In many novels, Communist Party persecutors who live long enough to experience the Cultural Revolution are persecuted in their turn (as in *Silver City*), allowing the reader to sympathize with them. Revolution, epitomized by mayhem and anarchy, becomes the oppressive force, not party dictatorship. Su Tong's *The Boat to Redemption* satirizes the Communist Party (more in the Chinese printing than in the award-winning English-language version), but his book highlights the party's weakness and vulnerability. Its abstract judgment on history, that the Ku family are not descended from a Communist martyr, and their acceptance of the importance of that, is what oppresses even those characters, not the party as such.

Mo Yan's *The Republic of Wine* may be counted as an exception. It gives a face to Communist Party corruption, which eventuates—perhaps—in cannibalism (the offense is never proved). However, a running joke is that the corrupt mine director and party secretary are so indistinguishable that even the narrative voice, taking the detective's drunken point of view, cannot tell them apart. The novel resorts to calling them "the mine director or party secretary, whichever." In notable historical works that illustrate the wielding of unjust power in the Mao era, such as Li Rui's *Silver City* and Mo Yan's *Big Breasts and Wide Hips*, the Communist Party members and their foes, the Nationalist, pro-Japanese puppet, and independent forces, are all related through ancestry or intermarriage. Mo Yan's other novels depict party members directing hysterical struggle sessions, but mostly as deviant personalities acting on personal grudges, and once more, the struggle is "all in the family"; in Zhang Wei's *September's Fable*, the source of persecution is quite mysterious.

Beyond the political, whichever era they portray, pre- or post-1949, China's new historical novels are reticent about collective institutions and groups as such. That includes social classes, voluntary organizations of civil society (religious organizations, professions, unions, women's groups, youth groups), even workplace groups. The ex–Red Guard generation to which the writers belong must surely be ambivalent about collective institutions organized from above; their relative invisibility in the novels, along with the absence of mid-level voluntary organizations of civil society, heightens the isolation, solitude, and oppression of the struggling heroes (and families) as they search for values, self-determination, and companionship. It is instead China's "realistic" anti-corruption novels that feature "good," though conspiratorial, cabals within the Communist Party, fighting bad local party tyrannies. That, to be sure, has many overtones of Mao-era conflicts between good and bad. Despite their jaundiced views of collectivism, the ex–Red Guard generation, by upbringing, must be conflicted about "individualism," too. García Márquez claims that "the Buendías' frustration comes from their solitude, that is, their lack of solidarity," though some critics contest his interpretation of his work.[10] It is hard to see where China's new historical novelists stand on this question.

The numerous seers, Daoists, and religious practitioners in the Chinese novels, like the midwives, veterinarians, rural doctors, and medicine peddlers, appear as rugged individualists maintaining private practices. The foreign Christian missionary in Mo Yan's *Big Breasts and Wide Hips* is a lone actor, except in his adulterous love affair, which leads to the birth of the novel's breast-worshipping hero.[11] Enterprises, whether prerevolutionary, like *Silver City*'s salt mines, *Rice*'s rice emporium, and *Red Sorghum*'s winery, or post-socialist, like the glass noodle factory in *The Ancient Ship*, are not so much sites of production and hard labor as property—objects of struggle for posses-sion. Many post-Mao private enterprises in *Brothers*, *The Ancient Ship*, *Big Breasts and Wide Hips*, and *Life and Death Are Wearing Me Out* are simply caricatures that reflect the eccentricities of their mock-heroic founders; they tend to sell fake or ridiculous products and services, such as hymen-restoring operations for women who want to appear to be virgins. Perhaps the most no-table act of productive labor in the novels, apart from Lan Lian's island of private farming in a sea of collectivized fields in *Life and Death Are Wearing Me Out*, is Yu Hua's commemoration of blood selling. But that is allegorical. Not only the crafts of the Latin American novels,[12] but the literary and "thought work" professions—so tortured in the Slavic and Anglophone dysto-pian classics and newer efforts like *The Unbearable Lightness of Being*, where they bear heavy symbolic and antiauthoritarian weight—are notable by their absence in the Chinese works. The dramatized "Mo Yan" of *Life and Death* and *The Republic of Wine* and "Shaogong" of *Maqiao* are exceptions, but their existential plight as writers is not dissected.

One might look to Shanghai for evidence of civil society organizations, hence to *The Song of Everlasting Sorrow*. Wang Anyi ostensibly tells a tale of an independent women's society that lies in the bedrock beneath, but ulti-mately transcends the perfidies of, the male world of politics. Her topology of Shanghai, old and new, is creative and unique, focusing on the *atmosphere* of the *longtang* row houses and their *types*, including "Wang Qiyaos." But the ethos of the row house localities is gossip and domestic mysteries. They are not social *neighborhoods*. And the focus is not on Wang Qiyao's low-profile indi-vidual practice as a nurse, but on leisure activities: mah-jongg in the Mao years and dance parties, post-Mao. Structured groups do not appear as much of a threat, outside of Cultural Revolution times—a citizen's ability to escape the consequences of politics in this novel by ignoring it verges on the incredi-ble—and groups and organizations do not offer a place of refuge or solidarity, either.

It is in the countryside that the word "collective," in life, was inseparable from productive and social life after the mid-1950s. Hero Lan Lian's refusal to join the collective is a major subplot in *Life and Death Are Wearing Me Out*, but this is a very unlikely, alternately pathetic and humorous story. Han Shaogong's disquisitions on local usage in *A Dictionary of Maqiao* put the word "collective" to sly, ironic use. Village women's indignation toward a handsome cadre who is oblivious to their charms "gradually took on collective (*jiti*) proportions" (249/229). And when a woman takes off with the "wrong" man, the village takes it as a "collective (*tuantide*) insult" (209/193).

The matter of class standing necessarily appears in portraits of mass criticism sessions, but to participate is not to be empowered; it is only to be submerged in mass hysteria. The unfortunate characters who are criticized often are not even correctly categorized, as in Su Tong's *Opium Family*. Class struggle thus is not really *class* struggle, but an act of political or personal vengeance. Many of those who actually are of landlord background, like Ximen Nao and Li Naijing, do not in any case deserve to be vilified, much less executed—even by Maoist standards, and certainly not by post-Mao standards. Evil landlords of the old society, like Su Tong's in *Nineteen Thirty-Four Escapes* and *Opium Family*, are diseased, addicted, and degenerate, not embodiments of power.[13] Organizations of both the proletariat (the Communist Party) and the rich are headed up by the powerful. Rural life is full of conflicts, insults, and injuries, but these are personal, not class-based. Says the sent-down youth chronicler of Maqiao, "Public ownership of land in Maqiao, right up to the early 1970s, was no more than a system. . . . It hadn't yet permeated to the depth of a feeling" (121/111).

For class consciousness, one looks again to Wang Anyi's Shanghai: the twentieth-century cauldron of China's modern capitalism and its modern proletariat, the major bridgehead of imperialism and the seedbed of early Communism. Yet the heroes of *The Song of Everlasting Sorrow* have little class consciousness. Most of them live a bourgeois life; Wang Qiyao gains full "independence" from her natal family by becoming the kept woman of a Nationalist official. Wang Anyi erects taste, connoisseurship, and above all an overarching concept of *fashion* as a substitute for class differences based on livelihood, income, or social role. Consumption, or rather the knowledge of how to consume, is the chief "social force" in the novel, and after that, generational identity. The heroes in Wang Anyi's great novel are but fellow refugees from socialism. Even more startlingly, the discourse of urban cadres in Ge Fei's *Land in Dreamland* is hardly more political.

Why, then, are Big Brother, his organizations and auxiliaries, and to some extent any group at all, so obscure in these novels, even in depictions and satires of the Mao era? Several factors may be adduced, first among them the continuing regime of China's literary control and its subtle aftereffects, including the authors' self-censorship.[14] Second, the modern Chinese state may be present symbolically, in representations of the Chinese family, an ancient Chinese philosophical device suggested by the contemporary novels' portraits of the family as a prison. Third, the bugbear of tyranny may be eclipsed by anarchy, a seemingly opposite trope of social breakdown that also has deep literary roots in China (anarchy is addressed in chapter 5). Fourth, *memories* of class consciousness in the Mao era, and perhaps actual class feelings in the Mao era, were "both state-centered and localized"; workers then and now had and have few direct, lateral connections; they visualized their connections only through the hierarchical and paternalistic state.[15] Gender solidarity was little different. This hierarchicalism is a manifestation of Big Brother, conscious or not. (To be sure, the new historical novelists are intellectuals and nearly all male.) Finally, there is the authors' ambivalence toward both collectivism and individualism. They were brought up on the idea that collectivism was a primary good and individualism a danger to self and society. The society that propagated those ideas then turned against their generation and their Maoist ideals, during and after the Cultural Revolution. And for one of their generation to take a stand on "individualism vs. collectivism" would be to call up their own implication in the society that created collectivism by mobilizing individuals to attack one another, while subordinating themselves to Big Brother's cult of personality. A major difference between the Chinese dystopian novels and the Slavic and Anglophone classics, and even the Latin classics,[16] is that the oppressed heroes, apart from Magistrate Tan, are seldom identified as belonging to Big Brother's lesser auxiliaries. Even if the reader sees them as auxiliaries of oppression, these heroes (including Tan) do not possess that self-recognition. If they escape from the one-world dystopia, it is by outliving it—an escape to a different time, not a different place. This denies agency to the hero, while obscuring his or her complicity in the old dystopia. And this escape is typically to another dystopia, without the hero's necessarily having achieved self-knowledge—even if he is Mo Yan's Ximen Nao, who has been reincarnated in a cycle of life.

What, then, would be proper individualism for these authors? Not passive revelry in consumerism, as currently sanctioned by the Communist Party. That sort of "individualism" appears to them as another mass illusion, invented by those above and enforced by social conformism. Moreover, it defeats Chinese intellectuals' utopian hopes, generated during the 1980s, of continuing political reform with *writers* at the center of the action—an old hope and, many might think, illusion of Leninist and Chinese revolution.

ALIENATION FROM THE "COMMUNITY"

Dystopian authoritarianism enters the Chinese new historical novels through the back door, in portraits of threats to the individual's autonomy from the community and the family. The settings of China's new historical novels are typically small, enclosed locales—villages, small towns, and self-contained urban neighborhoods. In the absence of larger, central structures of control and oppression, these places embody All Under Heaven. In ancient times, the self-sufficient rural community embodied arcadia, the Peach Blossom Spring, or Huajiashe; in Maoist ideology, the countryside was the font of revolutionary consciousness and the locus of recruitment for the revolution. In the new historical novels, it is dystopian, a place where utopianism is turned on its head. The village is not a place of refuge for the fictional heroes, not even for the community of natives in *September's Fable* who identify with their village. They are outcasts in the eyes of surrounding villagers, and their home territory is predestined for destruction within a larger economic plan. That China's villages were no arcadia, but a place to escape from, was of course the common feeling of city people, above all rusticated young folk of the Red Guard generation.

Among them, Han Shaogong and Li Rui, and the ex-peasant Mo Yan, became mainstays of the 1985 literary fad of seeking "roots" in the countryside, a way, it would seem, of salvaging something from their "wasted youth" there— except that Han Shaogong's signature roots-seeking short stories are already dystopian. Even earlier in the 1980s, Wang Anyi gained a reputation for conveying the flavor of Shanghai neighborhoods, her home before and after she was rusticated. Sent-down youth were rarely well integrated into the rural collectives where they resided. None bore the status of "member of the village." Mo Yan, the former peasant who re-created a fictionalized version of his native place, is the exception. Ge Fei chose to exclude a self-portrait from his *Southlands Trilogy*. His protagonists live south of the Yangzi; he was born in that locale, but he recasts it as dreamy and abstract even in its decadence.

One might apply Mikhail Bakhtin's concept of the chronotope to the settings of China's new historical novels, a gestalt of time and space coming together to define a unique locus in "time-space" (the literal meaning of "chronotope").[17] But Lin Qingxin and Howard Y. F. Choy, authors of erudite monographs on China's new historical fiction, counterpoise time to space, positing the supremacy of the latter, citing recent literary theories.[18] Choy opines that "writers are now seeking a new historical aura by evoking the feel of place and local community. This is a new narrative strategy that stresses the spatial dimensions rather than the temporal dimensions of history" (10). He finds that in most experimental fiction of the Deng Xiaoping era, "time provides only an entrance to historical landscapes. By changing the tradition of 'once upon a time' to the fiction of 'once in a place', the spatialization of history flattens the past into a plane surface or, more precisely, a map" (11). Lin Qingxin likewise feels that "in the space-time relationship, the NHF [New Historical Fiction] favors the spatial axis." He concurs with Edward Soja's notion (partly inspired by Foucault) that "the current era is more an age of geography (space) than one of history (time)" (85; also 21–22).

My view is the reverse; for one thing, localities in these novels are unpleasant and relatively undifferentiated, certainly not exemplars of local color.[19] Mo Yan's work is the exception, if there is one. Only of *Red Sorghum*, whose sorghum plants are rendered truly alive thanks to magical effects, can it be said that the "landscape is not a passive creature."[20] Han Shaogong's Maqiao speaks in an idiolect, not a dialect that conjures up regional images. It also represents Earthbound China and beyond that, humankind, not Hunan or the ancient region of "Chu."

Except in the period novels, time—historical change—is the mover of society and the provocateur of the hero. Writes Chi Li, a neo-realist and peer of the new historical novelists (b. 1957, in Hubei): "It is the age, instead of my hometown, that makes me grow into the person I now am." "I am a person who has no hometown!" she exclaims, citing the many dislocations of her family during Mao-era political movements.[21] The new historical novelists share this experience and this childhood sense of time, as filled with political "events" (and not technological change). To cite again a pronouncement by the narrator of Yu Hua's *Cries in the Drizzle*: "Our lives, after all, are not rooted in the soil as much as they are rooted in time" (31/34). The most important aspect of space in the new historical novels, it seems, is neither its site characteristics (local color) nor its relative location (e.g., distance from Beijing), but its small scope and inescapability—its confinement—a genuine aspect of Maoist China. Local life is not insignificant: it is paradigmatic, and in the case of both the countryside and the city under Maoism, truly a living experiment Every action is magnified, acts of tyranny and enslavement above all.

The locality as the scene of action in China's new historical novel is thus a locus of alienation and enisling typical of the dystopian imagination. This alienation takes at least three forms. The locality is itself isolated and inescapable—self-contained without being truly self-reliant or self-sufficient. Second, it is not a community, but a place divided against itself. Even the structures of local control—production brigades, communes, and in the cities, neighborhood associations and meetings—are nearly as occluded as the power structure above. (By contrast, these were not invisible in the "red classics.") Third, the hero (and sometimes his or her family or clan) is estranged from whatever is left of community at the local level. Each level of isolation has its own mixture of tyranny, alienation, and at times, anarchy.

The downtrodden heroes of Su Tong's *The Boat to Redemption* exemplify the elemental isolation of the locality. They are boat people, "enisled" because they are unwelcome onshore. Ku Dongliang, who with his father is exiled to life on the river and comes of age in the novel, reflects: "I didn't know then that it was to be a lifetime banishment. Boarding was easy, getting off impossible" (42/29).[22] From the decrees of local politics, which tighten as time goes by during the revolutionary years, as well as from traditional prejudice, the boat people become increasingly excluded from society on land. They have their own customs, mores, relationships, and hierarchy. To that extent they might be seen as a countercultural, if not fully utopian, part-society struggling alongside a dystopian, more urban world on land. Yet the world of the boat people declines and dissolves as history moves on.

The town of Wali in Zhang Wei's *The Ancient Ship*, too, may be considered an island of human existence, brought from a state of contact with the outside world into a kind of isolation not by engulfing waters, but by the retreat of the river waters that originally linked it to the outside through commerce and prosperity. The town in effect "ran aground" after the river dried up, as symbolized by the ancient ship the townsfolk unearth. Again, the story is of the decline of a formerly good society. Once Wali is cut off from the outside world, it is overcome by violent—and seemingly internal—social forces of rural revolution that it cannot resist.

The visionary but inadequate socialist modernizer Tan Gongda of Ge Fei's *Land in Dreamland* does not see isolation as idyllic; one of his grand schemes is to connect all the villages with roads, an echo of his mad grandfather's plan to connect all the houses of Puji with a walkway. The houses of Huajiashe are thus connected, but the community itself is secluded, and it has its own, literal island, representing the isolation of the human heart.

The actual figure of an island is evoked, metaphorically, in Su Tong's appalling *Opium Family*, when the ill-fated heir to the powerful Liu family of landlords comes home from school. Here he first confronts the reality that he will inherit acre upon acre of land planted in poppies. Knowing the nature of the scourge from word of mouth but not from experience, he muses,

> "This is my family's opium; this is the opium plant that always remained outside of the botanical curriculum; it comes from father's land, but it can turn your face ghostly pale and make you feel as though you're floating in a nightmare." The sweet, pungent odor of opium poppies rose up from every corner of the fields; Chencao discovered that he was standing on an isolated island; he felt dizzy; the murmuring sound of the waves of opium poppies pushes you onto an isolated island where everything is far far away from you and there is only that murderous odor penetrating your lungs. (9/192–193)

Thus does an idyllic and salvational—utopian—sense of perfected quiet and freedom, of separation from the mundane realm of worldly dust transform into its opposite, like withdrawal from addiction.

In these novels, cities as such are dystopian, and in a rather classical sense of entrapment, since peasants migrate there in search of utopia and have trouble going back. Five Dragons, the hero of *Rice*, makes his fortune in the city and at first considers it his own private "paradise" (18/18).[23] But in the end he thinks it "an obscene, sinful, huge, fucking trap ready to lure the unwary. For a handful of rice, or a few coins, or a moment of pleasure, pitiful people poured into the city by train and by boat, all bending their efforts toward finding paradise on earth. If only they knew it didn't exist" (185–186/217). He returns to his native village as a corpse. Ge Fei's *Southlands Trilogy* can be read as an extended tale of urbanization with an unhappy outcome. The razing of old homes then spreads to the countryside, and unwitting farmers welcome it.

The second form of alienation, the division of the locality against itself, begins with the artificiality of its political and territorial definition. The locality is no community, even in the countryside; it is constructed by invisible powers on high. Han Shaogong's Maqiao is the rare work that mentions official collective structures, but this brief appearance emphasizes their arbitrariness and instability in recent history. Maqiao has not constituted itself. Says the narrator:

—before 1956, [it was] called Maqiao Village, part of Tianzi Township;

—from 1956 to 1958, called Maqiao Group, part of Dongfeng Cooperative;

—in 1958, called 22nd production team, part of Changle People's Commune (Large Commune);

—from 1959 to 1979, called Maqiao Production Team, part of Tianzi People's Commune (Small Commune);

—since 1979, when the People's Communes were disbanded, up to the present day, Maqiao Village, along with a section of Tianzi Township, has become part of Shuanglong Township.   (11/8)

These novels' villages, however small, are rent by conflicts, political or not. In *Cries in the Drizzle*, arguments over private plots lead to violence that is "commonplace" in the 1950s (10/11). *A Dictionary of Maqiao* conveys occasional village solidarity, but usually negatively, by depicting inter-village antagonisms. Maqiao has its own dialect, but it is not necessarily a tool or emblem of the village's intellectual or social liberation. In daily life the denizens of Maqiao are divided against themselves, and they see their neighbors as oddballs, outsiders, or potential outcasts. Only the narrator, it turns out, cares about the village's "communal" knowledge. When the Mao-era controls come off, younger and more vigorous Maqiao natives migrate to the city. In this, they follow the path of "Shaogong" and his cohort.

Critical interpretations of *A Dictionary of Maqiao* tend to stress its implicit validation of local ("Maqiao") speech departures from Modern Standard Chinese and thus of Maqiao's unique ways of seeing and typologizing the world. Local consciousness cannot, it seems, be fully suppressed by the central power. Fair enough. But this is not to say that the Maqiao people are models for the rest of us, particularly if their more peculiar usages are, as I suspect, invented by Han Shaogong, the author, for critical, satiric, and even transparently pedagogic purposes. "Shaogong" the narrator/compiler cites several examples of Maqiao usage that he refers to as "Jasmine-Not-Jasmine," and also as "double-talk" (*moleng liangke*): "It's going to rain, it doesn't look as if it will"; "I'm full, I'm full, one more bowl and then I'll be full"; "I reckon the bus isn't going to come, you'd best keep waiting"; "This newspaper is well written, I can't understand a single word"; "He's an honest man, he just doesn't talk honestly" (318/289). When the Maqiao folk reverse some meanings of Modern Standard Chinese, they often "correct" the tergiversations of official double-think. They use the words "awakened" and "precious" to mean "stupid," "asleep" to mean "clever," and "get muddled" for "start school." When they use the standard word "indolence" to indicate a coveted state of ease and comfort, and "lawbreaking" for succeeding in life, one cannot so easily accept their world-view, but they are still performing linguistic acts of resistance.

And yet, the Maqiao folk also engage in doublethink, and not just in the popular sense of equivocating. "Doublethink" is something more complex in *Nineteen Eighty-Four*: "To know and not to know, to be conscious of complete truthfulness while telling carefully constructed lies, to hold simultaneously two opinions which cancelled out, knowing them to be contradictory and *believing* in both of them [my emphasis]."[24] This is to be self-contradictory, not simply duplicitous. It is what Han Shaogong the author is asking his readers to do when they learn "Maqiao usage" while not forgetting their Modern Standard Chinese: "knowing them to be contradictory and believing in both of them." Are not the Maqiao people the same as us, in this more complicated sense, then—forced into a state of self-contradiction and diminished integration of their personalities by their flawed society? They are playing its game, not their own.[25]

Mo Yan's novels create the most poignant images of the countryside, and not of communities, but of individual peasants with their own eccentric thoughts and habits, rather than "peasant masses." Their very diversity and eccentricity undermine a sense of community. The rural world of *Big Breasts and Wide Hips* features Mo Yan's typical cast of bullies, brawlers, antagonistic mutes and misfits, self-proclaimed Daoists, mystics, sorcerers, purveyors of odd customs, black market traders of women and children, plus a Swedish missionary who recites Confucius. Even more than in Macondo, odd family relations are at the center of the action. The Shangguan family's many females fornicate with diverse available males and marry into all political sides (bandit, Kuomintang, Communist, Japanese puppet), much as in *Red Sorghum*. The village—or really, the novel's heroine, "Mother"—manages self-defense when famine-ravaged outsiders try to steal meager food stocks after Japanese raids (1:129–130/143–144), but otherwise the locality is perpetually distracted by intra-village rivalries and enmities, as between the Sun family of mutes and the Shangguans.

The village as an entity is prominent by its absence until halfway through the novel, when the work presents its first synoptic view of it, as villagers gather to see their first movie. The audience consists of comic grotesques: a single-breasted shop proprietress, a man with half a face due to a past encounter with a bear, a deaf and crooked-leg man, a blind man, and "Little Cross Eyes" (1:242–243/239–240)—as well as a downed American flier who provides the equipment, and the Shangguans and their in-laws, themselves rather eccentric in habits and natal origins. Later, the aftermath of the revolution brings on the usual disgraceful meeting for struggling against and executing landlords and rich peasants (1:291–309/282–296). The main target, Sima Ku, is absent, so the assembly decides to execute his little daughters. One peasant finally "rediscover[s] his conscience" and retracts his accusations, confirming that they were lies from the start. During a subsequent mass evacuation occasioned by civil war, it is every man (or, in most cases, woman and child) for himself (1:309–329/296–313). Outsiders penetrate the shattered village to persuade its many widows to remarry (2:371–372/334), much as they did earlier in the century to persuade women to unbind their feet. The dystopian trend of history is not generated internally, but the local community is hardly a refuge from the horrors of social life; it is the medium in which they operate.

"Original" rural society as remembered by Ximen Nao in *Life and Death Are Wearing Me Out* resembles *One Hundred Years of Solitude*'s opening vision of utopia. Ximen pictures himself at the center of a benevolent manorial system that he created. This is nostalgic, for the former landlord recalls his idyllic local world as a donkey, reborn from hell after the human Ximen Nao came before the firing squad during the land reform.

> Back then I was on top of the world. Bumper harvests every year, and the tenant farmers eagerly paid their rent. The grain sheds overflowed. The livestock thrived, and our black mule gave birth to twins. It was like a miracle, the stuff of legend, not reality. A stream of villagers came to see the twin mules, and our ears rang with their words of flattery. We rewarded them with jasmine tea and Green Fort cigarettes.   (9/10–11)

This is an idealized, boastful, and self-serving account. The revolution has already begun to drag the world of the Ximens and their neighbors into dystopia, and Ximen Nao himself into hell. He finally works his way up to human again through good deeds in his successive reincarnations, but given the unedifying state of the post-Mao society into which he is finally reborn as a human in 2000, he may have to experience the misery of the wheel of life all over again.

Mostly, the animal narrator tells of inimical forces: humans who would geld Ximen Donkey or send him to the butcher's, hunters who would claim credit for his good deed in fending off wolves, and other hunters who would hunt down Ximen Pig; this is in addition to the pig-eat-pig and wolf-eat-donkey world that Ximen must contend with outside the human realm. Ximen Donkey is finally butchered by a mob of starving villagers during the famine after the Great Leap Forward (88/105); Ximen Ox is tortured and burned to death during the Cultural Revolution for his loyalty to a politically incorrect master.

Otherwise, the notable interpersonal activities of the non-leading villagers, apart from their sexual assignations, are activities like unending visits to Lan Lian's home to put round-the-clock pressure on him to join the people's commune. Local society tears itself apart again in the Cultural Revolution. The situation post-Mao is no better. Says Ximen Pig, looking at the locals chatting after a banquet, when Mao is gone and the electricity grid has reached Ximen Village:

> I knew the people who were sitting at the tables. A bad lot, all of them. The onetime puppet security chief Yu Wufu, the turncoat Zhang Dazhuang, Tian Gui the landlord, and the rich peasant Wu Yuan were seated at one table. Seated at one of the other tables were the onetime chief of security Yang Qi and two of the Sun brothers, Dragon and Tiger. . . . I later learned that Yang Qi was in the business of selling bamboo poles—he'd never been much of a farmer. (330–331/347)

Here is dystopia as restoration of the evils of the past, both in the larger sense of history and as embodied in individual characters. The local village is unrecognizable after the post-Mao reforms, but its moral character is all too familiar. And Ximen Pig has here unconsciously adopted the point of view of the previous "new" society, which despised landlords, rich peasants, and collaborators—a viewpoint contrary to Ximen's own past pride in his supposed community leadership as a landlord. But Ximen has been executed and suffered as an animal all these years. Is it right for the other former landlords and rich peasants to be able to lord it over others, now that the *new* New China has come?

Oddly, the countryside is seldom portrayed as the site of shocking poverty in these novels (as are the urban environments of *Nineteen Eighty-Four*, *The Handmaid's Tale*, *The Hunger Games*, and post-apocalypse films such as

Soylent Green and *Blade Runner*, with the exception of *September's Fable*. The stockpiling of rice, in several works by Su Tong, is less an indication of poverty than an emblem of addiction and sign of "species regression"; likewise, the wealthy landlord's idiot son's obsession with steamed buns in *Opium Family*. This is quite in contrast with the memoir literature of ex-Red Guards, ex-Rightists, and others who have told their personal tales of rustication poverty.

Urban neighborhoods offer no more comforts of belonging than the dystopian village. *Tattoo* begins with the main protagonist's mother falling into icy waters and drowning as she carries her just-born son, later called Limpy, while crossing a stream.

> She screamed for help and kicked her legs against the freezing water. Her screams were wild and despairing. Those who had windows facing the canal and could hear her were unable to tell whether they were the screams of a human being or of the legendary river goblins. No one even dared open their rear window to find out.   (133/153)

In the salt mines and compounds of Li Rui's *Silver City*, and in the one remaining glass noodle factory of Zhang Wei's *The Ancient Ship*, there is no enterprise or small-town sense of community. Wali is a battlefield, among political forces labeled according to their class background, and really, in Maoist as well as post-Mao times, among antagonistic clans. The postmodern world of Ge Fei's small city of Hepu, in *Southern Spring Played Out*, is utterly bereft of human compassion and beneficial cooperation.

The Song of Everlasting Sorrow is silent about the civilian "eyes and ears" of the police who keep citizens under surveillance in the big city, but Wang Qiyao's new abode in Shanghai of the Mao years, in an anonymous and confining "Peace Lane"—within a maze of other lanes with rotting exteriors ideal for losing one's way—is a place of vague apprehension for those like Wang who lead unconventional lives. The heroine forms her own part-society, keeping a low profile so as to escape notice. The Shanghai streets in the prerevolutionary era of Su Tong's *The Gardener's Art* are similarly unfriendly. They house families in walled-off compounds and shops of shyster lawyers and detectives and such. One can be murdered by a gang of common thieves in front of one's own house without anyone noticing. And yet a good deal of unfriendly "spying" goes on; Mr. Kong's dalliances with other women do not go unnoticed, and the young master of the household takes to spying on the dramatic troupe next door. The violent, gang-ridden ethos of *Rice* is even less civilized, and the two heroes of Yu Hua's *Brothers* are forced, during the Maoist chaos, to live on the street by their wits. The most positive, though highly ironic, depiction of an urban site is the town of Liquorland in Mo Yan's *The Republic of Wine*—a town known for its dedication to winemaking, but corrupt and besotted. It spreads a kind of transient global drunkenness to all who come to visit, the self-dramatized author Mo Yan included, much as Macondo once imparted transient global amnesia to all its townspeople.

The third kind of alienation, of the hero (with or without family) against the community, such as it is, needs little elaboration. "Shaogong" as a sent-down youth in Maqiao is alien to the community from the start, as is the detective investigating local reports of cannibalism in *The Republic of Wine*. The patriarchs Li Naijing and Ximen Nao are executed at the outset of the tales of their personal sagas; their kith and kin are in jeopardy ever after. The matriarch of *Big Breasts and Wide Hips* barely hangs on, and not all of her kin survive. Lotus, a former student out of place in an old-style family and at odds with its other concubines, goes mad in *Raise the Red Lantern*. The Suis of *The Ancient Ship* and the Kus of *The Boat to Redemption* struggle unsuccessfully to regain their lost status on land. Fugui barely manages "to live," and Yu Hua's "brothers" barely survive the Cultural Revolution. The young folk of *September's Fable* are alienated from their elders. Wang Qiyao's survival strategy is to go underground and create her own counter-society in the shadows of Shanghai.

A common goal, then, is to escape the claustrophobic locality, a ubiquitous theme of the classic Western dystopian novels and also the memoirs of China's former sent-down youths and ex-Rightists. Escape from Maple Village is the highlighted narrative thread of Su Tong's *Nineteen Thirty-Four Escapes*. Villagers in that year experience a plague of cholera and a famine that results in mass hysteria and mob violence. More surreally, "the rules of morality were overturned everywhere in Maple Village that autumn" (139/118); unmarried men and women left their farm work to couple in the fields, as if possessed. Family cruelty begins in childhood with the whipping of little brothers and sisters and culminates in rapes, murders, and attempted murders. It is hinted that the narrator's grandfather Chen Baonian may have copulated with his own sister. The escapes begin when Chen Baonian leaves his bride of seven days to set up a bamboo crafts shop in a city 450 miles away. Precisely 139 males escape Maple Village to set up shops, despite the wailing of their abandoned wives.[26]

Li Rui's *Silver City* and Yu Hua's *Brothers*, which continue their stories into post-Mao times, also end on notes of escape—the Yu Hua brother who succeeds in commerce buys a trip into outer space. The unsympathetic central character of Su Tong's *Rice* begins that novel as a typical rural migrant to the city. The narrator of *A Dictionary of Maqiao* and many of the natives finally leave Maqiao. The unlikely and politically insecure boy monarch of Su Tong's *My Life as Emperor* simply goes on the lam in the later chapters of that novel, traveling across his lost kingdom with a former servant and taking up a new vocation as—tightrope walker. That change of status is one of the closest approximations to the Western dystopian novel plot device of escape to an outer zone beyond the central command, one of savages and yet also of freedom. But in the novels about modern China, escape from the village or socialist neighborhood chiefly succeeds through an escape from Maoist *times*. The theme of escape may be attenuated by a more nostalgic feeling of a need not just to escape but to return, to better and more moral times. Yet in these novelists' worlds, though history does often repeat itself, the times never get any better or more moral.

The setting of *September's Fable* is the exception: a kind of community. Yet this miserable village, beset by poverty, ignorance, and pointless violence, in many ways epitomizes dystopia. Beatings over trivial matters are a way of life. The villagers repeatedly injure and mutilate themselves and each other. There is nothing of what a Chinese reader would call "culture." Surrounded by hostile villages, the villagers do not have the option of escaping. In Zhang Wei's novel, one must remain imprisoned in the village until it is destroyed by economic forces beyond its control.

And what if one does manage to escape to the city? In the frantic and run-on speech of the grandmother in *Nineteen Thirty-Four Escapes*, intended to prevent her son from fleeing, "How can you go to the city the city that miserable place good people go there and their hearts turn black evil people go there and pus flows out of the soles of their feet and their heads are covered with sores." (149/136–137).

The Family: A Prison

Confucian utopia is a harmonious patriarchal family with five generations living under one roof, self-sufficient and self-contained. In ancient philosophy and literature, the family's hierarchical but ideally reciprocal human relations were cited as a model for all social structures, particularly ruler-subject relations in the good state. Officials in imperial China were "fathers and mothers of the people," a conceit satirized by Mo Yan in *Life and Death Are Wearing Me Out*. Says the village head regarding his concern for the commune's pig-raising project, with old Ximen Nao listening in as a pig, "Young people who view our pigs as their mothers and fathers are exactly what we need" (196/225).

The breakdown of the utopian family, like the breakdown of all utopian institutions, is a foundation for dystopia. One sees two different forms of it in the Chinese novels.[27] The family may maintain its prescribed ideal outer form, while its inner workings and confinements make it hell on earth. As in any oppressive structure, the oppressed want to escape. This has been a common theme in Chinese literature since the May Fourth movement. More surprising for its ubiquity in the recent novels (even if some chapters unfold amid the chaos of war) is another form of perceived decline, in which male-female and parent-child relations become entirely "disordered" or disloyal. In the new historical novels, seldom is any family strong enough to afford its members protection from inimical social forces, much less joy or satisfaction.

Mo Yan's breakout novel, *Red Sorghum*, is prologue to his themes of irregular and improvised family relations. Granddad first takes the narrator's grandma by force in a sorghum field, prying her loose from her marriage to a leper, into which she had been forced against her will; he helps her by murdering that rich man, takes her as his common-law wife, and together they appropriate the rich man's legacy. Granddad ultimately takes two other wives, in a haphazard way far outside the formal polygamy of the landlord class. Sex in this novel is as passionate and heroic as the warfare.

Big Breasts and Wide Hips is ostensibly a tribute to China's strong females in time of war and peace. Shangguan Lu, known to the narrator as Mother, holds together a three-generation family, helping it survive Japanese invasion, civil war, migration as refugees, and finally the Communist struggle sessions that target the family because of its complicated landlord and political connections. She possesses the stabilizing power of an Úrsula Buendía during all social and family upheavals, lacking only Úrsula's 115-year life span. Shangguan Lu's mother-in-law, Shangguan Lü, is another strong figure, a blacksmith's wife "much better with a hammer and anvil than her husband could ever hope to be" (1:3/3). The men of the family are weak, incompetent, and dependent on women, up to and including the narrator, Jintong. According to a summary narrative comment expressed in a voice whose identity is uncertain, "Weak father, weak son, accomplish little with their soft hands—limp wicks, fluffy cotton, always careless and given to cutting corners" (1:11/9–10). This reversal of basic Confucian propriety occurs in the context of a long-term decline in efficacy of the Shangguan male line. Yet something similar could be said of the women. Mother hates her mother-in-law, as in many a Chinese novel, and finally cracks her skull with a rolling pin after the woman lives too long to suit her (1:218/219). The fathers of Mother's nine children indicate chaos in the family system as Mo Yan reimagines it. The eldest child is fathered by Mother's uncle (a relative by marriage), and likewise her second, another daughter. Mother's third daughter is fathered by a duck peddler, the fourth by an itinerant herb doctor, the fifth by a dog butcher, the sixth by a monk, the seventh by one of four army deserters who raped Mother, and the eighth, together with a twin brother, the only male child, by a Swedish missionary. The girl twin is born blind, joining Mo Yan's cast of crippled, mutilated, and disabled rural characters, and the boy, Jintong, the novel's chief focal consciousness and narrator, has blond hair and a breast fixation that keeps him on a milk diet into adolescence. That Mother's legal husband and father-in-law are both murdered by the Japanese is a minor fact next to her illicit hookups, some forced on her as rape, but others due to passion or happenstance or engineered by her as an act of defiance of the patriarchal family—and a way of fulfilling the requirement that she bear a male child.

Decline affects her daughters as much as the younger generations of men; some of their multiple hookups are with former lovers or husbands of their sisters. Madness, prostitution, murderous urges, opportunism, and physical disability run through the bloodline. The passions of coupling appear just as rife among the general population, according to Mo Yan's portrait of the assignations of a cross-eyed girl, including incest with her brother (1:244/240).

Non-monogamous and adulterous relations might be expected in novels depicting the "old society," particularly those with characters of the landlord class, but frequent premarital and adulterous couplings, many of them mutually consensual, are featured in depictions of *Maoist* society in the family sagas of Yu Hua, Mo Yan (in his contemporary satire, *The Republic of Wine*, too), Zhang Wei, particularly in *September's Fable*, and even among the peasants of Han Shaogong's fictional town of Maqiao. This does not accord with the memories of the authors of China's autobiographers, who recall having to go to a people's park to hold hands with a girl- or boyfriend even in the early 1980s, and rape charges' being leveled at those who lived together outside of marriage.

The characters pay a biological price for their conspicuous promiscuity. From early post-Mao times, madmen, the developmentally challenged, and particularly mutes have peopled Chinese fiction and film as symbols of the destruction of human nature by an inhumanly repressive Maoist society, which did not allow citizens to speak or always to choose their own mates. (In Ge Fei's trilogy, madness is brought out by inhumane social forces, but it also embodies genius.) The power of men over women in these novels leads to incest, and that or more mysterious outcomes due to promiscuity lead to defective human beings from birth. In *Opium Family*, the old landlord patriarch Liu Laoxia's first five children are defective. "The first four were placed in the river and allowed to float downstream; they looked like fish, having neither legs nor arms" (5/185). The peasants attribute these birth defects to the old man's lechery. In fact, he committed adultery with his father's concubine and took her as his own after his father's death, which he might have caused for that purpose. She, who might have been the mother of Liu Laoxia, was the mother at least of Laoxia's fifth child, an idiot who harbors murderous intentions. The Lius are the ultimate dysfunctional family; Laoxia's legal wife is drowned in a bathtub and the one normal son, Chencao, the heir, is suspected to be illegitimate, the son of a hired hand. The boy goes scot-free after stabbing the idiot to death. After the revolution, the former hired hand gets revenge. He and all the Lius perish in the end in a great fire at the scene of the old patriarch's lechery. The peasants are not entirely wrong that the Liu bloodline has turned decadent; there is an oedipal dialectic of violence when Chencao, spawn of a landlord's concubine-cum-mother who coupled with a proletarian, kills that hired hand to avenge the landlord family line; he does not recognize the worker as his father. He has, however, committed parricide.

"Mother," the heroine of Mo Yan's *Big Breasts and Wide Hips*, begins her long life of childbearing after being raped one night in bed by her guardian, Big Paw, her father's sister's husband. "Your aunt . . . made me do it," he stammers (2:688/59). This is not incest in the blood sense, but the shameful relationship leads to not one but two offspring. The pressure on Mother to bear a male heir, whoever the father might be, comes mostly from her harsh mother-in-law. More damaged physically, and perhaps genetically, are the "brood of five grandsons, all mutes," of the novel's Aunty Sun, the mother-in-law's great enemy. "The parents seemed not to ever have existed" (1:14/12).

An "eternally dissolute Chen family bloodstream" (171/173) in Su Tong's *Nineteen Thirty-Four Escapes* leads to a scenario in which the narrator's grandfather Chen Baonian implants a son in a mistress, who steals the legal wife's only surviving son (Father) after the wife has already buried her five other children during a cholera epidemic. The kidnapping is payback to the wife, who poisoned the mistress's own fetus in the womb. The mistress bears an uncanny resemblance to Chen Baonian's sister, a beauty with whom Chen may be suspected of having had incestuous assignations when he was a lad of seventeen; her subsequent "violent death" must have been his doing, too (140/121).

The nadir of Chinese family life is reached in Su Tong's longer work, *Rice*. In a plot worthy of a nineteenth-century European novel, the demonic character Five Dragons marries a rice merchant's elder daughter after she becomes a fallen woman, abuses her, forces himself on her younger sister, and then marries her, too, completing his conquest of the family. Five Dragons takes over the business, becomes an underworld boss after committing mass murder by arson, and fathers a son who smothers his little sister in a vat of rice. Five Dragons finally betrays all his gangster associates to occupying Japanese forces. His motive in all this, apart from acquiring a fortune in rice, is vengeance, though the perceived offense he has suffered from the proprietor family, and even the gangsters, is simply his lower social station. Injuries and gonorrhea rot his body away before he can be returned home atop a railway boxcar of rice. Enraged at being left with no inheritance, his greedy son, Kindling Boy, pries the gold teeth from his dying father's mouth. Decay and decline, both physical and moral, are the common threads of the family relations conjured up by Su Tong, Mo Yan, Yu Hua, Li Rui, and Wang Anyi. The coming of prosperity, whether after the war or after the Maoist social leveling, provides no comfort. Human nature has not changed.

Even the relatively conventional family is a prison in China's new historical novels, confining and oppressing the main protagonists as surely as any state-run regime. The flimsy housing interiors in these works do not afford overlooked corners where one can be alone from prying eyes, as do even the future-world residences with telescreens and so forth in *We*, *Nineteen Eighty-Four*, and *The Handmaid's Tale*. It is chiefly in *The Song of Everlasting Sorrow* that Wang Anyi's heroine Wang Qiyao finds in her lonely rooms a refuge from curious neighbors, and even from politics, so that she can carry on her friendships and trysts.

Chinese intellectuals have portrayed woman's lot as miserable since the May Fourth movement. Though some critics have called the male bravado of Mo Yan's fiction and the scenes of abuse of women in Su Tong's stories misogynist,[28] *Big Breasts and Wide Hips* comprehensively and sympathetically lays out the hell that is Mother's life, owing to her natal situation as well as to forces of war, civil war, and general social breakdown. This is not to say that she is a moral exemplar; she does after all kill her mother-in-law. In this epic novel, women have to do both "women's work" and men's work, in time of both war and peace. Aunty Sun is reputed in youth to have been "a renowned bandit who could leap over eaves and walk on walls" (1:15/14). But all the women suffer from the social duty and lesser status prescribed for their gender. "'Women are worthless creatures,' Shangguan Lü said, 'so you beat them. You beat a woman into submission the way you knead dough into noodles'" (2:701/68). Her daughter-in-law, Shangguan Lu, is accordingly subjected to physical and verbal abuse for bearing seven daughters in a row. She hates her husband and promises some of her own daughters to unsuitable men and sells one of them, perpetuating the cycle of conjugal misery. As property, then, women are not exactly worthless, except to themselves. Mother, with her beauty and tiny bound feet, once appeared to her guardian uncle as "a truly marketable treasure" (2:674/49).[29] The pressure to sacrifice oneself for the family is such that one of the daughters sells herself into prostitution. In a similar vein, of the better-off young Li women in Li Rui's *Silver City*, one marries a warlord to secure protection for her family, and another mutilates herself to make herself unmarriageable, thus sparing her family the cost of a dowry so that her younger brother may be educated.

This is the "feudal" family system of the old society, in which ducks were allegedly valued more highly than granddaughters (2:690/60) and "humans and animals are so much alike," according to Mother herself (1:73/94), a point that the author, Mo Yan, suggests at greater length in his *Life and Death Are Wearing Me Out*. We need not repeat the sad tales of concubines; all the women in Su Tong's *Wives and Concubines* and its film adaptation are emotionally mutilated, if not murdered. Hatred among multiple wives leads them to try to murder one another or their offspring by their own hands in *Silver City, Nineteen Thirty-Four Escapes*, and *Opium Family*. But wife beating continues after the revolution. In *September's Fable*, village wife beating is posed as a custom and a social necessity.[30] It begins with Jinyou. "People opened their windows and looked off in the direction of Jinyou's place and said, 'Jinyou's beating his wife again.' 'Wife's a pitiful thing. Has to be beaten from time to time.' Jinyou got tired of beating her so he sat down for a while" (52/86). The practice spreads and becomes general (62/102, 95/157–158). One autumn, "as night fell, every man was beating his wife, or cursing, and hitting his children until they started to bawl" (190/318). The cruelest family predicament, according to traditional lore, is the mistreatment of a daughter-in-law by her mother-in-law. In *September's Fable*, the behemoth of a woman Big Feet Fat Shoulders scares off her son's beloved and marries him to a woman of fallen reputation, Three Orchids, precisely because she knows she can break her. Indeed, she does; after torture, the girl takes poison and dies (248–249/419). Less surprisingly, high cadres rape women with impunity in *Land in Dreamland*, and in the final novel of the trilogy, extramarital affairs appear to be the new normal.

The women are no angels, but defects in the outwardly conventional family in China's new historical novels are more often traced to defective and oppressive fathers. This was a common theme in twentieth-century Chinese literature until the Communist revolution, which substituted the authority of the state for that of the father in literature and in life. In the post-Mao novels, most fathers are both oppressive and weak, if not absent—unable to fulfill a positive role. The mostly male novelists in this study have little to say about father-daughter relations. Lu Xiumi seems belatedly inspired by her father's idealism in *Bygone Beauty*, but that is after he has gone missing. Another exception is the love accorded—again, belatedly—to the former wastrel Fugui, in Yu Hua's *To Live*. Mo Yan's *Sandalwood Death* gives its daughter figure a strong voice, to express a forbidden love as well as an old-fashioned sense of filial piety toward her father (in the "old society" of 1900) after he kills German railway technicians in Shandong and is sentenced to a five-day lingering death by full-body impalement. The father has not been such a boon to the daughter. After being impaled and displayed aloft on a cross, he becomes a "saint" and an embodiment of the pathos of the local operatic view of life, since he once led an opera troupe. He dies for a déclassé folk ethos that transcends all family relations.

It is father-son relations that epitomize the perceived prison of the Chinese family. We need not reiterate the indecencies of the scheming and lecherous fathers in Su Tong's *Nineteen Thirty-Four Escapes*, *Opium Family*, and *Rice*. Among the many protagonists who grow up without a father: Commander Yu Zhan'ao; the young monarch Duanbai (fatherless from age fourteen, at which time he goes mad with power until he becomes a pauper and a wanderer); the Communist leader Li Naizhi; Dongliang's father, Ku Wenxuan, and the abandoned girl Huixian, who loses her mother, too; Mo Yan's Jintong, who is fixated on his mother's breast; "Fat," a major character in *September's Fable*; and in Ge Fei's trilogy, Magistrate Tan and his son, wife, mother, and Tan's unrecognized true love, Yao Peipei. The (step-)brothers in Yu Hua's novel of that name are soon fatherless, left to be raised by their mother, and neither boy is a credit to his ancestral line. Zhang Wei lets the Sui brothers of *The Ancient Ship* fight it out after the premature death of their father.

Fathers are notable for their absence in *The Song of Everlasting Sorrow*; one could analyze Wang Qiyao's story as a search for a strong substitute father figure. "Fathers of girls like Wang Qiyao always end up beaten into submission after years of being henpecked by their wives. This sets an example for Wang Qiyao of what it means to respect a woman" (20/23). A model of successful fathering among the new historical novels' orphans is Lan Lian, China's last independent farmer in *Life and Death Are Wearing Me Out*. He is a strong enough parent to keep his son at his side and stay out of the collective farm, but inevitably pressure mounts, the family splits, and the loyal son must draw a line against his father and abandon him for the collective. Yu Hua, more given to positive representations of fatherhood, creates a sometime blood seller, Xu Sanguan who, like Fugui in *To Live*, gains a human side as a family man, though only later in life. Before his reformation, he brings much gratuitous misery and shame to his son after he begins to believe rumors that the son's biological father was another man. Song Fanping in Yu Hua's *Brothers* is another strong, even heroic, father figure, rare in the new historical literature. He is persecuted and killed in the Cultural Revolution. Most unsettling of all is the belatedly positive father-son relationship in Mo Yan's *Sandalwood Death*, which represents a transmission of blood and culture that is strengthened by the commission of a historical crime. Xiao Jia, a slow-witted butcher and husband of the beautiful Sun Meiniang, considers himself an orphan until his father, Zhao Jia, arrives from Beijing to take up residence with him. Zhao is a famous retired executioner and torturer, commissioned to do away with Meiniang's father, a killer of Germans, in a way that will be long remembered. As the father oversees the gruesome task, letting the son do the actual reaming so that he may be apprenticed to the old society's terrible "art," the son at one point doubts the blood relation and wonders whether the father is a human, an animal, or a specter (403/347). However, most of the son's spoken lines, in the mock-operatic testimony that fills out the last third of the novel, are so fulsome in their praise of his controversial father, whom he accepts as a perfect role model, that they turn pathetically ironic. Meanwhile, the local magistrate sees the execution as an omen that the dynasty (the Qing, and symbolically the current regime, which authorized the 1989 massacre[31]) will soon end. There appears to be a sort of ironic Christian imagery as the folk celebrate their common, native culture below the cross, in defiance of the Qing-German alliance in Shandong. Xiao Jia almost loses faith in his father while carrying out his duty. The crucified Sun Bing is the *true*, universal Father, of Meiniang and of local opera. The entire morass of betrayal is internecine: senior and junior executioners, the executed and his wife, and her godfather the magistrate who fathered her unborn son, are all one family.

Yu Hua's early novel *Cries in the Drizzle* is such an extreme embodiment of "ordinary" Chinese family life as dystopia that the cruelty and neglect of the father for his children comes to suggest a general deterioration of human feelings. Narrator Sun Guanglin's foundational memory is of being abandoned by his family and sent to live with others, for no reason he ever understood. By the time he is in school, "it was almost unthinkable [he says] that I would receive any affection from my family" (83–84/87). The whole village sees him as a spectator of what goes on in his family, "operating outside the family circle" (33/37). Once his little brother bears false witness against him and his father thrashes Guanglin to within an inch of his life, with the village children looking on and his brothers maintaining "order," Guanglin keeps "a record of every beating I suffered at the hands of my father and big brother" (9/11). Guanglin's father is just as cruel to his own elderly father (164–165/172). Guanglin's young friends Su Yu, Guoqing, and Lulu, too, are emotionally or even physically abandoned by their fathers.[32]

The narrator, Guanglin, indicates his lack of respect for his father without ever having to state it, dispassionately telling of the latter's affair with a widow and then with his elder son's wife. Both sons nurse a grievance against their weak but bullying father. The family of Guanglin's boyhood is too "rent with divisions" even to prepare for New Year's celebrations. The narrator is himself so cynical that he cannot attribute an ounce of altruism to his deceased younger brother, who died trying to save another child from drowning. "My little brother had not reached a level of such lofty virtue as to be willing to exchange his own life for someone else's. It was his authority over the other boy that prompted his action" (32/35–36). This, however, suggests that Yu Hua is really talking about the Chinese state. All family relations appear to be power relations, mirroring society as a whole. As to the ungrateful boy who was saved, in time he becomes "unconvinced that the accident had ever occurred, as though the story was all cock-and-bull" (33/36; cf. the forgetting of the massacre of banana workers in *One Hundred Years of Solitude*). After the family and village community disintegrate in the early chapters of *Cries in the Drizzle*, the madness of Maoist politics moves in and continues the process of societal destruction.

The most complicated, if not really nuanced, portrait of father-son conflict and love-hate ambivalence is in Su Tong's *The Boat to Redemption*. It repeats the aforementioned theme, in *Cries in the Drizzle* and *The Song of Everlasting Sorrow*, of post-1949 citizens' seeking to inherit the political glory and high social status of relatives and ancestors who were great revolutionaries in history. Such fixations are yet another diminution of actual class identity as a force shaping posterity. In Su Tong's work, the father, Ku Wenxuan, was once celebrated throughout the town because his mother was a revolutionary martyr. He won official appointment on that basis, but when his connection to the martyr is denied in a rewriting of history, Ku Wenxuan becomes an outcast, and so do his wife and son, Dongliang, by association. Conversely, actually inheriting social status leads to the temptations of indolence and decadence—as is the case of the social parasite Sasha in *The Song of Everlasting Sorrow* and perhaps Ku Wenxuan himself, in his earlier, glory days as an official.

Ku Dongliang is ashamed of his father and even hates him: "The second half of [Ku Wenxuan's] life was like a rubbish heap, with no place to hide beyond the river and the barge," he feels (32).[33] The wife divorces Wenxuan, but only slowly, because she "wanted to make him suffer" (30/40). A social climber who made a good escape from her natal family in the first place to get free of its bad class standing, she treats her husband and son sadistically just to see the effect; she is "crestfallen over the docility of her husband" when he takes her punishments without objecting (31/41–42). He is another inadequate male—by action and by his historically revised, purely socially constructed political "bloodlines."

The son elects to stay with the father—whether because of feelings of inadequacy on his own part or his mother's self-centeredness and attitude of superiority—and yet father-son relations turn very sour. The father treats Dongliang like a "chunk of coal" and forces him off the barge at the age of fifteen (52–53/69–70). Onshore, Dongliang feels like an "exile" even from his subaltern status as a boat person already exiled from shore. Later, his father, in a fit of madness and guilt, mutilates his own penis by half cutting it off, thereby redoubling his humiliation and social isolation. Yet, paradoxically, this increases the self-abasing adolescent's identification with his father, for "my father's enemy was my enemy"; the forces inimical to his young adult status come to displace his childhood "enemies" (112). Dongliang's hatred of his mother and himself increases as he grows up, and so does the shame that comes from his obsession with a girl he grew up with on the boats—Huixian, a pursuit that "constituted the greatest betrayal of my father's wishes" (343). That is, however, nothing compared to the accumulating hatred and shame he communicates to his father: "You shame me by showing your face" (135/201). Dongliang feels a need to "escape Father's watchful eye," for his father puts him under surveillance (169–171/250–252). This heightens implications that the father might serve as an allegory of the state or the Communist Party. When Dongliang screams at his father, the boat people observe that he is "rebelling" (247/401); in one edition of the book, he himself loudly proclaims the unthinkable: "I'm rebelling! . . . I'm rebelling!" (402). Yet he also knows he has to "save father" (360). He does after all choose to serve his father rather than his mother (but then, she would never have him—if only because she lives onshore, and the shore would not have the boy). In the end, his father offers him his freedom (418), and Dongliang, after eleven years on the barges, finally "luxuriate[s] in the loving care of his father" (286/463). The Boat to Redemption does in the end offer a tale of partial reconciliation, but it is unclear if the hero has in fact been redeemed.

Another problematic relationship commonly portrayed in the new historical novels is that between brothers. The male novelists and Wang Anyi speak little of sisterhood, except for Mo Yan in Big Breasts and Wide Hips, in which the elder sisters, the first in particular, care for their younger sisters; the latter then conspire with the eldest to help her elope when Mother tries to force her into a bad marriage (1:99/117). As to brother-sister relations, the narrator, Jintong, recalls, unremorsefully, how as a baby he completely "stripped" his blind twin sister of her "right to nurse" (1:88/107). Rice Boy purposely buries his little sister, Little Bowl, alive in a giant pile of rice, in Su Tong's Rice

Confucian brotherhood is involuntary, and it is not in principle egalitarian, like the hopeful kinds of relationships discussed in the next section. In the Confucian family, the younger brother owes obedience to the elder. But in the worlds conjured up by the new historical novelists, the problem between brothers is not so much one of authority as one of rivalry, typically over a claim to property—no son inherits the traditional, but now much weakened ritual role of the father. These rivalries, which existed in the traditional family system, intensify as the market economy returns to China post-Mao; they may perhaps be seen as symbolic criticisms of post-Mao neo-capitalist relations.

Relations between brothers are unrelievedly dismal in Su Tong's works. The brothers Rice Boy and Kindling Boy have to flip a coin to see who will have to take on the burden of accompanying their father home to die. Liu Laoxia, the evil landlord of Opium Family, takes advantage of his brother Laoxin's philandering to repossess all his land; the latter takes comfort in mutual commiseration with the family idiot of the next generation, who for his part is stabbed to death by his own half brother, Chencao. Ge Fei's Tan Duanwu is of no help to, and seems to envy, his more inventive and idealistic, but "mad" half brother, Wang Yuanqing, who is ill-suited for the twenty-first century. The brothers Sui Baopu and Sui Jiansu of Zhang Wei's *The Ancient Ship* struggle over their competing visions of how to acquire and run the town's remaining glass noodle factory, splitting their "clan" even as it struggles to preserve itself from the Zhaos. At the end, Jiansu declares, regretfully, "I realized that my real foe wasn't Zhao Duoduo but you! You, my own brother! . . . You see, my brother, I lost my way and actually collaborated with the Zhao clan to fight you" (338/416). The middle son and narrator of *Cries in the Drizzle* has a miserable relationship with his brothers during childhood years. And much of the drama in *Life and Death Are Wearing Me Out* revolves around conflicts and rivalry between the all-too-clever Ximen Jinlong (who changes his name to Lan Jinlong), born of Ximen Nao's concubine Yingchun, and Lan Jiefang, son of the same mother, but whose father is Lan Lian. It is, ironically, the former hired hand Lan Lian and his son who are politically threatened by class struggle, simply because their family is not in power. Lan Lian's former *employment* by his old boss, Ximen Nao, is held against him, even if Lan Lian was theoretically the one exploited, and so is his post–land reform marriage to Ximen's former concubine. The rivalry of the brothers thus has a pseudo class-struggle aspect.

The landmark portrait of relations between brothers is Yu Hua's mammoth and bawdy novel of that title: *Brothers*. In the first volume, Song Gang is about eight and his stepbrother, Baldy Li, is a year younger and a head shorter. The stepbrothers are inseparable and bullied together, for apolitical reasons, before having to fend for themselves and suffer hardships of a more political nature during the Cultural Revolution. Its daily tortures and persecutions of the older generation finally kill off their father, Song Fanping, and fully demoralize their mother, Li Lan.

Song Gang is the quintessential "giver" in the brotherly relationship and Baldy Li the "taker," also given to misadventures with sexual overtones. The brothers appear to be on their own, without much parental supervision. They are successively thrown together, separated (Baldy Li goes to live in the countryside for years), and thrown together again in their old home of "Liu City," in a repeating pattern. On her deathbed in the mid-1970s, Li Lan makes her stepson Song Gang "promise to look after Baldy Li" (2:70/274). This injunction does not seem to come from the Confucian view that Song is the elder brother or from partiality on Li Lan's part because Baldy is her natural son. She loves both boys and asks that neither seek advantage over the other: "If there is one bowl of rice left, the two of you should split it; and if there's one shirt left, you should take turns wearing it" (1:242/206). This is not just familial sharing, but also, in a nutshell, socialism, suggesting a reading of volume 1 as an allegory of socialism. Li Lan's request to her stepson seems an acknowledgment that Baldy Li is after all the morally weaker and more erratic of the two—the one who may need to be forgiven: "Song Gang, promise me that, no matter what Baldy Li might do, you will take care of him" (1:243/206). Indeed, her request that the brothers share everything can be seen as a parental correction of Song Gang's altruistic promise to give *Baldy Li* his last bowl of rice, "and if I have just one shirt left, I'll give it to him" (1:243/206). Li Lan realizes that her birth son is a budding man on the make, unlike Song Gang, who is capable, morally upright, conservative, and a lover of book learning like his deceased father. Song's role as giver and Baldy's as taker endanger the former and threaten the moral compass of the latter.

Farcical subplots take off in volume 2, tragic only in their impact on the relationship between the two brothers and their implicit commentary on post-Mao, marketized China. Baldy Li manipulates Song Gang into becoming Baldy's surrogate suitor, or really stalker, of an unwilling beauty. After this proxy courtship fails, the brothers part ways over the woman, Lin Hong, whom they both love; Song finally marries her and they settle down to a re-spectable life of working in socialist factories. Baldy Li gets a vasectomy and leaves in a huff. He begins his career as an entrepreneur in increasingly unlikely and outrageous businesses and schemes, culminating in a National Hymen Olympics to pick the most beautiful virgin, partly to satisfy his own promiscu-ous urges and also to make a fortune in hymen reconstructive surgery, which confers on women the benefit of eternal return to virginity. As the plot reaches new heights of absurdity and hilarity, and also descends at times into bathos, even the stalwart Song Gang, ill-suited to the *new* New China, is desperate enough to become a sex-aid salesman, peddling breast-enhancement creams after getting breast implants himself to prove that even gender is no obstacle to growing D cups. Subplots depict still other snake oil salesmen and person-alities whose lives appear silly or meaningless once they acquire wealth. De-spite his good sense of the market, some of Baldy Li's entrepreneurial schemes do fail. When that happens, Song Gang saves his stepbrother from hunger by giving him his state-conferred grain ration coupons. Lin Hong simply cannot force the brothers apart. Moreover, Song Gang has ruined his back and lungs through good old-fashioned socialist factory work, even as society has begun to slough off his type. Baldy Li secretly gives Lin Hong money for his brother's medical treatment, a reciprocal turn. Yet, in the end, he steals Lin Hong during Song's absences from home to have orgies of sex with her, and she likes it. The self-abnegating Song Gang, true to form, acquiesces in this outcome and clears the way for the couple by committing suicide. The relationship between the brothers is perpetually symbiotic and mutually self-destructive. Both Maoist socialism and post-Mao "capitalism" have created dystopian societies that betray the ideals they claim to uphold, and they destroy morality, however conceived. Maoism is cruel, bullying, and yet weak in the knees; market society is corrupting and addicting. Both forms of utopia are unmasked, and with them, their motivations.

And the family, in Mao-era and post-Mao times? In the Mao years in this novel it appears to flourish in ways overlooked by the theorists of totalitarianism who speak of the state's wholly replacing the family. But the family cannot protect its members from the madness of Maoism. (The death of Mao, which occurs between volumes 1 and 2, goes unnoticed.) In the years after Mao's death, sustenance and survival are not so chancy, but family values can provide only a sense of guilt, for family solidarity has ruptured and family loyalties have been betrayed. The result is ruin (Song Gang commits suicide), degradation (Lin Hong becomes the madam of a bordello), and a desperate need to escape prosperity (the fantastically rich Baldy Li buys a trip into space). The family in Yu Hua's novel, like that in Ge Fei's trilogy, is no longer stifling, but that is the case only because it has disintegrated, under two different and adversarial social systems. Maoism leads to suicide for the old working class. Ge Fei's dystopian vision shows the leaders to be equally at risk.

RAYS OF HOPE: FRIENDS AND COLLABORATORS

The heroic protagonists in classic Slavic and Anglophone dystopian novels do not struggle alone. They remain social beings seeking allies and associates of their choice. Narrating *The Handmaid's Tale*, Offred observes of her closed and suffocatingly misogynist theocratic world: "There can be alliances even in such places, even under such circumstances. This is something you can depend upon: there will always be alliances, of one kind or another" (129). In or out of a totalitarian context, that sounds like an axiom of Chinese politics. Closest to the figurations of D-503's attempts to escape dystopia with I-330, Winston Smith with Julia, Offred with Nick, and Guy Montag in memory of Clarisse, is Yao Peipei's dream of escaping to a little island hidden from the rest of the world, where she might live out her life free of worldly cares. She dares Magistrate Tan to come with her if they should ever encounter peril. Peipei does encounter peril and she does flee; and Tan tries to meet up with her. But it is too late. Peipei's escape has taken her right back to Puji, and Tan Gongda has never fully realized the danger he is in, or even that he lives not in a playground for building utopias but in a real-world dystopia—partly of his own construction.

The protagonists of China's new historical novels do not, like the heroes of numerous other Chinese novels from the red classics to contemporary anti-corruption novels, seek to create new blocs, collectives, or revolution; those concepts are evidently anathema to this generation of writers. But friendships and alliances do appear. As in the Western dystopian classics, the Chinese alliances are voluntary, often heterosexual, not familial, and not based on *guanxi*, or "relations": natural or fabricated ties of blood, history, or organization. Having a friend or ally is also different from having a "backer," a protector in the bureaucratic or family hierarchy. Backers have their own ups and downs, a lesson learned by the orphan boat girl Huixian in Su Tong's *The Boat to Redemption* and by Lotus, who seeks friendship among more senior concubines in *Wives and Concubines*. (The master is the only backer who counts.) Forming an alliance or just a friendship is itself a measure of self-assertion against oppression. One does not, in these modern novels, define oneself just by playing one's role in the family and other social hierarchies. Forming alliances outside the family can even rival the comforts and protections that are commonly attributed to the problematic solidarity of family.

Zhang Wei's *September Fable* is particularly strong in showing the formation of group loyalties outside the mainstream and, paradoxically, within or beyond the village, which is jealous of outside loyalties. The outside loyalties are possible because they are largely unknown to the village as a whole. The young people make their own word (as if they were peaceful Red Guards) and thus resist the confinements of both the adults and the larger society that isolates the village and all villagers, keeping them in their place. The young people run wild at night while the elders are asleep, and two young women form romantic relationships with nearby, intruding engineers who come from a different world. The adult character Old Turtle reveals a paradigmatic situation in his tale of how he left the village to track down his missing common-law wife. Reduced to begging along the road, he came upon a band of beggars and was allowed to join them. "For the first time he felt the pride of belonging to a group" (220/371). That is, a group he chose to join.

Yu Hua pays particular attention to friendships outside the family, such as Fugui's brief comradeship in adversity with two soldiers during the civil war days and Xu Sanguan's friendship with fellow blood sellers, who help him adjust to the dreary society in which they all live. *Brothers*, by contrast, depicts few friendships in the years the stepbrothers are growing up, particularly during the Cultural Revolution, an age of bullying. Voluntary association awaits the post-Mao years, when Baldy Li gathers a circle of investors, made up of petty tradesmen, not ordinary factory workers. It is Yu Hua's early novel, *Cries in the Drizzle*, that pointedly focuses on friendship, but not adult or true friendship. The hero Sun Guanglin reflects that he tried to attach himself to one Su Hang "to put on a show and try to look cool" (81/84). After being rebuffed, Sun, who by then was already the black sheep of his family, "no longer [claimed] to have lots of friends; I returned instead to solitude and began an independent life as the true me" (81/85). Guanglin forms a more sincere friendship with Su Hang's younger brother, Su Yu. Appropriately, he feels sympathy for the boy when he is sentenced to a year of reform-through-labor for incautiously putting his arm around a girl. Sun is duly punished for his sympathy for this ostracized boy; he has to write a self-criticism. In this gloomy novel, a misunderstanding breaks up that friendship anyway, after Su is released from the penal camp. Sun then befriends another loner and unfortunate, a younger child named Lulu, but his mother is likewise sent away to reform-through-labor. *Cries in the Drizzle* gives some examples of friendship, but without any hope that they might contribute to resistance of bullying, snobbery, or power. Friendships are, on the other hand, potentially more fulfilling than the ascribed relationships within an unforgiving and inescapable family.

Li Rui's *Silver City* paints touching pictures of traditional quasi-familial relationships, as between the great family patriarch Li Naijing and his faithful adviser Zhao Pu'an, and an idyllic, "bourgeois" modern student relationship between two liberated young women who room together before the war and civil war, Bai Qiuyun and Li Ziyun. Their voluntary friendship ends even before they end up on opposite sides of the Communist revolution, for Li Ziyun sacrifices her individual happiness to protect the Li clan by marrying the local warlord. *Silver City* is one of the few novels to straightforwardly relate, however briefly, some of the social dynamics of revolutionary uprisings. Most of the partisans in the local uprisings join because of charismatic movement leaders; that goes not just for the poor peasants but also for Li Naizhi, the future Communist official and husband of Bai Qiuyun. The example of a radical teacher inspires him to enter the movement. Joining any of Silver

City's many uprisings, Communist or pre-Communist, always turns out to be a trap, leading to mass killings and still more cycles of revenge and counterviolence.

These political associations are voluntary, not determined by blood relationships or necessarily even economic or political "interests." Those most lacking in blood relations, the orphans, become emblems of a benevolent society that might have been but never was. The fortune of the great Li clan of Silver City comes from Li Naizhi's great-grandfather's having saved an abandoned child left at a ferry landing, who went on to pass the imperial examinations and become an official. Ximen Nao of *Life and Death Are Wearing Me Out* rescued the orphan Lan Lian, who became his hired hand and later his protector and an exemplar of political incorrectness as an uncollectivized farmer—without any of his own allies. Half sensing that his donkey and then his ox are reincarnations of his old boss, Lan Lian returns their favors. The raising of an orphan is not just an act of charity outside the requirements of the traditional or modern family system; it is an act of social wisdom. Ku Wenxuan and his father's assistance to the orphan girl Huixian might have had a good outcome, if only the Kus had not been so flawed in their other social proclivities.

At the extreme, in *Tattoo*, young people seek their own identity and escape from a bleak society by joining gangs. *My Life as Emperor*, also by Su Tong, is another tale, picaresque, of generally happy escapades furthered by the voluntary association of an ex-emperor and his servant. The basis of this relationship is the reduction of the ex-emperor to a status of equality with all men. He and a former servant travel the country and survive many hazards because of their mutual loyalty. In *Opium Family*, the idiot Yanyi and his uncle Liu Laoxin, though related, form another odd alliance because both have been betrayed by the patriarch, Liu Laoxia, Laoxin's brother. Both suffer a premature death. Su Tong's most intimate examination of alliance building is in *Wives and Concubines*. The confining and suffocating authoritarian family in this novella comes closest to approximating the stifling sense of total control of the individual (individual women, that is) that one sees in the older Western dystopian novels. Lotus, the educated fourth wife, forms an alliance with the third wife after rejecting a falsely proffered alliance with the second one, once it becomes evident that the second wife and her minions, including a servant, are plotting against the third and fourth. Escape in this case is impossible. The result is death for the third wife and insanity for the fourth; Lotus imagines a relationship with a son of the master, and the third wife actually has adulterous relations, but these liberties hasten their respective downfalls.

Wang Anyi's *The Song of Everlasting Sorrow* offers perhaps the most positive affirmation of the power of determining one's own friends and relationships—so positive that her heroine Wang Qiyao's insulation from political harm strains credulity. Her case remains tragic and her existence and milieu broadly dystopian, but her downfall is due to random factors involving evils of human nature, not the political superstructure. As a young woman just after the Sino-Japanese War, Wang Qiyao chooses a new family when she leaves home and takes up residence with her rich friend, Jiang Lili. Thereafter she maps out her own life, even when living as the kept woman of a Nationalist official, and more positively, when she puts together her own circle of friends, a quartet of mah-jongg players in the Mao era. Later she becomes the center of "salons" in post-Mao times. The "gossip" that *The Song of Everlasting Sorrow* expatiates upon at the beginning of the work in an almost exultant tone (7–11/8–13) is not always positive or empowering, but it is reimagined by Wang Anyi as a female activity possessing an inchoate power, subversive of the masculine world of politics, commerce, and current affairs. Wang Anyi's idea of gossip is like a Chinese echo of the information and rumor network among the oppressed females in *The Handmaid's Tale* that Offred comments on. If only momentarily, the Shanghai gossipers form an alliance outside of mainstream society. And yet, although the young maidens of prerevolutionary Shanghai may see themselves as privileged rather than confined, their world of *longtang* and trips outside to the movies is constricted. A possible way out is to become a model and a movie star, but Wang Qiyao does not quite make it; still less, the plainer girls.

China's new historical novels as a whole do not enter the postindustrial totalitarian worlds of the classic Slavic and Anglophone writers, or yet the pervasively magical and existentially arbitrary world of Latin American and Caribbean writers who see dystopia in peculiarities of their cultural, national, or postcolonial history. The family, and sometimes even the village that Chinese film adaptations have re-created with such poignant cinematography, is the unforgiving taskmaster of individuals and degrader of the humanity of both oppressor and oppressed. Dystopia is something the hero must try to escape, acquiring allies along the way as much as society allows—outside both the family and the state. The hero, however, even if an intellectual, seldom sees himself or herself as a former auxiliary of Big Brother—a participant in now discredited revolutionary actions.

5 ANARCHY

Social, Moral, and Cosmic

M ORAL AND SOCIAL ANARCHY, as in *Lord of the Flies*, Cormac McCarthy's *The Road* (2006), and post-apocalypse films like *Mad Max* and *The Book of Eli*, is a condition ostensibly opposite to totalitarianism, although both dystopian visions are filled with conflict, terror, and tyranny, which can flourish at the grassroots level when there is no larger governing force. Stories of local tyrannies amid nationwide anarchy are legion in China's ancient and modern historical record. Mayhem was employed by Big Brother himself in the Kristallnacht and China's Cultural Revolution, fueled by propaganda and rituals like *Nineteen Eighty-Four's* Two Minutes Hate. Local tyrannies in China hardly disappeared after 1949 and have flourished again in recent times, spawning local riots. Curiously absent from novels that depict the Mao era, in light of or perhaps because of China's current rising prosperity—in the cities—is the specter of mass poverty that often accompanies both totalitarian and anarchistic versions of dystopia.

Despite their evident ambivalence about social control, and thus about Confucian and Communist ideals with their respective utopias of collective harmony and collective class struggle, China's new historical novels appear to fear raw social chaos above all. In Chinese, *luan*, or chaos, generally signifies disorder, turmoil, confusion, arbitrariness, and other invariably undesirable conditions. Liberation from tyranny in the Confucian family (under the father, who may yet be deplorably weak) or Maoist commune may still leave one helpless. Even the hapless Ku Dongliang of *The Boat to Redemption* is enjoined, by another young person, to serve his father "no matter what you think of him. . . . People have only one father and one mother, and when they're gone, they're gone" (254/411). Surrounded by manifestations of chaos in modern history, one might well yearn for peace, unity, and harmony. But a Legalist or statist imposition of order by fiat and strict discipline, even if dressed up in more benevolent and modern garb than its original formulations two millennia ago, appears to China's new novelists to be unachievable or unsustainable. Their works often depict an absolute dearth of social peace; a lack of any center in leadership, political geography, or morality and ideology; and, in the end, a Hobbesian or pan-species "Darwinian" struggle of all against all. "Magical" interludes are of little comfort. In the Chinese new historical novel, magical realism can even accentuate social chaos.

Eternal Dearth of Social Peace

Mass violence appears endemic in China's new historical novels. In wartime, even the armies are disorganized and lack a higher cause. The pre-1949 native armed forces that wreak havoc in *Red Sorghum*, *Silver City*, and *A Dictionary of Maqiao* are short-lived and operate in a sub-warlord or "bandit" (*tufei*; highwayman) mode. In *Red Sorghum* (in the author's preferred edition), hints of the fighting forces' ideological affiliation as Nationalist or Communist are visible only through differences in the forces' motivation, appeals to locals, and formality of command structure, weapons, and uniforms. Armed forces, including those of the Communists, are quite willing to betray a temporary native ally just to acquire a weapons cache, even in the midst of war against the larger enemy, Japan. Writes one critic, "The portrait that emerges is of a society living on the precipice of anarchy. With no organized central government, every village has been left to fend for itself."[1] The victorious battle in the first chapter is countered in the fourth by a terrible defeat on the day of Grandma's funeral, a marker of Granddad's hubris, "yet another of his great mistakes" (407/297). The four-sided war leads to serial massacres of the innocent. Chaos becomes a force of nature untamed by human will and abetted by collective fanaticism, like that of the Iron Society, a gang of freebooters that Granddad is persuaded to join and lead. The surviving pro-Nationalist soldiers, cold and hungry, of necessity dress in dog skins. The locals call them dog soldiers, recalling the canine struggle to the death described in a previous chapter of the novel.

Japanese, Nationalist (KMT or Kuomintang; Guomindang), and Communist (CCP) armies are particularly undifferentiated in the barren wasteland of suffering, starvation, and refugees lacking refuge that Mo Yan describes in

Big Breasts and Wide Hips. The same sense of political dislocation characterizes Yu Hua's depiction of the KMT-CCP civil war in *To Live*, in which Fugui is involuntarily caught up through impressment into the KMT army. In Su Tong's *Opium Family*, a whole community that plants opium is outside the law. Gangs rule the streets in *Rice* and *Tattoo*, absent any kind of central authority.

To present the pre-1949 era as a time of armed conflict, with many of the combatants of uncertain loyalty and fighting only for personal gain, is realistic. But it is the new historical novelists' choice to take China's chaotic Republican era as the foundational and even representative period of modern Chinese history, and within that period, to select the most chaotic times and places of the Republican experiment—for instance, "1934"—*as* Su Tong reimagines it. The novelists might have begun in an earlier era, such as the "declining" but still unified days of the late Qing, when most historians feel modern Chinese history began. Like the textbooks, the novelists might have begun after 1840, so as to make Western imperialism the motive force of modern Chinese history. Or they might have started a century or more earlier with the reigns of the great Qing emperors that fascinate audiences of Chinese television serials: costume dramas about a time when Chinese power truly was great. The later films of Zhang Yimou, such as *Hero*, and Chen Kaige's *The Emperor and the Assassin*, depict the founding of the Chinese empire two millennia ago amid settings of splendid luxury. Li Rui's and Han Shaogong's novels cite Qing and earlier history, but not the standard conditions of imperial rule—rather, the rebellions and civil disorders. These are not the allegedly proto-socialist "peasant rebellions" previously sanctified in official Communist Party history, such as the Taiping Rebellion (a baseline in, for instance, Mao Dun's story "Spring Silkworms"). *Silver City* instead cites the reign of terror of Zhang Xianzhong as the precedent for twentieth-century violence; *A Dictionary of Maqiao* invents a fanatical Lotus Flower Rebellion of the 1890s. As local historian, the Maqiao narrator cites (fictitious) book references, stressing that the locals have no memory of it. Zhang Wei's *The Ancient Ship* mentions Wali's glorious past only briefly at the outset, to set the stage for its decline in the next several hundred pages. Even Su Tong's imaginative *My Life as Emperor*, situated in imperial times, depicts a chaotic world of assassinations, palace intrigue, and a young emperor's flight from responsibility as his empire disintegrates amid civil war. That the named dynasty of the action never existed in life furthers one's impression that the novel is a commentary on modern times.

Of special interest, then, is the new historical novels' nonpartisanship and reluctance to make too much of the transition from the "old society" to Mao Zedong's "New China." *Big Breasts and Wide Hips* marks the transition simply by going from volume 1 to volume 2 (in the original Chinese edition). The final pre-Liberation chapter features a desperate retreat by Mother and her starving family amid artillery fire. The year is noted: 1948 (1:344/320). The next chapter (2:347/321) proceeds to a panoramic account of a Snow Festival, necessarily attended mostly by widows and orphans, without any mention of the recent and momentous change of regime. *Brothers* marks the transition from classically dystopian Maoist times to post-Mao times similarly, with a change of volume and no attention to the political change. *Chronicle of a Blood Merchant* also passes from the prerevolutionary to the revolutionary society without segue. *Silver City* begins with a flash-forward to 1951 executions, but the subsequent narrative skips directly from 1946 to 1964, eliding the "Golden Years" of Communism. Revisionist history in the contemporary academy points out that there were indeed continuities among all three twentieth-century eras—pre-Mao, Maoist, and post-Mao—and revivals of old customs in the post-Mao years. But the novels leave the surprising impression that China, even after it reunited in 1949 and "stood up" by ousting the imperialist presence, remained a place of chaos and dystopian cacophony. One can read novels set in the Republican era, such as *Red Sorghum*, as allegories of post-1949 oppression under Communism. This is a historical revision as profound as the frequent reversal of "good" and "bad" actors among the various political "sides." Little attention is paid to the establishment of new institutions, except in name (such as the people's communes—but Lan Lian manages to stay outside them). As chapter 4 noted, even the Communist Party and the People's Liberation Army are seldom depicted, except insofar as they are represented by particular, usually minor, characters.

The focus on nonpartisan and even jubilant violence begins with *Red Sorghum*, whose war story unfolds in a context that is as much legendary as historical. The famous torture episode of Uncle Arhat being skinned alive by Sun Five on the orders of a Japanese commander (a major scene in Zhang Yimou's movie) is spectacular and heroic in its excess: "Sun Five no longer seemed human as his flawless knifework produced a perfect pelt." What is left of Uncle Arhat's corpse disappears, or so it was told "from this generation to the next, until it became a beautiful legend" (46/37). Horrible and nauseating violence, variously perpetrated by Japanese invaders and narcissistic armed marauders, becomes fascinating and even spellbindingly gorgeous, thanks to Mo

Yan's surrealistic descriptive talents. The narrator portrays history with the eyes of an aesthetician rather than as a real character raised after 1949. They are the eyes of the old society, able to take on the point of view of his ancestors, who could have had little notion of the future historical significance of their acts. That the narrator sometimes questions versions of events that have been passed down to him in no way marks him as an oral historian with the particular outlook of the Mao or post-Mao era.

Mo Yan narrates *Big Breasts and Wide Hips* with the same degree of morally nonjudgmental and nonpartisan wonder. ("All the Japanese—or maybe it was the Chinese—had left for us was a half cellar of sugar beets that had already begun to sprout" [1:127/141]). The Mao era in this novel has its own fearful political campaigns, divisive family accusations, and diverse kinds of misery that descend upon the family as history goes on as anarchically as ever. The post-Mao days are no happier or more harmonious. The specter of ferocious attacking dogs, notorious in *Red Sorghum*, enters this novel too at the end. The main protagonist, Jintong, by the 1980s a survivor of years of imprisonment, escapes being torn apart only because a wayward calf presents the dogs with an easier target. The class struggle of humans is joined, in *Life and Death Are Wearing Me Out*, by power struggles and outright warfare among animal comrades and enemies of the reincarnated hero in his successive animal bodies.

In *Big Breasts and Wide Hips*, emblems of the years of social and historical divisiveness come flooding back in 1993 as Jintong curses his wife using epithets that are out of context in post-Mao times and out of temporal sync with one another:

> you counterrevolutionary, you enemy of the people, you bloodsucking insect, you damned rightist, capitalist-roader, reactionary capitalist, degenerate, class outsider, parasite, petty scoundrel tied to the post of historical disgrace, bandit, turncoat, hooligan, rogue, concealed class enemy of the people, royalist, filial daughter and virtuous granddaughter of old man Confucius, feudalism apologist, advocate for the restoration of the slave system, spokeswoman for the declining landlord class. . . . Only one will be left standing. When two armies clash, victory goes to the most heroic! (2:641/524–525)

Class conflict in *The Ancient Ship*, with its complicated, fragmented plot, reduces political differences to subtle clan warfare in the narrative's vaguely post-Mao present, but these splits are reiterations or reprisals of armed class struggle that occurred in the late 1940s. The watersheds between pre-Mao, Maoist, and post-Mao eras are in the end erased in an unending parade of social conflict. It is in the post-Mao era that the Sui heroes' family itself splits, as do the inseparable eponymous heroes in *Brothers*. Anarchy in Zhang Wei's later novel, *September's Fable,* is just as pervasive, despite the lack of mass kill-ings and class enemies. The "folk" are constantly fighting against outsiders and among themselves, frequently becoming maimed or disfigured in the process. The unnamed village of the novel is, more than most, seemingly im-mune to political movements from above, yet in the end it is powerless to save itself from the total destruction that serves outsiders' economic development plans. In its helpless isolation, the unnamed village represents a Marxist spec-ter of rural "idiocy." Han Shaogong's village of Maqiao seems less anarchic in the age of Communism, but its identity, in the eyes of the sent-down-youth narrator, is heavily indebted to upheavals and identity formations of the past. Maqiao must enact the class struggles declared by the outside world, but it applies meanings to them from its own, idiosyncratic culture. Local feuds need no outside political mandates·to fuel them. Maqiao has no organic soli-darity to begin with.

China's new historical novels, including even some that unfold only in the Maoist years of central control, enforced unity, and uniformity, appear to be under the spell of the past—and not a Confucian, Legalist, or imperial past, but the violence and disorder of the early twentieth century's recent past (and social conflicts from time immemorial, in *Silver City*). Any sense of social unity in the Mao era appears simply to mask deeper social divides and blood debts. Even when the ostensible subject is Republican history, one must wonder if the real subject is the Communist era, and when the ostensible subject is the revo-lutionary era, old habits of conflict from the warlord and civil war years appear beneath the surface. The post-Mao consumerist years lack the political vio-lence of the Mao era, but they raise another specter, and it is not really tradi-tional, even if it seems like a "reversion" to capitalism: the moral disorder of a disintegrated center, from which it is impossible to derive ethical value.

ABSENCE OF A CENTER: OF A LEADER, A CAPITAL, A GUIDING ETHIC

Both the Nationalist and the Communist political and military cultures em-phasized heroism, but one cannot find great national leaders in the new his-torical novels. *Silver City* is the rare work that provides an image of Mao—as a statue. Duanbai, the title figure of *My Life as Emperor*, sloughs off his inherited role of leader. His career aspiration is to become an entertainer.

Even in their confined worlds, village leaders such as Benyi, the Communist Party secretary in *A Dictionary of Maqiao*, and Loose Fang, the village head in *September's Fable*, are more like firsts among equals than oppressive dictators of local policy and ideological teaching. Among the denatured and seemingly emasculated local leaders in the new historical novels, one might add Milltown's party secretary, Zhao Chuntang, in Su Tong's *The Boat to Redemption*. Moreover, his predecessor was the uniquely defective Ku Wenxuan, father of the narrator. The party secretary in Zhang Wei's *The Ancient Ship*, of the Li clan, is a minor figure, not the power behind the scenes in the local tyranny of the Zhaos. Magistrate Tan in the middle novel of Ge Fei's trilogy is reckless and ineffectual, not tyrannical; surely he is a party member, but party membership is occluded in the novel. Mo Yan's novels of village China and Yu Hua's mysterious *Cries in the Drizzle* offer no major exceptions. Local power is diffused and non-ideological, except for fulfilling outsiders' mandates for struggle sessions in *Big Breasts and Wide Hips*, and forcing the locals to collectivize in *Life and Death Are Wearing Me Out*. In chapter 4, we noted the lack of strong father figures. Defective fathers, such as those Su Tong created in *The Boat to Redemption*, *Opium Family*, and above all *Rice*, range from the unremarkable to the utterly reprobate.

Granddad and Grandma of *Red Sorghum*, though they have heroic moments, are morally questionable. Their role modeling exists primarily in legend. Granddad not only shifts his combat and marital allies from time to time, but on more than one occasion he nearly leads his armed band into annihilation. In *Big Breasts and Wide Hips*, Mother is courageous and a survivor, but she sells one of her daughters into slavery, serves the male-centered ideal of the old society by coddling and suckling Jintong, depriving him of his own manhood, and is powerless to have a larger impact on society; like Yu Hua's character Fugui, she can only promote primitive survival. Ximen Nao of *Life and Death Are Wearing Me Out* is a natural-born leader, but in the narrative he shows his mettle best as a leader of the four-legged. Ximen's hired worker and replacement as father figure after 1949, Lan Lian, is a rugged individualist true to his own values, but ultimately he is ground down by the system. Song Fanping of Yu Hua's *Brothers* is a short-lived role model not just to his young sons but also to his fellow factory workers, yet Cultural Revolution violence sends him down to the Yellow Springs. Li Naijing survives many challenges in Li Rui's *Silver City*, and so does his adviser Zhao, but they cannot survive the revolution. Most heroes of the past come to bad ends, even after sacrificing for the greater good. They are overpowered by the social system, not by better people. Society allows the bad to come out on top. Maqiao and Wang Anyi's Shanghai simply lack heroes at all.

Leaders and role models of the past stand out because their offspring are weaker. The exception is *Red Sorghum*, in which Father is treated as a war hero, though that novel's larger message is one of historical decadence and decline. Both sons of the good father Song Fanping, biological and adopted, prove inadequate in their different ways. Jintong, like most of the males in *Big Breasts and Wide Hips*, is a peculiar and selfish human being. The daughter of Wang Qiyao and all of her generation are but shadows of their forebears. So is Qiyao's friend Sasha, the son of a revolutionary martyr.

Designated leaders, even when exercising their power and thereby ruining lives and fortunes, tend to lose control, like Ge Fei's heroes and heroines. Many in these novels are displaced by warfare and political struggles. In *Wives and Concubines/Raise the Red Lantern*, the patriarch loses control of his very concubines; he can only resort to punishment. Five Dragons, though an underworld boss, loses control of his sons—as does Ku Wenxuan in *The Boat to Redemption*. Perhaps the most remarkable loss of self-control is that of the government prosecutor, sent with full authority from the outside, who sinks into a morass of corruption and drunkenness in Mo Yan's *The Republic of Wine*.

Most dispiriting of all is the fact that the absence of a leader brings with it little or no sense of freedom and self-determination. The very promise of "liberation" is hollow under such circumstances. Those who do escape the village or the family—and usually they do so simply by surviving to a new era—do not and cannot celebrate freedom, except perhaps the young people who run wild at night in *September's Fable*. The son of Ku Wenxuan in *The Boat to Redemption* is not empowered by leaving his father. On the national scale, if the national dictator is invisible, it is difficult to rebel against him and his utopia. One has to fight a shadow, and can only turn inward. The enemy is human nature.

The sense of social and existential chaos is furthered by the lack of a geographic center: a national or provincial capital, a Party Central, even a central bureaucratic authority to which one might appeal for justice. In this respect, the Chinese new historical novels are closer to the post-apocalyptic novels and ex-utopias in the wilderness like Macondo and the atoll of *Lord of the Flies* than the worlds of the Slavic and Anglophone classics, which tend to position their heroes near the center of their evil empires. Macondo knows something of the nation beyond the mountains and swamps. Colonel Aureliano Buendía starts thirty-two civil wars out there, and his father, founder of the town, once tried to send a marvelous invention to the capital city, "though a trip to the capital was a little less than impossible at that time" (3). Rural life in Faulkner's Yoknapatawpha County unfolds with full awareness of its center in the county seat of Jefferson. The local tyranny created by the populist despot Willie Stark in Mason City and Burden's Landing leads him into the governorship in the capital of a fictitious Southern U.S. state in Robert Penn Warren's *All the King's Men*. Likewise, China's plethora of "anticorruption novels" from the turn of the millennium take place on the shop floor and in the party branches, with eyes always turned upward toward the provincial capital and Beijing. Authorities from the political heights finally save the day, as dei ex machina. In China's new historical novels, Northeast Gaomi Township, Maple Village, Wali, Maqiao, Milltown (*The Boat to Redemption*), Liu Town (*Brothers*), Puji (*Bygone Beauty*), and diverse anonymous or undifferentiated towns and villages created by Su Tong, Yu Hu, Wang Xiaobo, and Zhang Wei may be visited or invaded by armies, warlord bands, counterrevolutionary forces, Communist Party work teams carrying out land reform, Red Guards, Revolutionary Rebels, outside mining engineers come to collapse the very land beneath their feet (*September's Fable*), even sent-down youths. Nevertheless, there is little or no reference in the new historical novels to the national capital, the provincial capital, the county town (except in Ge Fei's closing volumes), or other seats of higher civilization and political-social order. This lack of grounding may be as defamiliarizing to some readers as ambiguity about the era, perhaps socially dystopian on first principles.

Mo Yan's Northeast Gaomi Township is not too far from the Shandong capital and near a railway line and highways that allow the Japanese to penetrate during the wartime era, but battles come and go without much reference to the urban centers where political power and higher culture are based.[2] A more fully integrated, even if in its own way stereotypical, view of post-Mao rural-urban relations appears in Mo Yan's novel *The Garlic Ballads* (1988; banned for a time after 1989), which portrays the mounting anger of peasants against leaders who are safely ensconced in the county seat. The peasants descend on the town and burn down the government compound. The Gaomi county town is likewise a force inimical to the passions and local "culture" of its rural environs in *Sandalwood Death*. Political distance from mere county government is realistic even in later times; this heightens the verisimilitude of Northeast Gaomi Township's insularity in Mo Yan's fiction. In *Big Breasts and Wide Hips*, when Mother and her family flee the ravages of the war, the narrator,

Jintong, recalls, "It was the first time any of us had taken the road to the county seat" (1:141/155). They are on their way to town to visit the human slavery market. Earlier in the Republic, in 1917, a County Magistrate Niu who wanted to unbind Mother's feet while she was still young was driven off by the locals (2:674–680/49–53). As China quickly modernizes in post-Mao times, many of the Shangguans, like the Lans and Ximens, are urbanized. This allows Mo Yan to paint his signature portraits of Chinese decadence in the late twentieth century. The epitome is a plan "to build a theme park around [an] ancient pagoda as a tourist attraction for Chinese and foreigners" (2:610/509). An old "feudal" festival will be revived, too; the countryside will be colonized by the city for its entertainment. But this kind of subordination is less suggestive of good order than of an absurd inversion of urban-rural relations. The cadres in *Life and Death Are Wearing Me Out* go them one better, planning a Cultural Revolution Village that brings the urban disorders of that era into a pastoral rural setting. It will also have a casino and "modern-day adult entertainment complex" (419/422).

Zhang Wei's *September's Fable* tells of an even more down-and-out Shandong village, still more cut off from civilization. Hiking to other villages is a great adventure. The home villagers generally do not allow it, and surrounding villages are hostile. Given the absence in all these novels of reference to Beijing, Shanghai, or even provincial capitals, and the occasional marvelous intrusion of new technology in at least Mo Yan's novels (as in *One Hundred Years of Solitude*), one might wonder if the driver of China's modern history is in the national capital of Nanjing or Beijing or in an outer center of global technology—the West.

Lotus, the young educated woman who becomes a rich man's fourth concubine, first appears as a modern young woman strutting through an urban locale toward her unhappy future in a walled compound during a memorably lengthy and slow-moving scene at the start of Zhang Yimou's film *Raise the Red Lantern*. In the Su Tong novella on which the film is based, however, one can deduce her urban background only from her education. When her family's tea factory went bankrupt, her father committed suicide, going "effortlessly down to the Yellow Springs of the Dead" (6/19). Just so, Lotus descends into a square box, the living hell of a family compound that is her prison. Educated outsiders, including the master's son, materialize when they please within this closed world, only to wreak emotional havoc. The urban realm, whether miles distant or just outside the gate, is a world away and offers no salvation, either physically or spiritually.

Su Tong's "Bamboo Town" in *Nineteen Thirty-Four Escapes* is located by the author "on the lower reaches" of the Yangzi River (135/111), but like Maple Village in this novella, it is as devoid of character as its evidently fictional and generic name implies. The narrator tells the story while living in a city "450 miles from our Maple Village home," presumably the city of his birth. Aware of his Maple Village ancestry, the narrator notes that he began "from the age of seventeen or eighteen" to enjoy "telling my city friends, 'I'm an outsider'" (173/177). That is the universal relationship of one place to another, whether city, village, or town: each is any other place's "Other," and that is all. A somewhat different, even more isolated "Maple Village" is the setting of *Opium Family*. The 1949 Communist revolution comes to this opium-growing "island" community from previously liberated Horsebridge, seemingly the township headquarters. The "Liberation" of Maple Village is undertaken by a work team of outsiders, headed by a Communist named Lu Fang from the county seat (12/196) who became friends there with Liu Chencao, the recognized legitimate heir of the village's landlord dynasty, whom Lu Fang will one day execute. This is credible enough; probably the two met in school, in town. But the town, like the Communist work team, is simply one more Other. Lu Fang "compared the task of his 1949 work team to dredging a sunken ship up from the bottom of the ocean; you could see the ship lying there on the bottom, but you had no way to bring it up; it was like it was growing there. And besides, all of the inhabitants of Maple Village acted just like fish, seaweed, or submerged rocks, preventing you from diving down deeply; you were caught in treacherous, complex, and ever-changing currents—you didn't know how you were going to drag the ship up" (33/232–233). The metaphor bespeaks a literally high-low relationship, but this is overshadowed by its evocation of depth and alienness—of unfathomability. If the work team offers the comforts of a centering ideology, they are not strong enough to subordinate the countryside or the bedrock culture. Su Tong's community of boat people in his longer novel *The Boat to Redemption* is clearly subordinated to its onshore town, Milltown (a place name as generic as Bamboo Town or Maple Village), but the two subcultures are autochthonous. It is the boat people who sometimes travel and learn about goings-on upstream and downstream; the shore people seem, by contrast, enisled.

Villagers in these novels think about other villages, often rival villages—or culturally equivalent places like Bamboo Town—but not about the city and its new, modern culture. The towns are similarly self-absorbed, including Liu Town (Yu Hua's *Brothers*), Wali (not the prosperous Wali of yore, but the modern

Wali, whose main interaction with the provincial capital is when the latter's museum comes to remove and mummify its "ancient ship"), and the anonymous town in Yu Hua's *Chronicle of a Blood Merchant*. In that novel, as in *Brothers*, Shanghai is simply a faraway place where people go when they are sick or to be imprisoned. As in the masterpieces by Mo Yan, the Liu Town denizens of *Brothers* become fully, if not excessively, "globalized" as the post-Mao period progresses, but the outcome only marks their moral and physical decadence. In Yu Hua's *Cries in the Drizzle*, Beijing and the nearest county town find their way into the minds and dreams of the Southgate villagers as places where officials can give them redress for their grievances (45/49), confer on them honors for their heroic suffering (38/42), or lock them up. The city never renders real blessings. In the end, Southgate's land is requisitioned by county authorities for the construction of a textile mill (19/21), just as the mythic village of *September's Fable* is destroyed by a mining project authorized from an unknown place. The narrator of *Cries in the Drizzle* is by the time of his narration living in Beijing, at university. It was his escape.

Wang Anyi's *The Song of Everlasting Sorrow*, however, is set right in Shanghai. But it is not the Shanghai of neon signs, coffee shops, bright streets, and urban slums in the prerevolutionary age, or the Shanghai of factory workers and ex-bourgeois factory owners of the New China. Nor is it the headquarters of the Cultural Revolution Group or, two decades later, the spearhead of China's post-Mao commerce. Wang Anyi has deliberately defamiliarized Shanghai, even while heightening its myth as China's premier *modern* city, dominated by "old-fashioned" row house communities. Hers is a city of enclosed neighborhoods, gossip, young ladies' bedchambers, and pigeon's-eye views of the rooftops and balconies; in revolutionary times, of hushed mah-jongg games; and in post-Mao times, fashion again, and retro chic. Shanghai as a source of production and modernity scarcely appears. The capital, whether in Nanjing or Beijing, never enters the conversation or the gossip that the reader overhears. Shanghai is a stifling, tiny stage for Wang Qiyao, her fashion, and her falling-out from fashionableness. Reversing the usual pattern of urban migration, Wang Qiyao at one point escapes Shanghai for her grandmother's village of Wu Bridge, "the kind of place that exists specifically to be a haven for those trying to escape from the chaos of the world" (123/141). She wants to avoid gossip about her pregnancy. In the end, Shanghai with its "chaos" draws her back, like a moth to the flame, to her own form of hiding from Shanghai male-defined politics and production. Chaos, in its most elemental form of crime, kills her. Shanghai, in Wang Anyi's vision, is not a capstone central city and spearhead of China's progress, but a city ruled by ungoverned neighborhoods and streets, like one of Su Tong's cities. Wang Qiyao, unlike the partly comic protagonists of *Brothers, Big Breasts and Wide Hips, Life and Death Are Wearing Me Out*, and Wang Xiaobo's 2015, understands her insignificance in history. She comes closest to a genuine tragic figure.

Amid all the conflict and class warfare, the great conflict-based ideologies of the age, which rationalized Chinese Nationalism and Chinese Communism, are simply absent. (Magistrate Tan's vision of communism comes from his visit to the USSR, not the thought of Mao Zedong or perhaps even Marx; through one of his subordinates, he becomes curious about Tito, but only because Tito took a young wife.) The theme of conflict and competition among various social and moral systems and ideologies has been prominent in Chinese intellectual discourse and literature since the May Fourth era and also in Mao-era literature, which posited eternal conflict between progressives and reactionaries. In the new historical novels, there is no central ideology against which to "rebel." That is not necessarily comforting or liberating. It can lead instead to confusion and hopelessness.

Zhang Wei's *The Ancient Ship* is the rare new historical novel that dramatizes an ideological conflict, between its two Sui brothers, but Zhang's evenhandedness tends to dissolve the main bases of the ideologies. Sui Baopu, the elder, is enthralled with the altruism he finds in *The Communist Manifesto*. This puzzles his brother, Sui Jiansu, who has no ideology. He simply embraces the new entrepreneurialism, and not for any higher purpose than self-enrichment and glorification of the Suis, which is partly for revenge against the rival Zhao clan.

The novel does not let either ideology or developmental strategy "win," either in the brothers' debates or in the outcome of Wali's development. Entrepreneurialism lies in China's future, readers must have already surmised when the novel appeared in 1986, but Sui Jiansu's private enterprises fail, partly due to the cutting of corners and outright fraud committed by him and other private entrepreneurs. *The Communist Manifesto*, however sacred to Sui Baopu, enters the plot only in cameo appearances that make it appear less a lodestone for "correct" moral or ethical policy direction than a prognostication—of History, which in the 1980s has acquired weight, in Baopu's view, from the course of events. The *Manifesto* appears somewhat prescient, but unable to transcend the novel's larger dialectic of altruism (Baopu and Marx) versus self-interest (Jiansu and private property rights). That dialectic eventuates, I argued in chapter 3, not so much in an *aufhebung* (simultaneous fulfillment and transcendence) leading to a higher stage of history as in a circular pattern of struggle. Baopu "laugh[s] in agreement" with the *Manifesto's* prediction that "the less strength and skill required by manual operation, the more developed modern industry becomes, the more likely it is that male workers will be edged out by female workers" (147/181), which he witnesses happening before him. But the outcomes Baopu actually sees fulfilling the *Manifesto's* views are only these technical results, not a more comprehensive and optimistic, progressive outcome of historical dialectics. Class struggle has been tried and found wanting. Communism is reduced to idealism: opposition to greed and inequality.

The moral that Baopu underlines (literally, in his copy of the book) when *The Communist Manifesto* first enters the plot comes from Marx and Engels's very bleak summation of capitalist society, surely portrayed as a dystopia were it not to be superseded by socialism. Baopu reads this passage, without context: "It ruthlessly cuts out all the invisible feudal shackles that bind people to their natural leaders; it strips off all connections between people except those related to naked interests and cold, merciless 'cash exchange.' It submerges sacred emotional evocations such as religious faith, chivalric ardor, and petty bourgeois sentiment in the icy water of self-interest" (147/182). The subject of this bleak sentence is left ambiguous by Zhang Wei (in *The Communist Manifesto* the subject is "the bourgeoisie"). The reader of the novel might take "it" to be society or history as such—or even, allegorically and opposite to the drift of the original document, socialist or Maoist society as China has just experienced it. Further, the human relations being stripped off appear to have some good in them, whereas the original *Manifesto* marks these sentiments as hypocritical or self-deluding. "Petty bourgeois sentiment," for instance, or "the sentiments of the lower urbanites" (*xiao shimin*) as Zhang Wei's Chinese literally says, represents what the standard English translation of the *Manifesto* refers to as "philistine sentimentalism."[3] Jiansu notes that Baopu has underlined in his copy the words "religious faith," "chivalric ardor," and "petty bourgeois sentiment." These qualities, which are negative in *The Communist Manifesto* if not in other ethical and belief systems, have new meaning when Jiansu delineates Baopu's faith in Marxism. Baopu's socialist faith is religious in its force, chivalric in its ideals, and petty bourgeois as might be judged by Baopu's social role as the small-time manager of an enterprise in provincial Wali. "Now [Jiansu] understood. He knew that Baopu was in the grip of a peculiar, irresistible force that emanated from that thin book" (148/183).

Sui Baopu's further references to *The Communist Manifesto* affirm its role as prophetic utterance and evidence that past generations understood life better than moderns do. The document is not a moral or political road map here, though he uses it to rationalize his tendency to "despise people who want only to grab things, because what they take away actually belongs to everyone" (228/284). Baopu's main proffered reason for frequent reading of the *Manifesto* (and yet not Mao Zedong Thought) is that "it's so tightly bound up with our town and the misery of the Sui clan" (229/285).

One might conclude that the connection is that the *Manifesto* explains the ultimate outcome of the town's and the clan's flaw of "grabbing" things as their private property. But the connection might also be that the sorry fate of the Suis is "bound up" with the vengeance of the class warfare that the *Manifesto* inspired in China.

The end of the novel cites another passage of the *Manifesto*, which excoriates the union of certain nineteenth-century European aristocratic and conservative thinkers with fearful conservative workers to oppose the socialist movement. These critics seized on seeming flaws in the theory of socialism. Marx and Engels called those critics' thinking "feudal socialism: half lamentation, half lampoon; half an echo of the past, half menace of the future; at times, by its bitter, witty, and incisive criticism, striking the bourgeoisie to the very heart's core, but always ludicrous in its effect, through total incapacity to comprehend the march of modern history"[4] (347/427). In the 1980s, one might easily associate "feudal socialism" with the Mao era just past, since in 1979 the Communist Party had chosen the equally oxymoronic term "feudal fascism" to characterize the ideology of the Gang of Four. This passage of the novel could thus be interpreted as a searing criticism of Maoist collectivism and Chinese socialism. On the other hand, the phenomenon of seemingly rearguard elements lampooning socialism and sometimes hitting their target despite their poor understanding of history might suggest Deng Xiaoping's (and Jiansu's) post-Mao philosophy of mass consumerism, so indebted to "grabbing" things. It could be that Zhang Wei really does believe in a progressive march of history, but it might also be that he thinks the consumerists of today are simply ignorant of how their greed and lack of altruism will lead to another cycle of envy, violence, vengeance, and counter-vengeance.[5] The fact remains that in *The Ancient Ship*, belief in the market appears only to legitimize greed, whereas the most idealistic expression of Marxism, even without accretions from Leninism or Mao Zedong Thought, appears to be not a guide to action but a prophecy for the future, now turned bleak. How dystopian, if the inhumanities of nineteenth-century industrialism are re-created in the rice noodle factory, torn away even from the old utopian faith of both capitalism and Marxism-Leninism that deferred gratification might lead to a better future. Neither Marxism nor market consumerism offers a centering ideology for the post-Mao age.

A reduction of all political disagreement to a "two-line struggle" between Communists and reactionaries, good and evil, patriots and traitors dominated political discourse and literature in the Mao era. Several of China's new historical novels besides *The Ancient Ship* describe the perennial two-line struggle and sometimes the civil war that preceded it, but largely without putting the objects of battle in the ideological terms of the era.

Li Rui's *Silver City* is a seminal presentation of the civil war and its aftermath, with Communist and non-Communist forces in a two-line struggle fought with guns. The non-Communists are under the warlord Yang Chuxiong, who is ultimately co-opted by Chiang Kaishek and made one of his senior generals after he defeats other local armed forces, as is historically appropriate to the novel's setting in the upper Yangzi area, presumably Sichuan. Yet even the Communist protagonists are not depicted as motivated by ideology or other high values of life, so the ideological battle is quite indirect. The local Communist putsch or peasant insurrection of 1927, a subsequent salt miners' strike, and later conflicts are presented as historical recurrences of uprisings and insurrections perpetrated to achieve the ends of charismatic military leaders going back to Zhang Xianzhong (not Hong Xiuquan, leader of the Taiping Rebellion, the Chinese Communist Party's putative precursor), and as class struggles in which one class, defined as an *interest group*, simply tries to take land, money, and power from another interest group in a zero-sum game. There is no vision of building socialism or of collectivizing land and mines once they have been seized from the current possessors.

In the Cultural Revolution, Red Guards shout, "Workers, peasants, soldiers—unite, / Stride forward, kill the enemy!" But to what end? Li Jingsheng, a son of the revolution, yearns for a "historic gesture" of "a hand raised to the future" but does not see it, for it "had already been claimed: it belonged to every statue of Chairman Mao, large or small, concrete or stone, in every public square, large or small, in every town and city in the nation. It had become the exclusive property of the Great Teacher, the Great Leader, the Supreme Commander, the Great Helmsman" (7/9). (This is a rare reference in the new historical novels to the person of the chairman.) Li Jingsheng's father, Li Naizhi, converts to the Communist cause as a young boy after the example of his charismatic school principal. The latter quotes a line from the ideologist Li Dazhao, but again it is a call to arms, not an ideological guidepost: "Mark my word, red flags will fly over the world in the future!" (15/15). The Communist cause is embodied in its desire to join the winning side of history, not any ideology.

Continuing revolution in the later years of Maoism is similarly unmotivated by ideological commitment. Reflects Li Zihen, a longtime underground Communist Party member, "What purpose was served by making life a struggle?" (212/216). The old Bolshevik Li Naizhi finally expires in a May Seventh Cadre School, punished not for mistakes of "line" (policy), reassessment of his class background, or even guilt by association, but for the kind of "crime" typically found in East European dystopian novels that recall Stalin's trials of the 1930s: having betrayed the Communist Party by escaping execution in 1939 when his comrades did not.

Lack of an ideological, religious, or moral center casts a pall of anarchy and moral opportunism over most of the modern history retold in the novels. The characters are driven not by traditional or revolutionary values and ideals, but by primitive survival instincts (simply "to live," in Yu Hua's novel by that name), a desire for vengeance, or a selfish quest for domination. True ideological battles are notable by their absence. In the works that span the Republican and Communist periods, the ostensible ideology and guiding principles of society may change, but without altering larger patterns of historical stasis and circularity or fundamentally changing human motivation, much less human nature. The very utopianism of Maoism is nullified, including its hopes for development and the creation of a new socialist man. The contrary utopian promises of Deng Xiaoping's era, of widespread enrichment and consumerist acquisition, seem just as chimerical when their time comes.

Sometimes universally condemned values of the old society manage to overcome the bright hopes of the new. In Su Tong's *Wives and Concubines* and its film version, *Raise the Red Lantern*, patriarchal power and the jealousies provoked by polygamy not only defeat marital harmony and female self-fulfillment, but they also bring about a socially tolerated murder and drive a modern, educated woman insane. In *Opium Family*, the coming of Communism is simply a turn in the cycle of revenge and social enervation symbolized by the drug. In Mo Yan's *Red Sorghum*, invaders evoke a military heroism in response—of a mythic, not wholly believable kind—but for the sake of vengeance, not nation-building. The same is true in *Big Breasts and Wide Hips*, in which families divide and the sides turn on each other during foreign invasion, civil war, and Communist suppressions of counterrevolutionaries.

Maqiao's village society is relatively stable, but the narrator observes no system of ethics keeping it going. Ten years after the collectivization of the land, families still remember which lands belonged to them and accordingly treat those fields differently from other fields. Recalling the collective era, the narrator writes, patronizingly: "For as long as many Maqiao people would hold in their urine in order to release it over what had previously been their own private fields, . . . their grasp of the concepts of public ownership, of the 'public family' had to be a little shaky" (121/111). The narrator continues with a condescending view of the Maqiao people as submitting to collectivization out of an imperial-era idea that all land belongs to the ruler. They may have understood the word "public" in its even more ancient sense of belonging to the "lord" (122/112). The narrator cannot congratulate the locals for "ideological resistance," since their opposition appears to come from both "feudalism" (backwardness) and an anarchic tendency to go their own way no matter what— a tendency that might, in the modern world, lead to chaos. The Maqiao people are xenophobic, superstitious, and "backwards": "Women generally didn't have speech rights" (159/146). For all his celebration of "difference," Han Shaogong, the real author, betrays a fear like that of the May Fourth generation that the locals may be fully resistant to progressive views and national integration. Maqiao, like Zhang Wei's fictitious village in *September's Fable*, has its share of beatings and local violence, directly evoking the specter of social chaos that occurs when a locality is left to its own devices.

"Human Nature" Unmasked as Animal Nature

Monographs by Yomi Braester, Ban Wang, David Der-wei Wang, Xiaobin Yang, Michael Berry, and Sylvia Li-chun Lin (who treats Taiwan) note a preoccupation with violence in contemporary Chinese fictional and cinematic representations of twentieth-century Chinese history. These studies draw heavily on history and memory discourses, Holocaust studies, trauma theory, and cultural and psychoanalytic criticism from Adorno, Bataille, Baudrillard, Benjamin,[6] Lyotard, Žižek, Freud, and Lacan. All but Ban Wang's book have the word "trauma," "violence," or "atrocity" in the title or subtitle. David Der-wei Wang's *The Monster That Is History* is one of the few to mention the vengeful class violence that was actually sanctioned in "red classic" novels of the Mao period (73). These scholars' approaches make notable contributions, though they do not focus on the new historical novels and film adaptations, as does this book. And some of the scholars define violence figuratively, including institutional violence, symbolic violence, epistemic violence, spectral violence (wrought by ghosts), and representational violence,[7] or even identify trauma with modern life.[8]

The utility of analyzing *trauma* in modern Chinese history, besides its deepening of cultural theory's interest in the body, is that trauma is a psychological condition that lingers and may be socially "inherited," though it can change, like "memory."[9] "Trauma" may point to an ur-trauma instead of an event and be "a method of interpretation, for it posits that the effects of an event may be dispersed and manifested in many forms not obviously associated with the event."[10] It lends itself to the idea of a collective, national trauma, like that resulting from humiliations of the Chinese as a nation.[11] But authors of the Red Guard generation might well ask, Where *is* the recognition of trauma today? Prosperity and continuity of the reins of power have suppressed it. These authors' novels recall real violence—persistent, recurrent, and without particular ideological significance: physical attack and counterattack.

Trauma as "a method of interpretation" is not the primary lens through which the narrators of the new historical novels view history, unlike those of some of the more self-consciously avant-garde works. To be sure, psychological trauma enters the new historical novels. Sun Guanglin's family abandons him without explanation in *Cries in the Drizzle*, leaving him feeling guilty. The widow of the village miser gives away her three children, allegedly out of economic necessity—possibly in the post-Mao era—in Han Shaogong's Maqiao (292/266). Limpy is crippled, orphaned, and generally ostracized in *Tattoo*. There is the existential quandary of the landlord's son, Chen Mao, of *Opium Family*, who is denied his birthright and his inheritance, and the quandary of the recognized heir, Chencao, the hated son; the premeditated degradation of the rice shop owner's daughters in *Rice*, motivated by Five Dragons's sadism; the shunning of Xu Sanguan's eldest son because his father suspects he is illegitimate; the whispering campaign about Ku Wenxuan's backside in *The Boat to Redemption*, followed by the reputed lunacy of his obsessed son; and the victimization by gossip of women named and unnamed in *The Song of Everlasting Sorrow*.

A more prominent gestalt than abstract trauma in the new historical novels is that of humans as animals, struggling to the death: a Hobbesian image of all against all. The salient image in Mo Yan's *Red Sorghum* occurs in the chapter titled *"Gou Dao,"* or the "Way of Dogs," a play on the ancient philosophical ideal of *Ren Dao,* the Way of Humankind, and perhaps on a *Guo Dao* or way of the nation-state. In modern Chinese, *Ren Dao* denotes "humanitarianism" or "humanism." The Way of Dogs that Mo Yan describes is clever in its brutality; it is inhuman, or rather, "all too human."

Red, Green, and Blackie, formerly the family dogs of *Red Sorghum's* main protagonists, return to a feral state after having to forage for food amid the ruins of warfare and village destruction. A massacre by the Japanese has littered the ground with hundreds of human corpses for them to feed on. The three dogs rise to become leaders of a pack of some six hundred of their species. Emboldened by the call of the wild, the hungry dogs regress beyond all domestication and "civilization." A battle between humans and canines ensues, with both sides developing the theme of never-ending revenge common in the new historical novels. The soldiers on the human side are children, like William Golding's protagonists. The latter-day narrator calls Mo Yan's child soldiers Father and Mother, which is appropriate and respectful for him, but ironically anachronistic given the characters' age at the time of the action.

Anthropomorphically, the dogs' counter-revenge follows a "power struggle" for leadership of the pack that ultimately only Red survives; one of the losers commits suicide in order to avoid murderous torture and death (like many Chinese pursued by "Reds" in the Cultural Revolution). The narrator attributes the dog pack leaders' initial command position partly to their "willingness to martyr themselves by attacking with unparalleled ferocity" (277/214) in a seeming direct parody of the heroic Maoist red classics that celebrate revolutionary battles. In the final battle between dogs and children, the top dog Red brilliantly sends a "pointy-eared mongrel to lead half the dogs in a frontal charge," while he leads "sixty others in a flanking maneuver to the rear of the marshland, from where they could launch a surprise attack and tear those little [human] bastards, who had blood on their hands, to pieces" (284/218). The dogs represent humanity in a primal state.

The allegorical nature of the battle recalls Orwell's allegory of Communist revolution, *Animal Farm,* whose barnyard beasts overthrow their human oppressor. Says *Red Sorghum,* in a passage of uncertain narrative voice, "A hatred of humans—those two-legged creatures that walked erect—seethed in [the dogs'] hearts, and eating human flesh held greater significance than just filling their growling bellies; more important was the vague sensation that they were exacting terrible revenge upon those rulers who had enslaved them" (277/213).[12] Red's revenge takes on anachronistic tinges of Cultural Revolution chaos when Granddad curses him as a "Rebel bastard." Mo Yan returns to animal battles in *Life and Death Are Wearing Me Out*, of donkeys vs. wolves and pigs vs. pigs, in passages that provide virtuoso descriptions of heroic violence and anarchy: chaos that transcends experience and the understanding of humankind and its philosophers. These animal battles, too, are anthropomorphic. The ex-human Ximen Donkey leads one of the sides in the donkey battle; Ximen Pig is the general of a pig faction. The specter of humans treated as livestock appears in *The Republic of Wine*, in which young children, designated "meat boys," are raised for the dinner table.

Human behavior is portrayed as a sadistic struggle for dominance in many of the new historical novels. It is uniquely human only in that its cruelty and sexual irregularities are unworthy of animals.[13] One recalls Uncle Arhat's skinning alive in *Red Sorghum*; the ignoble thieves and bullies who take the means of survival from other refugees in *Big Breasts and Wide Hips* (324–325/309–310); the beating to death of the gallant father figure Song Fanping in *Brothers*; the reigning bullies who rape and extort favors from females in *The Ancient Ship*; the culture of beating and threatening to beat people in *A Dictionary of Maqiao* and *September's Fable*; the heroines' self-sacrifice and even self-mutilation in *Silver City*; the literal draining of the lifeblood from Fugui's beloved only son to provide a transfusion for a magistrate's wife in *To Live*;[14] and multiple incidents of children blinding and maiming one another, recalling the youthful savagery of *Lord of the Flies*, in *September's Fable*. There are murder and seeming cannibalism in *The Republic of Wine*; sadistic torture, on a whim, in *My Life as Emperor* spectacular torture as a symbol of traditional and post-Tiananmen social control in *Sandalwood Death*; incest and voyeurism in *Brothers*; and so forth. Robin Visser notes that the sadistic and at times masochistic protagonist of *Rice* is frequently likened to a beast; he has a "canine sense of self."[15] Human life in these novels lacks "humanity." The characters' socially disapproved but nonviolent comings-together, as in incest and prostitution, have joyous and happy outcomes in *One Hundred Years of Solitude*, but not in the Chinese novels it inspired.

These portraits of humanity as animalistic or worse stand in stark contrast to traditional Chinese concepts of human nature, rooted in Confucian views of reciprocity, benevolence, and responsibility on the part of superiors. The ideal was the "superior man" (but not an *übermensch*) who commanded respectful obedience from inferiors. The classic statement on human nature as sympathy for others comes from the Confucian sage Mencius, who extended it to the ideal of a commiserating government:

Mencius said, "All men have a mind which cannot bear to see the suffer-
ings of others. The ancient kings had this commiserating mind, and they,
as a matter of course, had likewise a commiserating government. . . . My
meaning may be illustrated thus: even now-a-days, if men suddenly see a
child about to fall into a well, they will without exception experience a feeling of alarm and distress. They will feel so, not as a ground on which they
may gain the favour of the child's parents, nor as a ground on which they
may seek the praise of their neighbours and friends, nor from a dislike to
the reputation of having been unmoved by such a thing. From this case we
may perceive that the feeling of commiseration is essential to man."[16]

To erase the line between humans and animals is to rob life of human-
heartedness and subordinate it to seemingly amoral constructs of "biology"
rather than national, cultural, or social-class norms. Confucian thought and
the idea of an essential "human nature" were heavily criticized in the Mao
era, refuted through reference to the putative "class nature" of society. Marx
and Engels in fact wrote of animal aspects of human behavior, but Chinese
Marxists emphasized transcendental—heroic or sublime—human potentials.[17]
Marxist ideological commitments expired for most Chinese in the 1980s,
though they may have left some residue in the generations educated under
Mao. "Humanity" became a mantra for Chinese intellectuals in the early
1980s as a non-religious font of post-Marxist values, as well as a source of optimism about China's capacity for renewal. Yet Chinese intellectuals also con-
templated the proposition that human nature was essentially evil. William
Golding's *Lord of the Flies* was a ready reference in the debates.[18]
 By the late 1980s, many of China's intellectuals had become pessimistic
and turned against "humanism" and affirmations of a positive human nature.
Academic debates in the 1990s again variously questioned or lamented China's
olden "humanistic spirit" as a lost ideal.[19] The intellectuals' own hopes that
they could and would lead China's modernization through their ideas and
writings, even in the absence of democracy—perhaps under a "new authoritarianism" without the burden of mass participation that seemingly got out of
hand in the Mao era—were dashed in the process. If human nature existed
but was in fact bad, then perhaps Mao was not wholly wrong in thinking "human nature" must be changed. However, that had failed. The idea of a fundamentally benevolent humanity that could restore balance and the good society in the aftermath of decline was displaced in the new historical novels by
visions of a universal potential for inhumanity—one knowable from history.

The age of permanent revolution may have passed, but the condition of un-principled struggle seemed permanent: it *was* human nature. This was the Darwinian truth of life itself.

Chinese social critics and satirists have of course observed and described inhumanity and pervasive corruption of institutions and morality from time immemorial. Lu Xun, China's preeminent writer of the early twentieth century, depicted inhumanity in the Chinese society of his day in figures of pervasive cannibalism and bullying, such as that suffered and in turn perpetrated by his iconic character Ah Q.[20] But Lu Xun attributed inhumanity to Chinese tradition and "national character," and he found it in everyday life and culture rather than in the vicissitudes of history as a great narrative. He believed in progress, Darwin, and progressive modernity coming to the world; in this context, China was simply backward. China's new historical novels of the late 1980s, 1990s, and beyond, composed during much better times for China as a nation, transcend such a national discourse. China's triumph in national terms simply confirms the universality of everlasting struggle and absolute lack of human sympathy. Violence is so pervasive that Mo Yan and Su Tong can portray it aesthetically, as gorgeous.

A view of life as struggle is the nexus of biology and images of decline in the new historical novels. The idea that struggle leads to progress appeared in China before evolutionary theories, prior to the twentieth century, James Pusey writes.[21] Darwinism then became "the first Western 'ism' to be widely accepted by Chinese" (241). Compatible premises from Herbert Spencer, Thomas Huxley, and Jean-Baptiste Lamarck accompanied this partly reimagined "ism." Darwin and his followers (and revisers) simply "proved" the universality of struggle, the inevitable supremacy of the strong, and the fated perishing of the weak. The weak died of their inability to compete; they did not have to be killed by their oppressors. Their demise was "natural." As Yan Fu put it in his seminal translation of evolutionary thinking, *wujing tianze* (things contend; Heaven [or nature] chooses).[22] The process was fated. Confucian literati and the old imperial regime did not mobilize against Darwin's principles, and in China, no great religious establishment opposed them.

Reformers and revolutionaries alike embraced the idea that species, individuals, and above all peoples and nations (as *qun*, groups) struggled for survival, the strong displacing the weak. "Bullying" was a particularly important keyword by the turn of the twentieth century. It conjured up images of physical, biological power as well as scientific truth conjoined with moral overtones. Social Darwinist ideas went hand in hand with theories of eugenics, racial characteristics, and human physiotypes.[23] Some welcomed the struggle, for when combined with belief in the efficacy of human will, it offered hope and a program of action for China.

Thus, "Darwin created the ideological vacuum that cried out for something like Marxism" (450), Pusey writes. Mao revised Darwin by heralding a world in which willpower had "the power to fitten the unfit" (451). Adds Frederic Wakeman, Jr., "Mao's Marxism was just another variation of Social Darwinism: if not a teleology, then at least a scientific theodicy" (236). "Struggle" became for Mao an end in itself, the motive power of history, the basis of "the entire structure of [his] thought and action" (236), and ultimately the means of eliminating the weak and bad from society, as judged by class analysis. The new belief in progress in turn confirmed the truth of "Darwinism."

Darwinian views of change through conflict were also widely accepted by those to Mao's right—and not just fascists. Yan Fu early on had been able to envision evolutionary struggle as embodying the Dao.[24] No new threats to Darwinian views of social change appeared after Mao's death; preoccupation with the idea of global competition continues today. Chinese citizens can finally exult that their nation is "winning." Merciless competition and struggle for success, a winner-take-all competition that leaves the loser behind in the dust, seems to increasing numbers of Chinese the implicit ideology of China's new way of managing individual needs, too.

The other element of optimism that came with Darwinism at the turn of the twentieth century was a belief that *groups* struggled for supremacy. Dismayed at China's lack of group solidarity above the family level, China's turn-of-the-century thinkers and their successors looked forward to new forms of solidarity through a Chinese *nation*. In the context of the biological and quasi-biological definitions of groups at the time, the Chinese nation was pictured as a Spencerian organic structure, interdependent parts struggling as one with other nations, as if nations were species.

In China's new historical novels, the association of pervasive biological and social struggle with inevitable progress is controverted, and so is the old optimism, which in the novelists' youth attached to the idea of social classes and an international proletariat—of strength in groups. In the new historical novels, no viable new social groups have formed, and a trans-Darwinian, animalistic, even sub-animalistic motive force of pure vengeance has reared its head, negating all humanistic group solidarity. Biology summons up images not of progress, but of secular and recurring decline, even regression. The idea of competition and social struggle, long condemned in traditional thought and discredited in the late twentieth century by Mao's unprofitable kinds of struggle, is not disproved but disapproved by the novelists.

Su Tong's fiction is best known for palpably linking decadence, decline, and domestic horror to biological causes unrelated to Maoism. Birth defects come from inbreeding in *Opium Family*. Mo Yan, too, lets human physical mutations, such as the one-breasted woman and the six-fingered girl of *Big Breasts and Wide Hips* (2:358/358) and the mute son and five mute grandsons of Aunty Sun, symbolize social-moral dysfunction. (A six-fingered character also appears in Su Tong's *The Boat to Redemption* [101/148], and still others are recurring figures in Ge Fei's *Southlands Trilogy*.) But such "defects" may be only quasi-biological. On closer inspection, oddities "inherited" from earlier generations come as much from karma (the past record of sinning by the protagonists and their ancestors) as genetics, in Su Tong's *Rice, Nineteen Thirty-Four Escapes*, and again, *Opium Family*. One might say Su Tong's imagination has created a modernized karmic Lamarckian principle of the inheritance of acquired sin (modernized because the figuration already existed in folk Buddhism). Intimations of accumulating physical degeneracy join with spectacles of moral and physical decline that resonate variously with dark and vaguely understood forces of heredity, transgenerational cosmic retribution, and worldly feuding—the pursuit of vengeance for past crimes and indignities. The narrator of *Opium Family* even imputes to primitive peasant mentality a genetic determinism contradicting the idea of hybrid vigor: "Maple Village grandfathers told their grandsons . . . When the pure, strong unmixed bloodline, passed on for generations, reached Chencao, it got mixed up and diluted; and when it got mixed up and diluted, it declined. That's just the way heredity works." (42/248) The sense of inevitable decline and dystopia compounds and becomes weighty, seemingly inescapable.

The mellower and more urbane tones of Wang Anyi's *The Song of Everlasting Sorrow* might appear to lie outside the rigors of competitive struggle to the death. Yet the heroine is eternally defined—trapped—by her status as a former beauty *contestant*, and not the real winner. Moreover, she is a type, one of many Shanghai "Wang Qiyaos." Lacking the protections of any biological family (indeed, from a traditional point of view she "sins" in her youth by moving out of her natural family's home), she struggles to form new social networks of her own choosing. They dissolve or go unnoticed, like the heroine, due to their formation for frivolous ends such as card playing and, later, partying and even self-display. To the Chinese reader who knows the political turmoil of Shanghai urban life under Communism and its dynamism in the "new era," it is clear that a Wang Qiyao can thrive only if she is sheltered from the outside world. In the end, the "real world" of materialism intervenes and takes her life.

Maqiao, too, is an isolated "population" with its own quasi-biological mutations of language and social custom. They seem fantastic in relation to the larger "genetic pool" of words in Modern Standard Chinese. But Maqiao is a place of social inbreeding, with its own linguistic and ritual adaptations, like a lost world of prehistoric residuals such as Jules Verne or Arthur Conan Doyle might have invented. Maqiao preserves certain proto-Chinese customs not only from the ancient kingdom of Chu but also the kingdom of Ba, "savage" customs that even today "arous[e] a certain savagery in people" (10/7). From the start, Han Shaogong takes pains to relate the community's "bloodlines," tracing them back to pre-Qin antiquity (9/5–6). He offers far-fetched, quasi-biological arguments about a local cultural lineage that follows lines of etymological descent through mutations. Maqiao is a community struggling for survival. In the "new era," it will not survive. The village is a museum of cultural leftovers, genetic oddballs, and freaks, including a man with a "third ear" under his arm and the seemingly obligatory mute.

Even isolated Maqiao is beset by internal, sometimes violent struggle. This takes the reader by surprise as it intrudes in the dictionary, spontaneously, in extended early entries that root Maqiao's past in incidents of bloodshed and fanatical struggle: the Lotus Flower Rebellion (13–14/9–10), the depredations of Zhang Xianzhong (14/11), whose example inspires mayhem also in Li Rui's *Silver City*, and the "banditry" and civil war battles of 1948 (97–104/88–94). Continuing political struggles under Communism are seen more obliquely, through offhand appearances of words like "labor reform," "revolution," "reactionary"; the placement of an entry on "Tiananmen" directly after "Democracy Cell (as Used by Convicts [as if it were a prison cell])"; and an entry on "Traitor to the Chinese" that, however idiosyncratic in its Maqiao usage, must send chills down the spine of the Chinese reader. Most internally generated struggle is apolitical, however, in this self-contained community: wife beating, marital betrayals, and elopements (one ends with a hand grenade lobbed into a cave; 208/192), and long-lived feuds. The narrator claims early on that "the importance [the Maqiao people] attach to blood ties doesn't equal the importance they attach to pots" (27/23). This is one more indication of cultural decay—of the unreliability of the biological tie. Animal images reinforce the idea that life at the grass roots is one of inherent struggle. The village's "Boss Hong" is a big ox thought to be the reincarnation of "a great bully"

(183/169). The modern struggle for survival is a new, scientific version of the ancient struggle, often unsuccessful, for beneficial rebirth.

MAGICAL REALISM

The end of the chapter 4 noted that some of China's new historical novels, however dystopian, hold out hope of escape from alienating social control through egalitarian and voluntary comradeship as in classic Euro-American dystopian novels, though without their themes of dissidence or revolt. *The Kingdom of This World*, *Men of Maize*, and *One Hundred Years of Solitude* instead depict escape, transcendence, or righteous vengeance through magical realism, witchcraft, and fantasy. Examining a much broader range of post-Marquezian novels by Salman Rushdie, Toni Morrison, Ben Okri, D. M. Thomas, and Angela Carter, certain international critics see in them a magical realism that expresses a general third-world, folk, and/or feminist postcolonial spirit of resistance to urban, core, patriarchal oppression.[25] (Günter Grass's and Milan Kundera's magical realisms oppose European totalitarianism.) Might evocations of divine intervention or fantasy offer a hint of deliverance from Chinese afflictions of social confinement and social anarchy?

Magical realism became prestigious in China after García Márquez won his Nobel Prize, but Chinese writers tended to inflate the concept into a broader Marquezian or even "Latin American" gestalt of epic, trans-realistic, and folkish allegory and fable making, while conflating it with avant-garde tendencies of fantasy, surrealism, absurdism, and Borgesian paradox. García Márquez had indeed reconciled magical realist, historical, folk, and allegorical tendencies that many readers had thought incompatible.[26] In fact, China's literati high culture as well as its folk had since ancient times blurred the boundaries that separated the cosmos, nature, living humanity, and spirits of the dead. Even so, it was attraction to "magical realism," not native folk or literati tradition, that led Mo Yan in three different novels to repeat the signature Marquezian miracle of a simple rural person departing the earth with wings like an angel.[27]

Defined by Matthew Strecher in a global and indeed East Asian (Japanese) context, "magical realism is what happens when a highly detailed, realistic setting is invaded by something 'too strange to believe.'"[28] Magical realism that does not convey a whole alien belief *system* empathetically, from the inside ("ontologically"), requires an unresolved incongruity of realistic and inexplicable plot elements, and the latter must not be simply extradiegetic. Alejo

Carpentier's seminal 1949 essay on "the marvelous real" associated the former syndrome, now sometimes called ontological magical realism, with New World spirituality, religion, indigenous cosmologies, and openness to paranormal phenomena and forms of consciousness. It is a belief *system* incompatible with the conventionally realistic European novel that modernists like Carpentier already considered passé. His invocation of the "real" also suggests a folk sensibility formed by a hybrid culture—in this case, from three continents. Many critics have since reasserted the linkage to Spanish American literature,[29] whereas postcolonial critics have globalized the concept. The children of Mao, however, tend to see paranormal folk perceptions as backward and incapable of thwarting central power with a more rural, "alternative modernity." The Chinese writers are more attuned to William Golding's figure of a deluded and evil childlike imagining of Beelzebub as a living and potent god (the lord of the flies)—one originating in the darkness of human nature, not "authentically," from a sacred book or tradition.

Those who value "magic" for the shock value of its intrusiveness may value magical realism not for casting an extrasensory "spell" directly over the reader, but for deepening and supplementing realism's powers of perception. There is support for this even in Carpentier. Celebrating "baroque" aesthetics and their "horror of the vacuum," his 1975 explication of "magical realism" recalled the German art historian Franz Roh's original, 1925, use of the term "magic realism," by which Roh criticized European Expressionism on behalf of "objective" *detail* in "magic realist" paintings. Carpentier's literary biographer, Roberto González Echevarría, credits Roh as Carpentier's predecessor in "having isolated a salient characteristic of avant-garde aesthetics—the aesthetics of the minuscule." What Carpentier loved about China in 1967 was not its Cultural Revolution, but its traditional, to him evidently baroque, architecture—its "medieval walls" and "gargoyles" on palace roofs.[30] That is an unlikely stance for a modern Chinese intellectual. In Latin America, likewise, detailed observation ("reconnaissance") can appear as European and colonizing, or in a Chinese context, Westernizing if not Orientalizing—or even "of the gentry"—belonging to the elite that colonized China's native rural subcultures.

By some anthropologists' accounts China's indigenes (such as the Miao and Yao) once lived in an enchanted world that was not wondrous—rather, was full of harmful spirits inspiring dread and needing to be appeased, as in Han Shaogong's novella *Pa Pa Pa*, which describes an ethos from the opposite end of Hunan province from Maqiao's. This fits a pervasively dystopian ethos as in Asturias's *Men of Maize*. A modern functional equivalent of *intrusive* magic in China's new historical novels that is frightening instead of wondrous is the totalitarian politics of hate. It appears to choose victims randomly, allegedly by a system, and yet a counterintuitive one. Magic in the novel is like politics in life, or politics in the novel as Stendhal allegedly described it: "like a pistol shot in the middle of a concert—loud and vulgar, yet impossible to ignore."[31] It was only in the red classics that politics was not an explosive or fearsome intrusion, since it belonged to the works' discursive fabric. Commentary on totalitarianism thus enters the new historical novel through the back door, when uncomprehending peasants see Maoist class struggle as evil and unmotivated black magic, coming from the urban culture, not their own spirits.

The broad love of everything Marquezian in China complicates identification of magical realist flourishes. It is surely magical, but not traditional or folkish—though very "human"—when youngsters in a Mo Yan story suffering from famine in the Great Leap Forward munch on scrap iron of the sort that fed the era's notoriously useless backyard steel furnaces.[32] When a present-day narrator created by Su Tong relates that precisely 139 craftsmen left a village in 1934 to pursue a particular trade, or a boy knows that exactly forty-nine drops fell from his granddad's head when he shook it decades ago (*Red Sorghum*, 83/95), those revelations are marvelous, the former example perhaps magical or "cabalistic," suggesting a folk or indigenous code that is alien to the high culture. When the nose of a woman turns into a beak and her arms change into wings to fly (*Big Breasts and Wide Hips*, 223–224/1:224), we are in the signature Marquezian territory of the folkish marvelous, matter-of-factly told. However, when Mo Yan's rural characters prognosticate using dead babies or tell of having become animal spirits and fortune-tellers, the reader attributes that to the characters' own subjectivity, but it seems a benighted subjectivity, not "ontological" magical realism empathetically conveyed, as by Carpentier or Asturias. To the Chinese authors, such beliefs still smack of "feudal superstition" as a Marxist worldview would put it, not native resistance. Chinese high literature has anciently assimilated beliefs in the supernatural and ghosts, or what David Der-wei Wang calls the "spectral," "uncanny," and "phantasmagoric." One finds these rationalized forms of fantasy more prevalent than "magic" even in modern works.[33] Mo Yan and Zhang Wei celebrate their Shandong fellow provincial Pu Songling (1640–1715) for developing the Chinese tradition of spectral fantasy,[34] as does Han Shaogong in *A Dictionary of Maqiao* (343/311).

Wondrous Chinese magical realism peaked in the 1980s, in short stories by the "Hunan Army" (Han Shaogong, Cai Cehai, Ye Weilin), in fiction about "mystical" Tibet by Tashi Dawa and Ma Yuan, and in works by Mo Yan and Jia Pingwa.[35] One also finds it in late 1980s works by Zhang Xianliang, an older writer (b. 1935) seldom considered Marquezian.[36] Chinese critics never recognized magical realism as a Chinese "school," and the trend has since declined in China, as it has in Latin America. The inexplicable (as in *Nineteen Thirty-Four Escapes*) occurs less frequently in Su Tong's and Yu Hua's later novels, if the latter's Kafkaesque 1980s short stories were ever realist in any sense. It is likewise a misnomer to describe as magical realism the outlandish exaggerations and black humor in *Brothers* or the dreams and recurrences in Ge Fei's *Southlands Trilogy*. Han Shaogong's *A Dictionary of Maqiao* lacks Han's earlier magical realism, except when its young intellectual narrator describes weird folk beliefs, sometimes with mock equanimity.[37] Zhang Wei's *September's Fable* (1992, but begun in 1987) might be called a 1990s throwback to Asturias-style, ontological magical realism.[38] But his subsequent Mao Dun prize-winning *roman-fleuve, You Are on the Highland*, returns his creativity to a more conventional path. It is chiefly Mo Yan who still deployed occasional magical realism—together with surrealistic and pantheistic description, fantasy, and black humor—in full-length novels of the 1990s.

Missing from China's new historical novels is a belief system equivalent to a totalizing mystical faith: the Latin American Catholicism of *One Hundred Years of Solitude,* or the indigenous beliefs in gods and *nahuales* and the syncretistic Catholicism of mestizos in *Men of Maize.* The Chinese counterpart, after Confucianism, would be Marxism-Leninism-Mao Zedong Thought. However, slyly depicting Maoist ideology with full-scale Marquezian or scriptural magic, allegory, parody, or satire, would mean fighting the censors and exploring the ex–Red Guard generation's own past beliefs. Mo Yan's satire comes closest. In *Life and Death Are Wearing Me Out*, Cultural Revolution loudspeakers blare out Red Guards' frantic denunciations of class enemies so loudly that wild geese fall dead from the sky. As potential food for hungry peasants, the birds cause a riot in which seventeen people are trampled to death. "In the months to follow, while there were pitched battles, with bricks and tiles flying in the air and an assortment of weapons, from knives to guns to clubs, the number of casualties paled in comparison to this incident" (133–134/158; the novel adds that local historical chronicles later attributed the deaths to bird flu!). Tropes of magical realism, which *supplement* detailed, mundane life even in most theories of magical realism, are merely incidental in China's new historical novels. Magical realities seldom bolster a sense of human agency or of a cosmos benevolent enough to protect humans from the follies of their dystopian society. At most, a sentient universe may bear witness to the pathos. In Mo Yan's later novels, "magic" provides comic relief or heightens a dystopian element of horror.

Magic and Fantasy in China's New Historical Novels

Mo Yan's early novel *Red Sorghum* has a panoply of "magical," fantastic, and humorous devices—above all, surrealistic description—although mostly in the first and second chapters. The amazing descriptions evoke a holistic and supernatural ethos rare in the Chinese new historical novel. But nature's pantheistic sympathy and even empathy for human suffering simply magnifies the absence of such traits in human society.

"Magic" in the first chapter inheres in a minutely described atmosphere of mystery and anticipation, synesthesia,[39] synchronizations of heavenly and human phenomena, and recurring personifications of sounds and of the sorghum, which in the season of battle has turned from green to red.[40] Its stalks "screeched in secret resentment" (4/6) when men bumped against them; in the mist, "one dew-soaked ear of sorghum after another stared sadly at Father" (9/10). Crushed and trampled, "sorghum everywhere was crying bitterly" (40–41/33); it "remained dignified and solemn" after Grandma's death (81/64); and as a hail of Japanese bullets rained down, "sorghum stalks wailed in concert, their shattered, severed limbs drooping low or arching high into the air" (82/65). Older critical parlance might have called this "the pathetic fallacy," but here it creates an animistic atmosphere.[41] It dawns on Father that the sorghum stalks are "living spirits: . . . they understood the ways of the heavens and the logic of the earth" (9/10). They are, moreover, "a collective body, united in a single magnanimous thought" (28/24). Gaomi's sorghum, like humanity, bleeds red (notable because Mo Yan's characters sometimes bleed green). Grandma, when she dies, sees the sorghum stalks "begin to moan, to writhe, to shout, to entwine her; they are demonic one minute, intimate the next, and in her eyes they coil like snakes" (92/73). Mo Yan animates the minutiae that Carpentier loved: in this novel, ants, grasshoppers, horseflies, toads, and "furry field voles" feasting on the bone marrow of mules worked to death by the foreign invaders (48/38). It is a pantheistic world both benign and terrible.

Mo Yan often trains his descriptive talents not only on the wondrous but also on filth, suppuration of the flesh, nausea, vomiting, and other forms of excretion.[42] Contrary to the image of Grandma's momentous wedding day in Zhang Yimou's film version, her sedan chair in the novel is "badly worn and terribly dirty; like a coffin. . . . The walls were festooned with yellow silk so filthy it oozed grease, and of the five flies caught inside, three buzzed above her head" (51/42). Like previous brides, she vomits from motion sickness (55/45). Father is alert to the aesthetics of the "minuscule"; he was "always slightly more alert than Granddad, perhaps because he concentrated on surface phenomena" (227/176). Mo Yan yet maintains a romantic, heroic tone in the first chapter by finding surrealistic beauty in ugliness and even pain, "satisfying pain" (116/94).[43] When "the bloated carcasses of dozens of mules" float down the Black Water River, "their distended bellies, baked by the sun, split and popped, released their splendid innards, like gorgeous blooming flowers" (48/39). At the time of her death, "two shells opened holes in the breast of Grandma's jacket. She cried out in ecstasy, then crumpled to the ground" (80/64). "Unfathomable mystery is embedded in [her dying] smile" (84/67).

These are literary effects of pathos in the narrator's voice rather than embodiments of the characters' worldview. And, like a traditional Chinese fiction writer, Mo Yan avails himself of the uncanny and the marvelous more often than the truly magical. Adjutant Ren kills himself in a spasm of heroic retributive justice when his Browning goes off as he cleans it (75/59). Fresh blood acquires the "aroma of sorghum wine" (84/67). Phenomena that suggest real magic are debunked. Granddad's piss gives the Gaomi wine its exquisite flavor, but the narrator explains it away with science: urine is alkaline (106/86). When later chapters dramatize supernatural folk beliefs, the narrator discounts them. An "Eighteen Stabs Geng" in the final chapter thus believes a fox fairy cured him of war wounds, but he turns into a pathetic figure who starves to death in 1973 and is discovered with his arms stretched out "like the crucified Jesus" (475/344–345). Passion (Second Grandma) is believed by her fellow villagers to have been possessed by a weasel spirit, but she was in "a deranged state" (438/318). Though the narrator says the weasel repossesses her body twice more, while Japanese soldiers gang-rape her and again when her corpse faces burial, he calls it a "legend" (492/356).[44]

A Boxer-like Iron Society deludes itself with absurd superstitious beliefs; Buddhist monks are hypocritical and licentious, as in much traditional Chinese fiction (353/265); and the narrator describes his grandmother's funeral in characteristically oxymoronic Marquezian terms as an emblem of an "ancient, resplendent culture, as well as a reactionary backward way of thinking" (335/254). His Second Grandma's practice of weighing infant corpses is a

ANARCHY 189

"unique and appalling method" of winning a lottery (462/334; "rich in magical coloration," says the Chinese text) Granddad's delusions of being destined to fulfill "Heaven's will," planted in his mind by an Iron Society stalwart called Five Troubles (lit., "Son of Five Forms of Chaos"), leads to the demise of most of his comrades and family. The skeptical narrator suspects that Granddad used folk sayings merely to "absolve himself" of his past and future crimes: he rationalized that "charity for the sake of karma doesn't mean you'll die in bed; murder and arson are a sure path to the good life" (137/110). The cosmos may be benign, but folk society is not.

Big Breasts and Wide Hips repeats the fantastic device of a preternaturally omniscient narrator (even in infancy), one Shangguan Jintong ("Golden Boy"), as well as florid, marvelous, and explosively oxymoronic descriptions; detailed observations of filth, poverty, and repulsive human injury and disability; and the natural world of animals and insects. Pantheistic attribution of sensibility to the inanimate world is, however, scarce, apart from a rare reference in the opening pages to a scream that "flew through the window lattice and bounced up and down the streets and byways, where it met Sima Ting's shout and entwined with it, a braid of sound that snaked through the hairy ears" of the local missionary (1:6/5).

The chief Marquezian aspects of this later novel are its emphases on the epic endurance of a large family, the peculiar, tragic fates and sexual intrigues of its increasingly eccentric younger generations, and the quiet courage of the family's matriarch. Other Marquezian figurations include a plague of locusts and a great flood; a family member who sprouts wings and flies; wandering outsiders; new inventions (unusual in China's new historical novels); incest; and other insinuations of decadence, decline, and circularity that lead to entropy even in a family and community that have survived multiple challenges to their existence.

Actual "magic" is largely confined to the early pages, and as in *Red Sorghum*, it accompanies violence and tragedy, often as comic relief rather than pathetic reinforcement. After a guerrilla soldier "puts back on" a piece of his shoulder that a Japanese sword sliced off, "it immediately hopped back off and burrowed into a patch of weeds. So he snatched it up and smashed it on the ground, over and over, until it was dead" (1:41/37). The return to life of an evidently dead Shangguan Lü (1:57/80) and Shangguan Jintong's vision of his father Pastor Malory returning from the dead (2:373/335) appear merely to be figments of the characters' imaginations. Folk beliefs in spider spirits, a cat that wreaks vengeance on its former tormentor after its death, and planchette prognostication are insufficient to divert one's attention from the omnipresent war and conflict. A description of a Snow Festival held shortly after the founding of the Communist regime in 1949 is eerie and unsettling, but more symbolic of the new political order than a journey into folk belief. Its unique custom is that no spectator may speak.

Some see magical realism in Mo Yan's *Life and Death Are Wearing Me Out* (2006), but the hero's entry into Buddhist hell and serial reincarnations are fantasy, not so obviously based on real religious belief. A touch of intrusive "magic" is Huang Huzhu's miraculously healing and "enchanting" hair. That it bleeds when cut is acknowledged with as much equanimity as the green hair of Rosa the Beautiful in *The House of the Spirits*. A cypress tree bleeds, too, when activists in the Great Leap Forward try to chop it down to fuel backyard steel smelters; this saves other trees in the grove (140/167). A local official, paraded in a papier-mâché donkey costume as part of his Cultural Revolution humiliation, grows long ears and actually acquires a donkey head (135/159–160). Ximen Pig can walk on his hind legs and jump over walls, as if he were a spirit like Pigsy in *The Journey to the West*, and he enjoys reading the Communist Party's classified *Reference News* (221/245). This, however, is extended fantasy, humor, and satire, not magical realism. As the arbitrariness of class-struggle politics recedes in post-Mao times, so do the miracles, except for Huzhu's miraculous hair. In place of politics comes the farce of market forces running amok.

Zhang Wei's *September's Fable* (1992) contains intimations of the supernatural, and it evokes a mystical and positive rural folk consciousness within its larger tragic context. More even than in *Red Sorghum*, the villagers possess organic solidarity, likened to a tree (24/39) and wrapped up in an expectant sort of mystery: "This little village had so many secrets hidden away!" (158/264). There is also a sense of being under surveillance, which makes the village seem more like a place of internment than a rural utopia. The character "Fat" senses that someone is constantly staring at her with a gaze that is "willful and fixed, rude and unreasonable" (10–11/17). Later, she warns Tingfang, an outsider, "Don't you know that tonight there is a pair of deep, dark eyes fixed on you? They will be there for thousands of nights to come. He's hidden in a place you can never know" (25–26/42).

As in *Red Sorghum* and *Men of Maize*, humans acquire special powers, inanimate objects have personalities, and the abstract becomes tangible. "Outside was the nighttime, black as pitch. If you grabbed at it, it was empty. You could neither wring water from it nor smell it. But it made people intoxi-

cated and stupefied" (11/18). Autumn, particularly September, becomes a nu-
minous entity. Most of the action takes place then; spring is never mentioned.
"Ask the moles in the fields, they'll sing the praises of autumn" (216/364). By
the end of the novel, the season has transmuted, more conventionally, into a
time of dying, after a particular "mournful autumn" (262/440). Says Fat, "I'm
afraid of the dark night . . . I'm afraid of these September days. I'm afraid of
these days of yam digging" (253/425).

More familiarly and comfortingly, *September's Fable* dramatizes the peasants' conversations with ancestors (291–292/491), communion with them in
daydreams (86–90/144–149), and visions of lost lovers or their spirits (110/183).
Fat's long-dead father, Old Roller, has a conversation in the underworld with
the more recently deceased Ox Pole, telling him how things are in the afterlife. Old Roller consoles him in tones reminiscent of Thornton Wilder's *Our
Town*: "The folks in our village can take care of just about anything. They
won't let things get out of hand" (260/437–438) Meanwhile, villagers blame
the departed for not helping them escape misfortune (284/478). Happy Property's deceased mother and Happy Years's mentor, the One-eyed Noble Man,
do materialize to help their former wards in their hour of need (267/450;
224/377). The One-eyed Noble Man, however, returns on the anniversary of
his death to haunt village leader Loose Fang's household, amid a profusion of
bad omens indicating a "mystic power" (235/396–397). The villagers exorcise
his spirit, with Big Feet Fat Shoulders providing him a paper horse to ride
away on.[45] If we are to imagine Chinese rustic natives as having a postcolonial
vitality that resists progress and science, this novel is the place to find it. Even
less than in Macondo or Tres Marías, however, can prayers and propitiations
ultimately deliver the folk from their wretched circumstances. Old Roller and
Ox Pole's afterlife is no paradise, and their forlorn "Our Town" will not survive in situ.

A rare vision of a folk ethos resisting imperialism is Mo Yan's image of mo-
bilization against German railroad builders in *Sandalwood Death*, a period
novel set mostly in Germany's Shandong sphere of influence, 1899–1900. Sun
Bing, a former opera troupe leader from Mo Yan's own Northeast Township of
Gaomi County, organizes resistance using his players and the survivors of a
German massacre, helped at one point by Boxers. But Mo Yan as usual ridi-
cules superstitious beliefs. The Boxer presence fades away, and Sun Bing pays
the price for the Gaomi community's "sins" of resistance during a lengthy
sandalwood torture as he looks down on the assembled folk while impaled
on a cross.

The apotheosis of local solidarity and group consciousness is not the Boxers and their pseudo-magic, but rather a mesmerizing and addictive local opera called *maoqiang*, with its repertory of tragic stories and screechy, "cat-intoned" melodies. Like the yams of Zhang Wei's mysterious September village, local opera casts a spell; it can make people do things they would not ordinarily do. Yet the unifying conceit of the novel, attributed again to local folk wisdom, is that all life, like an opera or an execution, is playacting. It is, however, performed for the folk and their culture, not for a divine, higher power.

Sandalwood Death is nominally divided into three sections, called the phoenix head, tiger belly, and panther tail, as in a classical conception of the ancient *yuefu* "folk songs"; each chapter in the head and tail sections is a lengthy soliloquy by one of the major characters, a prose rendition of one character's operatic lines. Together, the first-person narrations construct a nonlinear narration of a consistent storyline. Further, Mo Yan begins each chapter with the supposed "opera lyrics" of a latter-day *maoqiang* drama called *Sandalwood Death*.[46] These pithier narrations in the form of a sung soliloquy precede each prose soliloquy, as "ballads" do the chapters in Mo Yan's earlier novel, *The Garlic Ballads*. During the protracted torture, the sacrificial victim, opera players, and mass spectators not only sing opera lines in unison, they punctuate them with alternately piteous and triumphant "meows," which gradually acquire the force of "Alas!" "Behold!" or "Listen!" if not "Amen!" Some players dress up as cats and Mo Yan renders the term "*maoqiang* opera" in Chinese as "cat-inflected" or "cat-style" opera, although the standard way of writing it is with the homophonous word "*mao*" meaning "excellent" or "luxuriant." The association with cats evidences not only Mo Yan's affection for his local opera, but also humor; he compares the local music favorably to a nearby donkey-intoned opera (393)! This "subversive carnival"[47] is a benign and pacific response to real massacres perpetrated by the German imperialists and the Boxers. And yet, Mo Yan's "Afterword" to his novel makes a distinction between magic and apotheosized folk consciousness. It indicates that a previous draft of the novel had more magical realism, as in its depictions of the marvelous, overpowering sounds of the new locomotives. Mo Yan deleted that magic, letting the plaintive sounds of Gaomi's local opera prevail instead, to heighten the novel's folkish and purely native atmosphere (473). Moreover, politics in the novel also appears as theater, and this theater is cruel. Magic is not a substitute for politics.

Animal figurations and metaphors in the novel at times reinforce Mo Yan's familiar dystopian and Darwinist theme, that humans are animals at heart.

Xiao Jia, apprentice executioner, thinks he has a magic tiger whisker that allows him to see people's 'original nature"; his wife is really a snake, the executioner a black panther, and the magistrate a white tiger. However, although the novel introduces truly invasive, classically magical events, like decapitated heads hopping about to avoid dogs (11) and "cat opera" singing that charms sparrows out of the trees (396), Mo Yan usually takes his magic all back by indicating that the perception really comes from a dream, legend, or "superstition." When Gaomi's heroes dress up in operatic garb as Yue Fei and Guan Yu to resist the Germans, they look not like Boxers, but like children (204–206). They have their own way of seeing the world, but they are powerless before violence, anarchy, and injustice, and prone to wreak their own.

When the prestidigitation of Mao's class warfare invades China's new historical novels, it is not so benign: a systematic way of seeing the world, but an arcane one whose principles are unfathomable at ground level. In *September's Fable*, there is no visible ideology, Communist Party, socialism, or collectivization, hence no post-socialist decollectivization—until the end, one cannot be sure if certain episodes occurred before, during, or after the reign of Mao. *Landlords* are reimagined as magical beings during "remembering bitterness" meetings. Their kind could make wealth appear out of nowhere.

Contemporary politics as black magic catches the villagers unaware and unprepared, in a bout of recriminations so out of context that the reader associates them with the Cultural Revolution only because of the outcome: a suicide and the division of the village into factions, with the young men going wild, until one and all get a bellyful of buckshot (190–191/318–319). The episode is kept secret forever after, like the massacre of banana workers in *One Hundred Years of Solitude*. "The strange thing was that at the time nobody warned people to keep their mouths firmly shut. Yet even the children, who did not know any better, did not let out the secrets—if you could call them secrets. What sort of special tradition was this! This inexhaustible wisdom must simply have flowed through their veins" (192/321). So wrote Zhang Wei, after the Tiananmen massacre.

Mo Yan most poignantly depicts politics as a manifestation of evil magic. A rare concatenation of inauspicious events sets the stage for something more terrible than carnival, in *Big Breasts and Wide Hips*. The sun turns black; birds fall out of the sky; purple snakes wriggle down the street; and the narrator says his "goat's milk reeked of blood, and that truly was not normal" (1: 242/238–239). There follows a great slaughter of villagers in the compound of a Nationalist-affiliated Shangguan in-law, perpetrated by Communist forces led by another Shangguan in-law. Then comes a great flood, one of two in the novel. (The other coincides with the Great Leap Forward.)

What comes next, after the waters recede, is an exemplification of the terrible "political marvelous," seen through the lens of folk belief. A mysterious VIP is carried in on a sedan chair, like a god from on high. Accompanied by eighteen bodyguards, likened to the eighteen Arhats of Buddhist theology (1:294/284), he heralds a new era of *mysterious* bloodshed that will replace overt warfare. Class struggle follows, in which the VIP's words are likened by the narrator to white paper funeral streamers "filled with incantations to ward off evil spirits." "The villagers sat dumbfounded, wondering what was going on" (1:294/284). Selected villagers come up to bear false witness against their neighbors. A blind man calls for the extermination of the Simas' young twin daughters and also turns the tables on the meeting's organizers, who are after all related to the Simas by marriage. In a fit of fear, hysteria, and illogic, the innocent Sima twins, Feng and Huang (whose names make up the word for "phoenix"), are sentenced to death in lieu of their missing father. Then comes another concatenation of inexplicable events:

> What happened then remains a puzzle even now. At the moment when Pandi was facing the tear-washed, trancelike face of the mute; at the moment when Sima Feng and Sima Huang stood hand in hand, still terrified . . . ; at the moment when Mother came to her senses and began muttering as she ran toward the pond; at the moment when Xu Xian'er [the blind accuser] rediscovered his conscience and said, County Head, don't kill them . . . ; at the moment when a pair of dogs got into a fight . . . ; at the moment when . . . my mouth filled with the taste of ashes and the fragrance of elasticity of [First Sister's] nipple; at the moment when everyone was trying to guess where the VIP had come from and where he'd gone; at that moment two men on horseback rode in from the southeast like a whirlwind. (1:308/295)

They are two masked horsemen in black and white, who fire their pistols twice before vanishing "in front of our eyes, truly a case of coming on the winds of spring and leaving on the winds of autumn. They seemed like an illusion, though they were real enough" (1:308–309/296). They embody the new, revolutionary political magic, and the revolution itself, for the 1949 "Liberation" that is playing out here is never explicitly mentioned in the novel. When the people in the crowd look down, after the never-identified forces of nature disappear, they see the corpses of Sima Feng and Sima Huang, each with a bullet hole between the eyes.[48]

The story continues until this new, socialist era ends, but without any reference to the death of Mao. After being released from prison in the 1980s, Sima Jintong witnesses a newly chaotic and morally decentered society. The plot turns discursive, skeletal, and absurd, as Jintong is enlisted as an employee for successive post-Mao enterprises and scams. Magic is dead. There is no more need for it, indeed no more room for it. Proliferating new false gods of mammon have sucked up all the manna.

6 CONCLUSION

The End of History, Dystopia, and "New" Historical Novels?

D OES THE CHINESE new historical novel already belong to history now? Perhaps China has entered an age of postmodern prosperity—and political caution—indifferent to history, the quest for utopia, and the fear of dystopia. Will Mo Yan's Nobel Prize, awarded to him in mid-career, paralyze his muse and overshadow his colleagues' achievements?[1] The writers featured in this book dominate what the Chinese media call *shilipai zuojia* ("the strong writers"): powerful, canonical modern authors who have acquired status through their works, not their politics. In their fifties and sixties now, the new historical writers have kept alive the flame of "serious" literature in an age of unbounded commercialism and piracy and have given it global recognition. But the literary baton of contemporary literature is passing to younger generations and their tastes. In 2012 an online Chinese encyclopedia redefined the "strong writers" in favor of younger talents: Zhang Yueran, Qin Yu, Song Haohao, and Anni Baobei.[2]

Grand narratives of a past that many citizens find unbelievable or wish to forget; premonitions of gut-wrenching dystopia; idealisms promoting deferred gratification, a new transcendence, or a new sublime; literary novels that do not help the reader "get ahead"—such works do not reflect the current trend. This need not diminish the canonical status of the now mature authors' "new" historical novels. Their mission has always been to uphold art in literature, perfect it for the long term, and induce readers to take history seriously. It is a modernist quest for "a redemption of modern life through culture"[3] in a "postmodern" time when a sense of history and the search for utopia are supposedly dissolving. To Mo Yan's generation, the opposite of utopian idealism is not dystopian speculation, which is still idealistic, but cynicism and hedo-nism. They may still have hopes for humanism, but they cannot abide Men-cian "feudal humanism," Western individualistic "bourgeois humanism," or, in retrospect, the "Maoist humanism" that attributed to human will the power to remake the self and overcome physical reality. The novelists may, in the end, wish for a better kind of collectivism, one in accord with the transcen-dental, utopian aspirations of their youth. Stories of their own personal par-ticipation in an unhappy history, including reflections on the lot of the writer, are glossed over in their historical novels. Still, their devotion to historical, cultural, familial, and autobiographical themes goes forward.

Latin America's new writers of the later 1980s came to view Marquezian prose as passé, imitative, and culturally essentializing (the Latin American equivalent of alleged "self-orientalizing" in Asian fiction and film). Magical realism had become a fad. Some critics dismissed latter-day magical realists Isabel Allende and Laura Esquivel as "bestseller writers." A younger cosmo-politan wave of the Latin American Post-Boom, not so interested in any pecu-liarly Latin American syndrome, founded a new movement in 1996, in Chile. They called it McOndo, a label evoking the hipness (in their milieu) of a global world of McDonald's, Macintosh computers, and condos. The term also indicated deference, defiance, and anxiety of influence regarding the creator of Macondo and his generation. This is not to say that all "McOndo" works are uncritically immersed in sybaritic, postmodern global lifestyles and brands. Imaginary Latin American nations rendered dystopian by untram-meled global neoliberalism are the subject of *Death as a Side Effect* (1997) by Ana Maria Shua of Argentina and *Sueños digitales* (Digital dreams, 2000) by the Bolivian American author José Edmundo Paz-Soldán, a work indebted to *Nineteen Eighty-Four*.[4] Chilean Roberto Bolaño's (1953–2003) horrific and un-magical thousand-page novel, *2666* (Spanish, 2004; English tr., 2008; Chinese tr., 2011) has reportedly generated "another wave of Latin American literature heat" in China reminiscent of that touched off by *One Hundred Years of Solitude*.[5]

A kind of Chinese McOndo has arisen since the 1990s among writers vari-ously called new-born, later-born, new concept, alternative (*linglei*), rupture (*duanlie*, sometimes translated as "crack," as if borrowed by Chinese critics from the mid-1990s Mexican *literatura de la generación del crack*),[6] post-1980, and post-1990, all terms that are framed in relation to older "schools." At the high end of the McOndos in both hemispheres are, or were, labyrinthine works (a return to Borges) and at the low end, *Shanghai Baby* and novels that revel in a "celebratory representation of a consumer-flâneur lifestyle."[7] Some younger Chinese authors take pride in being hip and best-selling, unafraid of ephemeralism or kitsch. They glory in a sense of rupture not from Maoist discourse but from the children of Mao who use their literary celebrity to continue harping on politics and history. One might, on the other hand, see a Chinese McOndo among expatriate and ambiguously expatriate Chinese writers, some of whom write in English for the global Anglophone market, as certain McOndo authors native in Spanish write in English or Spanglish. Many of the young Chinese writers abroad, however, still set their stories in a distinctively *Chinese* society, with emphasis on their earlier years, which are increasingly not just post-Mao but also post-Tiananmen. The Western-language market may have as broad a reader interest in Maoist and Dengist China as the post-Deng domestic Chinese market.

Lively recent-history novels of India by India-born authors, such as *Midnight's Children*, suggest another comparison. Many are written in English, by "Indo-Anglian" authors. Against Rushdie's intellectual and international market dominance, Amit Chaudhuri has praised writing in India's "vernaculars,"[8] opposing a McOndo-like tendency of catering to cosmopolitanism and a global marketplace favoring English and linguistic hybridism. He also advocates writing about quotidian regional life, without so much allegory, exoticism, magic, or Anglophone figurations in which "modern Indian history has acquired the air of a fancy-dress party or the Mardi Gras."[9]

Critic James Wood has likewise criticized a breathless display of knowledge and trends (e.g., postmodernism) in a broader array of Anglophone novels by Rushdie, Zadie Smith, and Thomas Pynchon, calling the tendency "hysterical realism," which is "not exactly magical realism, but magical realism's next stop." "Stories and substories sprout on every page" in "a perpetual motion machine," with "dolls, puppets, allegories" (referring to another Rushdie novel). This hysterical realism is "a pursuit of vitality at all costs," with caricatures rather than dissections of character. The style is sensationalistic, ephemeral, affected, pedantic, and egotistical.[10]

When it conferred the 2012 Nobel Prize in Literature on Mo Yan, the Nobel Committee noted "hallucinatory realism" in Mo Yan's prose.[11] It is not a common critical term, but Chaudhuri, more than twenty years earlier, wrote of "Rushdie's hallucinatory prose," seemingly to criticize it as magical realism's "next stop."[12] Mo Yan is more often criticized for political caution than "hysterical" style, or certainly pedantry, and the Swedes no doubt meant to praise Mo Yan's imagination. But some of his writing, like Wang Shuo's and

Yu Hua's (in *Brothers*), may be too over-the-top, slapdash, and repetitious in its satire to survive changes in taste.

A difference between China's new historical novels and Anglophone works by South Asia–born authors is that the latter tend to be *national* allegories in Fredric Jameson's sense, about the destiny of a mere nation. However, the comparative advantage in competition with India need not go to China. In our age still dominated by nation-states, the Nation as an abstract, global construct can be allegorized. And India's "hysterical" vitality may reflect the richness of its pluralism and democracy. The Chinese novels are transnational partly because lack of democratic freedoms endangers exploration of China as a polity, as a nation. If a British or North American novelist of South Asian extraction won a Nobel Prize in literature, diverse readers and nonreaders of South Asian origin across the globe might well claim the writer for the glory of Bharat Mata, Pakistan, Bangladesh, or Sri Lanka, though most candidates one can imagine, from Rushdie to Ondaatje, would be in every sense less "Asian" than Gao Xingjian was when he won his Nobel Prize in 2000. The Chinese propaganda apparatus has persuaded most Chinese readers to ignore and disdain Gao as "not Chinese," because he turned his back on the Chinese *state*.

The Death of Utopia and Dystopia?

The "death of utopia"—not to be confused with Herbert Marcuse's "end of utopia," which envisioned the obsolescence of hypothetical plans for social perfection because Marcuse thought perfection (or really, material plenty) might finally be realizable—today refers mostly to disillusionment with Marxism as a utopian program. Such talk proliferated in the 1990s with the fall of the Soviet empire and the "end of history," though the discourse has earlier and broader referents.[13] Marxists (not including Ernst Bloch, Herbert Marcuse, or Fredric Jameson) and Karl Mannheim have generally seen both ideologies and utopias as distortions of reality, though Mannheim also viewed utopian visions as fruitful agents of change and ideologies as upholders of the status quo. His critic Karl Popper argued that, on the contrary, utopian aspirations lead to violence.[14] Chinese in the Mao era did not see Mao Zedong Thought as an ideology or utopia in those prewar negative senses, but in post-Mao times, the utopian or "sublime" elements of Maoism are in some circles celebrated, shorn of their historical outcomes. Mannheim is widely cited by Chinese cultural critics today, and others agree with Jameson's insistence on "the necessity of the reinvention of the Utopian vision."[15] China's new historical novelists, more like Popper, fear that utopian plans and resultant dystopias will never die.

Our Chinese novelists, like Jameson, now see unrecognized and harmful utopianism in the market economy rationales that have replaced Maoism in China.[16] The Mo Yan and Yu Hua burlesques about Cultural Revolution theme parks and so forth are humorous, but these episodes, at the end of their long novels, may strike future readers as shallow, derivative, overly topical, and "hysterical." Andreas Huyssen points out that "for Baudrillard, utopia is not to be realized, to be transformed from dream and fiction into reality, because it has already been realized in the opposite sense that in the society of the simulacrum reality itself has become u-topian ['a no- place'], hyper-real."[17] (That would spell dystopian.) Finding *unusual* incongruity worthy of satire in postmodern times is difficult due to aesthetic confusion. Chinese readers are interested in conventional dystopian novels full of stingingly realistic Orwellian political critique, like Chan Koonchung's *The Fat Years*, but the more literary (and more censored) in-country "strong" novelists feel they have a "deeper," cultural mission to fulfill. That puts them at odds not just with popular writers, but also with dissidents, who feel that political critique is more fundamental. This recapitulates a century-old split in the outlook of Chinese intellectuals: should critique of culture come first, or critique of politics? It is common readers, "protected" from political commentary, who may not appreciate dystopian critiques of their very own consumerist goals and accomplishments. Ge Fei himself has not asked the theoretical question of whether a reformed, self-sustaining, and replicable (if replication is not in principle dystopian!) Marcusean material utopia superior to Huaxi's parasitic one would be spiritually utopian or dystopian.[18]

The new historical novelists, like most people, require of life a sense of novelty and wonderment. Their magical realism, humor, and other fantastic and absurd touches endeavor to maintain and restore this "magic" by literary means. The need for a sense of wonder and magic in life unveils a weakness not just in most utopias, but also in "happiness" itself, if that happiness is cast as predictability, security, postmodern choice and freedom without limits, indeed fulfillment. Is the denial of change and uncertainty not a denial of wonder, novelty, and hope itself? If dystopia is embodied not only in Orwellian futurism but also in stability, recurrence, and "guaranteed happiness" safe from "anarchy" and disapproved trends in culture, how can one not be bored? This is a conundrum yet to be faced by the novelists. Moreover, in the cacophony of post-Mao, post-Deng, cybernetic, anything-goes times, satirical descriptions of current trends may simply reinforce an unwelcome sense of anarchy, confusion, and rampant copying of that which is mediocre in these still un-utopian times.

HISTORICAL NOVELS IN A POSTMODERN OR POST-POSTMODERN WORLD

Are China's new historical novels postmodern then? Terms like "postmodern historical novel" and postmodern "historiographic metafiction" (Linda Hutcheon, 5) have been applied to works by John Barth, Thomas Pynchon, Ishmael Reed, and Robert Coover, and also Carlos Fuentes, Gabriel García Márquez, and Salman Rushdie; indeed, these works have even been said to have a utopian variant when a counterfactual narrative of the past is happier than the real thing.[19] Nonlinear plotting, spectacle, pastiche, trauma, black humor, and carnival absurdity occurring in the Chinese novels previously analyzed, particularly as the timeline approaches the present, suggest postmodern "play" as much as modernist "subversion." The novels' quasi-biological determinism at times conspires to negate the psychological depth of canonical modernism or any sense of alienation beyond elemental suspicion of the group. Some works, on the other hand, remain true to "old-fashioned" realistic technique and social analysis. The deadly serious dystopian outlook is itself a major factor linking the novels to modernism. The sundry excesses, inward turns, and syncretism of Huaxi, Chinese McOndo, and even the metafictional and epistemological querying of China's 1980s avant-garde stories "about history" and Wang Xiaobo's continuation of their inquiries in his triple trilogy, seem more postmodern than the now "classic" and idealistic "new" historical novels.[20] Meanwhile, critics such as Xudong Zhang, Zhang Yiwu, and Jason McGrath have applied the postmodern label to indie cinema and elite fiction by authors such as He Dun, Chen Ran, and Han Dong who creatively deal with the complications and discontinuities of contemporary urban, globalized Chinese life.[21] Surely a new reincarnation of the serious political novel is waiting in the wings, too, when the political atmosphere unfreezes. It is too soon to tell whether these kinds of works, or yet another round of "neo-realism," memoirs, or other subgenres that competed with new historical novels for readers in the 1990s, will achieve a longer-lived ascendancy. Meanwhile, "postmodernism" must come to an end sometime, and some critics think it has.[22] For now, book publishing still flourishes—of "workplace novels" (*zhichang xiaoshuo*), for instance, a genre that contains self-help tips.

Liu Zhenyun's *One Word Is Worth a Thousand* (lit., "One Sentence Is Worth Ten Thousand"; 2009; Mao Dun Prize, 2011) is an acclaimed recent novel that might exemplify the Chinese postmodern. Its highly mannered, minimalist prose calls attention to itself; its subject matter folds in on itself; and its implied view of the "times" is so counterintuitive that some might think of it as "alternate history." Chen Xiaoming writes that this novel by a former "neo-realist" is so unrealistic as to be avant-garde.[23] If we stipulate that it fits the postmodern mold, the novel raises the question of whether the latter is compatible with conventional historical interests. I see Liu's masterwork as a postmodern "anti-historical novel," set in the past but unconcerned with the history that undergirds the new historical novel.

The setting of this work is a seemingly timeless rural China, viewed in anthropological, transhistorical terms reminiscent of 1980s Chinese avant-garde writing and also 1980s neo-realism, which detailed "quotidian," every-day culture. Liu's masterpiece is a quest novel, or rather two period quest novels in succession, with heroes from a further and a recent past linked by ties of blood—ties broken during a long historical gap in the middle of the work, as in Ge Fei's *Southlands Trilogy*. The picaresque heroes' perpetually unattainable quest is for confidants: folks to "talk to"—meaning, those one can "get along with," even see eye to eye with, though the linguistically obsessed omniscient narrator insists on tagging each character literally as "talkative" or "not talkative" when he or she enters the narrative.

The initial, 208-page piece of the saga is set in Liu Zhenyun's old home and favorite location for his fiction, Yanjin County, Henan. The work's older characters were born into a vaguely late Qing or early Republican era, as in the opening pages of Ge Fei's *Bygone Beauty*. A long and digressive trail of happenstance, *guanxi*, and petty disputes that destroy those *guanxi* cast the second-generation hero Yang Baishun successively as tofu maker, butcher, dyer, water carrier, festival player, gardener in a yamen, bamboo splitter (work introduced by an Italian Catholic missionary who renames him Yang Moxi, or Moses Yang), then steamed bun hawker (by way of an uxorilocal marriage that requires another name change, to Wu Moxi), and finally, refugee in Shaanxi under yet a third name, to escape ignominy after his dear five-year-old stepdaughter Qiaoling is stolen from him—during a trip taken on the false pretense of hunting for his truly unfaithful runaway wife. Moxi's quest is not to "only connect," but also to find a trade, a home, and a life "direction," as the priest puts it. Each compromise, each life and name change, threatens his dignity (recalling Lao She's character Camel Xiangzi). His original name, Baishun ("Always Going Along with Things"), suggests an intrinsic flaw of character or culture.

The hero of the second part is Niu Aiguo ("Patriotic" Niu, the surname meaning "Bull") of Shanxi province. His mother is in time revealed to be the former Qiaoling, who after being kidnapped was sold in Shanxi while still a child. She is the middle-aged Cao Qing'e as we meet her now, evidently in the early post-Mao era, as one may guess from a character getting her first perm (215). Aiguo, a truck driver who previously served in the army on the edge of the Gobi Desert (as did Liu Zhenyun in life), goes on many trips and makes many friendships, all destined to be severed. His wife cheats on him and abandons her family, just like Yang Moxi's wife decades before. When Aiguo's mother dies, he goes to seek his "roots" rather than his unfaithful wife and when that is frustrated, a lover whom he himself abandoned.

Critics are bound to dispute the work's multiple implied deeper meanings and allegories, and with difficulty try to reconcile them. Do the heroes, for instance, and should readers, go in quest of an essential single sentence or insight worth ten thousand?[24] The novel recalls old Ming-Qing novels and has simulated storyteller's patter. The plot is episodic and the characters numerous, with new ones appearing up to the end; each is schematically characterized and known forever after, reiteratively, with Homeric epithets marking his or her temperament, talkativeness, trade, family, *guanxi*, and grudges. One event simply leads to another, each of which has a backstory. Liu's mannered and repetitive prose, stripped of modifiers and details, is rich in Yanjin dialect usages, and an obliging narrator explains several of them.

Critics, the book jacket, and Liu Zhenyun's later commentary suggest that *One Word Is Worth a Thousand* is a pastiche not just of the Ming-Qing novel but also of *One Hundred Years of Solitude*. Human isolation is Liu's theme—a solitude evidently less abstractly existential than that explored by Ge Fei and García Márquez, though Liu's social version of it is panhuman, not just a narrowly national or cultural critique. Like García Márquez, Liu has composed a rambling and allegorical multigenerational family saga. The plot develops in concrete geographical places (actual, unlike Macondo), but the era is vague. The abundant cast of secondary characters—"Old Ma," "Old Yang," and "Old Pei," all small-time itinerant craftsmen and peddlers from their respective nondescript Ma Family Village, Yang Family Village, and Pei Family Village—recalls the monotony of the given names that recur in successive generations of Buendías. The Yanjin characters' hobbies and hobbyhorses, including funeral songs, non-Yanjin operas, and the game of go, likewise recall the Macondians' idiosyncratic penchants for astronomy, old manuscripts, and making golden fish.

The themes of *One Word Is Worth a Thousand* might well be considered postmodern, though its quasi-throwback style, largely mimetic, does not restructure one's view of "reality." A bigger question for us is whether it conveys any sense of history. The putatively old-fashioned narrator takes pains to explain chains of causation, often with formulaic and mesmerizingly repetitive grammar: "Old Yang's dispute with Old Pei was not (*bushi*) due to factors X or Y just related, but rather (*ershi*) because of Z, as follows." Liu's epic of quotidian events may even be called a grand narrative, a family saga like those of Mo Yan, Su Tong, Yu Hua, and Li Rui, with lively digressions about family offshoots and rivals worthy of Zhang Wei. The family and the neighborhood are broken and confining institutions as in the dystopian novels—given to feuds, fisticuffs, wife beating, and recurrence. Moxi, his father, and his wife keep making the same mistakes. And Aiguo and Moxi are driven by similar dysfunctional social expectations to leave town, under the same false pretense of tracking down their adulterous wives. Search for the woman who abandoned him by successive male heroes is the recurring theme not of *One Hundred Years of Solitude*, but *Men of Maize*. That quest symbolizes deteriorating male-female and man-land relations in three successive eras of Central American history.[25]

Unlike Guatemala as Asturias more fancifully and mythically describes it in roughly the same era, rural North China in Liu's novel has no evident center, national capital, or leader, not even a Nationalist or Communist Party. Yet, unlike the new historical novels, there are no hints in Liu's masterpiece of civil disorder or national policies. (The major clue that chapter 3 of the second section is a flashback to *pre*-post-Mao times is families with third and fourth children.) Human nature remains as dark and petty as in the new historical masterworks, even without social breakdown. Numerous characters, particularly Moxi and Aiguo, experience murderous urges. They rush out to act on them, but a chance encounter with a third party invariably prevents bloodshed.

That opportune legal and spiritual deliverance of a potential murderer separates Liu Zhenyun's novel from his colleagues' dystopian ones. Further, he "intentionally avoided mentioning historical events and their influence," he explains.[26] One can guess the era when a bicycle, train, or long-distance bus appears amid the donkey carts,[27] or Beijing is called Beiping (87), as it was from 1928 until 1949.[28] One gathers from the name "Patriotic Niu" that the second cast of characters inhabits post-1949 times and, later, that "present time" has already skipped ahead to "post-socialism," due to offhand mentions of a new superhighway, independent truckers (220), a "company" (292), and finally, cell phones. The late appearance of a character named Jiefang or "Liberation" (324), a name given to those born in 1949, establishes a more concrete time-line only retrospectively.[29]

Yet, important "history" was made in twentieth-century Henan. Much of *One Word Is Worth a Thousand*'s first section apparently unfolds in 1935, which was relatively peaceful. Still, there are no visible scars from Henan's decades of warlord turmoil and extreme poverty. The characters' descendants in the second part act as if they and their parents never experienced North China's eight-year Sino-Japanese War, Japanese occupation, the civil war, transition to socialism, Great Leap, post-Leap famine, Cultural Revolution, "post-socialist" turn, or innumerable floods and other disasters, like the devastating 1975 typhoon that washed out dozens of dams in Henan. Because the novel leaps over the entire Maoist era, Liu's post-Mao characters, like young readers today, have no occasion to recall cooperatives, people's communes, political campaigns, abolition of private commerce, or settling of scores with landlords and petty capitalists. Characters of those classes appear in the first section, but the second provides no clue whether they, including Moxi's immediate Jiang in-laws, survived the revolution.

This is not to charge Liu Zhenyun with timidity. In *Back to 1942* he re-awakened public memory of a great Henan famine and its political origins, and his Homeland series tells epic tales of dictatorship. But *One Word Is Worth a Thousand* is an "anti-historical novel" that takes pains to erase all "big events" and institutions.[30] *One Hundred Years of Solitude* has no "real" histori-cal events, either, but they appear symbolically, in recurring epidemics of mass amnesia, thirty-two civil wars between Liberals and Conservatives, the coming to town of the police and multinationals, and a hushed-up massacre of protestors in the town square. *Men of Maize* has concrete referents in his-tory and myth. *One Word Is Worth a Thousand* can be praised for its prose style, narrative ingenuity, and depth in understanding timeless, panhuman behavior. It is unlikely to be read as a comment on history. It seems to imply that social-historical context is irrelevant to individual life stories. And that opens the question of whether this particular novel, and Chinese postmodernism gener-ally, are all too well suited to ephemeral taste and ideological strictures. Postmodern or not, *One Word Is Worth a Thousand* helps define China's new historical novel because in some ways it is its antithesis.

Liu Zhenyun has said that "the loneliness of a society without religion" is that novel's "main theme. Without a trustworthy God or Buddha to talk to, lonely people turn to friends. But God keeps secrets while friends often don't."[31] Perhaps he means that in an atheistic, "humanistic" society, sharing confidences is difficult, for it can occur only between all-too-fallible peers. This is a fascinating argument, opening the door to a recasting of human isolation and egoism as a non-theistic, Chinese humanist variant of the idea of Original Sin. However, Liu's words, even without comparisons to Latin American and other global literature, surely overstates the place of religion in his novel, or any quest for supra-social justice. Yet his comment points to a broad concern of all "postmodern," global citizens.

The new historical novels, however desirous of eternal, unbounded, and transnational notions of history and morality, show no confidence or faith in larger, cosmic sources of meaning. (Works by Zhang Chengzhi, who converted from Maoism to a populist Islamic sect, are an exception.) Even in their comic and absurd variations, China's new historical novels fruitlessly yearn for transcendental justice and righteousness from above: from Heaven, God, the gods, or sage officials. They are nowhere to be found. Meanwhile, as literary novelists, the writers seek novelty and the ability to impart a sense of wonder. Precisely where in life and art to look for justice, goodness, and creativity, when in life one sees rampant unpunished evil, ecological catastrophe, conflicts among "the people," unfortunate outcomes in the grand sweep of history, and derivativeness and ephemerality in literature and literary fame is a question with no resolution on the horizon. Utopia lacks wonder; dystopia lacks justice. God is dead; "life" disappoints.

CHINESE CHARACTERS

Ai Qing	艾青	He Dun	何顿
Alai	阿来	Hong Xiuquan	洪秀全
Anni Baobei	安妮宝贝	*hua* (flower)	花
Ba (kingdom)	巴	Huajiashe	花家舍
Bo Juyi	白居易	Huaxi	华西
Cai Cehai	蔡测海	Jin Yong	金庸
changlang	长廊	Li Dazhao	李大钊
Changzhou	常州	Li Er	李洱
Chen Cun	陈村	Liang Shuming	梁漱溟
Chen Ran	陈染	Ling Yu	凌宇
Chu (kingdom)	楚	*linglei*	另类
Cui Hu	崔护	Liu Suola	刘索拉
Deng Youmei	邓友梅	Liu Zaifu	刘再复
Du Mu	杜牧	*longtang*	弄堂
duanlie	断裂	Lu Wenfu	陆文夫
Dushu	读书	Lu You	陆游
Gaomi	高密	Ma Junwu	马君武
Gou Dao	狗道	Ma Yuan	马原
Gu Changwei	顾长卫	*maoqiang*	猫腔 (茂腔)
Gu Jiegang	顾颉刚	*moleng liangke*	模棱两可
guanxi	关系	Ōe Kenzaburō	大江健三郎
Guo Dao	国道	Ouyang Xiu	欧阳修
Guo Moruo	郭沫若	*pai* (faction)	派
Han Dong	韩东	Pingyao	平遥

Qin Yu	秦豫	Yan Fu	严复
qun (groups)	群	Yang Guifei	杨贵妃
Ren Dao	人道	Ye Weilin	叶蔚林
Song Haohao	宋浩浩	Yen, James Y. C.	晏阳初
shilipai zuojia	实力派作家	*yiku*	忆苦
shiwai taoyuan	世外桃源	*yuefu*	乐府
suku	诉苦	*yuyan*	寓言
Tao Qian	陶潜	Zeng Guofan	曾国藩
Taohuayuan	桃花源	Zhang Ailing	张爱玲
Tashi Dawa	扎西达娃	Zhang Tianyi	张天翼
tufei	土匪	Zhang Xianzhong	张献忠
Wang Meng	王蒙	Zhang Xinxin	张辛欣
Wu Renbao	吴仁宝	Zhang Yueran	张悦然
wujing tianze	物竞天择	Zheng He	郑和
xiangtu xiaoshuo	乡土小说	*zhichang xiaoshuo*	职场小说
xin lishi xiaoshuo	新历史小说	Zhou Zuoren	周作人
Xu Zhimo	徐志摩	*zhuanyuan*	专员

NOTES

1. Introduction: Chinese Visions of History and Dystopia

1. Jonathan Spence, "Born Again," review of Mo Yan's *Life and Death Are Wearing Me Out*, *New York Times Book Review*, May 4, 2008, 8.

2. González Echevarría, *Myth and Archive*, 13–18. Coover suggests that literature was Latin America's "most dangerous export" and that the phrase "total novel" may come from "*futbol total*"—a quest leading to "beautiful consequences and ultimate frustration."

3. Visser, *Cities Surround the Countryside* (the book title reverses the geography of the Maoist military strategy).

4. A minor exception: Mo Yan's *Sandalwood Death* has cameo portraits of Yuan Shikai, Zhang Xun, Liu Guangdi, and the Empress Dowager. The plot of this period novel in the form of a popular saga mostly comes from Mo Yan's imagination and hometown stories from Gaomi, Shandong. In the novel, Gaomi County residents lead resistance to German colonial railroad building (as in life), suffer a retaliatory German massacre of twenty-seven Chinese in a fictitious walled town called Masang that the Germans later bombard with artillery (in life, it was twenty-five Chinese in three villages and subsequently a bombardment of another village, killing more than four hundred), and German occupation of the Gaomi county town, with its academy as German headquarters (in life, though not in the novel, the Germans burned its famous library as a reproof to China's Confucian *Weltanshauung*). On the history, see Mühlhahn, 46–47. Oddly, the novel asserts that 1899 was not "an especially bad year" (165/139). In life, there was a great famine. It also seems odd that a magistrate in those troubled times would

predict that the Qing court was about to abolish the traditional examinations (375/322). Mühlhahn in a personal communication adds that the German names are fictitious, except for Clemens von Ketteler, and so are most events in which Germans appear, although German railway workers' harassment of local Chinese women was real and did lead to the uprising. He finds the descriptions of Boxer rituals relatively realistic, and there was in fact a gathering of thousands of locals and a march toward the city. Mühlhahn cites a Sun Wen as a peasant leader. The counterpart in the novel is Sun Bing.

5. Film: *Chang hen ge*, 2005, *Everlasting Regret*, Stanley Kwan, dir. (Hong Kong).

6. Less well known is the adaptation of Su Tong's *Rice*, as *Dahong midian* (1995, Huang Jianzhong, dir., banned until 2003). Production of an adaptation of Su Tong's *Tattoo*, as *Ciqing shidai* (Jia Zhangke, dir.), once due out in 2007, has stalled.

7. Anita Chan's book by this title refers to the Red Guard cohort.

8. Zheng Yi (b. 1947) and Wu Tianming (b. 1939, in Shaanxi) are older than the others. Wu graduated from the Beijing Film School in the "Fourth Genera-tion," originally known for Soviet-style "realistic" cinema. On *Old Well*, see Jiayan Mi.

9. Kinkley, "Modernity and Apocalypse," discusses *Yellow Peril*. Song, guest ed., anthologizes utopian and dystopian science fiction.

10. On Wang Xiaobo's works, see Morrison and Lin Qingxin.

11. Gary Xu analyzes relevant Ye Zhaoyan works.

12. Li Yuchun, 32, and Fokkema, 332, call certain novels by Yan Lianke dystopian.

13. On the fantastic allegories in *The Republic of Wine*, see Shelley Chan; Xiaobin Yang, 207–229; my review in *World Literature Today* 74.3 (Summer 2000): 581–582; and Kinkley, "A Talk with Chinese Novelist Mo Yan."

14. Jameson, "Third World Literature."

15. Huyssen, "Memories of Utopia," in his *Twilight Memories*, 85–101.

16. Cowart, 4.

17. This book's chapters 3 and 5 discuss Zhang Wei's ambivalent treatment of *The Communist Manifesto*. The published version of Su Tong's *The Boat to Re-demption* (but not the English) has a brief, perhaps slighting reference to Ku Wenxuan carrying a copy of Engels's *Anti-Dühring* (101, 102, but not 147, 149).

18. Lukács, 183.

19. Wang Biao, ed., "Daolun," 1–13, argues this, as did Xudong Zhang when I presented an earlier version of this chapter to the Columbia Modern China Semi-nar, October 11, 2012.

20. One might add novels by Alai (b. 1959), Jia Pingwa (b 1952), Ma Yuan (b. 1953), Zhang Chengzhi (b. 1948), and Chen Zhongshi (b. 1942), even Bai Hua (b. 1930; author of *The Remote Country of Women*, 1988), and novellas by Tashi Dawa (b. 1955). Morrison convincingly includes novels by Li Er (b. 1966) and other novels by Liu Zhenyun and Wang Xiaobo (1952–1997). Payne analyzes other 1990s works by Ge Fei. Wang Biao and Jie Lu emphasize Qiao Liang's (b. 1968) 1986 novella *Ling qi* (Mourning flag).

21. Seymour Menton popularized the idea of a Latin American "new historical novel" in his book by that title. He traces the subgenre's ascendancy only to 1979 (Carpentier's *The Harp and the Shadow*), though *One Hundred Years of Solitude* (1967) and Carpentier's *The Kingdom of This World* (1949; Menton does list this work in his *"prependix"*) seem to fit the mold. Swanson, 92, like others, feels that novels of the new historical type date back to the Boom. I feel Menton defines the *historical novel* too broadly, to include any novel set in the past, and the *new* historical novel too narrowly. He finds six traits in the latter, "although all six are not necessarily found in each novel": 1. Philosophical ideas, 2. Conscious distortion of history, 3. Using famous historical figures as characters, 4. Metafiction, 5. Intertextuality, and 6. "Bakhtinian concepts of the *dialogic*, the *carnivalesque*, parody, and *heteroglossia*" (22–25).

22. "Umberto Eco to Receive Treaties of Nijmegen Medal," January 23, 2012, http://www.treatiesofnijmegenmedal.eu/news/umberto-eco-to-receive-treaties-of -nijmegen-medal/, accessed July 18, 2012.

23. Chinese Muslims in 1989 launched street marches protesting a novel they felt insulted Islam, citing Khomeini's 1989 fatwa against Rushdie as a precedent. The Chinese Communist state, then under assault during the Tiananmen democracy movement, redoubled efforts to "protect" Islam. See Gladney. But this does not explain previous Chinese neglect of modern Indian literature.

24. *Xiangzhengxing* and *yuyanxing changpian xiaoshuo*, from Lei Da.

25. See Wang Biao, ed.; Hong Zhigang; Chen Sihe, 306–310; Yan Min, *Posui*; Ouyang Ming. Choy, 20–25, Fu Shuhua, and Zhang Liqun summarize the many views. One can express "new historical novel[s]" in Chinese as *xin lishi changpian xiaoshuo*, but a Google search of that and similar terms in Chinese led to zero hits still in September 2011. On August 22, 2013, a search for the exact term yielded just four hits, and for *"changpian xin lishi xiaoshuo"* (in Chinese characters), just twenty-nine hits.

26. Zhang Qinghua, Yan Min, *Posui*. See Choy's clarifications, 20–25. Qiu Lan shows how ideas of writing the history of common people and their lives are identified with *yeshi, unofficial* history.

27. Chen Sihe, 306–310. Choy, 20, says Chen "formulated" the Chinese term, citing a 1992 article, but Hong Zhigang used the term in 1991. The Baidu definition is at http://baike.baidu.com/view/2564989.htm, accessed July 18, 2012. Lin Qingxin's major monograph in English defines new historical fiction as oppositional to the discourse of revolution, adding that it opposes the discourse of modernity and emphasizes "spatial narration" (11).

28. Wang Biao, ed., "Daolun," 1–13, emphasizes the metaphysical emphasis of the shorter works. See for instance Ge Fei's "Mi zhou" (The lost boat). A forerunner of the new historical fiction is the 1979 story "Open Ground" by Wan Zhi (pseud. of Chen Maiping). In the Mao years, such was the hold of revolutionary "realism" and the majesty of the historical subject (typically the Red Army vs. its foes) that some critics found it audacious simply for an author to enter the mind (or subjectivity, a concept popularized by the liberal critic Liu Zaifu) of a person who lived in a bygone era to imagine events not derived from "historical materials." It was, however, expected that authors would continue to write of warfare. See Hong Zhigang.

29. Mo Yan's full-length *The Garlic Ballads* (1988) pioneered use of folkish narrative devices.

30. Sommer, 1–3.

31. Henry Zhao, "Post-Isms"; Ben Xu.

32. He Zhenbang; Hong Zicheng, 443; Chen Mo; Lei Da on the conventional historical novels.

33. I agree with Chen Fong-ching and Jin Guantao, 142–148, 182–185, that 1984–1986 was a cultural "golden triennium," followed by a "looming crisis" of 1986–1987 and beyond, which presaged the 1989 massacre.

34. Wolfgang Kubin savages even Mo Yan's works, in "Interview: Mo Yan Bores Me to Death," interviewer Mathias von Hein, Deutsche Welle, October 12, 2012, http://www.dw.de/interview-mo-yan-bores-me-to-death/a-16301782, accessed February 28, 2013.

35. Donald L. Shaw, "The Post-Boom," entry in Smith, ed., 498. See also Peter Standish's "The Boom" entry, 70–71.

36. Shaw, "The Post-Boom," 499.

37. China's middlebrow and formulaic historical narratives appear in television serials about famous emperors, officials, and palace intrigues; in heroic post-Mao but still state-backed *zhu xuanlü* ("main melody" or leitmotif) films and television dramas about modern leaders; and in popular twentieth-century novels by Jin Yong and others set in imperial times, commonly thought of as chivalric or martial arts fiction. Historical novels set in ancient dynasties that are more of the

Graves and Renault type were written post-Mao by Tang Haoming, Er Yue He, Liu Sifen, Ling Li, Zhang Xiaotian, etc. See Lei Da.

38. Bowers, 39, 63, 84.

39. Jameson, "Third World Literature"; Hsia. Even Mo Yan's *Sandalwood Death* emphasizes how personal motivations, not German imperialism, led Chinese into the Boxer Rising.

40. Mo Yan has proclaimed Faulkner his favorite foreign author and indicated that his literary construct of Northeast Gaomi Township was stimulated by the example of Yoknapatawpha. Shelley Chan, 15.

41. Interview by anonymous reporter, "Mo Yan: Wo yiting 'maoqiang' jiu ganjue relei yingkuang!" (Mo Yan: The moment I hear "Maoqiang opera," my eyes fill with hot tears!), posted on Baicu Tieba, undated [2003?]. http://tieba.baidu .com/f?kz=142997189, accessed September 6, 2012.

42. In a jocular mood I meant to coin this term, but an Internet search finds it the subject of articles and theses in Chinese. Su Wei, 51, already used the term in 1991.

43. Entry for *fanwutuobang* (dystopia), Baidu, http://baike.baidu.com/view /525451.htm. Douban begins with the "trilogy," then proceeds to *Fahrenheit 451*, *Lord of the Flies*, and others, including the *Gulag Archipelago*. http://book .douban.com/tag/%E5%8F%8D%E4%B9%8C%E6%89%98%E9%82%A6. *Lord of the Flies* tops a popular, anonymous 2010 Chinese Web list of the "Twelve best-selling dystopian novels" that omits *We*. http://www.360doc.com/content/ 10/0308/12/655789_17979799.shtml. All sites accessed March 10, 2013. Chinese novels are conspicuous by their absence in these lists.

44. Eberlein says that *Nineteen Eighty-Four* and *Brave New World* appeared in mass printings in Chinese in 1985. A limited-circulation translation of *Nineteen Eighty-Four* "for reference" of CCP cadres was reportedly printed in 1979. The National Library in Beijing holds a 1989 copy of *Animal Farm* in Chinese but no reprints from the 1990s; they appeared only after 2003. Mo Yan told interviewer Kong Wuchen that his *The Republic of Wine* "is a political allegory similar to George Orwell's *Animal Farm*." Cited in Shelley Chan, 197.

45. The National Library in Beijing holds multiple translations, each by a different translator and published by a different press: one in 1984, two in 1985, two more in 1987, one in 1990, etc.; a Chinese adaptation for children appeared in 1990. The novel's view of human nature was debated in *Dushu* (Reading) in 1980–1981 (see Xue Dezhen; Chen Hun). In the 1990s, Ge Fei, Chi Li, and Wang Shuo were dismissive of *Lord of the Flies*—Wang, precisely because it has an allegorical message; more positive were Ma Yuan, Yu Jie, and Alai (who also liked *Animal Farm* and *Nineteen Eighty-Four*) (Zhang Helong, 59, 61).

46. E.g., Li Ruzhen's early nineteenth-century *Jing hua yuan* (Flowers in the mirror); Liang Qichao's *Xin Zhongguo weilai ji* (A future account of the new China, 1902); Wu Jianren's *Xin shitou ji* (New story of the stone, 1905–1908); Lao She's *Mao cheng ji* (Cat Country, 1933; banned during the Maoist years); and Bai Hua's (b. 1930) *The Remote Country of Women* (1988). Can Xue's (b. 1953) novellas *Old Floating Cloud* (1986) and *Yellow Mud Street* (1986) describe a dystopian contemporary Chinese urban scene, but are not historical. For analyses of premodern Chinese dystopias, see Hanan, 173–176; David Der-wei Wang, *Fin-de-siècle Splendor*, 252–312; and Fokkema, 284–287, 330–344. Excerpts of late Qing and recent science fiction are translated in Song, guest ed.

47. Jones, *Developmental Fairy Tales*, 39–40; Hanan, 76; quotation from Hill, 127. See also Kang Youwei's great nonfiction utopia, *Datongshu* (English translation, *Ta T'ung Shu*), which germinated ca. 1884 and was finally published in 1935.

48. Fokkema, 57, 83–93, etc.

49. Zamyatin's *We* begins the literary tradition of dystopia being under a dome, later seen in the film *Logan's Run* and many other sci-fi works.

50. *The Iron Heel* (London, 1907), *It Can't Happen Here* (Lewis, 1935), *Messiah* (Vidal, 1954), and *A Clockwork Orange* (Burgess, 1962). Ayn Rand's *Atlas Shrugged* (1957) is dystopian, but the work ends happily, for her true believers.

51. Ignatius Donnelly, *Caesar's Column* (1890). Edward M. House, *Philip Dru: Administrator* (1912).

52. Hayot, 148–167.

53. Gottlieb, 27–30.

54. Gottlieb, 10, 16–17.

55. The standard reference is Link, *The Uses of Literature*.

56. M. Keith Booker, *The Dystopian Impulse*.

57. The play contributed the word "robot" to the English language. The work is subtitled *Rossum's Universal Robots*; "R.U.R." is an abbreviation. Bulgakov's *The Master and Margarita* was published posthumously, in 1967, then enjoyed international éclat.

58. Napier, 186. Strecher.

59. Abe's dystopian *The Woman in the Dunes* and *The Box Man* do count among his most famous works. There is also a dystopian strain in Japanese graphic novels. Murakami Haruki's 1Q84 (2009–2010), a best seller in Japan, is arguably dystopian. According to Fujii Shozo, Murakami's novels were translated into Chinese only beginning in 1989. There was a "Murakami boom" after 1998.

60. Works about the future are sometimes revised to keep pace with actual technological and historical change ("retcon," or retroactive continuity—indeed,

"retcon" of historical records was the job of *Nineteen Eighty-Four*'s Ministry of Truth). Margaret Atwood and Wang Lixiong might wish they had not referred to the USSR in their futuristic novels, *The Handmaid's Tale* and *Yellow Peril*.

61. Anders sees the influence of Saramago's novels *Blindness* and *Seeing* on the Chinese mass amnesia depicted in Chan Koonchung's novel. But the mass amnesia in *One Hundred Years of Solitude* is better known in China.

62. Wu Liang et al., eds. Shaowen. Yang Shumao, 349, 371–374. On the work's global appeal, see Browitt.

63. Jing Wang, 38; Su Wei, 50; Shelley Chan, 74. The Communist Party helped fan and organize writers' desires for native, not Western "roots" of literature. Payne, 145–147, finds the roots-searching literature "quasi-utopian"—at pains to discover arcadian origins.

64. Shaowen writes of a surge of translations of Latin American works and collections of them in the ten years after García Márquez won his prize, academic conferences about him, etc. Zou Geben, 16, says 205 Latin American literary works were published in China in Chinese from 2000 to 2008. When asked in 1999 for "ten short stories that have influenced me," Mo Yan selected García Márquez's "The Old Man with Enormous Wings" and Cortázar's "The Southern Thruway." Shelley Chan, 5. On the Chinese Nobel mania, see Lovell, *The Politics of Cultural Capital*, 114, 123, 128.

65. On Carpentier's 1967 China trip, mentioned in my preface, see Anderson, 5, González Echevarría, *Alejo Carpentier*, 221, and Carpentier's own "The Baroque and the Marvelous Real" (1975). Asturias visited China on a 1956 invitation to attend commemorations of the twentieth anniversary of Lu Xun's death.

66. Patricia Murray, entry on *Cien años de soledad*, in Smith, 268.

67. Wu Ziru. Schiaffini writes that Tashi Dawa, a Tibetan who writes in Chinese, likes to think of himself as the Chinese García Márquez.

68. In *One Hundred Years of Solitude*, however, the execution never occurs. Li Rui's character Li Zihen, a spinster who sacrifices her marriageability for the sake of the family, like Férula of Isabel Allende's *The House of the Spirits*, recalls Amaranta of *One Hundred Years of Solitude*.

69. Bowers, 50–51.

70. Shelley Chan, 5, 15–16; Kinkley personal interview of Mo Yan, March 25, 2000.

71. Bowers, 32–82, considers these noted aspects of García Márquez's and Rushdie's writing as magical realism. So did early readers of *Red Sorghum*, who were amazed by a narrator who enters the minds of grandparents he has never met.

72. Zhang Wei, *The Ancient Ship*, 4/5.

73. In the novella "Tibet: The Mysterious Years" (1985), discussed by Choy, 104–113.

74. See Lupke on Chinese ideas of fate.

75. China of course has its own classic family sagas, notably Cao Xueqin's *The Dream of the Red Chamber.*

76. The *Men of Maize* translation was second in a series of works by Nobel laureates, published by Lijiang Press of Guilin.

77. Bowers, 91, citing a 1974 article in Spanish by Roberto González Echevarría.

78. A full, non-internal Chinese translation of *Men of Maize* appeared only in March 1986, from Guilin's Lijiang Press, the same month People's Literature printed Mo Yan's first two chapters of the larger work he later titled *Hong gaoliang jiazu*, so influence is hard to prove, but I presume excerpts, reports, and/or academic articles appeared earlier. Liu Xiliang and Sun Jiying (husband and wife) submitted the full translation after five years of work, in November 1984. See http://www.yilin.com/book.aspx?id=4805, accessed September 15, 2013. One wonders about Han Shaogong's *Pa Pa Pa* (1985), about aborigines practicing slash-and-burn agriculture.

79. Hong Zicheng, 266, 385.

80. Mo Yan praised Kundera's satirical critique, while preferring García Márquez's and Faulkner's literary qualities. "Mo Yan: Meiyou yilun jiu meiyou Milan Kundela" (Without critique, there would be no Milan Kundera), Ewen Web interview, July 29, 2003. http://www.ewen.cc/books/bkview.asp?bkid=42359&cid=77081, accessed February 9, 2013.

81. Iovene, 1–2, 6.

82. For instance, Kundera's novel details a practice in Communist Czechoslovakia that many Chinese novelists must have experienced just before going abroad—being invited to a friendly lunch by agents of the State Security Ministry.

83. Todd, 305.

84. Cited in González Echevarría, *Alejo Carpentier,* 233.

85. Link, *Evening Chats,* 249–290; Yue Daiyun; Davies.

86. Booker, *Dystopian Literature,* 3.

87. As in *The Garlic Ballads* and *The Republic of Wine* (the rebellion of the "meat boys").

88. Xudong Zhang, *Postsocialism,* 185, speaks of China's 1990s "fervor to embrace global capitalism and its ideology" as "utopian/dystopian."

89. The world of youngsters marooned on a Pacific atoll that Golding creates seems at first like a utopia, an Eden. In perfect isolation on an island, with all

necessities provided by nature, the children build a new society from scratch, in a place that is "all ours" (30), and in which they may work and play, relieved of school and grown-ups—as in some nostalgic Red Guard images of the Cultural Revolution. It comes to a bad end.

90. Jing Wang, 116.

91. It seems the China Spring (Democracy Wall era, 1978–1979) is erased from the memory even of these authors.

92. PEP, *Quanrizhi* . . . , Chinese edition and nearly identical translated English edition.

93. See Harrison.

94. On the idea of semicolonialism, see Karl, 172–188.

95. Shirk, 79–80. History as presented in Chinese museums and books is discussed by Zheng Wang, Denton, and Hilton.

96. Wang Anyi's *The Song of Everlasting Sorrow* has a half-Russian character.

97. Zheng Wang, 86–87, summarizes research findings to this effect by Parks Coble, William Callahan, Kirk Denton, and Ian Buruma.

98. The chapter 11 table of Chinese achievements in the 2011 Chinese printing has not been updated. It stresses Chinese achievements in outer space, but the Three Gorges Dam has not been added (2:143/2:232).

99. Literary production in post-Mao times is covered in one paragraph: "Since the end of the 'Gang of Four,' literature has recovered and revitalized as the number of publications has increased, and the subjects covered broader themes. Prosperity came. After the 1980s, the 'Mao Dun Literary Prize' was established in our country, and many excellent literary works have won prizes. This has further pushed forward the development in literary creativities" (2:148/2:241).

100. A required world history text (PEP, *Putong* . . .), vol. 3, however, embodies the Enlightenment discourse of developing humanism. It devotes a unit to "The Origins and Development of the Western Humanistic Spirit," beginning with a chapter 5 titled "The Origins of Western Humanistic Thought" (3:22–25), followed by a chapter each on the Renaissance and the Enlightenment.

101. See Kinkley, *Corruption and Realism*.

102. This was the peasant's outlook in North China, too, due to the Communist Party's relatively early, pre-1949 entry into the North China countryside. Pickowicz, 45. Ge Fei, in Zong Renfa et al., eds., 34, traces all problems of the Mao era to Mao's Yan'an period (1935–1947), though he does not write of Yan'an or the Cultural Revolution in his *Southlands Trilogy*.

103. As seen from the collective interviewing projects assembled in Ching Kwan Lee and Guobin Yang, eds.

104. The previously mentioned story of Wan Zhi created sympathy for Kuomintang (Guomindang) soldiers already in 1979.

105. Jian Xu, 248, sees Zhang Wei's *The Ancient Ship* as "putting down the peasantry and lifting up the bourgeoisie."

106. That World War II was a world war is indicated in two sentences in a brief overview of the Sino-Japanese War (2:26/2:45) and in one brief sentence at the chapter's end, which mentions the fall of German fascism, since "Japanese fascism" then "fell into complete isolation with no help at all" (2:42/2:74). There is no indication that the United States was a Chinese ally in the war.

107. Howard Goldblatt points out (in Lingenfelter) the need for professional editing in Chinese publication.

108. Erik Eckholm, "Secret Memoir [Zhao Ziyang's] Offers Look Inside China's Politics," *New York Times*, May 14, 2009. Perry Link, "Waiting for WikiLeaks: Beijing's Seven Secrets," *New York Review of Books Blog*, August 19, 2010. http://www.nybooks.com/blogs/nyrblog/2010/aug/19/waiting-wikileaks-beijings-seven-secrets/, accessed February 29, 2012.

109. Fugui of Yu Hua's *To Live* is an exception.

110. Gu Hua, *Rulinyuan* and *Zhennü*.

111. Yu Hua, *China in Ten Words*, 134. See Barmé, 316–344, and Ming-Bao Yue for others' nostalgia.

112. In the 1980s, nostalgia for "the old society" before 1949 was purveyed by Wang Zengqi, Deng Youmei, Feng Jicai (b. 1942; his *The Three-Inch Golden Lotus* might be called a historical novel, and some of his other themes, such as the Boxers, make him appear to be a predecessor of Mo Yan), and, arguably, some works by Lu Wenfu. For a different take on 1990s nostalgia, see Dai Jinhua.

113. Anon, "Ge Fei de xiezuo zhi lu" (Ge Fei's literary path), Wenhua Zhongguo, December 13, 2011, http://cul.china.com.cn/book/2011–2012/13/content_4693111.htm, accessed May 30, 2013.

114. Zhang Wei's early years are unclear, though Chinese critics identify him as a sent-down youth who put sent-down youth themes into his early fiction.

115. Hua Li, 92, 155. Yu Hua, *China in Ten Words*, 113–141. Choy, 156.

116. Shelley Chan, 7–8.

117. *Beijing News* columnist Cao Baoyin's transcription of a July 13, 2012, talk by Liu Zhenyun, *China Digital Times*, at http://chinadigitaltimes.net/2012/07/liu-zhenyun-oh-china-why-are-you-so-dirty/, accessed June 19, 2013.

118. Zhang Helong, 61. See also Jones, "The Violence of the Text."

119. Liu Kang.

120. Hong Zicheng, 385n7.

121. Ge Fei might have read the German utopian Marxist Ernst Bloch, who linked utopia and music. The ambiguous titles of all three novels in the trilogy suggest literary allusions, though they do not necessarily echo the original meanings of the ancient poets. The phrase *"renmian taohua"* appears in "Ti du cheng nan zhuang" (In a village south of the capital) by Cui Hu of the Tang, about a young man lovesick for a beautiful girl whose face he remembers in relation to peach blossoms when he first saw her. She was gone when he returned to her home a year later to propose marriage; he lost his opportunity. "Shiyiyue Siyue fengyu" (Rains and winds of the fourth of the eleventh month) by Lu You of the Song has the phrase *"tiema binghe rumeng"* ("in my dreams, I rode an armored horse over a frozen river"), the last three characters of which seem mimicked in Ge Fei's middle novel, *Shanhe rumeng*. *Chunjin Jiangnan* suggests a line in "Ji Yangzhou Han Zhuo Panguan" (A message to Yangzhou magistrate Han Zhuo) by Du Mu of the Tang, but with "autumn" (*qiu*) replacing "spring" (*chun*). In the Du Mu poem, *"qiujin Jiangnan"* means that "autumn has come to the Southlands [south of the Yangzi]," yet it remains green as the poet views it from the more desolate north. However, based on Ge Fei's frequent favored use of the word *jin* in his trilogy, and my sense of the novel, I prefer the translation "completed," "ended," or "exhausted." "Spring Comes to the Southlands" would be a grammatical and fully ironic alternative translation to my "Southern Spring Played Out."

122. Analyzed in Xiaobing Tang, 318–328.

2. DISCOMFORTS OF TEMPORAL ANOMIE

1. See Ching Kwan Lee and Guobin Yang, eds.

2. Note the importance of periodization to, for example, the theoretically conscious critic Wang Ning.

3. Kwong, 173–180.

4. The 1992 novel from which this 1993 film was adapted, *Farewell My Concubine (Ba wang bie ji)*, is by Lilian Lee (Li Bihua), who lives and published this book in Hong Kong. The film was made in China.

5. McDougall and Louie; Yibing Huang; Kinkley, *Corruption and Realism*.

6. The Chinese edition was accessed online as an unpaginated text. This description comes from the opening sentence of the second section.

7. Choy, 152–153.

8. See Knight, "Decadence," 108.

9. David Der-wei Wang, "Chinese Fiction for the Nineties," 245.

10. Choy, 147, likewise stresses the temporal ambiguity of the novel.

11. The Chinese text of the preface is at http://www.cp1897.com.hk/product _info.php?BookId=9622576494&cl=english, accessed February 29, 2012.

12. Translated in Deppman, 36.

13. Rong Cai. Vivian Lee compares the two novels and finds *Wu Zetian* less interesting.

14. Li Zhisui.

15. Knight, "Absolute Career Change."

16. Lin Qingxin, 108–110, finds the "ahistorical" repetition of these novels tedious.

17. See Morrison, 222.

18. Dai Sijie's *Balzac and the Little Chinese Seamstress* exemplifies this discourse (see Deppman, 141); an ironic twist on the latter phenomenon is Bai Hua's *Remote Country of Women*, which describes a utopian tribal matriarchal society to criticize Han China in the Cultural Revolution as dystopian.

19. Xiaobing Tang, 225–244, analyzes this work.

20. *Men of Maize* is read not only as an allegory of assaults on indigenous culture, but also of Asturias's battle with his own demons, including alcohol.

21. The novel does mention a young man sent down to the countryside after graduating from high school, evidently in the Cultural Revolution (281/290).

22. Fugui's past resembles that of Yu Hua's grandfather; Yu Hua, *China in Ten Words*, 64.

23. Fugui survives the Chinese Civil War and the harsh vicissitudes of the Communist years. He also has a faithful wife and children, though they die prematurely.

24. Richard King points out that blood loss also leads to two major deaths in *To Live*—that of Fugui's only son, from whom too much blood is drawn in order to save the life of the county magistrate's wife, and Fugui's deaf-mute daughter, Fengxia, who dies in childbirth from loss of blood.

25. Shen Congwen, "Life." An old puppeteer stages Punch-and-Judy fights between two puppets and has the underdog win in the end. The puppeteer finishes by calling the winner by the name of his deceased son, having dramatized a revision of history in which his son lives.

26. Xu Sanguan sells his blood the second time ten years after his first donation (136/96), just after he has sex with Lin Fenfang, who also relates that they were friends ten years earlier (131/92). More conclusively, in 1958 or later, in the Great Leap Forward, it is stated that the Xus have been married for more than ten years.

27. After the death of his father, Xu Sanguan's mother married a Nationalist company commander (65/25). It seems unlikely that Xu Sanguan could have later

escaped notice for this "bad class background" (however unfair that might be), particularly since he openly announced his origins—and we know, by dint of our calculations, that he did it before the revolution.

28. Yu Hua, "Xianshi yizhong." For similar stories in English translation, see his *The Past and the Punishments*.

29. Cited in Eric Abrahamsen, "Yu Hua Fun Fact," *Paper Republic* blog, December 22, 2008, http://paper-republic.org/ericabrahamsen/yu-hua-fun-fact/, accessed January 1, 2012.

30. Published respectively in *Renmin wenxue*, 1986, no. 3, and in *Jiefangjun wenyi*, 1986, no. 7.

31. Goldblatt's "Translator's Note" on the title page of the English edition indicates that Mo Yan asked him to work from that 1988 text, "which restores cuts made in the Mainland Chinese edition" of 1987. The translation also has deletions, made "with the author's approval," and the Taiwan Chinese edition itself lacks some passages of the mainland edition, such as praise of the Communist Party that may have been added to get the work published on the mainland (at Mainland 177–178/Taiwan 255/English 198). Only the Mainland edition identifies the Jiao-Gao troops as Communist and Pocky Leng's detachment as Nationalist. Examples, besides the above (citations are of Ml/Tw/Eng, respectively): 52/75/58, 176/253/196, 179/257/199–200, 217/312/240, 335/480/348, 339/485/351. The preferred text does have a few literal mentions of Communists and Nationalists, derogatorily.

32. Gaomi, Pingdu, and Jiao counties are real, though Saltwater Gap, Black Water River, Dalan (in *Big Breasts and Wide Hips*), and Masang River and Masang Town (*Sandalwood Death*) may all be fictitious. Characters from *Red Sorghum* are found in other stories by Mo Yan outside the series.

33. E.g., at 433–434/315. The first subchapter of chapter 2, "Sorghum Wine," in effect summarizes the narrative to come. See also the telegraphing of future action at 228/178, 245/190–191, 407/297.

34. Choy, 45–46, indicates that the incident is a fictionalization of fact.

35. Moreover, the later chapters identify the narrator's mother ("Mother") as Qianer ("Beauty"). A Qianer already appears in the second chapter (79/90–91), as a minor companion of Grandma; the two Beauties might be "the same woman," but this seems unlikely; probably Mo Yan picked "Beauty" to be the narrator's mother's name only when he wrote the later chapters.

36. Unlike Saleem Sinai, who narrates the exploits of his grandparents in Rushdie's *Midnight's Children* (which Mo Yan is unlikely to have read), Douguan does not explicitly claim telepathic powers.

37. This is my own translation, which follows the Chinese in opening with the word "1939."

38. This accords with calculations made possible at 370/273, in the fourth chapter.

39. This is characteristic also of Mo Yan's *Big Breasts and Wide Hips*, except for a depiction of a "speak bitterness" session staged by the Communists after the revolution, at 2:398–410/357–367.

40. Mo Yan leaves to the last chapter the solution of what happened to the "missing guns" that Granddad and Father hid in a dry well (481/349). A loose end, explained in another story outside the series, is Granddad's imprisonment in Hokkaido (99/78).

41. *Xing huo liao yuan.*

42. Notably, in the fifth chapter, Second Grandma's consultation of abandoned babies' corpses to get gambling clues.

43. Kenny Ng.

44. A counterintuitive suggestion that rural folk are freer than city folk appears in *Men of Maize*, 223–224. See also Yan Min, *Shenmei langmanzhuyi.*

45. Jie Lu, 156, points out that the seasons (and, I would add, the cultural ethos) are not clarified by references to holidays and festivals. This is quite unlike *Men of Maize*, which is full of overt references to Catholic holy days and inexplicit resonances of various phenomena with the names of the saints honored.

46. Given the grinding poverty, violence, and constant stresses and apprehensions of daily life in this village, I hesitate to call it utopian, as Jie Lu does (152–153, 166–173). It does seem to enjoy a premodern holistic worldview and communal solidarity against intrusions by rival villages and modern miners—who might be advancing either socialism or capitalism.

47. There are, however, friendships; see 103/171, 125/208, 162–163/304–305, and 200/336.

48. Repeated also by a major character in that novel, Sui Jiansu (223/278).

49. Xudong Zhang, *Chinese Modernism*, 310.

50. A. O. Scott sees in Zhang Yimou's cinematic oeuvre "just about every imaginable directorial trait except a sense of humor."

51. The film, unlike the novel, emphasizes that the sorghum grows wild. All the more does it represent vitality, but it is not the local people's "own."

52. Clark, 165.

53. The religious connotations of the number recur when 108 Buddhist monks attend a funeral service in *Silver City* (110/115).

54. Silbergeld, 74.

55. Jianying Zha, 97–99, interprets the film *Farewell My Concubine* as an allegory of the relationship between former filmmaking partners Zhang Yimou and Chen Kaige. Cited in Silbergeld, 108.

3. PROJECTIONS OF HISTORICAL REPETITION

1. As in Mo Yan, *Life and Death Are Wearing Me Out*. A variant expression is voiced by Uncle Maomao in Wang Anyi's *The Song of Everlasting Sorrow*, 176/158. For thirty years, see Su Tong's *The Boat to Redemption*, 70/97, 112/162, 252/407.

2. Bulman.

3. On Chinese utopias, see Bauer; Shiping Hua.

4. *Jiu zhi*, 2, in a preface titled "From Winter to Winter" that is not included in the English edition. The original, optimistic phrase comes from Percy Bysshe Shelley.

5. Shelley Chan, 122–136, addresses this.

6. Apart from Marquezian plot devices in this novel, Li Rui is linked to the Chinese avant-garde mostly through his 1980s roots-seeking fiction.

7. My original Taiwan edition, signed by Li Rui, says "October 23"; the translation and various Chinese editions available on the Internet say "October 24."

8. The references in the novel are vague, but the major Sichuan commanders in the 1930s were Liu Xiang and his nephew Liu Wenhui.

9. The relevant chapter, in the English (numbered chapter 14; 16, in the Chinese), newly inserts, on page 267, the sentence "Li Jingsheng [while being welcomed as a potential native-son returnee] felt in himself an ineffable sickness at heart, an unspeakable abhorrence of this vaunted dialectic of turning grief into strength" (absent from the Chinese pages 263–264). In the "Translator's Acknowledgment" (277), Goldblatt thanks Li Rui "for supplying clarifications and additional material."

10. Li Rui, *Jiu zhi*, 1.

11. It is unclear which level of government owns the glass noodle factory; perhaps it is the town.

12. The trope may seem patently Western, having originated with Plato, but a fully allegorized ship of state appears already in Liu E's *Travels of Lao Can* (1907).

13. Su Xiaokang and Wang Luxiang, English transcript, 120. Zhang Wei's views may have influenced the cultural critique of the old, Yellow River–based Chinese civilization in the television series.

14. The authors in the symposium of Wang Xiaoming et al. discuss the novel's many symbols and find them not to form a unified gestalt.

15. However, China is a big country; in several interviews, Mo Yan has attested that Lan Lian is based on a real person he saw in childhood. E.g., "Mo Yan: Wo yiting 'maoqiang' jiu ganjue relei yingkuang!" (Mo Yan: The moment I hear "Maoqiang opera," my eyes fill with hot tears!), posted on *Baidu Tieba*, undated [2003?]. http://tieba.baidu.com/f?kz=142997189, accessed September 6, 2012. Also "Ninety Minutes with Mo Yan, I," May 5, 2009, blog, at http://sinoafficionado .blogspot.com/, accessed July 7, 2012.

16. The narrative frequently refutes details in stories by "Mo Yan" and even quotes passages from them. However, apart from "Ling yao" (The cure) and "Baozha" (Explosion), the stories, including "Ren si, diao bu si" ("The man died, his dick lived on," as rendered by Goldblatt; 11/12), "Tai sui" (Wandering god; 13/15), and "Hei lüzi" (The black donkey; 32/39) were invented by Mo Yan when he wrote his novel.

17. Mo Yan's narrative at times mocks the idea of reincarnation or introduces jokes whose humor relies on a shared general view of its improbability, at 34/41, 56/67, 97/115.

18. As in *Sandalwood Death*, 372/319.

19. A historian would note that Shanghai is not only the seat and symbol of China's bourgeoisie, but also its proletariat, even if they were not in fact in the driver's seat under socialism.

20. Hockx. Regarding nostalgia in the novel, see Michael Berry's "Afterword" to the translation, 431–440, and Xudong Zhang, *Postsocialism*, 196–211.

21. Michael Berry and Susan Chan Egan, in their "Translators' Notes and Acknowledgments" to the novel, vi, indicate that they adapted the original novel's typesetting to that expected by Anglophone readers.

22. Karl Marx, *The Eighteenth Brumaire of Louis Bonaparte* (1852), opening line.

23. This is apparent already in the third entry, in which the narrator associates ancient geographical names with contemporary ones simply because they share a common character, without examining the history of place-names during the two millennia in between.

24. As Han Shaogong told Shen Congwen scholar Ling Yu, and Ling Yu related in a Changsha seminar previously cited in Kinkley, "Shen Congwen's Legacy," 98, 102, 399n71.

25. See Kinkley, *The Odyssey of Shen Congwen*, esp. 154–155, 231, 288n8.

26. That is a *Pingsui ting zhi* 平绥厅志 or *Gazetteer of the Pingsui Directly Controlled Prefecture*, which Han might have created from his knowledge of West Hunan's Miao districts, which were "pacified" and did have such a *ting*, but Ping-

sui could also be a pun on the Ping-Sui or Beiping-Suiyuan Railroad. Choy, 36n66, relates the fictional rebellion to actual Miao rebellions, but they were in West Hunan and Guizhou, not northeastern Hunan. The "Lotus Flower Rebellion" may suggest Lianhua (Lotus Flower) County, Jiangxi, and, by association, Mao's 1927 Autumn Harvest Uprising and 1930s KMT-CCP battles.

27. The narrator lists these movements at 37/33.

28. Payne, 155, 185, 196, finds that Ge Fei, dispirited by the commercialization of literature, temporarily withdrew from creative writing in the early 1990s.

29. When Chinese critics refer to Ge Fei's new exteriority, they refer not to his earlier, 1990s turn away from his 1980s avant-garde philosophical complexity (Payne, 184–224, even detects a gradual turn away from his 1980s multivocal view of history to a closer approximation of official history), but to a turn away from *Bygone Beauty*'s supposed "inward turn" of 2004, toward traditionally poetic and psychologically nuanced prose. Such a comparison takes avant-garde prose, whose *structures* cannot be ignored, to be as "exterior" as realism. See Li Yuchun, 33–34.

30. Cheng Yongxin speaking, in *Zuojia*, Zong Renfa et al., eds., 14. On Ge Fei's earlier works, see Xudong Zhang, *Chinese Modernism*, 163–200.

31. Oddly, but not uncharacteristically, Tan Gongda must deal with widespread famine in his realm during the mid-1950s, but there is no mention of the nationwide famine a few years later after the Great Leap Forward. This could be a chronological transposition to avoid commenting on the Leap, or typical Ge Fei mystification. Some commentators misconstrue the second volume as being about the Cultural Revolution.

32. Ge Fei has said that Pang Jiayu is a "failure" and Tan Duanwu an idealist, last of a kind (for this interpretation, see Liu Yueyue). I see Pang as the better-adapted, more vital force in Ge Fei's third novel, and Tan as a loser (from the start of the novel, when he abandons Li/Pang). Others agree; see Chen Xiaoming, mod. One can however be a noble *failure* *and* an idealist. Ge Fei says, in a blurb at http://www.books.com.tw/exep/prod/booksfile.php?item=0010563537: "My goal in writing [*Southern Spring Played Out*] was to go in quest of those not so interested in money, the so-called failures." That would include Duanwu.

33. "History repeats itself, or in other words is cyclical," says his colleague Shouren (3:234).

34. Yan Min, in *Shenmei langmanzhuyi*, and Li Yuchun, 32, identify utopianism, including that of premodern China, with romanticism.

35. Huaxi is ten miles south of the river, midway as the crow flies between Changzhou on the Yangzi southern shore and Nantong on the northern shore.

36. Griffiths.

37. *Want China Times* blog (Taiwan), November 28, 2011 (?), http://www.wantch-inatimes.com/news-subclass-cnt.aspx?id=20111128000048&cid=1103, accessed July 4, 2012.

38. *Shanghaiist* blog, http://shanghaiist.com/2011/10/18/photos_huaxis_50th _anniversary_-_gl.php#photo-1, accessed July 4, 2012.

39. Tina Tran, "China's Richest Village a Capitalist Commune," http://www .wessociety.com/News/World%20Entrepreneurial%20News/Economic%20 Development/China's%20village%20a%20capitalist%20commune.aspx, accessed July 4, 2012.

40. Coonan.

41. Griffiths.

42. Zhou.

43. Coonan.

44. Zhou.

4. ALIENATION FROM THE GROUP

1. Fokkema, 57, 83–93. Jameson, *Archaeologies of the Future*, 10–41.

2. Malmgren, 80.

3. E.g., *The Iron Heel* (Avis and Ernest), *We* (the male D-503, with the female I-330), *R.U.R.* (Helena and Domin), *The Kingdom of This World* (Ti Noel and his fellow-slave-turned-supernatural-spirit Mackandal), *Nineteen Eighty-Four* (Winston and Julia), *Fahrenheit 451* (Guy and Clarisse), *Atlas Shrugged* (Dagny and Hank), *The House of Spirits* (Blanca and Pedro Tercero; Alba and Miguel), *The Hunger Games* (Katniss and Peeta). In *The Handmaid's Tale*, Offred is inspired by her bisexual friend, Moira, and even manages to bind with her own Commander. In *One Hundred Years of Solitude*, too, the force that leavens the eccentricities of the Buendía patriarchs is their outside women: Pilar Ternera and Petra Cotes.

4. The National Library in Beijing has a 1984 Chinese-language Taiwan edition and two separate mainland translations, from Shanghai and Hangzhou, which appeared in 1985.

5. An allegory of the state, not the nation (as in Jameson's formulation); the worlds of rural China and neighborhood Shanghai, Macondo (the banana company notwithstanding), the Chilean realm of the Truebas, the fictional Dominican realms tyrannized by Trujillo, even Carpentier's Haiti (in parables of revolution and nation-building) are not beset primarily by foreign imperialism.

6. However, China has developed something of a "Leninist junta novel" in the separate anticorruption popular genre. See Kinkley, *Corruption and Realism*. After winning his Nobel Prize, Vargas Llosa went on a nine-day tour of China and in a Shanghai speech denounced dictatorship. "Mario Vargas Llosa Slates Dictatorships on China Trip," BBC News, June 15, 2011. http://www.bbc.co.uk/news /entertainment-arts-13776326, accessed September 3, 2013.

7. Mo Yan's later novels do mention Mao by name, as does Li Rui's *Silver City*. Pickowicz, 46, points out that Chinese peasants could consider the Chinese state their antagonist and still not blame Chairman Mao, whom they remembered as the victor in the revolution and war with Japan. But Mao does not appear as a protagonist or inspiration in the new historical novels about the pre-1949 period, either.

8. Menton, 39–64, 82, etc., points out this emphasis particularly in Vargas Llosa's writings.

9. Yu Hua, *China in Ten Words*, esp. 138. Yu Hua looked up to his own elder brother.

10. Ernesto González Bermejo, "And Now, Two Hundred Years of Solitude," in Bell-Villada, ed., 12–13.

11. The missionary, though a Swede called *Pastor* Malory, makes the sign of the cross and his convert, Mother, prays to the Blessed Virgin (1:43/39), which would indicate a Catholic identity uncharacteristic of Sweden, though Catholic missionaries were notorious in Shandong in the lead-up to the Boxer uprising. There was a Swedish Baptist mission in this part of Shandong, and the Swedes were interned by the Japanese in nearby Wei County. The Italian missionary in Liu Zhenyun's *One Word Is Worth a Thousand* is also a lone actor, largely abandoned by his church.

12. Fugui's craft of shadow puppetry in the film version of *To Live* is not present in the original novel.

13. Lin Qingxin, 126–128.

14. Link, *The Uses of Literature*.

15. Ching Kwan Lee, 157, and 160–161.

16. The Buendías, after all, bring about their own and Macondo's downfall. The Truebas, Cabrals, etc., are deeply implicated in the old order that readers associate with Pinochet and Trujillo.

17. Bakhtin, 84–258.

18. When Jie Lu, 109–145, refers to "the spatial representation of time," she is referring to nonlinear plots, not to emphasis on space at the expense of time.

19. Mo Yan and Zhang Wei write of different areas in Shandong, which are partly fictionalized and generalized. Su Tong's locales often lie along a Suzhou-Shanghai-Zhejiang axis, as do Wang Anyi's, though Su Tong's fictional Maple Village is of uncertain location somewhere north of the Yangzi River and its characteristics vary from story to story. Li Rui's Silver City, without its salt mines, like Northeast Gaomi Township without its sorghum, can easily be taken as a Chinese Everyplace. Yu Hua's novels analyzed here are rooted in a particular place, but without geographical distinctiveness.

20. These are the words of Guyanese novelist Wilson Harris, cited by Delbaere-Garant in Zamora and Faris, eds., 253.

21. Chi Li, "Houji yu xiaozhuan," *Chi Li wenji*, 4: 404–405, cited in Gong, 74. I have added two commas to Gong's translation.

22. John Boland's July 25, 2010, blog reports on a 2010 Sydney Writers' Festival session featuring Su Tong and Linda Jaivin that discussed extensive differences between the English and Chinese versions of the novel: "The explanation was that the English translation was taken from his [Su Tong's] second draft, and not his final draft [which went to the Chinese publishers], as the [English] publishers were anxious to get the book out!" Howard Goldblatt in a personal communication confirmed that Su Tong sent him different drafts of the book even as he was translating it.

23. Goldblatt's translation actually says: "A private utopia was taking shape in his head." The word *tiantang* can be translated as "utopia," but in the context of my book's argument, that English word may be too loaded. Visser, in "Displacement," analyzes images of city and country in this work and finds both depleted of "their existential value" (136). This sounds like the negative, literal meaning of "utopia" as no-place; she emphasizes the urban and country places' connectedness.

24. Orwell, *Nineteen Eighty-Four*, ch.1, subchapter 3, 32.

25. I am not sure whether Han Shaogong read Orwell before writing his novel, but we know he was familiar with *The Unbearable Lightness of Being*, which he translated. See Barmé, *In the Red*, 301.

26. Other escapes follow. The narrator's uncle Dingo escapes at the age of fifteen, to find his father, and his father's concubine also escapes Maple Village; her visit there to bear Chen Baonian's child is thwarted when Grandma poisons the fetus.

27. Chinese critics emphasize the breakdown of the family as a major wellspring of Chinese new historical fiction; see Wang Biao, ed., and Zhang Liqun.

28. Lu Tonglin.

29. My Taiwan edition of the Chinese text and the translation diverge here, but the phrase in question is similar.

30. Yan Min, *Shenmei langmanzhuyi*, 123–124, seems to see primitive vitality in this. I disagree.

31. The novel dramatizes the Qing massacre of the "Six Gentlemen" in 1898.

32. Hua Li, 158–168.

33. This and the other translated phrases with only one page reference are among the intense passages that appear only in the draft that Goldblatt translated, not the final Chinese edition.

5. ANARCHY: SOCIAL, MORAL, AND COSMIC

1. Hampton.

2. In *Red Sorghum*, the county town is briefly mentioned, as the seat of the magistrate Nine Dreams Cao. A County Chief Chen helps the good Lan Lian in *Life and Death Are Wearing Me Out*.

3. Quoting chapter 1 of the original, in the 1888 translation from the German by Samuel Moore in cooperation with Frederick Engels: "The bourgeoisie, wherever it has got the upper hand, has put an end to all feudal, patriarchal, idyllic relations. It has pitilessly torn asunder the motley feudal ties that bound man to his 'natural superiors,' and has left remaining no other nexus between man and man than naked self-interest, than callous 'cash payment.' It has drowned the most heavenly ecstasies of religious fervour, of chivalrous enthusiasm, of philistine sentimentalism, in the icy water of egotistical calculation."

4. Here, Goldblatt had no difficulty matching Zhang Wei's Chinese translation to Moore and Engels's version, word for word.

5. The novel has a seemingly tacked-on bit of optimism for the future.

6. "Illuminations" in the title of Ban Wang's English book pays homage to Walter Benjamin. The title of his similar book in Chinese is "History and Memory"; only Wang cites Pierre Nora's history-and-memory theories. Few of the authors cite Bourdieu, Ricoeur, or trauma theorist LaCapra.

7. Theorization of "symbolic violence" is typically traced to Pierre Bourdieu, who published his *Outline of a Theory of Practice* in 1972, but the phrase may have entered the vernacular long before; a major work on representational violence is that of Nancy Armstrong and Leonard Tennenhouse.

8. The violence that most concerns David Der-wei Wang is perceptual or epistemological "rupture" and "the violence of representation" (4). Power structures suppress personal testimony, distorting it or reducing it to silence. Ban Wang cites

others' ideas of *trauma* that include "unemployment, the polarization of the population, and the erosion of the social fabric," or "the trauma of the 'excess of individualism' of 'normal' middle-class life in the Eisenhower years" (*Illuminations*, 10). Whole generations in various countries may be survivors of trauma. Braester and Ban Wang acknowledge a debt to Cathy Caruth, who in effect sees modern history itself as trauma and thus potentially extends the idea of the traumatized, of the survivor, to all of us. Braester refers to an even more radical view from theologian Emanuel Lévinas, who "has gone so far as to state that one's very existence constitutes an act of violence" (7). My concern is that abstract ideas of violence not drown out the memories of the physically and mentally injured, which are already subject to doubt due to the sufferers' past mental injuries, and thus vulnerable to revisionist doubts denying the Holocaust, Nanjing Massacre, Beijing massacre of 1989, etc. Revisionism about the reality of the violence of the Cultural Revolution has emerged, since idyllic conditions during that era did exist for some. Some Germans had idyllic experiences during the Holocaust, as evidenced by Karl Höcker's album of pictures of happy SS workers at Auschwitz. See "Auschwitz through the Lens of the SS," at the website of the United State Holocaust Memorial Museum. http://www.ushmm.org/museum/exhibit/online/ssalbum/?content=2, accessed November 27, 2011.

9. Michael Berry aptly extracts Joshua Hirsch's definition of trauma. Hirsch tries to grasp it as something that can be essentialized or materialized, like a memory. Yet trauma is something ineffable, indeed a "crisis of representation." Says Hirsch, "Trauma, first of all is not a thing, . . . not even an event, not even a genocide, which cannot in itself be relayed, but which—perhaps this is too unthinkable—merely happens. Rather, trauma, even before being transmitted, is already bound up with the realm of representation. It is, to be more precise, a crisis of representation." Hirsch, 15–16, cited in Berry, 16–17. An irony that many a historian would raise (noted by Braester) is that "history," too, whether defined as the past or as representations of it, is by most recent philosophies of history subject to multiple crises of representation, due not necessarily to shock but simply to the multivariate and uncapturable nature of existence as it unfolds before a mere individual, not to mention the further limitations on how it is remembered, reconstructed, and represented.

10. Berger, 570, quotation 572.

11. Zheng Wang.

12. The animals' slogan in Orwell's classic is "Four legs good, two legs bad." The Chinese texts of *Red Sorghum* refer to humans only as those who walk erect; the translation adds that they are "two-legged."

13. Yan Min, *Shenmei langmanzhuyi*, 114–115, discourses on animalistic savagery in *The Ancient Ship*.

14. Yu Hua's earlier short stories, such as those translated in *The Past and the Punishments*, are even better known for their violence.

15. Visser, "Displacement," 127.

16. Mencius, ch. 6, 1–4; James Legge, tr., 2:77–79.

17. Ban Wang, *The Sublime Figure*, 2. Wang prefers to relate this more to Kantian aesthetics than to Nietzsche's idea of an *übermensch*.

18. Chen Hun; Xue Dezhen; Li Xin; Zhang Helong.

19. See Xudong Zhang, 38–39 and 115–117, McGrath, 25–58, and Wang Xiaoming, ed. The 1990s debate was largely a reaction to unbridled market forces unleashed amid a vacuity of ideology, faith, and social trust.

20. Foster.

21. Pusey, 9–47. Yan Fu's seminal introduction of Darwinian ideas in his translation of Thomas Huxley's *Evolution and Ethics* was completed in 1896, read by Liang Qichao the next year, and published in 1898 (Pusey, 89, 155); Ma Junwu published chapters of Darwin's *The Origin of Species* in 1903 and 1904 and the complete book in 1919.

22. Pusey, 61. On Yan Fu's thought, see Schwartz.

23. Dikötter.

24. Pusey, 77.

25. See numerous essays in Zamora and Faris, eds., and William Rowe, "Magical Realism" entry in Smith, ed., 373, citing J. Martin-Barbero and Ángel Rama. Bai Hua's *The Remote Country of Women* (which has no magical realism) suggests that tribal, matriarchal Mosuo culture may offer a local antidote to patriarchal culture.

26. Bowers, 27, 30.

27. Like Remedios the Beauty, Grandma in *Red Sorghum* dies and flies to heaven, "spreading her newly sprouted wings to glide weightlessly in the air" (93/73). Third Sister in *Big Breasts and Wide Hips* becomes a bird fairy with wings and "soars" off a precipice, though she falls and dies (1:224/223–224). In *Sandalwood Death*, a dead human transforms into a cat and flies to the moon (392/337). Further, in *The Republic of Wine*, the dwarf Yu Yichi spreads his arms "like the wings of a falcon ready to fly off" (179/149). When asked in 1999 to select for republication in Chinese "ten short stories that have influenced me," Mo Yan included García Márquez's "A Very Old Man with Enormous Wings." Mo Yan, ed., *Suokong li de fangjian*, cited in Shelley Chan, 5.

28. Strecher, 267.

29. Beginning with Flores.

30. González Echevarría, *Alejo Carpentier*, 115. Reprints of the seminal article by Roh and the two by Carpentier, "On the Marvelous Real" (1949) and "The Baroque and the Marvelous Real" (1975), appear in Zamora and Faris, eds.

31. The source of this often cited observation and its exact wording appear vague and variant on the Internet, in French and English.

32. Mo Yan, "Iron Child." The story also has elements of realism and the absurd.

33. Wang, *The Monster That Is History*, esp. chapter 8. See also Wedell-Wedellsborg.

34. Sinoafficionado, "Ninety Minutes with Mo Yan, I," May 5, 2009, blog, at http://sinoafficionado.blogspot.com/, accessed July 7, 2012. Zhang Wei, "Fiction and Animals," *Chinese Literature Today* 2.2 (2012): 32.

35. Chen Dazhuan; Schiaffini.

36. I thank Jennifer Ruth of Portland State University for this observation.

37. Zou Geben, 17, cites only a folk belief in Han's later novel as "magic."

38. "Translators' Note," Zhang Wei, *September's Fable*, xi.

39. As Chinese bandit-soldiers "marched through the heavy mist, [Father's] nose detected a new, sickly-sweet odor, neither yellow nor red, blending with the smells of peppermint and sorghum to call up memories deep in his soul" (3/4). A bugle that signals an assault plays "scarlet notes" (97/76, 97/77).

40. "Another long-drawn-out 'Mom' escaped from [Father's] lips [as he beheld his dying mother], fanned out, and glided unsteadily in the ear like a scarlet butterfly, its wings carrying it to the southwest." (347/261).

41. Similarly, farmers' rakes set to puncture Japanese truck tires "must have reached the limits of their patience" (77/61).

42. Not excluding lactation (228/177), which of course is also a major theme of *Big Breasts and Wide Hips*.

43. Less surprisingly, when Grandma whips a drunken Granddad before they become regular lovers, he experiences "ecstasy" (182/143).

44. Mo Yan's preferred text, published in Taiwan, accentuates this with a line deleted from the mainland edition, which suggests alternative folk versions: "Some people say that when she was placed in the coffin she was still cursing and kicking the lid" (492/356, last line of section 9).

45. The strange former closeness of the One-eyed Noble Man and Big Feet Fat Shoulders, and her statement that she has repaid him all she owed him (397/235–236), suggest that she and he tacitly recognize her as the woman that the blinded man has sought all his life to return to his hearth.

46. Mo Yan's "Hou ji" (Afterword) says that the story of Sun Bing resisting the Germans was a local legend commemorated in an actual local opera called *Sandalwood Death* (472/406).

47. Shelley Chan, 166; also 146–153.

48. In the order of the chapters in the Chinese edition printed in Taiwan, political magic, or at least arbitrary mischief, intrudes much earlier, at the start of the second chapter.

6. CONCLUSION: THE END OF HISTORY, DYSTOPIA, AND "NEW" HISTORICAL NOVELS?

1. Salman Rushdie and Herta Müller thought Mo Yan insufficiently dissident to win the prize. For Sinologists' views, see Perry Link, "Does This Writer Deserve the Prize?" *New York Review*, December 6, 2012, 22–24. Charles Laughlin, "What Mo Yan's Detractors Get Wrong," http://www.chinafile.com/what -mo-yan%E2%80%99s-detractors-get-wrong, with Link's response, at http://www .chinafile.com/politics-and-chinese-language, accessed February 6, 2013.

2. E.g., Baidu, http://baike.baidu.com/view/424727.htm, accessed September 18, 2012. For an excellent overview of current generational splits among Chinese writers, and some institutional advantages of Mo Yan's generation, see Lovell, "Finding a Place."

3. Huyssen, *After the Great Divide*, 152.

4. On the latter, see de Fays. Great poverty exists amid the wealth, as in Orwell's classic, not the Chinese works.

5. Wu Ziru.

6. The Crack Manifesto (Mexican; there is a pun on crack cocaine) is translated in *Context*, no.16, http://www.dalkeyarchive.com/book/?GCOI=15647100 103320&fa=customcontent&extrasfile=A1261091-B0D0-B086-B6AC69050 AD298EB.html, accessed July 25, 2012. Han Dong and Chu Chen edited collections of "rupture" stories in 1999 and 2000, respectively; see also Gao Yuanbao, McGrath, 59–94, and Zhu Wen's questionnaire, with predictably iconoclastic responses. Most rupture writers denied influence from anybody and probably most had never heard of the Mexicans. However, some Chinese thesis and article writers translate "*duanlie*" as "crack."

7. Phrase borrowed out of context, from Kaldis, 52.

8. This is illustrated by dueling anthologies of modern Indian literature by Rushdie and West, eds., and Chaudhuri, ed. Critics note that Chaudhuri's selections favor works in Bengali, and English.

9. Chaudhuri, ed., 484—referring to the influence of *Midnight's Children*.

10. Wood, "Tell Me How Does It Feel?" I thank Julia Lovell for this reference.

11. Official Nobel announcement, http://www.nobelprize.org/nobel_prizes/literature/laureates/2012/, accessed February 6, 2013.

12. Chaudhuri, ed., 484.

13. E.g., Derrida's 1982 essay "Of an Apocalyptic Tone," on the end of everything, and Kolakowski's 1982 lectures.

14. Mannheim, *Ideology and Utopia*; Popper, *The Open Society and Its Enemies*. John Gray's 2007 *Black Mass*, a general condemnation of utopias, echoes the Chinese novelists in its view of humans as animals and history as cyclical.

15. Jameson, *Postmodernism*, 159; see also his *Archaeologies of the Future*.

16. Jameson criticizes "anti-Utopian thought" (not "dystopian" thought) because he sees it as an attack on Marxism and not capitalism, in *Postmodernism*, 334–340, 401–406.

17. Huyssen, *Twilight Memories*, 90.

18. If Huaxi were more democratic, pluralistic, and inclusive, and produced for a Chinese socialist state instead of global capitalism to better suit Fredric Jameson, it might still represent what he calls Disneyfication (in his *Archaeologies of the Future*, 215–216).

19. Wesseling.

20. Morrison and Lin Qingxin convincingly find postmodern traits in Wang Xiaobo's narratives, but his absurdism also suggests high modernism.

21. Xudong Zhang, *Postsocialism*. McGrath. Zhang Yiwu calls such works "antiallegorical" because they "deconstruct" (though sometimes allegorically) the old Chinese national (Maoist?) allegory. See also Hong Zicheng, 447–449.

22. Davis, 297.

23. Chen Xiaoming, "'Hansang.'"

24. "One sentence [of Mao's] is worth ten thousand" is an obsequious comment by the now disgraced Lin Biao, an allusion that is surely parody in this novel. The linguistically obsessed narrator continually refers to "one sentence" here and "ten sentences" there, but the key one may be Niu's mother's seemingly carpe diem admonition (359), which evidently inspires Niu Aiguo suddenly to abandon his search for "roots" and seek his ex-lover. However, that may lead to a replay of the pathos of his own history.

25. Gerald Martin, Introduction to Asturias, *Men of Maize*, xvi–xvii. The formerly blind Indian beggar, Indian coyote-postman, and mestizo muleteer who search for runaway wives are moreover preceded by a legendary Mayan rebel chief who is also abandoned by "his woman."

26. "Liu Zhenyun's New Novel: Nowhere to Turn," *China Daily*, April 7, 2010, http://news.cultural-china.com/20100407165142.html, accessed June 19, 2013.

27. And yet, the nearby Zhengzhou Railroad Bureau was established as early as 1904.

28. I find no historical counterpart to Henan Governor Fei (149). Below him is a Commissioner (*zhuanyuan*, a post established in 1933) of Xinxiang named Geng. A Geng Qichang once took that very title, but that was in the 1950s, under Communism.

29. If Song Jiefang was born in 1949, Niu Aiguo was born about 1971 (see 327). Qiaoling was born about 1930, kidnapped in 1935, and died about 2005, the final "present time." Yang Baishun would have been born about 1914 (see 351), his father in the late Qing.

30. This brings Chinese literature full circle, back to Yu Hua's early short stories, described as "antihistory" by Henry Zhao, "Yu Hua: Fiction as Subversion," 118.

31. "Liu Zhenyun's New Novel." I substituted the word "without" for "sans" in the translation of Liu's words.

BIBLIOGRAPHY

Abe Kōbō 安部公房. *The Box Man* 箱男. E. Dale Saunders, tr. New York: Knopf, 1974 [Japanese, 1973].

———. *The Woman in the Dunes* 砂の女. E. Dale Saunders, tr. New York: Knopf, 1964 [Japanese, 1962].

Akutagawa Ryūnosuke 芥川 龍之介. *Kappa* 河童 (Kappa). New ed., rev. Seiichi Shiojin, tr. Tokyo: Hokuseido, 195 .

Allende, Isabel. *The House of the Spirits*. Magda Bogin, tr. New York: Dial Press, 2005 [1985; Spanish, 1982].

Anders, Charlie Jane. "The Dystopian Novel That's Turning China Upside Down." *Io9*, July 29, 2010. http://io9.com/5600012/the-dystopian-novel-thats-turning-china-upside-down, accessed August 16, 2011.

Anderson, J. Bradford. "The Clash of Civilizations and All That Jazz: The Humanism of Alejo Carpentier's *El reino de este mundo*." *Latin American Literary Review* 35.69 (January–June 2007) 5–28.

Armstrong, Nancy, and Leonard Tennenhouse. *The Violence of Representation: Literature and the History of Violence*. London: Routledge, 1989.

Asturias, Miguel Ángel. *Men of Maize: The Modernist Epic of the Guatemalan Indians: Critical Edition*. Gerald Martin, tr. Pittsburgh: University of Pittsburgh Press, 1995 [prior Martin ed., 1975; Spanish, 1949].

———. *The President*. Frances Partridge, tr. Long Grove, IL: Waveland, 1997 [1963; Spanish, 1946].

Atwood, Margaret. *The Handmaid's Tale*. New York: Anchor Books, Random House, 1998 [1986].

Ba Jin [Pa Chin; pseud. of Li Feigan 李芾甘]巴金. *Family*. Garden City, NY: Anchor Books, 1972 [1958].

———. *Jia* 家 (Family). Shanghai: Kaiming, 1949 [1933].

Bai Hua 白桦. *The Remote Country of Women*. Qingyun Wu and Thomas O. Beebee, tr. Honolulu: University of Hawai'i Press, 1994.

———. *Yuanfang you ge nüer guo* 远方有个女儿国 (The remote country of women). Beijing: Renmin wenxue, 1988.

Bakhtin, M[ikhail] M. *The Dialogic Imagination: Four Essays*. Michael Holquist, ed. Caryl Emerson and Michael Holquist, tr. Austin: University of Texas Press, 1981.

Barmé, Geremie. *In the Red: On Contemporary Chinese Culture*. New York: Columbia University Press, 1999.

Baudrillard, Jean. *Jean Baudrillard, Selected Writings*. 2nd ed. Mark Poster, ed. Stanford: Stanford University Press, 2001.

Bauer, Wolfgang. *China and the Search for Happiness: Recurring Themes in Four Thousand Years of Chinese Cultural History*. Michael Shaw, tr. New York: Seabury Press, 1976 [1974].

Bell-Villada, Gene H., ed. *Conversations with Gabriel García Márquez*. Jackson: University Press of Mississippi, 2006.

Bellamy, Edward. *Looking Backward: 2000–1887*. New York: New American Library, 1960 [1888].

Berger, James. "Trauma and Literary Theory." *Contemporary Literature* 38.3 (Autumn 1997): 569–582.

Berry, Michael. *A History of Pain: Trauma in Modern Chinese Literature and Film*. New York: Columbia University Press, 2008.

Boland, John. "The Boat to Redemption by Su Tong." *Musings of a Literary Dilettante's Blog*, July 25, 2010. http://musingsofaliterarydilettante.wordpress.com/2010/07/25/the-boat-to-redemption-by-su-tong/, accessed March 4, 2012.

Bolaño, Roberto. *2666*. Natasha Wimmer, tr. New York: Picador, 2008 [Spanish, 2004].

Booker, M. Keith. *The Dystopian Impulse in Modern Literature: Fiction as Social Criticism*. Westport, CT: Greenwood Press, 1994.

———. *Dystopian Literature: A Theory and Research Guide*. Westport, CT: Greenwood Press, 1994.

Bourdieu, Pierre. *Outline of a Theory of Practice*. Richard Nice, tr. Cambridge: Cambridge University Press, 1977. Translation of *Esquisse d'une théorie de la pratique: Précédé de trois études d'ethnologie Kabyle*. Genève: Droz, 1972.

Bowers, Maggie Ann. *Magic(al)Realism: The New Critical Idiom*. London: Routledge, 2004.

Bradbury, Ray. *Fahrenheit 451*. New York: Ballantine Books, 1991 [1953].

Braester, Yomi. *Witness against History: Literature, Film, and Public Discourse in Twentieth-Century China*. Stanford: Stanford University Press, 2003.

Browitt, Jeff. "Tropics of Tragedy: The Caribbean in Gabriel García Márquez's *One Hundred Years of Solitude*." *Shibboleths* 2.1 (December 2007): 16–33.

Bulgakov, Mikhail Afanasyevich. *The Master and Margarita*. Michael Glenny, tr. New York: Harper and Row, 1967.

Bulman, Raymond F. *The Lure of the Millennium: The Year 2000 and Beyond*. Maryknoll, NY: Orbis Books, 1999.

Burgess, Anthony. *A Clockwork Orange*. New York: W. W. Norton, 1962.

Cai, Rong 蔡蓉. Review of *My Life as Emperor*, by Su Tong, tr. by Howard Goldblatt. MCLC Resource Center, 2006. http://mclc.osu.edu/rc/pubs/reviews/cai.htm, accessed October 3, 2010.

Can Xue 残雪. *Old Floating Cloud: Two Novellas*. Ronald R. Janssen and Jian Zhang, tr. Evanston, IL: Northwestern University Press, 1992.

——. *Yellow Mud Street*. In Can Xue, *Old Floating Cloud: Two Novellas*. Ronald R. Janssen and Jian Zhang, tr. Evanston, IL: Northwestern University Press, 1992.

Čapek, Karel. *R.U.R. (Rossum's Universal Robots)*. Paul Selver, tr. Garden City, NY: Doubleday, Page, 1923.

——. *War with the Newts*. M. and R. Weatherall, tr. Evanston, IL: Northwestern University Press, 1996 [1985, 1937; Czech, 1936].

Carpentier, Alejo. "The Baroque and the Marvelous Real" (1975). In Zamora and Faris, eds., 89–108.

——. *Explosion in a Cathedral*. John Sturrock, tr. London: Gollancz, 1963 [Spanish, 1962].

——. *The Kingdom of This World*. Harriet de Onís, tr. New York: Farrar, Straus, and Giroux, 2006 [1957; Spanish, 1949].

——. "On the Marvelous Real in America" (1949). In Zamora and Faris, eds., 75–88.

Caruth, Cathy. *Unclaimed Experience: Trauma, Narrative, and History*. Baltimore: Johns Hopkins University Press, 1996.

——, ed. *Trauma: Explorations in Memory*. Baltimore: Johns Hopkins University Press, 1995.

Chan, Anita 陈佩华. *Children of Mao: Personality Development and Political Activism in the Red Guard Generation*. Seattle: University of Washington Press, 1985.

Chan Koonchung 陈冠中. *The Fat Years*. Michael S. Duke, tr. London: Doubleday, 2011.

—— [Mandarin: Chen Guanzhong]. *Shengshi: Zhongguo 2013* 盛世: 中国2013 (The fat years: China in 2013). Hong Kong: Oxford University Press, 2009. Electronic version: 盛世——中国 2013 年 *sheng.shi.2013.CN[1].pdf*, published by the author, as at http://ishare.iask.sina.com.cn/f/7181823.html, accessed September 28, 2011.

Chan, Shelley W. 陈颖. *A Subversive Voice in China: The Fictional World of Mo Yan*. Amherst, NY: Cambria Press, 2011.

Chang, Jung 张戎. *Wild Swans: Three Daughters of China*. New York: Simon and Schuster, 1991.

Chaudhuri, Amit. "I Wish Indian Writing in English Were Less Triumphant." Interview at the 2006 Frankfurt Book Fair. http://www.dw.de/i-wish-indian-writing-in-english-were-less-triumphant/a-2186200, accessed February 5, 2013.

——, ed. *The Picador Book of Modern Indian Literature*. London: Picador, 2001.

Chen Dazhuan 陈大专. "Han Shaogong jinzuo he La Mei mohuan jiqiao" 韩少功近作和拉美魔幻技巧 (Latin American magical technique in Han Shaogong's recent works). *Wenxue pinglun* 1986, no. 4: 135–136.

Chen Fong-ching 陈方正, and Jin Guantao 金观涛. *From Youthful Manuscripts to River Elegy*. Hong Kong: Chinese University Press, 1997.

Chen Hun 陈焜. "Renxing'e de youlü" 人性恶的忧虑 (Anxiety about the evil of human nature). *Dushu* 1981, no. 5: 107–111.

Chen Mo 陈墨. "Jiushi niandai changpian xiaoshuo" 90 年代长篇小说 (Novels of the 90s). *Baihuazhou* 百花洲 1996, no. 2: 181–198.

Chen Sihe 陈思和. *Zhongguo dangdai wenxueshi jiaocheng* 中国当代文学史教程 (A course on the history of contemporary Chinese literature). Shanghai: Fu-dan Daxue, 1999.

Chen Xiaoming 陈晓明. "'Hansang,' xingcun yu youai de xiandaixing" '喊丧,'幸存与友爱的现代性 (The modernity of "mourning singing," survival, and love of friends). Chen Xiaoming's Blog, May 28, 2013. http://blog.sina.com.cn/s/blog_473fffb401017s5i.html, accessed June 29, 2013.

——. "'Lishi zhongjie' zhi hou: Jiushi niandai wenxue xugou de weiji" "历史终结"之后: 九十年代文学虚构的危机 (After "the end of history": The crisis of fictionality in nineties literature). *Wenxue pinglun* 1999, no. 5.

——, [moderator]. Liu Yueyue, Cong Zhichen, Liu Wei, et al. 刘月悦, 丛治辰, 刘伟 等. "Xiangwaizhuan de wenti yu maodun de shidai shuxie—Ge Fei *Chunjin Jiangnan taolun*" 向外转的文体与矛盾的时代书写—格非《春尽江南》讨论 (An exterior turn in literary style and in writing about a contradictory era: Discussion of Ge Fei's *Southern Spring Played Out*). *Xiaoshuo pinglun*, 2012, no. 1: 105–116.

Chen Zhongshi 陈忠实. *Bai lu yuan* 白鹿原 (White deer plain). Beijing: Renmin wenxue, 1993.

Cheng Naishan 程乃珊. *The Banker* 金融家. Britten Dean, tr. San Francisco: China Books and Periodicals, 1992.

Cheng, Nien 郑念 (pseud. of Yao Nianyuan 姚念媛). *Life and Death in Shanghai*. New York: Grove Press, 1986.

Chi Li 池莉. *Chi Li wenji* 池莉文集 (The works of Chi Li). 6 vols. Nanjing: Jiangsu wenyi, 1995.

Choy, Howard Y. F. 蔡元峰. *Remapping the Past: Fictions of History in Deng's China, 1979–1997*. Leiden: Brill, 2008.

Clark, Paul. *Reinventing China: A Generation and Its Films*. Hong Kong: Chinese University Press, 2005.

Collins, Suzanne. *The Hunger Games*. New York: Scholastic, 2008.

Coonan, Clifford. "Huaxi: The Socialist Village Where Everyone Is Wealthy." *The Independent*. http://www.independent.co.uk/news/world/asia/huaxi-the-socialist -village-where-everyone-is-wealthy-6290583.html, accessed July 4, 2012.

Coover, Robert. "The Writer as God and Saboteur." *New York Times on the Web*, February 2, 1986. http://www.nytimes.com/books/98/06/28/specials/llosa-real .html, accessed July 18, 2012.

Cowart, David. *History and the Contemporary Novel*. Carbondale: Southern Illinois University Press, 1989.

Dai Jinhua 戴锦华. "Imagined Nostalgia." Judy T. H. Chen, tr. *boundary 2*, 24.3 (Fall 1997): 143–161.

Dai Sijie 戴思杰. *Balzac and the Little Chinese Seamstress*. Ina Rilke, tr. New York: Knopf, 2001. Translation of *Balzac et la petite tailleuse chinoise*.

Davies, Gloria 黄乐嫣. *Worrying about China: The Language of Chinese Critical Inquiry*. Cambridge, MA: Harvard University Press, 2007.

Davis, Robert Murray. "When Was Postmodernism?" *World Literature Today* 75.2 (Spring 2001): 295–298.

de Fays, Hélène. "From 1984 to *Sueños digitales*: The Dystopian Novel in the Age of Globalization." *A contracorriente* 3.1 (2005): 114–147. http://www.ncsu.edu /project/a contracorriente/fall_05/de Fays.pdf, accessed May 30, 2012.

Denton, Kirk A. "Museums, Memorials, and Exhibitionary Culture in the People's Republic of China." *China Quarterly* 183 (Fall 2005): 565–586.

Deppman, Hsiu-Chuang 蔡秀妆. *Adapted from the Screen: The Cultural Politics of Modern Chinese Fiction and Film*. Honolulu: University of Hawai'i Press, 2010.

Derrida, Jacques. "Of an Apocalyptic Tone Recently Adopted in Philosophy." *Semeia* 23 (1982): 63–97.

Díaz, Junot. *The Brief Wondrous Life of Oscar Wao*. New York: Riverhead Books, Penguin, 2007.

Dikötter, Frank. *The Discourse of Race in Modern China*. Stanford: Stanford University Press, 1992. *why not other 义...？*

Donnelly, Ignatius. *Caesar's Column: A Story of the Twentieth Century*. Walter B. Rideout, ed. Cambridge, MA: Belknap Press of Harvard University Press, 1960 [1890].

Eberlein, Xujun. "China 2013." *Foreign Policy* (July 30, 2010). http://www.foreignpolicy.com/articles/2010/07/30/china_2013?page=0,1, accessed September 28, 2011.

Eco, Umberto. *The Name of the Rose*. William Weaver, tr. San Diego: Harcourt Brace Jovanovich, 1983 [Italian, 1980]. Translation of *Il nome della rosa*.

Feng Jicai 冯骥才. *San cun jinlian* 三寸金莲 (The three-inch golden lotus). Chengdu: Sichuan wenyi, 1986.

———. *The Three-Inch Golden Lotus*. David Wakefield, tr. Honolulu: University of Hawai'i Press, 1995.

Feuerwerker, Yi-tsi Mei 梅仪慈. *Ideology, Power, Text: Self-representation and the Peasant "Other" in Modern Chinese Literature*. Stanford: Stanford University Press, 1998.

Flores, Angel. "Magical Realism in Spanish American Fiction" (1955). In Zamora and Faris, eds., 109–117.

Fokkema, Douwe. *Perfect Worlds: Utopian Fiction in China and the West*. Amsterdam: Amsterdam University Press, 2011.

Foster, Paul B. *Ah Q Archeology: Lu Xun, Ah Q, Ah Q Progeny, and the National Character Discourse in Twentieth-Century China*. Lanham, MD: Lexington Books, 2006.

Fu Shuhua 傅书华. "Xin lishi xiaoshuo yanjiu zongshu" 新历史小说研究综述 (Roundup on research on new historical fiction). *Zuopin yu zhengming* 2003, no. 2. http://cacl.literature.org.cn/2005–7-21%5C13–50–18.html, accessed November 19, 2011.

Fujii Shōzō. "The Reception of Murakami Haruki in Taiwan." Abstract of paper presented at the Yale University conference "Taiwan and Its Contexts," April 26–28, 2007. http://research.yale.edu/eastasianstudies/Taiwan/fujii.pdf, accessed May 2, 2011.

Gao Xingjian 高行健. *Ling shan* 灵山 (Soul mountain). Taibei: Lianjing, 1990.

———. *Soul Mountain*. Mabel Lee, tr. New York: HarperCollins, 2000.

Gao Yuanbao 郜元宝. "Zai 'duanlie' zuojia 'mei yisi de gushi' beihou" 在'断裂'作家'没意思的故事'背后 (Behind the "meaningless stories" of the "rupture" authors). *Dangdai zuojia pinglun* 103 (January 25, 2001).

García Márquez, Gabriel. *The Autumn of the Patriarch*. Gregory Rabassa, tr. New York: Harper and Row, 1975.

——. *One Hundred Years of Solitude*. Gregory Rabassa, tr. New York: HarperPerennial, 2006 [1970; Spanish, 1967].

Ge Fei 格非. *Jiangnan sanbuqu* 江南三部曲 (Southlands trilogy). Consists of *Renmian taohua* 人面桃花 (Bygone beauty), *Shanhe rumeng* 山河入梦 (Land in dreamland), and *Chunjin Jiangnan* 春尽江南 (Southern spring played out). Shanghai: Shanghai wenyi, 2012 [2004, 2007, 2011].

——. "The Lost Boat." Caroline Mason, tr. In Henry Zhao, ed , *The Lost Boat: Avant-Garde Fiction from China*. London: Wellsweep, 1998, 77–100.

——. "Mi zhou" 迷舟 (The lost boat). *Shouhuo*, 1987, no. 6.

——. *Xiaoshuo xushi yanjiu* 小说叙事研究 (A study of fictional narrative). Beijing: Qinghua Daxue, 2002. http://ishare.iask.sina.com.cn/f/4_04960.html, accessed June 2, 2013.

Gilman, Charlotte Perkins. *Herland*. New York: Pantheon, 1979 [1915].

Gladney, Dru C. "Salman Rushdie in China." In Charles F. Keyes, Laurel Kendall, and Helen Hardacre, eds., *Visions of Authority in Asia: Religion and the Modern States of East and Southeast Asia*. Honolulu: University of Hawai'i Press, 1994, 255–278.

Golding, William. *Lord of the Flies*. New York: Perigee, Penguin 1954.

Gong, Haomin. *Uneven Modernity: Literature, Film, and Intellectual Discourse in Postsocialist China*. Honolulu: University of Hawai'i Press, 2012.5

González Echevarría, Roberto. *Alejo Carpentier: The Pilgrim at Home*. Ithaca, NY: Cornell University Press, 1977.

——. *Myth and Archive: A Theory of Latin American Narrative*. Cambridge: Cambridge University Press, 1990.

Gottlieb, Erika. *Dystopian Fiction East and West: Universe of Terror and Trial*. Montreal, Quebec, Canada: McGill-Queen's University Press, 2001.

Gray, John. *Black Mass: Apocalyptic Religion and the Death of Utopia*. New York: Farrar Straus and Giroux, 2007.

Griffiths, Mark. "Huaxi: Secrets of China's Richest Village." CRI Webcast, 2004? video attached to Ryan Swift, "Chinese Village of Huaxi: Utopia or Dystopia?" *Swift Economics Blog*, November 7, 2010. http://www.swifteconomics.com/2010/11/17/huaxi-utopia-or-dystopia/, accessed July 4, 2012.

Gu Hua 古华. *Furongzhen* 芙蓉镇 (A small town called Hibiscus). Beijing: Renmin wenxue, 1981.

——. *Rulinyuan* 儒林园 (Garden of the scholars). Taibei: Haifeng, 1990.

——. *A Small Town Called Hibiscus*. Gladys Yang, tr. Beijing: Panda Books, 1983.

——. *Virgin Widows*. Howard Goldblatt, tr. Honolulu: University of Hawai'i Press, 1996.

——. *Zhennü* 贞女 (Virgin widows). Guangzhou: Huacheng, 1985.

Ha Jin 哈金. *Waiting*. New York: Vintage, 2000.

Hampton, Wilborn. "Anarchy and Plain Bad Luck" (review of Mo Yan's *Red Sorghum*). *New York Times Book Review*, April 18, 1993.

Han Shaogong 韩少功. *Ba ba ba* 爸爸爸 (Pa Pa Pa). Beijing: Zuojia, 1993 [1985].

——. *A Dictionary of Maqiao*. Julia Lovell, tr. New York: Columbia University Press, 2003.

——. *Homecoming? And Other Stories*. Martha Cheung, tr. Hong Kong: Renditions, Research Centre for Translation, Chinese University of Hong Kong, 1992.

——. *Maqiao cidian* 马桥词典 (A dictionary of Maqiao). Shanghai: Shanghai wenyi, 1997 [1996].

——. *Pa Pa Pa*. In his *Homecoming? and Other Stories*. Martha Cheung, tr. Hong Kong: Chinese University of Hong Kong, 1992, 35–90.

Hanan, Patrick. *Chinese Fiction of the Nineteenth and Early Twentieth Centuries*. New York: Columbia University Press, 2004.

Harrison, James P. *The Communists and Chinese Peasant Rebellions: A Study in the Rewriting of Chinese History*. New York: Atheneum, 1968.

Hayot, Eric. *The Hypothetical Mandarin: Sympathy, Modernity, and Chinese Pain*. Oxford: Oxford University Press, 2009.

He Zhenbang 何镇邦. "'Changpian re' dailai de fengshou" "长篇热"带来的丰收 (The bumper harvest from the "mania for full-length novels"). *Xiaoshuo pinglun* 2001, no. 2: 34–40.

Hill, Michael Gibbs. *Lin Shu, Inc.: Translation and the Making of Modern Chinese Culture*. Oxford: Oxford University Press, 2013.

Hilton, Isabel. "China: At War with Its History." Followed by Shen Jun [pseud.]. "Chinese History: A Personal View." *Prospect*, September 21, 2011. http://www.prospectmagazine.co.uk/magazine/china-history-cultural-revolution/, accessed July 7, 2012.

Hirsch, Joshua. *Afterimage: Film, Trauma, and the Holocaust*. Philadelphia: Temple University Press, 2004.

Hockx, Michel. Review of *Song of Everlasting Sorrow: A Novel of Shanghai*, by Wang Anyi. MCLC Resource Center. http://mclc.osu.edu/rc/pubs/reviews/hockx.htm, accessed December 2, 2010.

Hong Ying 虹影. *Luo wu dai* 裸舞代 (Summer of betrayal). Tainan, Taiwan: Wenhua shenghuo xinzhi, 1992.

——. *Summer of Betrayal*. Martha Avery, tr. New York: Farrar, Straus, Giroux, 1997.

Hong Zhigang 洪治纲. "Xin lishi xiaoshuo lun" 新历史小说论 (On new historical fiction). *Zhejiang Shi Da xuebao (shehui kexue ban)* 1991, no. 4: 22–25.

Hong Zicheng 洪子诚. *A History of Contemporary Chinese Literature*. Michael M. Day, tr. Leiden: Brill, 2007 [Chinese, 1999].

House, Edward Mandell. *Philip Dru: Administrator: A Story of Tomorrow, 1920–1935*. New York: B. W. Huebsch, 1912.

Hsia, C. T. 夏志清 "Obsession with China: The Moral Burden of Modern Chinese Literature." In Hsia, *A History of Modern Chinese Fiction*. 3rd ed. Bloomington: Indiana University Press, 1999, 533–554.

Hua, Shiping 华世平. *Chinese Utopianism: A Comparative Study of Reformist Thought with Japan and Russia, 1898–1997*. Stanford: Stanford University Press, 2009.

Huang, Yibing 黄亦兵. *Contemporary Chinese Literature: From the Cultural Revolution to the Future*. New York: Palgrave Macmillan, 2007.

Hutcheon, Linda. *A Poetics of Postmodernism: History, Theory, Fiction*. London: Routledge, 1988.

Huxley, Aldous. *Brave New World*. New York: Modern Library, 1956 [1946].

Huyssen, Andreas. *After the Great Divide: Modernism, Mass Culture, Postmodernism*. Bloomington: Indiana University Press, 1986.

——. *Twilight Memories: Marking Time in a Culture of Amnesia*. New York: Routledge, 1995.

Iovene, Paola. "Authenticity, Postmodernity, and Translation: The Debates around Han Shaogong's *Dictionary of Maqiao*." *Annali dell'Istituto Orientale di Napoli* 62 (2002): 197–218. http://ealc.uchicago.edu/faculty/files/7%20Iovene%202002.pdf, accessed November 20, 2011.

Jameson, Fredric. *Archaeologies of the Future: The Desire Called Utopia and Other Science Fictions*. London: Verso, 2007.

——. *Postmodernism, or, The Cultural Logic of Late Capitalism*. Durham: Duke University Press, 1991.

——. "Third World Literature in an Era of Multinational Capitalism." *Social Text* 15 (1986): 65–88.

Jia Pingwa 贾平凹. *Fei du* 废都 (The abandoned capital). Beijing: Beijing, 1993.

——. *Fuzao* 浮躁 (Turbulence). Beijing: Zuojia, 1987.

——. *Turbulence*. Howard Goldblatt, tr. Baton Rouge: Louisiana State University Press, 1991.

Jiang Rong 姜戎. *Lang tuteng* 狼图腾 (Wolf totem). Wuchang: Changjiang wenyi, 2004.

——. *Wolf Totem*. Howard Goldblatt, tr. New York: Penguin, 2008.

Jones, Andrew F. *Developmental Fairy Tales: Evolutionary Thinking and Modern Chinese Culture*. Cambridge, MA: Harvard University Press, 2011.

——. "The Violence of the Text: Reading Yu Hua and Shi Zhicun." *positions* 2.3 (1994): 570–602.

Kaldis, Nicholas. "Infectious Postmodernism in/as *Notes of a Desolate Man*." *Taiwan Journal of East Asian Studies* 9.1 (June 2012): 47–77.

Kang Youwei 康有为. *Ta T'ung Shu: The One-World Philosophy of K'ang Yu-wei*. Laurence G. Thompson, tr. London: Allen and Unwin, 1958.

Karl, Rebecca E. "On Comparability and Continuity: China, circa 1930s and 1990s." *boundary 2*, 32.2 (Summer 2005): 169–299.

King, Richard. Review of *To Live* by Yu Hua, translated by Michael Berry, and of *Chronicle of a Blood Merchant* by Yu Hua, translated by Andrew Jones. MCLC Resource Center, March 2004. http://mclc.osu.edu/rc/pubs/reviews/king.htm, accessed November 26, 2011.

Kinkley, Jeffrey C. *Chinese Justice, the Fiction: Law and Literature in Modern China*. Stanford: Stanford University Press, 2000.

——. *Corruption and Realism in Late Socialist China: The Return of the Political Novel*. Stanford: Stanford University Press, 2007.

——. "Modernity and Apocalypse in Chinese Novels from the End of the Twentieth Century." In Charles Laughlin, ed., *Contested Modernities in Chinese Literature*. New York: Palgrave Macmillan, 2005, 101–120.

——. *The Odyssey of Shen Congwen*. Stanford: Stanford University Press, 1987.

——. "Shen Congwen's Legacy in Chinese Literature of the 1980s." In Ellen Widmer and David Der-wei Wang, eds., *From May Fourth to June Fourth: Fiction and Film in Twentieth-Century China*. Cambridge, MA: Harvard University Press, 1993, 71–106.

——. "A Talk with Chinese Novelist Mo Yan." *Persimmon* 1.2 (Summer 2000): 62–65.

Knight, Deirdre Sabina. "Absolute Career Change" (review of *My Life as Emperor* by Su Tong). *PRI's The World*, website of Public Radio International. June 4, 2008. http://www.pri.org/theworld/?q=node/18538, accessed October 4, 2010.

——. "Decadence, Revolution and Self-Determination in Su Tong's Fiction." *Modern Chinese Literature* 10.1–2 (Spring/Fall 1998): 91–111.

Koestler, Arthur. *Darkness at Noon*. Daphne Hardy, tr. New York: Modern Library, 1968 [1941].

Kolakowski, Leszek. *The Death of Utopia Reconsidered*. The Tanner Lectures on Human Values. Australian National University, 1982. http://www.arisbe.com

/detached/wp-content/uploads/2009/09/kolakowski-the-death-of-utopia-recon
sidered.pdf, accessed July 14, 2013.

Kundera, Milan. *The Unbearable Lightness of Being*. New York: HarperPerennial,
2009 [1999, 1984].

Kwong, Luke S. K. "The Rise of the Linear Perspective on History and Time in
Late Qing China c. 1860–1911." *Past and Present* 173 (November 2001): 157–190.

Lao She 老舍. *Cat Country: A Satirical Novel of China in the 1930s*. William
A. Lyell, Jr., tr. Columbus: Ohio State University Press, 1970.

Lary, Diana. *The Chinese People at War: Human Suffering and Social Transformation, 1937–1945*. New York: Cambridge University Press, 2010.

Lee, Ching Kwan 李青群. "What Was Socialism to Chinese Workers? Collective
Memories and Labor Politics in an Age of Reform." In Ching Kwan Lee and
Guobin Yang, eds., 141–165.

Lee, Ching Kwan 李青群, and Guobin Yang 杨国斌, eds. *Re-envisioning the Chinese Revolution: The Politics and Poetics of Collective Memories in Reform
China*. Washington, DC: Woodrow Wilson Center Press, 2007.

Lee, Lillian (Li Bihua). *Farewell to My Concubine*. Andrea Lingenfelter, tr. New
York: W. Morrow and Co., 1993.

Lee, Vivian Pui-yin 李佩然. "Omens of History: Su Tong's Southern Landscape
and Dynastic Histories." *Journal of Modern Literature in Chinese* 10.2 (December 2011): 38–59.

Lei Da 雷达. "Disan ci gaochao" 第三次高潮 (A third high tide). *Xiaoshuo pinglun*, 2001, no. 4: 4–11.

Lévinas, Emanuel. *Entre nous: On Thinking-of-the-Other*. Michael B. Smith and
Barbara Harshav, tr. New York: Columbia University Press, 1998.

Lewis, Sinclair. *It Can't Happen Here*. Garden City, NY: Doubleday, Doran, 1936.

Li Bihua 李碧华. *Ba wang bie ji* 霸王别姬 (Farewell my concubine). Hong Kong:
Tian di, 1985.

Li Hangyu 李杭育. "Wo de Gechuanjiang" 我的葛川江 (The Gechuan River I
know). *Wenhuibao*, October 4, 1984.

Li, Hua 李桦. *Contemporary Chinese Fiction by Su Tong and Yu Hua: Coming of
Age in Troubled Times*. Leiden: Brill, 2011.

Li Ju-chen [Li Ruzhen]. *Flowers in the Mirror*. Lin Tai-yi, tr. Berkeley: University
of California Press, 1965.

Li Rui 李锐. *Hou tu: Lüliangshan yinxiang* 厚土: 吕梁山印象 (Thick earth: Im-
pressions of Lüliang Mountain). Taibei: Hongfan, 1988.

——. *Jiu zhi* 旧址 (Silver City; lit., "Former Site"). Taibei: Hongfan, 1993 [1990].

——. *Silver City*. Howard Goldblatt. tr. New York: Henry Holt, 1997.

———. *Trees Without Wind*. John Balcom, tr. New York: Columbia University Press, 2013.

———. *Wu feng zhi shu* 无风之树 (Trees without wind). Taibei: Maitian, 1998 [1996].

Li Ruzhen 李汝珍. *Jing hua yuan* 镜花缘 (Flowers in the mirror). Changsha: Yuelu shushe, 2005 [1827].

Li Xin 李欣. "Xiandai yuyan xiaoshuo *Ying wang* zhong renwu de xiangzheng yiyi" 现代寓言小说 "蝇王" 中人物的象征意义 (Symbolism of characters in the modern allegorical novel *Lord of the Flies*). *Shandong Shida Waiyu Xueyuan xuebao*, 2000, no. 2: 102–105.

Li Yuchun 李遇春. "Wutuobang xushi zhong de beifan yu lunhui—Ping Ge Fei de *Renmian taohua, Shanhe rumeng, Chunjin Jiangnan*" 乌托邦叙事中的背反与轮回—评格非的《人面桃花》《山河入梦》《春尽江南》 (Subversion and cyclicalism in utopian narrative: Critiquing Ge Fei's *Bygone Beauty, Land in Dreamland*, and *Southern Spring Played Out*). *Zhongguo xiandai wenxue yanjiu congkan* 2012, no. 10: 31–43.

Li Zhisui 李志绥. *The Private Life of Chairman Mao: The Memoirs of Mao's Personal Physician*. Tai Hung-chao, tr. New York: Random House, 1994.

Liang Qichao 梁启超. *Xin Zhongguo weilai ji* 新中国未来记 (A future account of the new China). Taibei: Guangya, 1984 [1902].

Lin Qingxin 林庆新. *Brushing History against the Grain: Reading the Chinese New Historical Fiction (1986–1999)*. Hong Kong: Hong Kong University Press, 2005.

Lin, Sylvia Li-chun 林丽君. *Representing Atrocity in Taiwan: The 2/28 Incident and White Terror in Fiction and Film*. New York: Columbia University Press, 2007.

Lingenfelter, Andrea. "Howard Goldblatt on How the Navy Saved His Life and Why Literary Translation Matters." *Full Tilt* 2. http://fulltilt.ncu.edu.tw/Content.asp?I_No=16&Period=2, accessed November 17, 2010.

Link, Perry. *Evening Chats in Beijing*. New York: W. W. Norton, 1992.

———. *The Uses of Literature: Life in the Socialist Chinese Literary System*. Princeton, NJ: Princeton University Press, 2000.

Liu E 刘鹗. *Lao Can you ji* 老残游记 (The travels of Lao Can). Ji'nan: Ji'nan, 2004 [1907].

———. *The Travels of Lao Ts'an*. Harold Shadick, tr. Ithaca, NY: Cornell University Press, 1952.

Liu Kang 刘康. "The Short-Lived Avant-Garde Literary Movement and Its Transformation: The Case of Yu Hua." In Liu Kang, *Globalization and Cultural Trends in China*. Honolulu: University of Hawai'i Press, 2004, 102–126.

Liu Yueyue 刘月悦. "Cong Ge Fei 'sanbuqu' lun xiaoshuo chuangzuo de zhuanbian—Jian ping *Chunjin Jiangnan*" 从格非 "三部曲" 论小说创作的转

变—兼评《春尽江南》 (On changes in fictional creation seen in Ge Fei's "trilogy"—With criticism of *Southern Spring Played Out*). *Zhongguo zuojia* 2012, no. 3: 81–87.

Liu Zhenyun 刘震云. *Guxiang sanbuqu* 故乡三部曲 (Homeland trilogy [unofficial critics' title]). Consists of *Guxiang tianxia huanghua* 故乡天下黄花 (Homeland: Faded flowers under heaven). Beijing: Zhongguo qingnian, 1991; *Guxiang xiangchu liuchuan* 故乡相处流传 (Homeland: Contact and transmission). Beijing: Renmin wenxue, 2009 [1993]; and *Guxiang mian he huaduo* 故乡面和花朵 (Homeland: Flour and flowers). Beijing: Huayi, 1998.

———. *Wengu yijiusier* 温故一九四二 (Back to 1942). Fukuoka, Japan: Chūgoku shoten, 2006.

———. *Yi ju ding yiwan ju* 一句顶一万句 (One word is worth a thousand; lit., "One sentence is worth ten thousand"). Wuhan: Changjiang wenyi, 2009.

London, Jack. *The Iron Heel*. New York: Macmillan, 1907.

Lord, Albert B. *The Singer of Tales*. 2nd ed. Stephen Mitchell and Gregory Nagy, eds. Cambridge: Harvard University Press, 2000 [1960].

Lovell, Julia. "Finding a Place: Mainland Chinese Fiction in the 2000s." *Journal of Asian Studies* 71.1 (February 2012): 7–32.

———. *The Politics of Cultural Capital: China's Quest for a Nobel Prize in Literature*. Honolulu: University of Hawai'i Press, 2006.

Lu, Jie. *Dismantling Time: Chinese Literature in the Age of Globalization*. Singapore: Marshall Cavendish, 2005.

Lu Tonglin 吕彤邻. *Misogyny, Cultural Nihilism, and Oppositional Politics: Contemporary Chinese Experimental Fiction*. Stanford: Stanford University Press, 1995.

Lu Xun 鲁迅. Preface [to *Outcry*]. In *The Real Story of Ah-Q and Other Tales of China: The Complete Fiction of Lu Xun*. Julia Lovell, tr. New York: Penguin Books, 2009, 15–20.

Lukács, Georg. *The Historical Novel*. Hannah Mitchell and Stanley Mitchell, tr. New York: Humanities Press, 1965 [1962].

Lupke, Christopher, ed. *The Magnitude of Ming: Command, Allotment, and Fate in Chinese Culture*. Honolulu: University of Hawai'i Press, 2005.

Lyotard, Jean-François. *The Postmodern Condition: A Report on Knowledge*. Geoff Bennington and Brian Massumi, tr. Minneapolis: University of Minnesota Press, 1984.

Ma Jian 马建. *Beijing Coma*. Flora Drew, tr. New York: Farrar, Straus, and Giroux, 2008.

Malmgren, Carl Darryl. *Worlds Apart: Narratology of Science Fiction*. Bloomington: Indiana University Press, 1991.

Mannheim, Karl. *Ideology and Utopia: An Introduction to the Sociology of Knowl-edge*. Louis Wirth and Edward Shils, tr. New York: Harcourt, Brace, and World, 1966 [1936].

Marcuse, Herbert. "The End of Utopia." In his *Five Lectures*. Jeremy J. Shapiro and Shierry M. Weber, tr. Boston: Beacon, 1970.

Marx, Karl. *The Eighteenth Brumaire of Louis Bonaparte*. http://www.marxists.org /archive/marx/works/download/pdf/18th-Brumaire.pdf, accessed November 26, 2011.

Marx, Karl, and Friedrich Engels. *Manifesto of the Communist Party*. http://www .marxists.org/archive/marx/works/1848/communist-manifesto/ch01.htm, ac-cessed November 26, 2011.

McDougall, Bonnie S., and Kam Louie. *The Literature of China in the Twentieth Century*. New York: Columbia University Press, 1997.

McGrath, Jason. *Postsocialist Modernity: Chinese Cinema, Literature, and Criti-cism in the Market Age*. Stanford: Stanford University Press, 2008.

Mencius. *The Works of Mencius*. James Legge, tr. In *The Chinese Classics: With a Translation, Critical and Exegetical Notes, Prolegomena, and Copious Indexes*. Vol. 2. London: Trübner and Co., 1861.

Menton, Seymour. *Latin America's New Historical Novel: 1949–1979–1992*. Aus-tin: University of Texas Press, 1993.

Mi, Jiayan 米佳燕. "Entropic Anxiety and the Allegory of Disappearance: Hydro-Utopianism in Zheng Yi's *Old Well* and Zhang Wei's *Old Boat*." *China Infor-mation* 21.1 (March 2007): 109–140.

Min, Anchee 闵安琪. *Becoming Madame Mao*. Boston: Houghton Mifflin, 2000.

——. *Red Azalea*. New York: Berkley Books, 1994.

Mo Yan 莫言. *Big Breasts and Wide Hips*. Howard Goldblatt, tr. New York: Ar-cade, 2004.

——. *Fengru feitun* 丰乳肥臀 (Big breasts and wide hips). 2 vols. Taibei: Hong-fan, 1996.

——. *The Garlic Ballads*. Howard Goldblatt, tr. New York: Penguin, 1995.

——. *Hong gaoliang jiazu* 红高粱家族 (Red sorghum; lit., "Red sorghum clan[s]"). "Taiwan edition" preferred by the author, cited in this monograph's main text and notes: Taibei: Hongfan, 1989 [1988]. "Mainland edition," cited in some notes when so indicated: Beijing: Renmin wenxue, 2007 [1987].

——. "Iron Child." In his *Shifu, You'll Do Anything for a Laugh*. Howard Gold-blatt, tr. New York: Arcade, 2001, 97–111.

——. *Jiu guo* 酒国 (The republic of wine). Taibei: Hongfan, 1992.

———. *Life and Death Are Wearing Me Out*. Howard Goldblatt, tr. New York: Arcade, 2008.

———. *Red Sorghum*. Howard Goldblatt, tr. New York: Viking, 1993.

———. *The Republic of Wine*. Howard Goldblatt, tr. New York: Arcade, 2001.

———. *Sandalwood Death*. Howard Goldblatt, tr. Norman: University of Oklahoma Press, 2013.

———. *Shengsi pilao* 生死疲劳 (Life and death are wearing me out). Beijing: Zuojia, 2006.

———. *Tanxiang xing* 檀香刑 (Sandalwood death). Taibei: Maitian, 2001.

———. *Tiantang suantai zhi ge* 天堂蒜薹之歌 (The garlic ballads). Beijing: Zuojia, 1988.

———. "Tie hai" 铁孩 (Iron child). In his *Yu dashi yuehui* 与大师约会 (Meeting with the master). Beijing: Zuojia, 2012, 121–131.

———, ed. *Suokong li de fangjian: Yingxiang wo de shi bu duanpian xiaoshuo* 锁孔里的房间: 影响我的10部短篇小说 (A room seen through a keyhole: Ten short stories that have influenced me). Beijing: Xin shijie, 1999.

More, Thomas. *Utopia*. New Brunswick, NJ: Transaction Publishers, 1997 [1516].

Morrison, Alastair. "Farewell to 'History': New Historical Fiction's Alternative Visions of Twentieth Century China." Ph.D. dissertation, University of London, 2012.

Mühlhahn, Klaus. "Negotiating the Nation: German Colonialism and Chinese Nationalism in Qingdao, 1897–1914." In Bryna Goodman and David S. G. Goodman, eds., *Twentieth-Century Colonialism and China: Localities, the Everyday, and the World*. New York: Routledge, 2012, 37–56.

Murakami, Haruki 村上 春树. *1Q84* Jay Rubin and Philip Gabriel, tr. New York: Knopf, 2011 [Japanese, 2009–2010].

———. *Hard-boiled Wonderland and the End of the World*. Alfred Birnbaum, tr. London: Vintage Books, 2003 [1991; Japanese, 1985].

Napier, Susan Jolliffe. *The Fantastic in Modern Japanese Literature: The Subversion of Modernity*. London: Routledge, 1996.

Ng, Kenny 吳國坤. "Review of Mo Yan's *Big Breasts and Wide Hips*." MCLC Resource Center. July 2005. http://mclc.osu.edu/rc/pubs/reviews/ng.htm, accessed October 18, 2010.

Nora, Pierre. *Realms of Memory: Rethinking the French Past*. Lawrence D. Kritzman, ed. Arthur Goldhammer, tr. 3 vols. New York: Columbia University Press, 1996–1998. Translation of *Les Lieux de mémoire*. 3 vols. Paris: Gallimard, 1984–1992.

Orwell, George (pseud. of Eric Blair). *Animal Farm*. New York: New American Library, 1964 [1956, 1946].

———. *Nineteen Eighty-Four*. New York: New American Library, 1962 [1950, 1949].

Ouyang Ming 欧阳明. "Lishi de yanjing zai zheli gewai mingliang—Xin lishi xiaoshuo lüe lun" 历史的眼睛在这里格外明亮—新历史小说略论 (Here the eye of history is unusually clear—A brief discussion of new historical fiction). *Jinyang xuekan* 晋阳学刊 1995, no. 2: 81–86.

Pavić, Milorad. *Dictionary of the Khazars: A Lexicon Novel in 100,000 Words*. Christina Pribićević-Zorić, tr. New York: Vintage, 1988 [Serbian, 1984].

Payne, Christopher Neil. "History in Varied Voices: Alternative Ways of Remembering in Wuhe, Ge Fei, and Xu Xi." Ph.D. dissertation, University of London, 2010.

Paz-Soldán, José Edmundo. *Sueños digitales* (Digital dreams). La Paz, Bolivia: Alfaguara, 2000.

PEP (People's Education Press). *Putong gaozhong kecheng biaozhun shiyan jiaokeshu: Lishi (bixiu)* 普通高中课程标准试验教科书: 历史 (必修) (Common high school curriculum standard trial textbook: History [required]). 3 vols. Beijing: Renmin jiaoyu, 2011 [2007].

———. *Quanrizhi putong gaojizhongxue jiaokeshu (bixiu): Zhongguo jindai xiandaishi* 全日制普通高级中学教科书 (必修): 中国近代现代史 (Full-time common high school textbook [required]: Modern and Contemporary Chinese History). 2 vols. Beijing: Renmin jiaoyu, 2011 [2nd ed., 2006]. English translation of nearly identical edition: *Quanrizhi putong gaojizhongxue jiaokeshu (bixiu): A Modern and Contemporary History of China*. 2 vols. Beijing: Renmin jiaoyu, 2002.

Pickowicz, Paul G. "Rural Protest Letters: Local Perspectives on the State's Revolutionary War on Tillers, 1960–1990." In Ching Kwan Lee and Guobin Yang, eds., 21–49.

Popper, Karl R. *The Open Society and Its Enemies*. 5th ed., rev. 2 vols. Princeton, NJ: Princeton University Press, 1966 [1945]. http://www.inf.fu-berlin.de/lehre /WS06/pmo/eng/Popper-OpenSociety.pdf, accessed December 21, 2012.

Pu Songling 蒲松龄. *Liaozhai zhiyi* 聊斋志异 (Strange tales from a Chinese studio). Changsha: Hunan shaonian ertong, 2006 [written ca. 1679?, first published 1766?].

———. *Strange Tales from a Chinese Studio*. John Minford, tr. and ed. London and New York: Penguin, 2006.

Pusey, James Reeve. *China and Charles Darwin*. Cambridge, MA: Council on East Asian Studies, Harvard University, 1983.

Qiao Liang 乔良. *Ling qi* 灵旗 (Mourning flag). In Wang Biao, ed., 1–48.

Qiu Lan 邱岚. "Zhongguo xin lishizhuyi xiaoshuo zhong de lishi qingsi" 中国新历史主义小说中的历史情思 (Historical sentiments in Chinese new historicist fiction). *Dangdai wentan* 2012, no. 6 (December 29, 2012). http://www.xzbu.com/5/view-3832433.htm, accessed September 22, 2013.

Rand, Ayn. *Atlas Shrugged.* New York: Random House, 1957.

Rege, Josna E. "Victim into Protagonist? *Midnight's Children* and the Post-Rushdie National Narratives of the Eighties." In M. Keith Booker, ed., *Critical Essays on Salman Rushdie.* New York: G. K. Hall, 1999.

Ricoeur, Paul. *Time and Narrative.* Kathleen McLaughlin and David Pellauer, tr. 3 vols. Chicago: University of Chicago Press, 1984–1988 [French, 1983–1985].

Roh, Franz. "Magic Realism: Post-Expressionism" (1925). In Zamora and Faris, eds., 10–31.

Rüsen, Jörn, Michael Fehr, and Thomas W. Rieger, eds. *Thinking Utopia: Steps into Other Worlds.* New York: Berghahn Books, 2005.

 Rushdie, Salman. *Midnight's Children.* New York: Knopf, 1981.

Rushdie, Salman, and Elizabeth West, eds. *The Vintage Book of Indian Writing, 1947–1997.* London: Vintage, 1997.

Saramago, José. *Blindness.* Giovanni Pontiero, tr. San Diego, CA: Harcourt Brace, 1997 [Portuguese, 1995].

———. *Seeing.* Margaret Jull Costa, tr. Orlando, FL: Harcourt, 2006 [Portuguese, 2004].

Sarmiento, Domingo Faustino. *Facundo: Or, Civilization and Barbarism.* Kathleen Ross, tr. Berkeley: University of California Press, 2003 [Spanish, 1845].

Schiaffini, Patricia. "Reconsidering the Origins of Tibetan Magical Realism: *Lo real maravilloso* and magical realism in Tashi Dawa." *Margin* (2006). http://www.angelfire.com/wa2/margin/nonficDawa.html, accessed February 2, 2011.

Schwartz, Benjamin I. *In Search of Wealth and Power: Yen Fu and the West.* Cambridge, MA: Belknap Press of Harvard University Press, 1964.

Scott, A. O. "Remade in China: Coen Brothers' Tale of Infidelity and Revenge." *New York Times*, September 2, 2010. http://movies.nytimes.com/2010/09/03/movies/03woman.html, accessed November 26, 2011.

Shaowen 绍文. "Mohuan xianshizhuyi laidao Zhongguo zhi hou" 魔幻现代主义来到中国之后 (Since magical realism came to China). *Zhonghua dushu bao,* June 22, 2005. http://www.gmw.cn/01ds/2005–06/22/content_256726.htm, accessed July 18, 2012.

Shen Congwen 沈从文. *Imperfect Paradise.* Jeffrey Kinkley, ed. Honolulu: University of Hawai'i Press, 1995.

———. "Life." Peter Li, tr. In Shen Congwen. *Imperfect Paradise,* 257–265.

———. "Sheng" 生 (Life). *Shen Congwen wenji* 沈从文文集 (The works of Shen Congwen). Vol. 5, 304–310. Hong Kong: Sanlian, and Guangzhou: Huacheng, 1982–1985.

Shirk, Susan L. *China: Fragile Superpower.* Oxford: Oxford University Press, 2007.

Shua, Ana Maria. *Death as a Side Effect.* Andrea G. Labinger, tr. Lincoln: University of Nebraska Press, 2010 [Spanish, 1997].

Silbergeld, Jerome. *China into Film: Frames of Reference in Contemporary Chinese Cinema.* London: Reaktion Books, 1999.

Sivin, N[athan]. "On the Limits of Empirical Knowledge in the Traditional Chinese Sciences." In J. T. Fraser, N. Lawrence, and F. C. Haber, eds., *Time, Science, and Society in China and the West.* Amherst: University of Massachusetts Press, 1986, 151–169.

Smith, Verity, ed. *Concise Encyclopedia of Latin American Literature.* Chicago: Fitzroy Dearborn Publishers, 2000.

Sommer, Doris. *Foundational Fictions: The National Romances of Latin America.* Berkeley: University of California Press, 1993.

Song, Mingwei 宋明炜, guest ed. *Chinese Science Fiction: Late Qing and the Contemporary. Renditions* 77, 78 (2012).

Strecher, Matthew C. "Magical Realism and the Search for Identity in the Fiction of Murakami Haruki." *Journal of Japanese Studies* 25.2 (Summer 1999): 263–298.

Su Tong 苏童. *The Boat to Redemption.* Howard Goldblatt, tr. London: Black Swan, 2010.

———. *Ciqing shidai* 刺青时代 (Tattoo). In Su Tong. *Su Tong zuopin jingxuan* 苏童作品精选 (Select collection of works by Su Tong). Wuhan: Changjiang wenyi, 2009, 133–157.

———. *The Gardener's Art.* Josh Stenberg, tr. In Su Tong, *Tattoo: Three Novellas.* Portland, ME: MerwinAsia, 2010, 75–150.

———. *He an* 河岸 (The boat to redemption; lit., "On the riverbank"). Rev. ed. Beijing: Renmin wenxue, 2010 [2009].

———. *Mi* 米 (Rice). Shanghai: Shanghai wenyi, 2008 [2005]. Taibei: Yuanliu, 1991.

———. *My Life as Emperor.* Howard Goldblatt, tr. New York: Hyperion East, 2005.

———. *Nineteen Thirty-Four Escapes.* Michael S. Duke, tr. In Su Tong. *Raise the Red Lantern,* 101–178.

———. *Opium Family.* Michael S. Duke, tr. In Su Tong. *Raise the Red Lantern,* 179–268.

———. *Qiqie chengqun* 妻妾成群 (Raise the red lantern; orig. and lit., "Wives and concubines"). In Su Tong. *Su Tong zuopin jingxuan* 苏童作品精选 (Select collection of works by Su Tong). Wuhan: Changjiang wenyi, 2009, 3–41.

——. *Raise the Red Lantern*. Michael S. Duke, ed. New York: William Morrow, 1993.

——. *Raise the Red Lantern* [*Wives and Concubines*]. Michael S. Duke, tr. In Su Tong. *Raise the Red Lantern*, 11–99.

——. *Rice*. Howard Goldblatt, tr. New York: William Morrow, 1995.

——. *Tattoo*. Josh Stenberg, tr. In Su Tong. *Tattoo: Three Novellas*. Portland, ME: MerwinAsia, 2010, 151–203.

——. *Wives and Concubines*. See under new title, *Raise the Red Lantern*.

——. *Wo de diwang shengya* 我的帝王生涯 (My life as emperor). Shanghai: Shanghai wenyi, 2009 [2005]. Taibei: Maitian, 1992.

——. *Wu Zetian* 武则天 ([Empress] Wu Zetian). Taibei: Maitian, 1994.

——. *Yijiusansi nian de taowang* 一九三四年的逃亡 (Nineteen thirty-four escapes). In Su Tong. *Yingsu zhi jie* (Opium family), 129–174.

——. *Yingsu zhi jia* 罂粟之家 (Opium family). In Su Tong. *Yingsu zhi jia* (Opium family). Shanghai: Shanghai wenyi, 2004, 1–54.

——. *Yuan yi* 园艺 (The gardener's art). http://www.xs007.com/xiandai/s/shutong/hyjj/03.htm, accessed November 27, 2011.

Su Wei 苏炜. "Xifang xiandaizhuyi wenxue dui Zhongguo bashi niandai zuojia de yingxiang" 西方现代主义文学对中国八十年代作家的影响 (The influence of Western modernist literature on Chinese writers of the eighties). *Zhishifenzi* 7.1 (Fall 1991): 45–52.

Su Xiaokang 苏晓康 and Wang Luxiang 王鲁湘. *Deathsong of the River: A Reader's Guide to the Chinese TV Series Heshang*. Richard W. Bodman and Pin P. Wan, tr. Ithaca, NY: Cornell University East Asia Program, 1991.

——. *He shang* 河殇 (River elegy, OR Deathsong of the river). Beijing: China Central Television, 1988. Television series in six parts.

Swanson, Philip. "The Post-Boom Novel." In *The Cambridge Companion to the Latin American Novel*. Efraín Kristal, ed. Cambridge: Cambridge University Press, 2005, 81–101.

Takami, Koushun 高見 広春. *Battle Royale*. Yuji Oniki, tr. London: Gollancz, 2007 [Japanese, 1999]. Translation of *Batoru rowaiaru* バトル ロワイアル.

Tang, Xiaobing 唐小兵. *Chinese Modern: The Heroic and the Quotidian*. Durham, NC: Duke University Press, 2000.

Todd, Richard. "Narrative Trickery and Performative Historiography: Fictional Representation of National Identity in Graham Swift, Peter Carey, and Mordecai Richler." In Zamora and Faris, eds., 305–328.

Vargas Llosa, Mario. *The Feast of the Goat*. Edith Grossman, tr. New York: Picador USA, 2001 [Spanish, 2000].

Vidal, Gore. *Messiah*. New York: Dutton, 1954.

Visser, Robin. *Cities Surround the Countryside: Urban Aesthetics in Postsocialist China*. Durham, NC: Duke University Press, 2010.

——. "Displacement of the Urban-Rural Confrontation in Su Tong's Fiction." *Modern Chinese Literature* 9.1 (Spring 1995): 113–138.

Vonnegut, Kurt. *Player Piano*. New York: Scribner, 1952.

Wakeman, Frederic, Jr. *History and Will: Philosophical Perspectives of Mao Tse-tung's Thought*. Berkeley: University of California Press, 1973.

Wan Zhi 万之 (pseud. of Chen Maiping 陈迈平). Bonnie S. McDougall, tr. "Open Ground." *Bulletin of Concerned Asian Scholars* 16.3 (July–September 1984): 6–7. From *Jintian* 5 (1979). http://criticalasianstudies.org/bcas/back-issues.html?page=16, accessed September 10, 2011.

Wang Anyi 王安忆.*Chang hen ge* 长恨歌 (The song of everlasting sorrow). Beijing: Zuojia, 2000 [1995].

——. *Shushu de gushi* 叔叔的故事 (Uncle's story). Taibei: Yeqiang, 1991.

——. *The Song of Everlasting Sorrow*. Michael Berry and Susan Chan Egan, tr. New York: Columbia University Press, 2008.

Wang, Ban 王斑. *Illuminations from the Past: Trauma, Memory, and History in Modern China*. Stanford: Stanford University Press, 2004.

——. *Lishi yu jiyi: Quanqiu xiandaixing de zhiyi* 历史与记忆;全球现代性的质疑 (History and memory: Interrogation of global modernity). New York: Oxford University Press, 2004.

——. *The Sublime Figure of History: Aesthetics and Politics in Twentieth-Century China*. Stanford: Stanford University Press, 1997.

Wang Biao 王彪, ed. *Xin lishi xiaoshuo xuan* 新历史小说选 (Selections from the new historical fiction). Hangzhou: Zhejiang wenyi, 1993.

Wang, David Der-wei 王德威. "Chinese Fiction for the Nineties." In David Der-wei Wang with Jeanne Tai, eds., *Running Wild: New Chinese Writers*. New York: Columbia University Press, 1994, 238–258.

——. *Fin-de-siècle Splendor: Repressed Modernities of Late Qing Fiction, 1849–1911*. Stanford: Stanford University Press, 1997.

——. *The Monster That Is History: History, Violence, and Fictional Writing in Twentieth-Century China*. Berkeley: University of California Press, 2004.

Wang, Jing 王瑾. *High Culture Fever: Politics, Aesthetics, and Ideology in Deng's China*. Berkeley: University of California Press, 1996.

Wang Lixiong 王力雄 (pseud. Bao Mi 保密). *Huang huo* 黄祸 (Yellow peril). 3 vols. Taibei: Fengyun shidai, 1991.

Wang Ning 王宁. "Rethinking Modern Chinese Literature in a Global Context." *Modern Language Quarterly* 69.1 (March 2008): 1–11.

Wang Shuo 王朔. *Please Don't Call Me Human*. Howard Goldblatt, tr. New York: Hyperion, 2000.

——. *Qianwan bie ba wo dang ren* 千万别把我当人 (Please don't call me human). Changsha: Hunan wenyi, 1993 [1989].

Wang Xiaobo 王小波. "2015" (Chinese). In Wang Xiaobo. *Baiyin shidai* 白银时代 (The age of silver). Beijing: Beijing wenyi, 2006, 168–223. Illustrated by Tian Ying.

——. "2015" (English). Hongling Zhang and Jason Sommer, tr. In Wang Xiaobo, *Wang in Love and Bondage*. Albany: State University of New York Press, 2007, 1–59.

——. "The Silent Majority." http://media.paper-republic.org/files/09/04/The _Silent_Majority_Wang_Xiaobo.pdf, accessed November 20, 2011. Translation of "Chenmo de daduoshu" 沉默的大多数.

Wang Xiaoming 王晓明 et al. "Gu chuan de daolu" 《古船》的道路 (The Ancient Ship's path). *Dangdai zuojia pinglun* 1994, no. 2: 17–27.

——, ed. *Renwen jingshen xunsi lu* 人文精神寻思录 (Inquiry on humanist spirit). Shanghai: Wenhui, 1996.

Wang Zengqi 汪曾祺. "Shou jie" 受戒 (Ordination). *Beijing wenxue*, 1980, no. 10.

Wang, Zheng 汪铮. *Never Forget National Humiliation: Historical Memory in Chinese Politics and Foreign Relations*. New York: Columbia University Press, 2012.

Warren, Robert Penn. *All the King's Men*. New York: Harcourt, Brace, 1946.

Wasserstrom, Jeffrey. "Hot Dystopic: Orwell and Huxley at the Shanghai World's Fair." *Los Angeles Review of Books*, May 20, 2011. http://lareviewofbooks.org/ post/5665989087/hot-dystopic-orwell-and-huxley-at-the-shanghai, accessed August 17, 2011.

Wedell-Wedellsborg, Anne. "Haunted Fiction: Modern Chinese Literature and the Supernatural." *International Fiction Review* 32.1–2 (2005): 21–31.

Wells, H. G. (Herbert George). *The Time Machine*. New York: Berkeley, 1963 [1895].

Wesseling, Elisabeth. *Writing History as a Prophet: Postmodernist Innovations of the Historical Novel*. Amsterdam, Netherlands: John Benjamins, 1991.

White, Hayden. *Metahistory: The Historical Imagination in Nineteenth-Century Europe*. Baltimore: Johns Hopkins University Press, 1973.

Wilder, Thornton. *Our Town, a Play in Three Acts*. New York: Perennial Library, 1985 [1957].

Williams, Raymond. *Keywords: A Vocabulary of Culture and Society*. 1976. Rev. ed. New York: Oxford University Press, 1983.

Wood, James. "Tell Me How Does It Feel?" *The Guardian*, October 5, 2001. http://www.guardian.co.uk/books/2001/oct/06/fiction, accessed February 6, 2013.

Wu Liang 吴亮, Zhang Ping 章平, Zong Renfa 宗仁发, eds. *Mohuan xianshizhuyi xiaoshuo* 魔幻现实主义小说 (Magical realist fiction). Changchun: Shidai wenyi, 1988.

Wu Ziru. "The Chinese Edition of Bolaño's 2666 Newly Released. *Global Times*, December 25, 2011. http://www.globaltimes.cn/DesktopModules/DnnForge%20-%20NewsArticles/Print.aspx?tabid=99&tabmoduleid=94&articleId=689780&moduleId=405&PortalID=0, accessed February 20, 2013.

Xing huo liao yuan 星火燎原 (A single spark can start a prairie fire). 7 vols. Beijing: Renmin wenxue, 1958–59.

Xu, Ben 徐贲. "'From Modernity to Chineseness': The Rise of Nativist Cultural Theory in Post-1989 China." *positions* 6.1 (Spring 1998): 203–237.

Xu, Gary G. 徐钢. "The Writer as a Historical Figure of Modern China: Ye Zhaoyan's Passionate Memory and Fictional History." *Neohelicon* (January 2009): 405–418.

Xu, Jian. "Body, Earth, and Migration: The Poetics of Suffering in Zhang Wei's *September Fable*." *Modern Language Quarterly* 67.2 (June 2006): 245–264.

Xue Dezhen 薛德震. "Guanyu renxinglun de yici duihua" 关于人性论的一次对话 (A dialogue on theories of human nature). *Dushu* 1980, no. 1. http://www.imagecode.net/service/reading.aspx?ID=430, accessed October 13, 2012.

Yan Lianke 阎连科. *Ding zhuang meng* 丁庄梦 (Dream of Ding Village). Hong Kong: Wenhua yishu, 2005.

——. *Dream of Ding Village*. Cindy Carter, tr. New York: Grove Press, 2011.

——. *Si shu* 四书 (Four books). Hong Kong: Mingbao, 2010.

Yan Min 颜敏. *Posui yu chonggou* 破碎与重构 (Smashing and reconstructing). *Chuangzuo pingtan* 创作评谭, 1997, no. 3: 54–59.

——. *Shenmei langmanzhuyi yu daode lixiangzhuyi: Zhang Chengzhi, Zhang Wei lun* 审美浪漫主义与道德理想主义: 张承志, 张炜论 (Aesthetic romanticism and moral idealism: On Zhang Chengzhi and Zhang Wei). Beijing: Huaxia, 2000.

Yang Shumao 杨树茂. *Xin shiqi xiaoshuo shigao* 新时期小说史稿 (Draft history of fiction of the new era). Guangzhou: Huacheng, 1989.

Yang, Xiaobin 杨小滨. *The Chinese Postmodern: Trauma and Irony in Chinese Avant-Garde Fiction*. Ann Arbor: University of Michigan Press, 2002.

Ye Zhaoyan 叶兆言. *Nanjing 1937: A Love Story*. Michael Berry, tr. New York: Anchor, 2004.

——. *Yijiusanqi nian de aiqing* 一九三七年的爱情 (Nanjing 1937: A love story; lit., "A love story from 1937"). Nanjing: Jiangsu wenyi, 1996.

Yu Hua 余华. *Brothers*. Eileen Cheng-yin Chow and Carlos Roas, tr. New York: Pantheon, 2009.

——. *China in Ten Words*. Allan H. Barr, tr. New York: Pantheon, 2011.

——. *Chronicle of a Blood Merchant*. Andrew F. Jones, tr. New York: Pantheon, 2003.

——. *Cries in the Drizzle*. Allan H. Barr, tr. New York: Random House, 1997.

——. *Huozhe* 活着 (To live). Shanghai: Shanghai wenyi, 2007 [2004].

——. *To Live*. Michael Berry, tr. New York: Random House, Anchor, 2003.

——. *The Past and the Punishments*. Andrew F. Jones, tr. Honolulu: University of Hawai'i Press, 1996.

——. "Xianshi yizhong" 现实一种 (One kind of reality). *Beijing wenxue*, 1987, no. 10.

——. *Xiongdi* 兄弟 (Brothers). 2 vols. Shanghai: Shanghai wenyi, vol. 1: 2007 [2005], vol. 2: 2006.

——. *Xu Sanguan mai xue ji* 许三观卖血记 (Chronicle of a blood merchant; lit., "Chronicle of Xu Sanguan Selling His Blood"). Taibei: Maitian, 1997. Nanjing: Jiangsu wenyi, 1996.

——. *Zai xiyu zhong huhan* 在细雨中呼喊 (Cries in the drizzle). Shanghai: Shanghai wenyi, 2007 [2004]. Previously titled *Huhan yu xiyu* 呼喊与细雨 (Cries and drizzle). Taibei: Yuanliu, 1992.

Yue Daiyun 乐黛云. *Intellectuals in Chinese Fiction*. Berkeley: University of California, Berkeley, Center for Chinese Studies, 1988.

Yue, Ming-Bao 余明宝. "Nostalgia for the Future: Cultural Revolution Memory in Two Transnational Chinese Narratives." *China Review* 5.2 (Fall 2005): 43–63.

Zamora, Lois Parkinson, and Wendy B. Faris, eds. *Magical Realism: Theory, History, Community*. Durham, NC: Duke University Press, 1995.

Zamyatin, Eugene. *We*. Gregory Zilboorg, tr. New York: E. P. Dutton and Co., 1952 [1924].

Zamyatin, Yevgeny. *We*. Natasha Randall, tr. New York: Modern Library, 2006.

Zha, Jianying 查建英. *China Pop: How Soap Opera, Tabloids, and Bestsellers Are Transforming a Culture*. New York: New Press, 1995.

Zhang Chengzhi 张承志. *Xinlingshi* 心灵史 (History of the soul). Guangzhou: Huacheng, 1991.

Zhang Helong 张和龙. "Renxing'e shenhua de jian'gou—*Ying wang* zai xin shiqi Zhongguo de zhuti yanjiu yu jieshou" 人性恶神化的建构—《蝇王》在新时期中国的主题研究与接受 (Constructing a myth of the evil of human nature: Study and reception of the themes of *Lord of the Flies* in new-era China). *Zhongguo bijiao wenxue* 2002, no. 3: 52–63.

Zhang Henshui 张恨水. *Ti xiao yinyuan* 啼笑姻缘 (Fate in tears and laughter). Shanghai: Sanyi, 1931.

Zhang Liqun 张立群. "Chongdu 'xin lishi xiaoshuo'" 重读"新历史小说" (Rereading "new historical fiction"). *Tianjin shehui kexue* 2007, no. 6: 112–115. http://www.china001.com/show_hdr.php?xname=PPDDMV0&dname=8K19141&xpos=90, accessed July 17, 2012.

Zhang Qinghua 张清华. "Shi nian xin lishizhuyi wenxue sichao huigu" 十年新历史主义文学思潮回顾 (Ten-year retrospective on new historicist literary thought). *Zhongshan* 1998, no. 4. http://www.dic123.com/A/8/80/806_192263.html, accessed July 19, 2012.

Zhang Wei 张炜. *The Ancient Ship.* Howard Goldblatt, tr. New York: HarperCollins, 2008.

——. *Gu chuan* 古船 (The ancient ship). Beijing: Renmin wenxue, 2009 [1987].

——. *Jiuyue yuyan* 九月预言 (September's fable). Beijing: Zuojia, 2009.

——. *Ni zai gaoyuan* 你在高原 (You are on the highland). 10 vols. Beijing: Zuojia, 2010.

——. *September's Fable.* Terence Russell and Shawn Xian Ye, tr. Paramus, NJ: Homa and Sekey, 2007. (Lacks author's postface).

——. *You Are on the Highland.* Not translated. See *Ni zai gaoyuan.*

Zhang Xianliang 张贤亮. *Half of Man Is Woman.* Martha Avery, tr. New York: W. W. Norton, 1986.

——. *Nanren de yiban shi nüren* 男人的一半是女人 (Half of man is woman). Beijing: Zhongguo Wenlian, 1985.

Zhang, Xudong 张旭东. *Chinese Modernism in the Era of Reform.* Durham, NC: Duke University Press, 1997.

——. *Postsocialism and Cultural Politics: China in the Last Decade of the Twentieth Century.* Durham, NC: Duke University Press, 2008.

Zhang Yiwu 张颐武. "Postmodernism and Chinese Novels of the Nineties." *boundary 2,* 24.3 (Autumn 1997): 247–259.

Zhao, Henry Y. H. 赵毅衡. "Post-Isms and Chinese New Conservatism." *New Literary History* 28.1 (1997): 31–44.

——. "Yu Hua: Fiction as Subversion." *World Literature Today* 65.3 (Summer 1991): 415–420.

Zheng Yi 郑义. *Lao jing* 老井 (Old well). Zhengzhou: Zhongyuan nongmin, 1986.

——. *Old Well*. David Kwan, tr. San Francisco: China Books and Periodicals, 1989.

Zhou, Raymond. "It Takes Brains and Guts." *China Daily* (Hong Kong edition), August 19, 2003. http://www.chinadaily.com.cn/en/doc/2003-08/19/content _256229.htm, accessed July 4, 2012.

Zhu Wen 朱文, ed. "Duanlie: Yi fen wenjuan he wushiliu fen dajuan" 断裂：一份问卷和五十六份答卷 (Rupture: a questionnaire and 56 responses). *Beijing wenxue*, 1998, no. 10.

[Zong Renfa 宗仁发 et al., eds.] "Ge Fei *Jiangnan sanbuqu*: Que you keneng chengwei yibu weida de xiaoshuo" 格非《江南三部曲》确有可能成为一部伟大的小说 (Ge Fei's *Southern Spring Played Out*: Quite possibly a great novel). *Zuojia* 2012, no. 19: 12–34.

Zou Geben 邹戈奔. "Mohuan xianshizhuyi yu Han Shaogong de chuangzuo zhuanxing" 魔幻现实主义与韩少功的创作转型 (Magical realism and the transition in Han Shaogong's writing). *Zuojia* 2012, no. 3: 16–17.

Zouxiang gonghe 走向共和 (Towards the republic). Zhang Li 张黎, dir. Beijing: China Central Television, 2003. 60 episodes (59, after mainland censorship).

FILMS

Ba wang bie ji 霸王别姬 (Farewell my concubine). Chen Kaige 陈凯歌, dir. Hong Kong: Tomson Films/Beijing: China Film Co-Production Corporation and Beijing Film Studio, 1993.

Chang hen ge 长恨歌 (Everlasting regret). Stanley Kwan 关锦鹏, dir. Hong Kong: JCE Entertainment, 2005.

Da hong denglong gaogao gua 大红灯笼高高挂 (Raise the red lantern). Hong Kong: ERA International/Beijing: China Film Co-Production Corporation, 1991.

Dahong midian 大鸿米店 (Dahong rice shop). Huang Jianzhong 黄健中, dir. Beijing: Beijing Film Studio, 1995; banned until 2003.

Feng yue 风月 (Temptress moon). Chen Kaige, dir. Hong Kong: Tomson Films, 1996.

Furongzhen 芙蓉镇 (A small town called Hibiscus). Xie Jin 谢晋, dir. Shanghai: Shanghai Film Studio, 1986.

Hong gaoliang 红高粱 (Red sorghum). Zhang Yimou 张艺谋, dir. Xi'an: Xi'an Film Studio, 1987.

Huang tudi 黄土地 (Yellow earth). Chen Kaige 陈凯歌, dir. Nanning: Guangxi Film Studio, 1984.

Huozhe 活着 (To live). Zhang Yimou 张艺谋, dir. Hong Kong: ERA International/Shanghai: Shanghai Film Studio, 1994.

Jing Ke ci Qin Wang 荆轲刺秦王 (The emperor and the assassin). Chen Kaige陈凯歌, dir. Beijing: Beijing Film Studio, 1998.

Ju dou 菊豆 (Ju Dou). Zhang Yimou张艺谋, dir. Beijing: China Co-Production Film Corporation/Xi'an: Xi'an Film Studio, 1990.

Lan fengzheng 蓝风筝 (The blue kite). Tian Zhuangzhuang 田壮壮, dir. Hong Kong: Longwick Film Studio/Beijing: Beijing Film Studio, 1993.

Lao jing 老井 (Old well). Wu Tianming 吴天明, dir. Xi'an: Xi'an Film Studio, 1986.

Mancheng jindai huangjinjia 满城尽带黄金甲 (Curse of the golden flower). Hong Kong: EDKO Film and Beijing: Beijing New Picture Film Co., 2006.

Qiu Ju da guansi 秋菊打官司 (The story of Qiu Ju). Zhang Yimou, dir. Hong Kong: Sil-Metropole/Beijing: Youth Film Studio of the Beijing Film Academy, 1993.

Yao a yao, yao dao waipo qiao 摇啊摇, 摇到外婆桥 (Shanghai triad). Zhang Yimou, dir. Shanghai: Shanghai Film Studio, 1995.

Yingxiong 英雄 (Hero). Zhang Yimou, dir. Hong Kong: Sil-Metropole/Beijing: China Film Co-Production Corporation, 2002.

INDEX

historical novel: defined, 2, 4. *See also* anti-historical novel; "costume drama" historical fiction and film; metahistory; new historical novel (Western concept); period novel; postmodern historical novel

historicism, xiii, 7, 14, 33, 34; new historicism, 7

history: concepts, theories, discourses of, 4–5, 6, 7, 9, 14, 17, 27, 33–34, 36, 43, 48, 73–74, 79, 102, 109, 130, 159, 180, 200; "history and memory," xi, 119, 174, 231n6; Marxist, 4, 33, 86, 103, 169–170; official, 21–25, 59, 105, 111, 159; revisionist, 34, 160. *See also* alternate history in the novel; amnesia; cyclicalism; documentaries, documentary aspects of fiction; grand narratives; memoirs and autobiographies (Chinese); memory; metahistory; myths, mythmaking, legends; oral history; periodization; revolutionary history, writing of in China; textbook history in China

Hobbes, Thomas, and Leviathan imagery, 67, 120, 158, 175

Höcker, Karl, 232n8

Hockx, Michel, 94, 96, 97

Holocaust, 119, 174, 232n8

Hong Ying, 26

Houellebecq, Michel, xi

House, Edward M., 216n51

Huaxi, Jiangsu, 115–17, 201, 202, 236n18

human nature, humanism, humanistic spirit, xi, xiii, 5, 6, 10, 11, 20 21, 27, 43, 67, 120, 132, 142–143, 184–183, 198, 207, 219n100; biological, animal nature of humans, 21, 61, 62, 90, 91, 144, 146, 173, 174–183, 190, 192, 193, 236n14; debates about, 12, 178, 215n45; mean side of, 2, 36, 39, 42, 45, 56, 75, 85, 104, 112, 137, 147, 156, 164, 184, 205; traditional belief in goodness of, 74, 177–178. *See also* class analysis; Mencius

humor, comedy, 9, 17, 30, 39, 68, 103, 169, 201, 207; black humor, 186, 202; farce, 30, 44, 62, 68, 88–89, 98, 151; of language, 48, 56; in Mo Yan's fiction, 30, 44, 62, 63, 68, 88–90, 127, 135, 187, 189, 190, 192, 201, 226n17; tragicomedy, 51. *See also* absurd, the; satire

Hunan and ancient Chu kingdom, 28, 100–105, 130, 182

Hunan Army (of post-Mao writers), 186

hunger, starvation, 28, 151, 158, 160, 188; famine, 3, 34, 41, 42, 65, 108,112, 134, 138, 206, 211n4; post-Great Leap famine, 23, 26, 52, 82, 90, 95, 102, 108, 136, 185, 206, 227n31

Hutcheon, Linda, 202

Huxley, Aldous, xi, 3, 13, 14; *Brave New World*, 12, 17, 20, 120, 215n44

Huxley, Thomas, 179

Huyssen, Andreas, 4, 201

ideologies, 12, 14, 21, 77, 180, 186, 200–201, 206; absent in fiction, xiv, 24, 27, 29, 122, 158, 163, 169, 172–73, 174, 175, 193; change in, 8, 27, 178; conflicts of, 16; dramatized in fiction, 24, 169–72. *See also* communism; Mao Zedong, Mao Zedong Thought; Marx, Karl, and Marxism; nationalism; Nationalist regime (Kuomintang)

imperialism, 11, 16, 22, 24, 62, 75, 127, 159, 160, 191–192, 228n5

incest, 17, 41, 141, 142, 143, 177, 189, 124

Indian and other South Asian literatures, xiv, 6, 199–200. *See also* Chaudhuri, Amit; Rushdie, Salman

indigenous peoples and cultures, 7, 11, 13, 18, 28, 64, 184, 185, 186

inheritance of physical and mental characteristics, 179, 181

"intellectual youth." *See* rustication of Chinese youth

Wei-Jin era literature, 100, 101
Wells, H. G., xi, 12
White, Hayden, xi
wife beating, 66, 144, 182, 205
Wilder, Thornton, 191
Williams, Raymond, 101
women and gender, xiii, 93–100, 102, 120,
125, 126, 127, 128, 140, 143–144, 146,
151, 156, 205; change in gender
relations, 64, 140, 205; companions,
120, 156, 228n3; female characters, 37,
47, 59, 60, 93–100, 106, 107, 110, 114,
120, 134, 135, 137, 140, 151, 153, 166, 181,
185; female rivalry, 98, 99, female
symbolism, 63; historical scapegoats,
44; lot of women discussed, 25, 39,
93–100, 112, 140, 141; matriarchy,
222n18; oppression of women
dramatized, 41, 49, 53, 55, 75, 87, 113,
134, 142, 143–145, 149, 155, 156, 173,
174, 177; sisterhood, 74–75, 128, 149,
154, 155; widows, 51, 80, 107, 135, 147,
160, 175; women as oppressors, 141,
143, 145, 175; women as rulers, 43;
women workers and professionals,
170; "women's world," 43, 94, 126, 156.
See also concubines; family; feminism;
friends; misogyny; rape; sex; wife
beating; women writers
women writers, xiii, 80. *See also* Atwood,
Margaret; Collins, Suzanne; Gilman,
Charlotte Perkins; Rand, Ayn; Wang
Anyi
Wood, James, 199
workers, 152, 168, 172; as characters in
novels, 11, 54, 76, 78, 142, 147, 163,
193; in life, 24, 28, 65, 115–116, 128,
168; Marxist references in novels,
170–171; the proletariat, 7, 8, 22–23,
63, 96, 127, 142, 180
workplace novels, 203

xiangtu xiaoshuo (rural or native-soil
fiction), 10

Xie Jin, 25
xin lishi xiaoshuo (new historical fiction),
6–7, 213n25

Yan Fu, 172, 180, 233n21
Yan Lianke, 3, 26, 28, 29, 212n12
Yang Guifei, 94
Yang, Xiaobin, x, xi, 174
Ye Weilin, 186
Ye Zhaoyan, 28, 29, 212n11; *Yijiusanqi
nian de aiqing* (Nanjing 1937: A love
story), 3
Yellow Earth (film), 3, 11, 45, 69, 70
Yu Hua, xvi, 1, 7, 143, 230n19; biography,
x, 28–30, 63, 124; and film, 3, 229n12;
influences from and comparisons
with world authors, 16, 17; political
commentary by, 56; style, 7, 29, 30,
49–50, 52, 55–56, 63, 151, 186, 200,
201; on time, 50, 130; treatment of
time, 49–56. *See also* allegory;
avant-garde; Cultural Revolution;
generational conflict; Great Leap
Forward; heroes and heroism;
narrators, narrative viewpoint;
politics; revolution of 1949; sex;
symbols and symbolism
Yu Hua, works of: *Huozhe* (To live), 30,
52, 53, 122, 145, 146, 154, 159, 163, 173;
"Xianshi yizhong" (One kind of
reality), 56; *Xiongdi* (Brothers), 107,
124, 138, 139, 146, 150–152, 163, 167,
168, 200; *Xu Sanguan mai xue ji*
(Chronicle of a blood merchant), 30,
35, 52–56, 122, 126, 146, 154, 168; *Zai
xiyu zhong huhan* (Cries in the
drizzle), 17, 49–52, 122, 124, 130, 147,
154, 163,168
Yuan Shikai, 211n4
Yunnan, 106, 114–115

Zamyatin, Yevgeny (Eugene), 13, 120;
We, 14, 101, 216n49
Zhang Chengzhi, 11, 207, 213n20